The Complete Works of Kuo Pao Kun

| Volume FOUR | Plays in English |

General Editor　Quah Sy Ren

Editor　　　　　C.J.W.-L. Wee

Preface

Tan Swie Hian

Not everyone has the innate sense and the subsequent training to be able to read the state of mind of a dolphin through the expressions of its eyes. It takes spiritual merits for an era to witness the coming into being of core artists who were born with the particular artistic sense. He learns and creates doggedly, rain or shine. Oblivious of himself, he is always on the job, with or without others' appreciation, letting his works unfold as naturally as flowers. In the end, the entire era wafts a particular fragrance because of the flowers he has left behind. Kuo Pao Kun allows us to realise this fact. His life is one of the most important chapters in the art history of Singapore.

There is always an ever-metamorphosing constellation in the mind of Pao Kun, enabling him to see new things, to listen to new sounds and whatever he touches has turned to gold. *The Collected Works of Kuo Pao Kun* ranks among the masterpieces throughout history that readers find it hard to close once they are open at hand. And under its glow, we have realised that life, in the words of Eugene O'Neill, is for each man a solitary cell whose walls are mirrors.

General Editor's Preface

Quah Sy Ren

Kuo Pao Kun is one of the most important cultural symbols of Singapore. Born in 1939, he passed on in 2002. In the short span of 63 years, he left Singapore and the world a rich legacy, which includes tangibles, such as theatrical productions, writings, commentaries and cultural institutions, as well as intangibles, such as communication that transcends communities and countries, his influence on his peers and the younger generations, and his gracious and inspirational dealings with individuals, among others. Part of Pao Kun's legacy was recorded in writing and other various media, while others could not be recorded in any form, and were instead etched in various cultural spaces and in the hearts and minds of individuals.

The editorial team of *The Complete Works of Kuo Pao Kun* comprises individuals from all walks of life, who identify with certain beliefs of Pao Kun. They converged proactively shortly after his demise, preparing earnestly to publish his works. What we could do was to set perimeters and to collate the best of the tangible materials, hoping to leave records of Pao Kun's works on one hand, and using this as the foundation for more reflections, thoughts and research on the other.

The Complete Works of Kuo Pao Kun has a total of ten volumes. Volumes One to Eight are collections of Pao Kun's creative, reflective and critical writings. With an introduction in each volume, it is hoped that some forms of engagement and dialogue could be provided for the general reader and the researcher. Volume Nine, *A Pictorial Record*, offers glimpses of his persona and showcases his works through selected photographs. This is to allow the reader to move beyond his writings and to appreciate the versatility of Pao Kun, and to offer the researcher an opportunity to read him from a visual perspective. Volume Ten, Chronology and Bibliography, details a chronology of the man's life, and puts together published research materials on him.

Many of Pao Kun's commentaries were written either in Chinese or English, while several languages were woven into some of his plays. To preserve the authenticity of the works, apart from his own translations when he was alive, the rest were kept in their original languages. In Volume Three, *Plays in Chinese 3*, and Volume Four, *Plays in English*, the texts were kept in the original English, Chinese and Malay languages, with translations provided for the readers' reading convenience. Volumes Six to Eight, on the other hand, collected the original texts with no translations. Volumes Nine and Ten, with texts written by the editors, are bilingual versions in Chinese and English.

The process of collation, sorting and publishing was complicated and difficult. Many people were involved. It is simply impossible to acknowledge everyone who has contributed in one way or another. That being said, I wish to extend my special appreciation to Pao Kun's family, Goh Lay Kuan, Jian Hong and Jing Hong. Their support helped to realise this otherwise impossible project.

The fact that we have had Pao Kun puts Singapore on the international cultural map. However, the significance of Pao Kun — the breadth and depth of his works and thoughts — has yet to be fully understood. *The Complete Works of Kuo Pao Kun* only marks a beginning. I strongly believe that the figure of Pao Kun continues to expand, in Singapore and beyond.

Acknowledgements

The assistance and patient support of many persons went into this edition of the plays Kuo Pao Kun wrote in English.

Thanks go to the following for many of the translations from Chinese and Malay: Chan Cheow Thia, Kamsiah Abdullah, Quah Sy Ren and Lee Chee Keng.

For help over many years with the varied and multitudinous historical and cultural references that appear in the plays, thanks go to Kevin Y. L. Tan, above all, and to Chan Theow Chia, Charlene Rajendran, Koh Guat Hua, Alexius Chia, Peter Teo, Wee Bee Geok, Christine Pelley, Anthony Seow, Joyce James, Tan Kar Lin, Peter Gu Yongqi, Cheng Hui Cheng, Larry Zhang Jun, Pang Tit Khuen, Chua Seok Hong, Xiao Lan Curdt-Christiansen, Alvin Leong, Yio Siew Koon, Lubna Alsagoff, Jessie Png, Wee Joo Liat, Shirley Lim Low Lan, Antonia Chandrasegaran and Cindy Tan Siew Lee. The range of persons mentioned here, and the different sorts of knowledge their lives embody, is suitably in accord with the varied, dense, embedded cultural life manifested in Kuo's plays.

Quah Sy Ren's support in every aspect of this volume cannot be understated.

Much thanks must also go to Haresh Sharma and Chong Tze Chien, for permission to include *One Hundred Years in Waiting* in this volume.

Thanks also go to the Division of English, Nanyang Technological University, and its head, Neil Murphy, for research leave that significantly assisted with the completion of the edition; to the Department of Asian and Middle Eastern Studies, Duke University, and its chair, Leo Ching, where I proceeded to for the leave period, for strong institutional and other support; and to the Asia Research Institute, National University of Singapore, and to Professors Chua Beng Huat and Prasenjit Duara, where the manuscript was finalised.

C. J. W.-L. Wee

Contents

Preface   iii

General Editor's Preface   v

Acknowledgements   vii

Introduction: Kuo Pao Kun's Contemporary Theatre   xi

The Coffin is Too Big for the Hole   1

No Parking on Odd Days   11

Kopitiam (The Coffee Shop)   25

Day I Met the Prince   61

Mama Looking for Her Cat   81

The Silly Little Girl and the Funny Old Tree   99

The Eagle and the Cat (A Monodrama)   115

0Zero01   133

The Evening Climb   143

Lao Jiu — The Ninth Born   181

Descendants of the Eunuch Admiral   235

Geylang People in the Net   255

The Spirits Play   289

Sunset Rise   329

One Hundred Years in Waiting   385

Production Information   437

Introduction: Kuo Pao Kun's Contemporary Theatre

C. J. W.-L. Wee[1]

Kuo Pao Kun (1939–2002), arguably, was the most important practitioner of contemporary theatre in Singapore from 1980 to 2002. He possessed a profound humanistic sensibility and sensitivity to culture, which engaged with the positive and negative aspects of modern developments in Singapore and beyond. Indeed, we could say that he placed his considerable artistic and intellectual capacities in the service of an expanding engagement with the recent historical and contemporary upheavals that trying to become modern — broadly taken — has entailed. From Singapore's postcolonial nation-building during and after the years of the Cold War, to cultural and linguistic diversity and histories in an era of standardised homogenisation, to Asian nationalism in the age of colonial empires, Kuo's artistic work concerned itself with peoples and cultures unhoused or displaced. There is a persistent and moving recurrent interest in the multiplicity of things, and with the scarcity of shared ideals on culture and society. And yet, despite the difficulty of thinking new versions of wholeness — itself potentially oppressing, Kuo was aware — the plays imply that being unhoused and displaced can force us to look for new places to stand and in which to live.

Kuo's theatre from the 1980s could be described, paradoxically, as neo-traditionalist contemporary theatre with experimental impulses that valued the experiences of daily life. He was no advocate of 'art for art's sake,' or of the beautiful in art. Historically, in the European West, in Peter Bürger's account, the primary concern of avant-garde artistic

---

[1] C. J. W.-L. Wee teaches literature and cultural theory in the Division of English, Nanyang Technological University, Singapore. He is the author of *Culture, Empire, and the Question of Being Modern* (2003) and *The Asian Modern: Culture, Capitalist Development, Singapore* (2007).

critique was with the bourgeoisie and art institutions.[2] In Kuo's case, a major object of critique in the 1980s and 1990s was the state-driven modernising process, with its impulse to standardise daily existence and its link to global capitalist development. To try to counter the homogenising cultural and other negative aspects of economic development in the city-state of Singapore, his theatre and intellectual work emphasised the need for, first, diverse cultural and multi-lingual complexities and, second, the historical memory of intertwined cultural connections (both in the *high-cultural* and *way of life* meanings of the term *culture*); these two components could contribute to the regeneration and reinvention of contemporary man's creative capacities. (These emphases in his later plays widened to cover the broader region.) The result was that various traditional theatrical forms were incorporated into his theatre practice to give us *not* traditional art but instead *contemporary* art. Distinctively, Kuo's aesthetic iconoclasm demanded a *newness* of art through traditional forms (e.g., Chinese puppetry; Noh minimalism) that, by and large, were stripped of exoticism and nostalgia to engage with present-day challenges.

As might be guessed from the above, Kuo's *oeuvre* was not invested in the bourgeois principle of aesthetic autonomy (that is, the idea that art possesses its own realm separate from other human activities): life and experience should be integrated into the arts, and so, like the artistic avant-garde before him, he wanted the arts to be a valuable social institution in a society in which 'pragmatic' and hyper-petit-bourgeois values were valorised by the state. Being a natural institution builder, Kuo founded Singapore's first independent arts centre, The Substation, in 1990. This arts venue, under his leadership, became a safe place where theatre, visual, performance and literary artists could create new work and have conversations across artistic boundaries. An integrated art, he also felt, should have a truth-telling capacity that, at the minimum, was nominally distinct from the region of politics.

Kuo Pao Kun, from his release from detention without trial in 1980, seemed to see that in a world increasingly dominated by global capital, simple oppositions of resistance and complicity, liberation and control, were false. Contemporary art and theatre had to think of the transversal connections between artistic practice and the fraught terrain of either capitalist and/or state-led socio-cultural relations. His art and orientation to culture suggest that the modernising moment we live in demands both reflexivity and artistic experimentation so that a freedom linked to cultural reinvention, in the face of either social-engineering or capitalist forces with totalising tendencies, remains possible.

---

[2] Peter Bürger, *Theory of the Avant-Garde*, trans. Michael Shaw (Minneapolis: University of Minnesota Press, 1984), p. 22.

Pre- and Post-Detention Theatre Practices

Chinese-educated but bilingual and bicultural playwright-director Kuo Pao Kun was born in Hebei province, China, in 1939, and emigrated to colonial Singapore in 1949. In the Foreword to one of the anthologies of his plays in English, *Images at the Margins* (2000), Kuo writes:

> I was born in a poor village in Hebei and was later taken to classical Peiping [now Beijing], then to cosmopolitan Hong Kong, then to multicultural Singapore, then to the massive Down Under, then back to Singapore, and for good. As someone who has been almost permanently on the move, the journey has been more than tolerable.
>
> The different places have been enriching, the people inspiring, the diverse cultures exhilarating. But it was at the margins of all these individually brilliant experiences that I found the most enlightening of spaces and moments. They were so singularly beautiful that one had to invent vocabularies to describe them, these uncharted territories, unexperienced happenings, unfathomed depths, these images at the margins.[3]

These words sum up Kuo's unique life experience and work. To a fair extent, it is *because* he occupied various locations at various margins in his lifetime that this Singaporean playwright, director, teacher and intellectual progressively attempted to break through the walls that surrounded not only him, but the society he lived in. He asked us to see *past* the identity and location we might be occupying, and realise that cross-cultural translation — moving from one regime of language and culture to another — has its rewards. Kuo's experimentation with aesthetic form was a type of contemporary theatre that was, as it were, an avant-garde theatre — that is, a theatre transgressive in some respects that engaged with daily life — that welcomed pluralism and difference. The result has been a body of humanistic work that is verily the result of Kuo's own insistence that he *himself* constantly not only accept but see beyond the limits of race, language, religion, the nation-state, and the cultural fragments created by modernisation and capitalism. Aesthetic experimentation reflects Kuo's own need to re-invent himself artistically and intellectually because of the various places he has occupied, voluntarily or otherwise.

Kuo's moral and authoritative stature among theatre and visual artists came from his combined activist and artistic record. He was a minor high-school activist in the turbulent

---

[3] Kuo Pao Kun, 'Foreword', in *Images at the Margins: A Collection of Kuo Pao Kun's Plays* (Singapore: Times Books International, 2000), p. 8. From the 1980s, Kuo wrote all his plays both in Chinese and English. In general, Kuo wrote the Chinese versions first.

1950s, against the Cold War backdrop of the Malayan Emergency. In 1962, he attended the National Institute of Dramatic Arts (NIDA), Sydney. Returning to Singapore in 1965, the year Singapore left the Federation of Malaysia that was constituted only in 1963, he set up the Singapore Performing Arts School (later renamed the Performing Arts Studio, and thereafter the Practice Theatre School). In 1976, along with his wife, Kuo was interned without trial for allegedly being a member of the Malayan People's Liberation League (MPLL).[4] Among other things, he had a radical social-theatre practice that, during the height of the Cold War, directly criticised the displacement and the exploitation that were linked to state-driven, post-independence modernisation linked with capitalist imperatives.

Kuo's own pre-detention work had been agit-prop theatre in the modern Chinese line that believed art must be deployed in the larger national and community interests, though Chinese activist theatre's social-realist edge was aesthetically modified because he became influenced by Bertolt Brecht — there was experimentation with form.[5] Among his early plays were *The Struggle* (1969) and *The Sparks of Youth* (1970). The first play deals with an exploitative landowner who evicts villagers from the land he owns so that factories can be built — and later, when the former villagers end up working in these new factories, they are again exploited by industrialists. However, during this second round of exploitation, they manage to stand up to their oppressors. The second play — which the state did not allow to be performed — outlines the story of a poor young man who had the good fortune to study out of Singapore. Unfortunately, he forgets his origins, and upon his return to Singapore, he works with capitalist roaders rather than take the side of the workers. His girlfriend, in contrast, has found the ability to identify with the masses, and ends up denouncing the man she once loved. The early work was an extension of politically committed modern art that hailed from the May Fourth Movement of 1919 in China; this was an art far removed from any notion of art as an autonomous bourgeois space, and

---

[4] The following accusation was made public: 'KUO PAO KUN, 37, was born in China and was arrested on March 17, 1976. At the time of his arrest, he was an Assistant Secretary of the Chinese Chamber of Commerce. ... His conversion to communist ideology was by self-indoctrination from the books he read in Australia. ... He returned to Singapore in 1965 and set up a Performing Arts Studio to propagate leftist dance and drama. The Performing Arts Studio was renamed the Practice Theatre School. ... He was inducted into the MPLL in August 1974, four months ahead of his wife, GOH LAY KUAN' ('The Faces of Subversion', *Straits Times* [Singapore], 28 May 1976, p. 30).

[5] Kuo's 1960s and 1970s theatre practice was a radicalism driven by the notion that art was 'useful'. Kuo's use of the Brechtian 'alienation effect' served a pedagogical purpose — to cool down the emotions so that the audience could be clear in assessing the current socio-political circumstances that framed their lives. See Yu Yun, 'The Soil of Life and the Tree of Art: A Study of Kuo Pao Kun's Cultural Individuality through His Playwriting', trans. Kuo Jian Hong, in Kuo Pao Kun, *Images at the Margins: A Collection of Kuo Pao Kun's Plays* (Singapore: Times Books, 2000), p. 22.

instead was undertaken according to the materialist dictates of a revolutionary vision of society.[6]

The PAP government releases Kuo in October 1980, but does not reinstate his revoked citizenship until 1992 — and then only upon application. After his release, Kuo moves away from a singular approach to theatre based on the revolutionary need to transform society to a more plural comprehension of art's relation to society, one not tied in to specific ideological goals and in which art needed its own realm free from specific political agendas: culture must *not* take specific or ideological political stances — not because politics do not matter, but because he felt that art's complicit role within the failed Cultural Revolution in China had undermined art's capacity for independent truth-telling. However, his work still did not subscribe to any notion that art functioned as the cultural-artistic manifestation of an individual ego, and avant-garde or iconoclastic experimentation with form also continued.

The Shanghai theatre critic Yu Yun writes that Kuo had told her that 'all of a sudden, [during his detention,] he began to understand an essay written by Lu Xun [1881–1936],[7] "The Divergent Ways of Art and Politics".'[8] The essay in question was based on a December 1927 talk by Lu Xun, and the novelist-essayist critically says that:

> I have always felt that art and politics are often in conflict. At first, art and revolution were not opposed to each other; they shared the same discontent with the status quo. Yet politics attempts to maintain the status quo, so it naturally stands in the opposite direction of art, which is discontented with reality. ... Art brought forth ruptures to society, but only through ruptures could society progress. Since art is a thorn in the eyes of the politicians, it had to be eliminated.[9]

---

[6] See *ibid.*, pp. 21–22. The Chinese-language tradition in theatre in Malaysia and Singapore partook of the modern progressiveness of the May Fourth movement, and Kuo himself further was influenced by the Cultural Revolution. The earlier plays have not been translated into English, but the Chinese texts can be found in *The Complete Works of Kuo Pao Kun, Vol. 1: Plays in Chinese 1 — The 1960s and the 1970s*, ed. Quah Sy Ren and Pan Cheng Lui (Singapore: Practice Performing Arts School and Global Publishing, 2005).

[7] Lu Xun was the author of short stories such as *The True Story of Ah Q* (published in instalments from 1921 to 1922); he was also an essayist, a translator of literature and a literary editor. He became the titular head of the Chinese League of the Left-Wing Writers in Shanghai in the 1930s.

[8] Yu Yun, 'Soil of Life', p. 31.

[9] Cited by Liu Kang, *Aesthetics and Marxism: Chinese Aesthetic Marxists and their Western Counterparts* (Durham, NC: Duke University Press, 2000), p. 58. The translation from Chinese is Liu Kang's; as far as I know, no English translation of the essay as yet exists.

The post-detention belief in the need for art to have its own space — and not a space to be eliminated when it no longer served propaganda purposes — did not signify some new belief in the bourgeois principles of autonomous art and the expressive artist, for Kuo remained committed to the artist 'still carrying the people and society in his bosom'.[10] He came to feel, though, that there needed to be room for the individual and individual critique, given the dangers of mind-numbing ideologies. His detention coincided with the collapse of the Cultural Revolution in mainland China, and in the process he thought through the vision of socio-political art that had previously sustained him and concluded that it no longer applied.

Kuo's artistic experimentation continued in the 1980s with a multilingual form of theatre first started in the mid-1960s.[11] He proceeded with groundbreaking multilingual theatre which conceived that the legacy of Singapore's multi-ethnic past could generate present-day trans-ethnic understanding in the face of the state's ongoing homogenising formation of national culture. *Mama Looking for Her Cat* (1988) was one result. This is a play where a Hokkien-Chinese speaking Mother who feels abandoned by her now Mandarin-Chinese and English-speaking offspring — the result of the state's educational policy for language learning — is able to sympathetically communicate with a Tamil-speaking man in a similar dilemma, even though they do not share a spoken language. The inter-ethnic link, however, does not dispel the new socio-cultural divide between the generations that language policy has created. *Mama* was workshopped (or devised), rather than being a play written solely by Kuo: workshopped theatre was a means by which he could integrate into a play the personal and the representative feelings of a multi-ethnic cast on the question of inter-connected cultural identity and a need for solidarity.[12] Other forms of inter-ethnic commonality also occur in Kuo's plays; for example, a primordial vitality seems to drive the English-speaking Chinese, Chinese-speaking Chinese and two Malay characters in the devised *0Zero01* (1991) as, salmon-like, they search for the source of life. Other plays examined the linked issues of the

---

[10] Yu Yun, 'Soil of Life', p. 33.

[11] For an account of Kuo's pre-detention work, see Quah Sy Ren, 'Evolving Multilingual Theatre in Singapore: The Case of Kuo Pao Kun', in *Ethnic Chinese in Singapore and Malaysia: A Dialogue between Tradition and Modernity*, ed. Leo Suryadinata (Singapore: Times Academic Press, 2002).

[12] Here is Kuo (in 1988) on the workshop process for *Mama Looking for Her Cat*: 'I can only work out a structure. The multi-lingual cast of 12 is asked to devise the play. The spoke English, Mandarin, Tamil, Malay, Hok[k]ien, Cantonese and Teochew. Many improvisations. Thoughts and feelings flowed, characterising their individual experience and vantage points, each a unique ethnic and linguistic sensitivity. I gave the play a unity, drawing freely from all their resources and my own' ('*MaMa Looking for Her Cat*: The "MaMa" Process', in *The Complete Works of Kuo Pao Kun, Vol. 6: Commentaries*, ed. Tan Beng Luan [Singapore: Practice Performing Arts School and Global Publishing, 2007], p. 263).

weakening, if not actual erasure, of the city-state's multi-cultures and the weakening of socio-cultural memory and identity in the wake of a statist capitalist modernisation that seemed to treat the built environment of the city-state (and the citizens in it) as a metaphorical or literal razed plane (or *tabula rasa*[13]) suitable for bureaucratic management and socio-cultural reinscription (e.g., *The Coffin is Too Big for the Hole* [1985]; *Kopitiam* [Coffeeshop; 1986]; *The Silly Little Girl and the Funny Old Tree* [1988]; *Lao Jiu: The Ninth Born* [1990]).

Kuo's work from the mid-1990s, though, notably started to think of the impact of various aspects of modernity in larger regional or even global dimensions. *Descendants of the Eunuch Admiral* (1995) uses the figure of the Ming Dynasty admiral Zheng He (Cheng Ho) — born Muslim, then forced into being 'Chinese' so as to represent the Ming state, and neutered in the interests of creating a reliable state servant — as an allegory of the fate of man's cultural identity when put in the high service of a 'globalising' state. The Singapore Condition of emasculated modernity was transposed to an allegorical level via an almost mythic 'Chinese' personality to indicate what is increasingly a general condition. In *The Spirits Play* (1998), five Japanese spirits are thrown collectively into recalling their life experience in the Second World War, and they wonder how to make sense of the war and its atrocities inflicted upon them by their own government and army; the attempt to create an assertive modern nation-state and the use of unrestrained nationalism in Japan — or anywhere else, Kuo implies — has its costs. I will return to his distinctive move towards a larger analysis of nationalism and national identity at the end of the Introduction.

In terms of aesthetic formats, traditional theatre forms from the East and the South-east Asian region were reworked and used by Kuo for the positive thinking through of the present moment, not for the purpose of nostalgia for a past world (though some have observed a streak of sentimentality in his work), but in order to imagine the possibilities that the contemporary world held for humankind. Despite this, his theatre and plays on Singapore possess a semi-tragic vision, one in which capitalist modernity is dominant: resistance is not futile, and the diverse reinvention of selfhood remained uppermost in the artistic outlook on human potential; but the displacements of capitalist modernisation and the scarcity of shared values, at the same time, are palpably displayed.

---

[13] See Rem Koolhaas, 'Singapore Songlines: Portrait of a Potemkin Metropolis … or Thirty Years of *Tabula Rasa*, Reconstruction, 1995', in Rem Koolhaas and Bruce Mau, *Small, Medium, Large, Extra-Large*, ed. Jennifer Sigler (Rotterdam: 010 Publishers, 1995), for a now well-known critique of the city-state's urbanism. For a response to Koohaas's argument, see Chapter 4 of C. J. W.-L. Wee, *The Asian Modern: Culture, Capitalist Development, Singapore* (Hong Kong: Hong Kong University Press, 2007), 'The Homogenised Urban Environment and Locality,' pp. 77–98.

Neo-Traditional Theatre as Experimentation

Traditional theatre practices (and especially Chinese theatre practices) are the backbone of Kuo Pao Kun's post-detention aesthetic experimentations. On occasion, the manifestation of the 'traditional' is extremely pointed; *Lao Jiu* — a play in which a teen-aged boy forfeits the blandishments of examination-based meritocratic success for a dissipating and seemingly irrelevant puppetry tradition and its imaginative world — would be a case in point here. Kuo writes in the 1990 programme for the Chinese-language version of the play that *Lao Jiu* featured various types of 'artistic and cultural resources':

> Here, three types of puppetry are being incorporated: the *Fujian* hand puppetry directed by Lee Chye Ee, shadow puppetry directed by Somsak Kanha of MAYA, Thailand,[14] and man-sized puppets choreographed by Goh Lay Kuan. Low Ee Chiang taught the cast pugilistics, Phoon Yew Tien composed and arranged the music, and Choo Ping Chyuen coached us on [Chinese] dialects.[15]

He observes that putting together an 'indigenous drama' was a 'risk', for traditional arts practitioners, in a world where their art seems less relevant, 'never seem to be able to agree anymore nowadays...'.[16] *Lao Jiu*, one could say, is indigeneity worn on one's sleeve.

In many of Kuo's other plays, though, the innovation of the old for the new is less obvious. In his monologues, such as *The Coffin is Too Big for the Hole* (1984), in which bureaucracy tries to reject the use of a traditional Chinese coffin that does not fit into newer, standardised cemetery plots, or *The Eagle and the Cat* (1990), in which the protagonist gets turned into a cat who meets an eagle trying to gain freedom against the constraints of a vast net cast across the skies, the actor is simply in present-day dress. We do quickly see, though, that the actors are not playing fully formed and psychologically realised characters, as we often see in the cinema or on TV; as with the numerous actors who are the 'children' of a single Mother in *Mama Looking for Her Cat*, such characters are expressionistic rather than naturalistic. The playwright-director says of *Mama*: 'We

---

[14] MAYA: The Art and Cultural Institute for Development, Bangkok, is an alternative theatre institute and NGO that was founded in 1981.

[15] Kuo, '*Lao Jiu*: The Lao Jiu Attempt', in *The Complete Works of Kuo Pao Kun, Vol. 6: Commentaries*, ed. Tan Beng Luan (Singapore: Practice Performing Arts School and Global Publishing, 2007), p. 267. The English-language version was directed by TheatreWorks' Ong Keng Sen in 1993.

[16] *Ibid.*

intentionally ventured beyond the naturalistic, learning to "express" rather than just be "natural". ... We also explored the verbal and visual language. We found silence seemed poignantly louder [sic], and the expressionistic more beautiful than the representative.'[17] How do we understand this expressionism in theatre?

From a 1994 article for the key performance studies journal, *The Drama Review*, 'Time/Space with a Simple Gesture', we get a direct articulation of the fundamental innovation that occurs in Kuo's theatre practice from the 1980s, particularly from 1985, he himself notes. He writes that when he was in detention, he evaluated the sort of realist theatre he had made in the 1960s and the 1970s, with Ibsen and Stanislavsky as the dominant models. This approach, as we might expect, was the legacy of May Fourth reformism in China, which 'upheld modern Western concepts as progressive and classical Chinese Art and traditional concepts (Chinese opera included) as conservative, feudalistic, reactionary'.[18] The enforced interregnum in his life led to an awareness that his Chinese and 'Mao-inspired' (156) cultural background — given the 'westward-looking' (156) nature of the May Fourth Movement — had led to a 'bias against traditional forms and concepts' (156), and also against the 'folk traditions' (157) that the German playwright Bertolt Brecht had shown an interest in. The anti-colonial moment of modern Chinese cultural history ironically had led to an absorption of Western high-cultural practices inimical to the local. Rereading Jerzy Grotowski's *Towards a Poor Theatre* (1968), with Grotowski's conviction that 'essential theatre [w]as nothing more than a confrontation between a naked actor and a single spectator' (157), in particular, lead Kuo to a conviction that the actor could become 'almost the sole instrument of expression', and that (*pace* Grotowski's own method) 'training should be a subtraction exercise (dispelling tension and releasing inhibitions) rather than an additional exercise (acquiring skills and technique)' (157). Chinese theatre tradition before the advent of modern *huaju* (or spoken) drama (vs. sung drama, or Chinese opera-theatre) offered precedents for new theatre experimentation in 'subtraction'.

Kuo further became convinced that the theatrical and artistic *process* could be more important than having a finished mental image of the production, for the interaction between director and actors could result in a 'mutual[ly] enriching/inspiring/developing process' (157). These ideas of 'developing process' had gone into the devising of *0Zero01*, which he elaborates upon in the article in *Drama Review*. This 'process' would lead to the

---

[17] Kuo, '*MaMa Looking for Her Cat*', p. 262.

[18] Kuo, 'Time/Space with a Simple Gesture', in *The Complete Works of Kuo Pao Kun, Vol. 7: Papers and Speeches*, ed. Tan Beng Luan (Singapore: Practice Performing Arts School and Global Publishing, 2008), p. 156. All page references will be given hereafter in the main text, within brackets. The original article appeared in *The Drama Review* 38, no. 2 (T142) (Summer 1994): pp. 59–63.

actor's body becoming expressive enough to evoke time and space, freeing theatre from the need of realistic sets:

> On reflection, Chinese classical [sung] theatre has influenced me most in its concepts of a flexible space/time. Rooting its expressive power almost entirely in the performers acting in an empty space, gestures alone create the entire universe of a traditional Chinese play. Such poverty/richness cannot communicate realism. ... *Xuni* (literally meaning omitting and suggesting) allows the performer to create any time/space with a simple gesture. And the audience responds/participates with an equally rich imagination. All the major Eastern theatres share this 'empty space' aesthetics. As I am constantly exposed to Indian and Indonesian theatre which are also part of Singapore's culture, it has become more and more difficult to say that my influence has come solely from the Chinese theatre. (160)

The impetus for artistic iconoclasm comes about from both reading Western theatre thinkers and reassessing the value of traditional Chinese theatre forms in the context of the discrediting of certain revolutionary imperatives. Kuo's sweeping re-evaluation of theatre practice finds inadequate modern cultural formations both in Western-European, First-World modernity and in China's socialist, Second-World modernity.

The question then follows, naturally, is how is this revivified notion of the traditional pertinent to contemporary theatre and human existence? In a keynote address to the Asian Art Festival in Tokyo, on 29 October 2000, Kuo tells his audience:

> For 100 years, new theatre in Asia drank from the spring well [sic] of the West — Europe and America. ... The larger and deeper reason for this [artistic-cultural] development was Asia's entry into the Modern Age. In Japan, the process was voluntary. For almost all the other Asian countries, the process was often a violent engagement with the colonial powers, including those of Japan.[19]

This context of the new and the imposed demands to be modern that existed in the colonial era, European and Japanese, though, had now passed — and in the newer post-war 'new' that Asia now exists in, many postcolonial societies have 'achieved varying degrees of economic affluence' (199). And 'riding on the crest of this new[er] wave [of the new], a deep transformation is, again, radically reshaping theatres in Asia' (199), with 'Non-Realistic' (200) theatre formats coming to the fore. Kuo resorts to Chinese terminology to describe

---

[19] Kuo, 'A Reflection of Theatre in Asia: One Voice from Singapore. Finding a New Role/Meaning for 21st Century Theatre', in *The Complete Works of Kuo Pao Kun, Vol. 7: Papers and Speeches*, ed. Tan Beng Luan (Singapore: Practice Performing Arts School and Global Publishing, 2008), pp. 198–99. All page references will be given hereafter in the main text, within brackets.

the new developments: citing Huang Zuolin (1906–1994), who had studied theatre in England and helped establish the Shanghai People's Art Theatre, Kuo uses the term *xieyi*, 'the theatre of the East, which he [Huang] also called "ideographic theatre"' (200). The description here is of what I think may be called the *suggestive* or perhaps *gestural form of body expressiveness* theatre form that I have already referred to, at the start of this section, in relation to plays such as *Mama Looking for Her Cat*. Such experiments with the neo-traditional, Kuo suggests, have become pronounced in the region:

> Modern Noh (or Noh-inspired) plays and the rise of Butoh in Japan, the creative works of Rendra of Indonesia, Lanling Theatre's return to the simplicity of Beijing Opera in Taiwan, and the more experimental works such as Ong Keng Sen's *Lear*, and Chen Shizheng's monumental staging of *Mudan Ting*, a 14-hour contemporary recreation of the 400-year-old Chinese classic written by Tang Xianzu (who died in the same year as Shakespeare), are all expressions of this new trend. (200)

However, the trend is not only manifested by Asian practitioners but also by Western intercultural practitioners such as Peter Brook and Ariane Mnouchkine. Brecht, as far back as the 1930s, Kuo goes on to say, 'had effectively subverted realism' (201). So, from Kuo's point of view, gestural-body theatre is a gathering force, and his own aesthetic experimentation is part of the gathering force of a newer new that has displaced an older, colonial-era version of modern cultural formation.

The reason for this focus on the body in indigenous art forms, Kuo speculates, is not due to some sort of revivified nationalistic nativism.[20] Kuo is, in fact, critical of nationalism, for the point of coming to terms with suppressed Asian traditional cultures is 'not to establish a[n artistic] system to counter the West's. ... Indeed, in this day and age, if a renaissance [of culture] is at all possible anywhere in this [homogenised] world, ... it would have to be a renaissance of world cultures' (203). Cultural renaissance should benefit everyone. A 'deeper reason for this profound change' in artistic practice is that

> people living in urban centres, where information technology has increasingly become a fact of life, have been increasingly drawn to a new mode of work which uses almost only the head and the hand. ... I believe that this new mode of working and living has in turn given rise to a new appreciation of the human body. ... Because the development of human

---

[20] Kuo probably would not have supported, say, Leopold Senghor's idea of *Négritude*. The French philosopher Jean-Paul Sartre, in the Preface ('*Orphée noire*') to Senghor's *L'Anthologie d'un nouvelle poésie nègre et malgache de langue française* (Anthology of a new negro and Madagascan French-language poetry; 1948) famously defined *Négritude* as the '*négation de la négation de l'homme noir*' (i.e., the negation of the negation of the black man).

body-centred theatre arts is very much in harmony with this new awareness, it enhances appreciation of the human as an individual. (201)

The above passage shows an unexpected comfort with the new global forces of knowledge production, with its emphases on 'knowledge-based industries', given Kuo's humanism. But while he does see new human possibilities that new knowledge economy offers, the main need is to foster what he calls an 'intellectual life force' (205) that working up of a gestural-body theatre will help into being, for such theatre forms help us to remember, and actually instruct us not to forget, our collective identities and the creative capacity of culture in the information age. What must be resisted is not newness per se but 'the consumerist market' and the 'culture of entertainment,' for they expel 'memory' (205): the 'colossal global market force ... has seduced theatre to play the short-term memory game' (206).

We might, as a consequence, even forget twentieth-century violence committed by states:

[We have witnessed] the most murderous one hundred years in history: more wars have been fought and more people have been killed than ever before. This has been especially true in Asia — even till today. ... The bizarre destruction of China's Cultural Revolution and the Tiananmen Square suppression, along with recent happenings in Afghanistan, Iraq, Myanmar, Indonesia and Timor are histories that are hardly complete; in fact, they are all crying to be remembered and made sense of. (205)

The body, gestural-expressive theatre, cultural memory and freedom — they all are linked in Kuo's understanding of the calling of contemporary theatre in a world where the arrival of modern developments both created violence and offered (and still offers) new possibilities of nurturing human potential: 'Finding itself a new role in the globalising and consumerist world seems to me to be the fundamental crisis our theatre is going through now. How will it resolve this crisis?' (208). He had, as yet, no answer: 'All I have to share with you are these questions and concerns' (209). For Kuo, our moment of the present requires both reflexivity and ongoing artistic-cultural experimentation, not a narrowly recuperative or nostalgic look at previous cultural forms. The difficulty for art lies in the ahistorical and anti-historical impulses of the Consumerist Now.

The Spirits Play and National Identity

We now turn to Kuo Pao Kun's move to examine the links of nationalism and national identity to state violence. In 1998, he authored what appeared to be a universal anti-war play, one in which nationalism is viewed with suspicion, written in a highly expressionist and symbolist manner. As I have mentioned, this play was part of a later development in his work, which thinks through the modernising impact in larger dimensions. However, such dimensions will reveal a *specificity* of the regional and the historical in universal themes, as the presence of a universal theme does not necessarily mean that the local is transcended. The playwright's refusal to be too exact in making clear that Japan is at the centre of *The Spirits Play* transforms it away from being primarily a denunciation of the lack of Japanese remorse for its colonialism during the Pacific War. This is unusual, given that that the war is usually seen in the region as an unjust war. Kuo deploys Japan as a strong indicative case study for the universal dangers of nationalism. But such 'universalism' is gained only through reaching back first through a shared East and South-east Asian history, one connected with the pain of becoming modern in a world dominated by the great Western colonial powers. *Spirits Play* reveals that Kuo's humane values exist on a level where the human has been brutalised palpably, and that new versions of wholeness should not be too easily proclaimed.

The Call of the Nation

Descendants of the Eunuch Admiral and *The Spirits Play* come out of the expansive last period of Kuo's *oeuvre*, and look at multicultures, memory and identity beyond Singapore-related contexts. Also, his plays in general from the mid-1990s manifest a sharper sense of life's tragic dimensions, and moved towards the metaphoric and the epic in format, though his work never abjures the need for human responsibility. *Spirits Play* was inspired by a historical fragment in Singapore: the garden-like Japanese Cemetery in the Serangoon Gardens housing estate in the north-east part of Singapore — where Marshal Terauchi, Supreme Commander of the Japanese forces in South-east Asia, is buried, Kuo has noted — provided him with the germ of the play's concept. He later developed the concept in the remote village of Niino in Nagano, Japan, while on an official Japan Foundation Asia Center (JFAC) trip to Japan in 1997–1998.

Spirits Play examines five Japanese spirits — a General; a Man; a Mother; a Girl; and a Poet — trapped on the island on which they died. They recall their life experiences during the Pacific War. These characters are de-individualised types; and while we are offered some background to each of the spirits, it is clear that such knowledge is to be taken as representative, rather than the specific information we need for well-rounded, properly psychologised characterisation. We can take the Girl as an example. The Girl's high-school boyfriend decides that his love for her was unimportant, given the national challenges of the moment, and joins the army. She becomes a nurse in response to the same call of the Nation, and later is gang-raped on the island by 18 soldiers. Instead of getting official support, she is persuaded to drop all the charges at hand, and then is duped, because of her patriotic fervour, into becoming a comfort woman. The stranded spirits are collectively thrown into turmoil by the process of recollection and by their wish to make sense of the war and its atrocities inflicted not only by the foreign enemy but, crucially, by the Japanese government and army. The Girl was tricked by the General — and until late in the play, the other spirits do not know his relationship to their suffering. They discover that the old man was in actuality the Commander-in-Chief of the forces on the island. The betrayal inflicted on them was in spite of the fact that the spirits had patriotically accepted the colonial war's nationalist imperative.

Home for the spirits is lyrically distilled in the symbol of a romanticised, single white crane in a poem by the Poet:

> 'High above me the sky is all blue
> All around me there is absolute silence
> A single white crane flashes over my head
> Painting the entire world with peace and tranquility' (scene 7)

Home therefore is the (seemingly) authentic counterpoint to the martial commitment to national salvation and Asian empire building. The play in general makes no specific references to Japan or Nippon (or any other such terms) in the text, in the setting, or in the dress of the characters (they are almost continuously dressed in nondescript white robes), though the use of evocative symbols like the crane make the implicit reference clear enough.[21] How, then, does one's spirit finally rest — especially as one finally realises that the gentle images of home are verily *part* of the General's fraught ideological paean to 'the Great Nation'? He had brought up the myth of a bird called *Can* ('brutality' in Chinese) that would devour everything and everyone to survive. The Poet, as a rejoinder, brought up another bird myth — that of *Xiang* ('auspiciousness') — to counter the General's myth. As the Chinese theatre critic and dramaturg Lin Kehuan observes, '*Can* stands for a dark

---

[21] Writing of the Hong Kong production of the play in 1998, directed by Kuo, Lin Kehuan tells his readers that: 'To avoid the audience being fixated on any specific historical association, the actors were made not to flaunt their Japanese costumes. Importantly, when the play ended, a stagehand all dressed in black placed five clothes-hangers at the front of the stage, and all the actors then hung their costumes on them before they faded into the darkness wrapped in white. This clearly informed the audience that costumes were nothing but an external signifier of identity. What the playwright was more concerned with was not the duality of the innate evil and good, or even the moral judgment over what was right or wrong. Neither was he merely concerned about Japanese culture, or the ills of the Japanese national psyche. While the play is about Japanese culture and national character, it transcends it' (Lin Ke Huan, 'Spiritual Wanderings and Confessions of the Soul,' in *Two Plays by Kuo Pao Kun*: Descendants of the Eunuch Admiral *and* The Spirits Play, ed. C. J. W.-L. Wee and Lee Chee Keng [Singapore: SNP Editions, 2003], p. 138).

fable of existentialism, while *Xiang* stands for a golden fairytale of romanticism. However, in the texture of the play, one sees *Xiang* as yet a kind of *Can* (*zican*: "self-brutality"). The difference is that *Can* can undertake its actions so as to proliferate its own species, while *Xiang* does what it does for altruistic idealism.'[22] The apparent difference between the two myths collapses when the General asks the other spirits if they 'really believe the [*Xiang*] story when it is a matter of *life* and *death*' (scene 7), when being 'a pack of wolves' might be better than being 'a herd of cattle' (scene 7), for, after all, each of them had responded to the call of the Nation. The negative epiphany leads the spirits to momentarily discard their white clothes to reveal a primal savagery lying underneath: 'Instinctively, impulsively, they begin to undress, revealing bodies painted in primal, savage colours. They all look the same. Tattoos bear individual designs of a unified primitive style' (scene 7). The collective deception by the Nation is also at least an unaware complicity in aggressive national aggrandisement. Too easy an acceptance of 'home' — one that blithely disregards the dangers of uncritically conjuring up images that speak of unsullied national purity — is dangerous.

Beyond Dichotomous Japanese Identity

Spirits Play challenges the clichéd yet long-lasting idea of Japan as a dichotomous culture and society possessing *both* a national culture without excess *and* a monstrous nationalism and desire for empire. Kuo's play cautions that gentle reflections on home can slip into and become part of harmonious fascist fantasies. It is from this indictment, however, that he moves on to *further* suggest that such a deviant nationalism does *not* only articulate Japan's supposed incomparable singularity, and is possible *anywhere*, which then makes Japan an object lesson for all — and this remarkably from a Chinese intellectual and artist (even though also a South-east Asian and a Singaporean) who experienced the war at first-hand.

Unsurprisingly, Kuo's play was not entirely well received — this reception itself being a mark of a successful cultural-artistic provocation. When the Chinese-language version of the play was performed in Singapore (directed by the noted Taiwanese director Stan Lai) and in Hong Kong (directed by Kuo) in 1998, many immediately saw that the play as an allegory of Japanese aggression in Asia. It was criticised it as being too soft on Japan's wartime belligerence, which still vexes many in East and — to a rather lesser extent — South-east Asia. A contrasting reaction occurred in Japan that was essentially the obverse of such reactions. When the Black Tent Theatre in Japan made a proposal in 1999 to invite three directors from Asian countries to direct different versions of *Spirits Play* for a 2000 theatre festival that was to be sponsored with official Japanese funding, the proposal met

---

[22] *Ibid.*, pp. 137–138.

with vague but persistent resistance. In the end, an alternative plan involving three of Kuo's other plays was submitted.

The 'classical' articulation of Japan's incomparable dichotomous identity was most famously voiced by the anthropologist Ruth Benedict (1887–1948) during the Second World War, the result of work associated with the U.S. Office of War Information. The opening of Benedict's *The Chrysanthemum and the Sword* (1946) tells us:

> All these contradictions, however, are the warp and woof of books on Japan. They are true. Both the sword and the chrysanthemum are a part of the picture. The Japanese are, to the highest degree, both aggressive and unaggressive, both militaristic and aesthetic, both insolent and polite, rigid and adaptable, submissive and resentful of being pushed around, loyal and treacherous, brave and timid, conservative and hospitable to new ways. They are terribly concerned what people think of their behavior, and they are overcome by guilt when other people know of their misstep. Their soldiers are disciplined to the hilt but are also insubordinate.[23]

Kuo did indeed have some queries about some jarring unevenness in Japanese culture, particularly the fact that the highly modernised society could have committed atrocities towards even its own people during the war. In 'Challenges to Asian Public Intellectuals: Asia Leadership Fellow Program 1997 Report,' which was a reflection on his experiences during the programme organised by the JFAC and the International House of Japan, Kuo remarks:

> If I have come to understand the Japanese better, I have also found them that much more enigmatic. Here they are: hardworking, disciplined, courteous, well educated, having successfully scaled the highest peak of material achievement and civility. … And yet, this is the same people who have committed some of the most heinous atrocities ever towards their fellow humankind [sic] — against not only other nations but also to their own people [during the war]![24]

Here is the contrast of the chrysanthemum and the sword, re-cast in terms of an achieved material modernity and high politesse that stood in stark relief to the fact that their own people had been violated during the war. Elsewhere, Kuo writes: 'I felt much closer and

---

[23] Ruth Benedict, *The Chrysanthemum and the Sword: Patterns of Japanese Culture* (1946; Boston: Houghton Mifflin, 1989), pp. 2–3.

[24] Kuo Pao Kun, 'Challenges to Asian Public Intellectuals: Asia Leadership Fellow Program 1997 Report', in *The Complete Works of Kuo Pao Kun, Vol. 7: Papers and Speeches*, ed. Tan Beng Lan (Singapore: Practice Performing Arts School and Global Publishing, 2008), pp. 239–240.

very related to the Japanese people because they are no less than the Na[n]king massacre, no less than the Manchurian germ warfare experimentation, and no less than the massacre of civilians in Singapore. ... This knid [sic] of suffering in Japan is no less than what the Japanese military caused outside Japan in Asia.'[25] Suffering links all in the region. What he gains during his fellowship in Japan is a discovery of intra-regional connections, ones that occurred during the wartime, and ones also linked to the literal and cultural journey Kuo had made from China to Singapore; and these discoveries — really unexpected excavations of history and of a larger cultural memory of unhoused and displaced cultures — helped re-work how war and nationalism might be thought as challenges to be faced within East and South-east Asia as a problem of what Kuo thought to be incomplete versions of regional modernity.

During the JFAC fellowship, Professor Ogawa Hiroshi of Kansai University had offered Kuo the opportunity to stay in his house in the quiet rural town of Niino, an offer accepted so as to complete the script for *The Spirits Play*. There he experiences a sense of Japan's 'spiritual dimensions' — 'a strong sense of unity with the land, the sky, the plants, the animals, the elements and their fellow humans'.[26] While wandering in the village, Kuo sees a tablet which informs him that a 'young man had died in Henan province in China in 1937, only a few hundred kilometres of where he will be born two years later in Hebei province.' He continues, 'How incredible! Here I was, deep in the mountains of Nagano, feeling so remotely away from everything I was familiar with, and suddenly something that close to my early childhood exploded right in front of me. Of course, there was the bond of the war which had fatally and intricately tied us together.'[27] The very next day, Kuo is invited to lunch at the home of a Niino master builder, and through writing in *kanji* to communicate, he learns that the old Grandpa in the house had fought in Manchuria before being transferred to Pekan: 'Yes, the town of Pekan in the [West] Malaysian [then actually Malayan] state of Pahang! Of course, I need not have asked, he must have gone up to Pekan by way of Singapore.'[28] When Kuo leaves, he finds the old man first looking at him intently through his window — 'He must have known that the man he was looking at — me — had come from two countries where he had waged war with the local people' — and

---

[25] Kuo Pao Kun, 'Keynote Address at the Southeast Asian Theatre Seminar on War', in *The Complete Works of Kuo Pao Kun, Vol. 7: Papers and Speeches*, ed. Tan Beng Lan (Singapore: Practice Performing Arts School and Global Publishing, 2008), p. 185.

[26] Kuo, 'Challenges to Asian Public Intellectuals', p. 238. This 'sense' of Japan enters *Spirits Play* in the images of Home that are created.

[27] *Ibid.*

[28] *Ibid.* Singapore and Malaya — later in 1963 to become West Malaysia — were effectively one country during the colonial period that Kuo speaks of.

then the old man waves to him with his one good arm: 'It was the most poignant moment of my entire stay in Japan.'[29]

How then, do the above experiences feed into a larger conception for culture and the arts in the region, and more broadly, in a global context? In terms of East and South-east Asia, Kuo notes:

> I have found a curious affinity with Japan, as I have earlier found with the Southeast Asian countries and peoples. It's a cultural one. Specifically, I feel we are all still, in different degrees, prisoners of semi-feudal culture. We are all still locked in a mode of thinking and behaving subject to the control of hierarchical and patriarchal systems. The leading figures or institutions of these hierarchies still dominate our psyches, restraining us from transcending our narrow interests and nationalistic views.[30]

The problem with Japan is, after a point, a lack of 'autonomous thinking', criticality and creativity[31] — a lack which then enabled the almost unthinking national complicity with the pre-war and war-time desire for empire. Present-day Japan still manifests a 'siege mentality': 'It [Japan] seems to verge close to a statement close made by Singapore architect Tay Kheng Soon: "Modernization without modernity", a comment he coined for his own country Singapore.'[32] Modernisation is incomplete until a critical level of reflexivity is reached. Japan, Kuo believes, still has a yet-to-be-fully-developed leadership capacity in the region: 'But, without a doubt, Japan, in Asia, still possesses the resources and potentials [sic] for advancing fully into modernity — in the liberation of the self, in the democ-

---

[29] *Ibid.*, p. 239
[30] *Ibid.*, p. 243.
[31] By 'autonomy', as I have earlier discussed in the Introduction, Kuo does not refer to individualistic bourgeois notions of the self, as he is interested in larger class and particularly cultural and artistic configurations and collectives; see his 'A Reflection of Theatre in Asia: One Voice from Singapore. Finding a New Role/Meaning for 21st Century Theatre', in *The Complete Works of Kuo Pao Kun, Vol. 7: Papers and Speeches*, ed. Tan Beng Lan (Singapore: Practice Performing Arts School and Global Publishing, 2008). Kuo here outlines how the diversity of traditional East and Southeast Asia theatre forms and practices can unexpectedly lead to a stronger artistic engagement with contemporary consumerist capitalism, and its homogenising tendencies, while yet not being an exercise in nostalgia but in the practice of cultural memory. He is not advocating an anti-Western theatre, for modern Asian theatre and culture, more generally, are the result of the colonial age, and served an important role in the drive to create modern societies and in the struggle against Western colonialism itself. But to ignore older cultural forms would also be a loss to the working out of Asian contemporary theatre that could encompass the greater historical and cultural experience of its people, and so be better placed to rupture the mass-cultural norms of high liberal capitalism.
[32] Kuo, 'Challenges to Asian Public Intellectuals,' p. 241.

ratization of society and in the realization of the knowledge-based mode of production and exchange.'[33] Significantly, both modern goals of self-reflexivity *and* post-industrial goals of new knowledge production go into and form Kuo's conceptions of the 'present', or perhaps what can be called 'the contemporary'. Intellectually and culturally, his work manifests a commitment to Progress, but *not* to a teleology that ends with the nation-state, or to global capitalism, for that matter. Nationalism is linked with an incomplete modernity in the region, and the memory of war should lead those in the region to pay attention and come to terms with to the more unfortunate common cultural affinities within the region.

But if the above gives us the various links that connect the diverse region, where is the final leap to the 'universal'? Kuo adds: 'we [in East and South-east Asia] also share a body of rich cultural resources ... which could offer the world now dominated by western culture a treasure of wisdom and experience with the complementary energy to help evolve a global or earthian [sic] fellowship, of peace and harmony'.[34] Is this a call for a pan-Asian supremacy? No, for Kuo is concerned with encouraging Asian multicultures to flower in their full complexities, and global fellowship should be one in which there is space for the full play of diversity, including diversity from the New Asia — even given the ideological claims to 'alternative' Asian values and modernities that existed up to the 1997 Asian financial crisis, when the West denounced such values as 'corruption, collusion and nepotism'. Kuo has no truck with such assertions.

The Artist-Intellectual as Regional Extraterritorial

Kuo's outlook on war and the region was possible because, in the layered cultural make-up of his sensibility and in his bilingual literary capacities (writing both in his native Mandarin-Chinese and in English, with a willingness to incorporate Malay and Tamil-language elements into his work as well), he is what the literary-cultural critic George Steiner calls an *extraterritorial*. Steiner has in mind polylingual writers such as James Joyce, Samuel Beckett and Vladimir Nabokov, who found homes in languages rather than in nation-states; and this type of writer has a symbolic value: 'A great writer driven from language to language by social upheaval and war is an apt symbol for the age of the refugee.'[35] Kuo was not a literal refugee, but he was born in Hebei, China, and was raised in Peiping, Hong Kong and Singapore during the years of anti-colonial struggle and

---

[33] *Ibid.*, p. 243.
[34] *Ibid.*
[35] George Steiner, *Extraterritorial: Papers on Literature and the Language Revolution* (New York: Atheneum, 1976), p. 11.

revolution, amidst the tumultuousness of the Cold War. He was detained without trial for alleged communist activities for four-and-a-half years, and thus was made an internal refugee in his own city-state. His extraterritoriality was therefore the result not of European and Russian socio-political upheavals, but of a set of inter-related East and South-east Asian socio-political upheavals, in a region where there was the pre- and post-war struggle to attain the 'modern' condition and nationhood.

The artist's own artistic and intellectual formation was complex, and these complexities make it difficult to describe exactly what 'modern Asian culture' was (and is): Kuo's early theatre practice drew from the energies of China's May Fourth Movement, but inflected by Stanislavski and Brecht. While in detention, he found himself disappointed with the Cultural Revolution, and subsequently abandoned his earlier theatre practice not just because of his detention, but because he felt that the agit-prop theatre practice of the 1960s and 1970s no longer fitted the Brave New high-capitalist world of the 1980s. Kuo Pao Kun's distinctive humanistic sensibility and distinguished artistic achievement are the result of the shared cultural capacities of and experiences of displacement in an interconnected East and South-east Asia. To come to terms with his cultural legacy for us means that we also need to grapple with the revolutionary and other upheavals that have shaped our shared contemporary cultures.

The Coffin is Too Big for the Hole

I don't know why, but it keeps coming back to me. This dream. Every time I get frustrated, it comes back to me.

It's the funeral. My grandfather's.

We were all at the cemetery. All my folks — my wife, my kids, my brothers, sisters, my cousins and their kids. There were so many people that I couldn't even say for sure who was a relative and who wasn't.

You see, my folks started drifting apart when they got married, one after the other. Grandfather was very annoyed at first, about the breaking up of the extended family.

You see, there were so many rooms in our old house. It could accommodate at least 50 people. But when he died, there was only my family still living there — and the two old servants who had been with him from more than 50 years ago.

Yeah, the funeral.

You see, the coffin was too big. It was so big we had to hire 16 coolies to carry it from the funeral coach to the grave.

But the problem was not so much the weight although it was very heavy all right. It was so damn heavy that the 16 of them nearly dropped it on the ground when they got it off the coach. And we men from the family had to rush over to save it.

You don't want the coffin to crash down. I'm sure you understand that. What if the thing gets busted open, right there in front of all the people?

There were at least 200 of them there. I don't know who most of them were. But I just had this feeling that most of them didn't really belong to the family. I had a feeling that we were being watched. I don't know why, but looking back, I still feel that way. Being watched.

Anyway, we saved the coffin from crashing down and prevented the possibility of the thing getting busted open. Then the lot of us carried the damn thing to the grave.

1

As we carried, we were cursing inside why grandfather had to get such a heavy solid thing and why the damn coolies were not strong enough to bear it. No wonder, you know. Most of them were opium addicts and just out there to make a fast buck when a coffin needed carrying. I'm sure they didn't know this was going to be a real heavy thing.

But we were feeling proud too. I did, anyway. I mean, how many people had a grandfather who enjoyed the honour of getting buried in such a rare, refined, solid, polished, grand and heavy coffin?

I'm sure many had got the news about the special-ness of the coffin and went to see just that.

Yeah, I remember some people were carrying cameras. Yeah! Come to think of it, I remember they were clicking away when we were biting our lips trying to keep the damn thing off the ground.

But, as I said, the problem was not so much the weight. It was the size. It was big. Unusually big. We knew that all along. But we never knew it was so big that it won't get into the hole!

Yeah, can you imagine? Can you imagine that the coffin of your grandfather cannot get into the hole specially dug for him on the day of his funeral? And in front of 200 people?

We were speechless. We were literally stunned. We just stood there and looked at each other. Nobody said a word. It must have been the funniest thing that had ever happened in the entire funeral history of mankind.

You invest so much time and money and energy and emotions in a grand funeral that 200 people had come to see and what happens? The coffin won't get into the grave because the hole was too small — or the coffin was too big. Anyway, they didn't fit. They didn't fit!

So we stood there. We looked at the coffin. We looked at the hole. We looked at each other. All the crying suddenly stopped. But no one dared to laugh. Mind you, if you were a member of the family, how can you laugh?

I mean, if this is your father, your grandfather or your granduncle getting buried and his coffin won't fit into the grave, what do you do about it?

You take him out and dump him into the hole without the coffin? You bring the coffin back with his body and go bury it in some other cemetery? Or do you come another day when the hole is made bigger?

You see, it's serious. You can't laugh. You just can't! I felt more like crying!

You see, I'm the eldest grandson and I was in charge there since my father and his brother had all 'gone' before my grandfather. You see, I was the head of the family. How can I cry? I had to do something!

So I called over the funeral parlour man in charge and I said to him, 'Hey, how come the hole is so small?'

'No, sir!' he said. 'No, sir! The hole is not too small. The coffin is too big!'

My god, I was furious. I mean, what the hell? This was serious business, man. My grandfather was lying there in a coffin unable to get into his grave and this damn funeral man wants to talk relativity with me! I mean, whether the coffin was too big or the hole was too small, what's the difference? It didn't fit, did it? That's the problem, wasn't it?

I tell you, I was boiling mad! But there were so many people there and everyone was watching me. Waiting for me to make a decision because I was the head of the family. So I said quietly and politely, 'Now, never mind which is too small or which is too big. The thing is, the coffin cannot go in. Tell me: Why didn't you measure the hole?'

'But sir, this is standard size,' he said. 'We didn't know your grandfather has such a big coffin. To tell you the truth, I have never seen such a grand, big coffin until this day. But I believe in my father's day …'

'OK, forget it!' I stopped him. I think he was going to tell me that his father had managed such big coffins before his day. You see, he was also a new generation undertaker. But I stopped him. I said, 'OK, forget it! Hurry up and dig the hole bigger.'

He fell silent and looked very surprised. He looked at me for a moment. Then at the coffin. Then at the hole. And then at me again, and said, 'But sir, I'm afraid it can't be done.'

'What do you mean it can't be done?' I said. 'You mean you won't dig?'

'No, sir!' he said. 'But I don't think the plot is wide enough if we dig so big as to get the coffin in. The wall of the next grave might collapse if we do that. You see, sir, we have to work according to a standard size.'

'All right, then. Get another plot. That would solve the problem, wouldn't it?'

Oh, I was deft! I thought. I was able to solve a nasty problem right there on the spot even in my deepest moment of grief, I could.

But I was wrong.

'I'm afraid you can't, sir,' he said. 'You see, sir, the regulation says one dead person is allotted one plot. How can you have two graves for one coffin?'

'Who said anything about two graves? One man. One body. One coffin. One grave. Only double the size.'

'But, sir, that is exactly what I mean,' he said. 'It's not allowed, sir. You look at all these other graves in the cemetery. See? All same size. No two graves for one person. Everyone standard size!', he said.

'What are we going to do, then?' I began to feel desperate.

'I know, sir,' he said. 'Change to a smaller coffin. We have a wide range of coffins. We have very big ones too, although not so big as this one, but which would fit the standard holes. We even have teakwood ones. Very lasting ...'

'Now, wait!' I stopped him before he could go any further.

Can you imagine the embarrassment? The whole of our extended family stranded at the cemetery with grandfather's coffin sitting protestingly beside us listening to a funeral parlour man doing a promotion on his range of coffins!

'Wait!' I said. 'I've got my coffin. All want now is an extra plot of land. Can you understand that?'

'But that's impossible as I've been trying to tell you! See for yourself, sir. Row upon row upon row of graves. As far as your eye can reach. Do you see anyone of them sitting on two plots? Sir, you must understand, there is no room for exceptions!'

It was quite clear that this young funeral manager was at his wits' end. But was I going to be at mine too?

For a moment I thought it was. And I began to sweat.

But somehow, at this, my moment of crisis, the sight of grandfather's big coffin became a source of strength and inspiration. As I looked at it, I felt as if the coffin was speaking to me, persuading me not to give it up. Not to give up this big, grand old thing. Immediately, my mind was made up, and I resumed my confident self again.

'Come!' I said to the funeral man. 'Let's go and see the officer-in-charge,' I said, as I dragged him along to make for the car. But before we drove off, I turned to the crowd and offered my apologies. I said, 'Dear relatives and friends, ladies and gentlemen. We apologise for the interruption in the funeral proceedings due to a technical fault. We shall resume the service as soon as possible and we are sorry for any inconvenience caused. In the meantime, the band will entertain you with a few numbers and I'll be back as soon as possible.'

But I soon realised that my decision was made too hastily because when I walked into the department office I found everyone staring at me wide-eyed. It was only then that I realised I was still wearing my full set of funeral costumes that becomes a pious grandson!

'Oh, never mind,' I said to myself. 'Since I'm here, I might as well get on with it. After all, the poor old man is still lying there in the big coffin unable to get into the hole!'

But, to be polite, I stayed outside and asked the funeral man to go in and talk to the officer-in-charge. I decided that I should not show my unusual disposition unless it became absolutely necessary.

Unfortunately, he got into trouble the moment he stepped into the room. You see, the place was not totally soundproofed, so I heard most of their conversation, especially the officer's hard scolding

'You really disappoint me. You really make me angry. That you should raise such a request. Of all the new generation of undertakers, it had to be you to ask a stupid thing like this. You are well aware of our policy. Irrespective of the person's status and condition, everyone is treated in exactly the same manner. You go there just about every day. Row upon row upon row of graves. As far as your eyes can reach, do you see anyone grave sitting on two plots? There is no room for exceptions!'

'Eh?', I said to myself. 'Eh? I think I've heard that one somewhere before, but where ...?'

But I had no time to work that out, because I had become so concerned and so anxious that I just marched into the office without even knocking.

'Sir, please allow me to draw your attention to a very grave situation.' I tried to be as firm as possible without being discourteous. 'Please take note,' I said, 'that my grandfather has been put into a very, very big coffin and now, because the hole is too small, he cannot get into the grave. We relatives are all, to say the least, feeling very uneasy. Please show your understanding and sympathy by allocating us another plot!'

I said that almost in one breath. And, frankly, I was a bit surprised afterwards by the eloquence I was able to command without rehearsing beforehand. And you know what?

The officer was awestruck. He stood up and just stared at me. At first, I really thought it was my eloquence which had captivated him. But his scanning eyes soon told me that it was actually my funeral costume which had caught his attention. Anyway, he had a good look at me, turned to the funeral man, sat down again, pondered for a while, and raised his head.

'The coffin is too big?' he asked.

'Yeah. Too big.'

'The hole too small?'

'Yeah. Too small.'

'Umm ...' His large, intelligent eyes rolled from side to side, betraying the powerful intellect of an obviously high-IQ person.

'Umm,' he said. 'According to the data you two have provided me with, several options exist.' He started to explain in a masterly, cohesive manner.

'One, change to a smaller coffin.'

'Two, change to a private cemetery.'

'Three, chop off the extra wood on the sides of the coffin.'

'Four, simply remove the body and bury it wrapped in bamboo sheets. Umm ... Come to think of it, this fourth option has an added advantage. You could donate this unique coffin to our newly renovated National Museum of History for perpetual admiration by our own people and the tourists from all over the world.'

Before I could respond, he swung around and said to me, 'But I suppose none of these sounds very sympathetic to a newly bereaved family.'

'Well,' I thought to myself, 'this officer is OK. He sounds sympathetic all right, Humane and sympathetic!'

So I butted in and said, 'Well, yes, sir. As you know, the coffin is already by the grave. We can't very well change a place or alter the burial. I think now the only way out is for you to give us another plot ...'

'No, no, no, no! That will be running against our national planning. You are well aware of the fact that we are a densely populated nation with very limited land resources. The consideration for humanity and sympathy cannot overstep the constraints of the state policy!' he declared.

Well, I can't say anything against that. 'But what about my grandfather?' I thought to myself. 'Constraint or not, the old man's big coffin still has to have a hole big enough to go into, doesn't it?'

Before I could get to open my mouth again, the stern look on his face suddenly changed to a near smile. A sparkle appeared in his eyes as he went on to say, 'But, wait. I think there could be a compromise.'

His apparent softening attitude prompted a surprised look on the funeral man's face.

'It would be nice if a little one is buried next to your grandfather's coffin, you know. To avoid you people digging too close to the wall and risk a collapse in the next wall, I could allow you two families to dig a big common grave. Put your grandfather's and the little one's coffins in together, cover them up and then mark the standard boundaries according to the regulation plot. That way, both your family and the state will be satisfied. But the pity is ... we have no little ones for burial at the moment ...'

'Yes, yes! There is, there is!' shouted the funeral man in excitement. 'But, there is a hitch, though,' he said.

'You see, we have a little boy, but he won't be ready for burial until tomorrow. However, if you are prepared to delay your burial until then, sir, we will be pleased to provide accommodation for your respected late grandfather at our parlour tonight free of charge!'

'No. No. No! I can't delay it and I won't delay it!' I declared with all the firmness I could summon within me.

I don't know where I got the passion and where I got the courage. I just went on declaring bluntly, 'You know, this is my grandfather getting buried. It is not the bottling of soya sauce; it is not the canning of pineapple cubes; it is not the laying of bricks for your HDB flats[1] and it is not the drawing of rectangles for your parking lots. Let me remind you, sir, there are 200 people standing and waiting there at the cemetery with my grandfather lying there in his big coffin without a hole to get in to. If you don't give me another plot so that we can give him a decent burial and put him to rest, I'll ... I'll ... I'll get the whole family to camp overnight right there in the middle of the cemetery!'

Aiyoh! I don't know how I got the compulsion to say all that. But I really did. I was really brave!

I was really excited but I also got a bit worried afterwards. I'm sure you know what I mean. That kind of straight talk could very well get you into trouble.

Only for a brief moment, though. Because I then said to myself, 'So be it. I mean, what the heck. I mean, how many times in your life can you get a chance of burying your grandfather decent-like? So, while I'm at it, shouldn't I just do it right and proper? If not, how am I going to face my ancestors when my day of reckoning comes?'

---

[1] HDB: Housing and Development Board. This is the Singapore government agency responsible for building subsidised public housing (in the form of modernist tower or slab blocks) in the city-state.

So I kept firm and stood my ground.

And you know what? The officer-in-charge didn't rebut. He seemed to have been stunned by my sudden outburst. He looked at me for a brief moment, swung around and marched out of the room! To consult his superior, I suppose. It took him quite a while to return. And his face seemed even longer as he walked into the room again.

'All right. Since you are already at the cemetery, and since the coffin has proven itself too big for the hole, we'll make this case a very special exception. Because we don't want people to misunderstand us, to read us as being disrespectful of traditions, as being hard and unaccommodating to even the dead. But listen, and listen well!'

He looked straight into the funeral man's face as he continued, 'There will only be this one exception and no such requests will be entertained ever again. One man, one grave, one plot! See that you make sure each and every one of them will be put in a coffin that is just right for the standard size of my graves!'

And so, my grandfather was safely put to rest in his hole at last. It was a very special burial to the very last. Because of the extra big size of his coffin, while everyone else slept north-south, he slept east-west.

It was a truly grand, solemn, colourful burial. By the time I got back to the cemetery the crowd had grown from 200 to about 800. And, to my utter surprise, all the newspapers, news agencies, radio, TV and Rediffusion people had arrived.

It made headlines all around. In the end, it was also voted one of the Top Ten National News Stories of the Year.

But, all the same, the crowd and the presence of the media got me worried for a while. Because I feared the officer-in-charge might think that it was I who had called them over. And since he had given me an extra plot, he might blame me for giving him so much publicity.

But my mind was put at ease soon afterwards when he was awarded a prize in recognition of the exceptional sympathy and understanding he had shown towards my grandfather's extra big coffin: He was voted the Most Humane Personality of the Year!

As for me, the funeral somehow stuck in my mind and it would often come back to me. In a dream. Especially when I'm frustrated.

I'm sure you'll agree with me that grandfather's coffin had its special charisma and unique character. But the problem was it was too big for the hole. So, under the circumstances, to be pragmatic, it seems I have to get a standard sized one.

But then, whenever I get to the cemetery and see those graves — the row after row of standard sized graves — I cannot resist thinking about the other problem, and this is what really bothers me a lot: Now, with them all the same size and the same shape, would my sons and daughters, and my grandsons and granddaughters after them, be able to find me out and recognise me?

I don't know ... I just don't know ...

(*End of Play*)

No Parking on Odd Days

Do you drive? I mean, do you drive a car? Or ride a motorcycle?

I do. But not much nowadays 'cos I get very nervous now. It's ... not that I'm afraid of the traffic — you know, too many cars on the road; no, I'm not afraid of that. I can handle heavy traffic. That's no problem ... What I'm afraid of is stopping. Parking. You know, leaving your car behind. Here cannot, there cannot. It's all written down, they say. But still I get mixed up. And end up parking in the wrong place. And you know what happens *lah*.[1] Fine. Fine. Fine. Fine. Fine *lah*.

I mean, what can you do? When you get fined, you get fined. Pay up *lah*, what else can you do? Isn't that right? I'm sure that's what you do also; I mean, we're so used to getting fined sometimes we just don't think about it any more. I have done it so many times my son made a jingle for me for comic relief: '*Kena*.[2] Pay up. It's part of our lifestyle. Ha ha ha ha!'

I know, it's funny. The first time he said it to me I was really amused. And I said to my wife afterwards, I said, 'Hey, this boy is creative, man. Maybe one day he'll become a writer. At least a copywriter.' This boy is OK, I thought to myself. That was a few years ago.

But something happened recently and I'm worried ... It's ... now, how should I describe it ... Well, it has a lot to do with driving, and parking ... and, of course, fining. Well, it's got to do with a whole series of events ...

Let me start with this parking offence — that time I got a ticket when I left my car at the end of the street when I went to visit this friend of mine in Bukit Timah.[3] He lives in a

---

[1] Editor's note: Malay: *lah*, '[A] particle emphasising the word to which it is appended' (*A Malay-English English-Malay Dictionary*, ed. A. E. Coope [revised edn.; London and Basingstoke: Macmillan Education, 1991]).

[2] Playwright's note: *Kena*, 'to get something'; 'affected by'. Editor's note: Malay: literally 'contact'. It carries the sense here of 'ran into trouble', or 'that went home'.

[3] Editor's note: Malay: *Timah*, literally meaning tin, lead or zinc. *Bukit* is 'hill', so here literally 'tin hill'. Refers to the central part of Singapore; it is now an upper-middle-class residential district.

rented garage of one of those old, pre-war bungalows. When I came out, there was this ticket waiting for me tucked under the windscreen, you know how they do it. The ticket says I committed an offence leaving my car too close the end of the street.

'*Alamak*![4] Father, *kena* again?' my son asked me. See, he was with me that time. He and my friend's son are also good friends, same age. 'What's wrong this time, father? No parking lots here, what?' My son asked me. Very observant boy, this fellow, although he was only nine then.

'Parking less than six metres away from the road junction.' I have always done that because my friend's house is right on the corner. This time just bad luck.

'Damn it! What to do? Pay *lah*,' I said.

'*Kena*. Pay up. It's part of our lifestyle. Ha ha ha ha.' My son repeated his joke and we laughed and I felt better. And we decided to pay up on our way home to avoid forgetting afterwards and end up *kena* a bigger fine.

But then, as we were on my way to a parking kiosk where I knew I could settle the ticket, my boy screamed, 'Father, look, look there! Stop! Stop!' He shouted so suddenly I nearly bumped into the bus in front.

'Look, father. Did you say six metres? That's not six metres! Not even three, man! How come they can, we cannot?'

For a moment, I was confused. And when I understood what my son was saying, I felt disturbed. I was disturbed because my boy, only nine, saw something which I meet so many times every day but don't see anymore.

'Go and fight *lah*, father. If this can, why you cannot? Go and fight *lah*!'

I looked at my son and I felt good. Boy only nine, already so observant. Even just for him I should, man!

Although deep down there in my mind I had my reservations, I drove straight to the head office of the parking authorities. And I felt very excited when I got into the officer's room — you know, they put officers there to meet people who go to plead for mercy. You know, there they call it compounding an offence. You pay money so they don't prosecute you. You know, you pay money to keep your record clean.

Anyway, as I sat down with my son beside me, the officer said, 'Yeah, what's your problem?'

---

[4] Editor's note: Malay: *Alamak*, exclamation of surprise.

'Sir, you see, I ah …' I showed him the ticket and tried to explain. But before he heard me to the end he cut in, 'Did you park your vehicle there or not?'

'Er … I did. But you see —' I didn't finish that sentence either before he cut in again, 'OK, compounded, $20.' And he waved as if I should go away.

'But sir, is it wrong to park there under all circumstances?' I refused to 'get lost'.

'Eh? What do you mean?'

'I mean, is it always wrong to park there, to park less than six metres away from a road junction?'

'Of course! Don't you know your *undang-undang*?'[5]

'But what about your own parking lots? Sir, on my way here I saw many streets got public parking lots drawn to the very end of the streets. Some are not even three metres from the end.'

'We measured, you know! …' my boy cut in, 'Are they all wrong?' He asked the officer all earnest-like, you know how little boys like that behave when they get onto a bright idea.

'Yeah?' The officer looked at him with a funny stare. 'You measured, uh?'

'Yeah, I did. Don't believe, you go and measure yourself!' my son said. I tried to stop him but too late. You understand *lah*, it's not wise letting a little boy go tell an officer what to do when you need his sympathy in a situation like this.

'Yes, sir,' I continued, 'some are actually less than three metres from the junction. Now, sir, if the authorities can draw their parking lots up to less than three metres from the end of the street, is it wrong for us to park there?'

I tried very hard to be polite. Actually what I wanted to say was: If you can draw parking lots in an illegal place, invite us to park there and charge money for it, why can't I park my car like that somewhere else?

I was feeling quite confident. I felt I had a fair chance of getting off the hook this time. I mean, what could the officer say? He couldn't say the authorities had always been wrong — not only wrong in drawing parking lots right up to the end of the street but also charging people money for parking there! And if they were not wrong, how could I be wrong?

But I got happy too early.

---

[5] Playwright's note: [Malay:] *undang-undang*, law or rules.

'Well, I can't speak on behalf of the authorities concerned. They have their own jurisdiction. I tell you what. Since you are so interested in legalities, why don't you go and talk to the magistrate in the traffic court? Or ask the relevant authorities about their illegal behaviour. You know, you are free to ignore our ticket and we will send you a summons in due course informing you of the date when your case will be mentioned in the traffic court.' He said this in a very polite and official manner.

What bothered me then was not the $20 I finally paid but the look on my son's face. He didn't say anything there in the office. And because I became very long-faced,[6] he didn't ask me anything on the way home, either. But I could see he didn't understand why the officer was so unreasonable. And he didn't understand why I just paid the fine and didn't fight on any further.

When later he finally asked me why, I simply told him the world was more complicated than he thought and people were not as simple as they looked. I knew it wouldn't satisfy him but it stopped him from asking me more questions.

Well, that was when I first got a bit uneasy. I mean, it shook my confidence a bit. The next time I had this problem was when the new airport had just opened. I went there one evening to pick up one of my in-laws who had gone for a short holiday in Hong Kong. I brought my son along 'cos he hadn't had an opportunity to see the big new airport yet.[7]

When I arrived at the airport parking area — Area A, you know, the expensive one nearest the terminal — I was shocked to find that instead of 60 cents per hour you had to pay $1.80 per hour and I had only two 60-cent coupons left in the car.[8] What to do? My son came to the rescue again.

'Look, father, we can stay in the car until the aeroplane lands and then leave and tear our coupon. One hour, $1.80; 60 cents, 20 minutes, right? Do you think we can get *Ah Chek*[9] out in twenty minutes?'

---

[6] Editor's note: Colloquialism, meaning 'unhappy' or 'dissatisfied'. It would seem to be a Singapore adaptation of the English expression, 'made/pulled a long face'.

[7] Editor's note: The father is referring to Changi International Airport, which replaced the older Paya Lebar Airport (now Paya Lebar Air Base) as the city-state's international airport in 1981.

[8] Editor's note: Singapore uses a pre-paid system of coupons that motorists have to buy if they wish to use municipal or state-provided public parking.

[9] Editor's note: A term in *minnan hua* or *minnan* language, a non-Mandarin-Chinese language, strictly speaking referring to an uncle on one's father's side of the family, but used more generally as a term of respect for a male who might be close to one's father's age.

'Very good idea, boy!' I said. 'But, just to be safe, let's put two 60-cents and give us 40 minutes. OK?'

OK. We waited until the plane's arrival before tearing two 60-cent coupons and dashing into the terminal.

And we made it. In fact, we brought them out within 30 minutes and we all said the airport was very efficient. But, when I got back to the car? Yeah! There was a ticket stuck under my windscreen: 'Insufficient amount displayed.'

'What do you mean insufficient amount?' I asked the kiosk attendant. Before the man could, my son cut in, 'One hour, $1.80; $1.20, 40 minutes, you think our arithmetic so lousy ah?'

'$1.80 per hour means you got to put three 60-cent coupons and tear them together. Identical. Otherwise how do you get $1.80? Complain to my senior officers in headquarters *lah*!'

'What if I don't want to park one hour, how? If I only want to park 20 or 40 minutes, how? You know, even in those places where you say $1.20 per hour I can still use one 60-cent coupon to park half an hour. So why not two 60-cents here for 40 minutes? ... Look, my pay is $200 a month, but I never get a full month's pay if I work only two weeks a month! Do you?'

He had no patience for me and I had no patience for him. Encouraged by my son, 'Go and fight *lah*, father, go and fight *lah*. This time sure win. That fellow don't even know Primary One[10] arithmetic. Go and fight *lah*.' I really went to the parking people's headquarters. Again, I had my reservations deep down but I went all the same because this seemed a much clearer case. It's only a matter of arithmetic, what? And again my son came with me.

As usual there was a long queue and when it came to my turn I made myself very polite and carefully worked out the sums again about $1.80 for one hour and $1.20 for 40 minutes.

'That it not how we calculate. If you want to complain you can write in officially. And if you want to take it further, you can wait for the summons to appear in court and present your case to the magistrate.'

Well? ... You guessed tight again. I paid him the compounded amount of $10.

---

[10] Editor's note: Reference to the first year of primary school education.

'Father, why don't you go ahead and write in?' My boy couldn't take it anymore. I think my face was even longer than the last time but that didn't stop him from complaining this time. Maybe because he is older now, almost 11, and not so afraid of me like before.

'No use *lah*, son. No use, I tell you.'

'If no use, go to court *lah*! I bet you the judge can do better arithmetic than these fellows!' he said in all eagerness.

My boy's seriousness, that bright spark in his eyes, the fighting spirit in his voice hit me hard somewhere inside. But somehow I felt I couldn't tell him again that the world was more complicated than he thought or that people were not as simple as they looked.

Downstairs in that parking headquarters building is a snack bar. I took him there, bought ourselves some drinks and cakes and told him something which happened to me some years ago.

This was quite a few years back, even before I got married. One day, I drove my car to Telok Ayer[11] — not my own car, that time I was working as a travelling salesman using the company's car. The place was crowded and I was so happy to find an empty lot. There was a sign saying 'Parking on Even Days Only'. Well that day was the tenth. Even day. You know, one, three, five, seven are odd numbers and two, four, six, eight are even numbers. OK, so I left my car and went to do my business.

When I came back? Yeah, a ticket! How come? Is this not an even day? Tenth? Right, what. I checked my watch, I checked my calendar and I checked with the *mamak*[12] corner store man about the date and I looked at the signboard again.

Right, what? That's what it said, 'Parking on Even Days Only.'

That means can park on even days, right?

I was very certain the parking attendant got it wrong. And that's what I told the compounding officer later when I got into his office.

'The parking attendant must have got his dates wrong. Maybe his watch stopped that day. Ha ha ha ...' I said jokingly, trying to look as casual and as relaxed as possible. Trying to

---

[11] Editor's note: Malay: Telok Ayer, literally 'water gulf'. An area of the city located in its central core.
[12] Playwright's note: *Mamak*, polite [Malay-language] term for an Indian-Muslim man, usually a paternal type of figure.

hide any nervousness. Don't know why, but every time I go to Maxwell Road[13] or when I see a traffic policeman in white and black uniform I get nervous.

'No, my friend, he didn't get it wrong. You did. The place is for lorries only.'

'For lorries only? But there's no other sign, what. Don't believe, you go and see yourself. "Parking on Even Days Only". Nothing else, I looked!'

'You go and look better. The parking lots so big, can't be for cars, what? I know the place. You go and check. Next!'

Of course I went to check. No, no other sign. Only 'Parking on Even Days Only'. I was right, what? Left and right, no other signs!

'I am right. For once, I am dead right and the traffic people are wrong. Ha, I'm going to tell them good this time!'

But as I was driving away, something caught my eye at the end of the street. I quickly stopped my car. It was a small blue sign. As I walked close, I saw the words clearly: 'For Lorries Only.'

My god, you can imagine how disappointed I was. I felt punctured. Ssss, I was like a balloon with my air gone. All my happiness gone with the wind.

But then as I stood there looking at the signboard again and again, something came to me.

'Yeah ... yeah ... That's right. That's right! It doesn't make sense,' I said to myself. 'Right, must go and fight the case. It doesn't make sense.' And I quickly drove back to see the same officer again.

'Look, sir, I went back to see. And you are right, there is a sign saying the place is for lorries only.'

'Of course, I told you what! Why come and see me? Go pay *lah*. And look better next time!' He waved me off again.

'But wait, sir. I have something to tell you. Do you know where is the "Lorries Only" signboard? It is at the end of the street.'

At least 50 yards from where I parked my car. Now listen to this. Near my car there were signs saying 'Parking on Even Days Only', but there is that 'For Lorries Only' sign at the

---

[13] Editor's note: The then-location of the Traffic Police headquarters.

end of the street 50 yards away. 'You see, sir, when I park my car and see a sign nearby, I naturally take advice from this sign. If there is no sign saying there is another sign somewhere else I must read, how would I know there is another sign somewhere there telling me something else? Do you know what I mean, sir?'

It's a simple matter but it sounded very complicated and I tried to be as clear as I could. When I finished, I could see the man was impressed. He stared at me, with no expression.

Now, that's good. You know, when they stare at you and give no expression, it means they are trying to think of something to tell you, something different from what they always tell you day in day out.

'I mean, sir, look at it this way. Say you are driving, and you park your car like me. Now, after you have parked your car, and you see a sign next to you with something like "Parking on Even Days Only", would you go on marching 50 yards each way to see if there is another sign which might say something else?'

He stared at me for a moment, really looking straight into my eye. I didn't blink, 'cos I wanted him to see how serious I was. But do you know what he said after all that? 'If you have a complaint, you can write in.'

Aaagh ... You bet I will write in! And I really did. Because this time I was sure I was right. And since I had investigated so much, I felt too strongly about it to give it up. I'm sure you know what I mean. When you honestly believe in something, when you really feel you know for certain you have been wronged, you want to go on, to clear up the problem and come out clean. Don't you?

I haven't been writing composition for a long time, but I wrote all right. I spent a whole week writing and re-writing, I filled my wastepaper basket twice, three times over with torn pages. To make it extra impressive, I borrowed a typewriter and spent a whole evening making it pretty and tidy.

My letter ran to two pages long, single spacing. I described the place and explained the situation in great detail. I even drew a diagram. I didn't cheat. I didn't tell any lie. I told them exactly what I did. I admitted I parked my car there and that there was a sign at the end of the street saying the place was for lorries only. And then I explained that it wasn't really entirely my fault. Very frankly and politely, I said the sign was a bit misleading.

I ended the letter by saying the words 'For Lorries Only' should have been written on the same sign 'Parking on Even Days Only'. In that way, I said, everything would be clear, and there would be no room for misunderstanding. And I suggested they should either change the sign, or paint something on the road to indicate that place was for lorries only. Oh, yeah, I was so caught up in explaining I nearly forgot to ask them to excuse me this once.

I treated the whole thing with lots of honesty and frankness. I wanted to come clean and I wanted to help make the signs clearer. Not only to clear my name but also to prevent other people from getting into that kind of mix-up. I promised also to be more careful next time.

I waited patiently for their reply. You really got to have patience with them. When they write to you they say you must reply within a week, two weeks or one month. Otherwise, fine. But you can't do the same to them. You can't ask them to give you a reply within such and such a period. I think you all understand that *lah*.

Anyway, I waited very patiently for many weeks and at last the letter came. No, my explanation not accepted. I still had to pay. If not, they would charge me in court.

I was very disappointed, and then very angry. I mean, I didn't want to break the law, and I honestly went down to find out whether that place was OK to park or not. Let's be fair *lah*, you can't expect me to see one sign saying something and still go a long way to see if there is another one saying something else. I mean, that is not human, man! I got very angry and I refused to pay. 'Go to court, go to court *lah*! I want to fight this case to the end!'

I was very worked up. I was very confident. I was very, very committed to this case because deep, deep down there in my heart I knew I was right. I never felt more sure that Truth with a capital 'T' was on my side.

The summons came about three months later. The court date was another six months away.

When I arrived at the traffic magistrate's court, I found a long queue outside. I showed the policeman there my summons and he told me to line up also. When the line started to move at about 9 o'clock, it moved very fast. I had never been to court so I thought to myself, '*Wah*, this is efficient, man. Not like the American courts we see in the movies, our court is fast, man!'

But when I got inside the room, I found it wasn't really like the trial we see in films or TV. Everyone said 'guilty' when their offences were read out to them and the magistrate just said, 'Fine $30, $40 or $50', or something like that.

Of course, when my turn came, I said, 'Not guilty,' and began to give my reasons. But before I finished my first sentence the clerk stopped me. The magistrate mentioned a date and the clerk told me to come again on that day to stand trial and state my case then.

That was my first ever appearance in court; I was all prepared to defend myself; I tried very hard to remember how Perry Mason[14] behaved in court but I didn't even finish my first sentence! Of course I was disappointed. But I was also relieved because I was already getting too nervous. So I thought to come another day would be better still.

But it was nearly a year afterward when my trial came. By that time, I had already forgotten many of the details of the day I parked my car at this place with a sign saying, 'Parking on Even Days Only.' So I decided to pay a visit there before going to court. Off I went to Telok Ayer.

When I found the place I parked my car more than two years ago, *aiyah*, I was so happy! You know what? The place was painted now! I mean, the road near the kerb was painted. In yellow stripes, with the words 'For Lorries Only' written down there.

'*Alamak!*' I said to myself, 'This time sure win.' They have painted the place just like I suggested. That means they have admitted the previous sign arrangement was not good enough. This is the best evidence to prove I was right. I mean, if they were right, why would they change? I mean, if this is right now, how could I be wrong then. Whichever way you look at it, I am a sure winner!

So when I walked into the court room I was full of confidence, very sure I would come out a proud, innocent man.

After I took my oath in the defendant's box and pleaded not guilty, the prosecution brought in their witness. A parking attendant. I knew only then that this was the man who booked me. Short chap, wearing spectacles, with a round face.

After the police inspector finished asking him questions to confirm the date and time of my offence I was told that I could ask questions of the witness.

I didn't expect this, honestly. Me question the witness? No, I didn't know I had to do this. But Perry Mason immediately came to my mind. Cross-examination! Yeah, that's what it is! Now I remember.

So I asked him, 'Can you tell me exactly where you found my car parked. I mean, in exactly what part of the street. And where were the signs placed? And were there other signs nearby —'

---

[14] Editor's note: A fictional lawyer character created by American mystery writer Erle Stanley Gardner in 1933. The reference here is more probably to the American CBS televsion serials — adaptations of the books (1957–1966; 1973–1974) — featuring the late Raymond Burr as Perry Mason. Both series were screened in the city-state by the then-Radio Television Singapore.

'Slowly. One question at a time,' the magistrate waved his hand at me without lifting his head.

'Er ...' The chap looked at me and then started to look at the ceiling. And then he looked into his notebook, flipping through the pages. But he kept repeating, 'Err ...' and no answer came. He began to get red in the face, the magistrate began to get impatient and the police inspector began to get uneasy. As for me, I felt more and more optimistic of winning my case.

According to one of my friends later, I had won the case that moment. He said if I had shut my mouth then I would probably have been let off within the next minute. But I made the mistake of playing it straight and honest. I wanted to make a bigger issue than just clearing my ticket.

So instead of enjoying the fruits of the poor parking attendant's bad memory, I opened my big mouth and went on to say, 'Let me remind you, I parked my car before such and such a number and just beside a sign saying, "Parking on Even Days Only", right?'

'Yeah, yeah, yeah! That's right, that's right!' The parking attendant smiled at me gratefully. The magistrate, always with his head down writing in his notebook, raised his head and looked at me as if with disbelief. The police inspector prosecutor also looked at me, his long face changed to a smile. And I smiled back at him.

I felt good. I felt my honesty was appreciated all round! And when the parking attendant left the witness box. I began to explain. What I did was simply this: I admitted everything they accused me of doing. And then I said I parked wrong because the signs were misleading.

'Look, sir,' I said this directly to the magistrate, 'when you park you car, you naturally take the advice of the nearest sign you see. You never go 50 yards each direction to find out whether there is another sign saying something else, would you? Like in this case, when I saw the sign "Parking on Even Days Only", I naturally thought I could park there on even days. You don't expect me to go to the end of the street to see the other sign saying all the parking lots are for lorries only, do you? And also, they have now painted the street just as I suggested; now everyone can see clearly that the place is for lorries only. It proves they admit that when I parked it there the signs were not clear. In fact it was really misleading. So, sir, please excuse me this once and I promise to be more careful next time.'

I had a very good feeling after saying all this. Although I wasn't as smart as Perry Mason, I felt I more or less said what I wanted to say. And in a very frank and honest way. To tell the truth is a damned good feeling, you know — the whole truth and nothing but the truth!

When the magistrate began to give sentence on my case, I felt a sense of great satisfaction.

'It is accepted that the sign display was somewhat inadequate,' he began softly. 'And it is to the credit of the relevant authorities that amends have been made to correct the situation. The court appreciates the honesty and frankness of the accused. I'm sure the authorities feel the same way about his readiness to make constructive proposals for improving the sign display in the said street. Nevertheless, the fact remains that on the said date and place the defendant was guilty of parking his vehicle in an unauthorised place. I sentence him to a fine of $30 or three days' imprisonment.'

I … I … What can I say? What can I do? What should I have done? Should I have kept quiet? Should I have cornered the poor parking attendant? Or should I have told some lies just to get off? …

I posed these same questions to my young son sitting in that snack bar. 'The world is more complicated than you think and people are not as simple as they look.' Yeah, I know it's a damned old cliché, but can you think of anything better to tell the boy?

My son kept quiet. As if he understood my difficulties; as if he understood why I didn't fight further when he thought I should have in some things — like this damned parking thing.

We went home quiet. And he didn't ask me about these things again. That suited me fine, 'cos it's not always easy to explain to your son why you didn't stand up for things the way the story books say every respectable person should.

Now, that's a sign of him growing up, I said to my wife. He's maturing, I said. That's normal, they get more quiet as they grow, as they get wiser. You know, wise men are always more thoughtful, quieter characters.

Well, he didn't ask me about that story again. He became more and more quiet and gradually the questions didn't come any more.

And then, recently, he got his driving licence and I had a competitor for the use of our family car. I don't mind that because I don't care much for driving now anyway. But he received his first traffic offence ticket on the third day — for parking without displaying a coupon.

He was just unlucky. When he parked the car, there were no coupons left in the car and as he went to buy some, the attendant booked him. *Kena*. Perfect timing.

Thirty dollars. And he promptly paid up.

I said, 'Son, why don't go and negotiate? I think you might have a case here.'

'No use *lah*, dad. You know very well what? *Kena*, pay up, it's part of our way of life. Ha ha ha ha.'

He shrugged his shoulders, laughed a bit and walked away. Boy eighteen now.

But, I don't find that jingle funny anymore ...

(End of Play)

Kopitiam (The Coffee Shop)[1]

Part 1
Scene 1

Darkness. Silence.

Poignant music is heard. Spotlight reveals a kopitiam[2] *banner pasted over with a white paper cross. Shouts by shop assistants are heard ordering drinks and snacks; they get louder, then gradually fade.*

Light falls on Gong Gong[3] *sitting by a marble-topped* kopitiam *table.*

Total silence.

He takes out a cigarette. Picks up a strip of paper from a can on the table, lights it at the top of a kerosene lamp and then lights up his cigarette.

GRANDPA   (*As if trying to capture something from way back in time.*) *Kopi,*[4]
                 teh o[5] ...

---

[1] Playwright's note: This play was inspired by Mr Liu Renxin's play *Spring in the Kopitiam*, written in 1985, which I directed for the Singapore Hock Chew Coffeeshop Owners Association in celebration of its 70th Anniversary. The play has also benefitted from a workshop conducted with the 1986 cast.

[2] Editor's note: *Minnan hua* or *minnan* language, a non-Mandarin Chinese language: Coffeeshop. *Kopi*, however, is an Anglicism or a loan word from English for 'coffee.'

[3] Playwright's note: [Either Mandarin-Chinese, or *minnan hua* or *minnan* language:] *Gong Gong*, Grandpa.

[4] Playwright's note: *Kopi*, coffee with [condensed] milk.

[5] Playwright's note: *teh o*, tea without milk. Editor's note: Literally, 'tea black.' *Teh* is the term for tea in a number of Chinese languages, including *minnan hua* or *minnan* language; here it is *minnan hua*, and the adjective *o*, 'black,' is not in that language but in Teochew-Chinese, or *chauzhou hua* or language, another non-Mandarin Chinese language. The mixing up of language is not untypical in language usage in Singapore.

HEAD ATTENDANT   (*Walking into the light, bringing Grandpa a cup of* kopi o.) What Jia Cai said is true. You know, *towkay,*[6] I have also wanted to quit long ago but I cannot make myself say it. My son, he has no one to mind his son. He and his wife both have to work. It's very hard to get someone to mind my grandson. You know my woman passed away a long time ago. And I've wanted to retire long ago. To help my son and ... It's been very difficult to tell you this ... *Towkay*, it's been so many years now. Such a long time ... But what Jia Cai said is quite true, you know ... But also such a pity ... *Towkay*, the keys ...

He takes out a bunch of keys, puts them on the table and withdraws into darkness.

GRANDPA   I have always hoped you would one day take over from your Father. Carry on this business ...

JIA CAI   Be practical, *Gong Gong*. I really think this is for the best. Neither *Meimei*[7] nor myself are suitable for the business. And you are getting old and *Mama* is not in good health.

GRANDPA   Jia Cai. It's been 50 years now, almost. One cup by one cup, one cent by one cent we saved up for this place ...

Unyielding, he lifts up his kopi o. *But his hand starts to tremble and the cup and saucer start to clatter. He tries hard to steady them but fails. Giving up, he drops the cup, exhausted.*

Yes, we're old!

Poignant music. An erhu[8] *playing the melody of 'Remembering'*[9] *is suddenly heard. It comes from another table where an old man is entertaining himself on the instrument with another old man.*

Maybe, very soon, you'd have to go some other place to play your *erhu* and read your newspapers ...

---

[6] Editor's note: *Minnan hua* or *minnan* language: boss.
[7] Playwright's note: [Mandarin-Chinese:] *Meimei*, younger sister.
[8] Playwright's note: *Erhu*, two-stringed Chinese musical instrument.
[9] Playwright's note: [Music from] *Si xiang ji*. Editor's note: The music is drawn from a famous operatic and dramatic work, *Romance of the West Chamber (Xi xiang ji)*. It was written by the Yuan Dynasty playwright Wang Shifu (*ca.* 1260–1336) and set during the Tang Dynasty.

OLD TEACHER   White-haired old men bidding goodbye to black-haired young men — it makes you feel that much older, and sadder. It's a blessing that Yin Guan has passed away peacefully, unlike this old friend of mind. *Lao Li*[10] and us taught in the same school for more than 30 years. He has always been a highly intelligent man. I never thought he would end his life like this. So tragic. What has the world come to? ... Well, I guess you just have to relax and accept it, don't you, if you want to go on.

Gets up, goes over to Jia Cai.

Jia Cai, if you hadn't come up to say 'hello' to me the other day, I would never have recognised you. But I'm not a bit surprised at your achievements. You always had a good imagination, always liked to dream. In fact, more than once Mr Li had told me you would go very far one day ... Come, Jia Cai, let me tell you something. I know it's very convenient for you to stay in the hotel. But you must understand, old people have their peculiar feelings. (*Indicating Grandpa.*) They need a special kind of understanding, and attention ...

OK, *Lao* Luo,[11] let's go and see *Lao Li*. We're going to Mr Li's house to pay our last respects. You are in mourning yourself, so you needn't go. According to our Chinese custom, it's not appropriate for someone in mourning to go visiting others in mourning.

Luo hangs up his erhu *on the wall and exits with Old Teacher.*

GRANDPA   White-haired old men bidding goodbye to black-haired young men. Yes, they make you feel even older. (*Pours* kopi o[12] *into saucer and drinks from saucer.*)

JIA CAI   *Gong Gong*, time has no mercy. Things are bound to happen when they have to happen and there's nothing we can do about it. But I'm really curious, *Gong Gong*, so many years have gone by, so many things have changed around us and yet our family has changed so little. Compared to ten years ago, we're almost exactly the same. *Baba*[13] was as stubborn he's always been. I asked him to see a Western doctor but he never

[10] Editor's note: Mandarin-Chinese: *Lao Li*, 'elder' Li, or less literally, 'brother' Li, as this is an honorific that can be used to address a contemporary and not only an older person.
[11] Editor's note: see note 10.
[12] Editor's note: Black coffee; see note 5.
[13] Playwright's note: [Mandarin-Chinese:] *Baba*, Father.

took any notice. *Meimei* said she and *Mama* were never told by *Baba* that I made the suggestion.

GRANDPA   Too many things have changed already ... Those which have not changed, it seems, are not going to be around ...

JIA CAI   *Gong Gong*, you mustn't mix up business with your everyday living or get emotional about it. So many times I have asked *Baba* to come and visit me, to take a look around. And he always said he had no time.

Grandpa lights up a cigarette with his lighter.

He always said he couldn't get people to relieve him and so couldn't leave this place even for a day. But he went to China and stayed on for three months! I'm not saying he shouldn't, I'm just saying he's too emotional. You can't do business like that.

GRANDPA   Your Father's a good man. This *kopitiam* has been his life. He stayed here every day. Every day of every year, for as long as I can remember, he worked in this *kopitiam*.

JIA CAI   But *Gong Gong*, man is not machine. Man needs to rest. You can't work every day. And from the time you wake tip until the time you go to bed.

GRANDPA   What would you do if you don't work?

JIA CAI   Go home? Take an afternoon nap. Go to the community centre: Play chess, watch TV.

GRANDPA   Go home! Everybody locks up their door — front door, back door, even their windows, nobody wants to talk to his neighbour. You don't even know who lives next door! You want to play chess in the community centre? Everyone is so *kiasu*.[14] They start quarrelling before you finish even one game. Watch TV? So noisy ... So many programmes speak languages which I can't understand.

JIA CAI   The greatest regret for *Baba* is that, all his life, he never enjoyed one relaxed moment. Honestly, I don't know how you all can go on like this

---

[14] Playwright's note: [*Minnan hua* or *minnan* language:] *kiasu*, literally, afraid to lose out.

every day, every year, repeating the same chores again and again and again. You never stop! ...

GRANDPA   (*Lights his cigarette again.*) We're born like this. So used to it ... If we don't work, what can we do? ... You know, your Father came to work for me when he was only ten. Washing cups and saucers, cleaning the floor, collecting the rubbish — all the dirty work. His Mother and Father had both died. He was very hardworking, very honest, very good to people. During the Japanese Occupation, they took him to Endau in Johor[15] to clear the jungle. He lived alone, a young man, but never took up any bad habit. He lived very clean. And when the war was over, he opened his own *kopi* stall.

Entering into his memory ...

When I went to seek him out to marry your Mother, he was only 20.

Yin Guan and his kopi *stall appear. Someone shouts 'Kopi, collect money here!'*

YIN GUAN   (*Offstage.*) O, *lailo!*[16]

After a moment, Yin Guan enters carrying a tray of empty cups and saucers.

Towkay-pek,[17] I want to work a few more years on my own before I move on. You know I have known Yao Di several years now. After I came back from Endau, you also asked me to work in your *kopitiam*. You have all helped me so much ... I won't forget. I have no one left in my own family now. You have all cared for me, more than anyone else ...

Serve a cup of kopi o *to Grandpa.*

GRANDPA   Yin Guan, you're the only one left in your family. Come to my place and life won't be so hard for you. Now you must work from sunrise to midnight, you want to pass water also have to wait for someone to look out for you.

---

[15] Editor's note: Johor is a state in southern end of West Malaysia, a short distance across the Johor Straits from the northern shore of Singapore.
[16] Playwright's note: [*Minnan hua* or *minnan* language:] *lailo*, coming.
[17] Playwright's note: [*Minnan hua* or *minnan* language:] *towkay-pek*, 'boss-uncle'.

YIN GUAN   Everybody's life is hard. Although it's peace time, now we have the Emergency.[18] Everybody's nervous; market very bad. At night very few people want to go out. My area here is not so bad, quite safe. During wartime, everybody want peace. Now peace is here, still confusion everywhere. Earning a living is really tough.

GRANDPA   If Yao Di can marry now, my heart will find rest. You know, her Mother died a few years ago. I've been so worried Japanese will spoil her. Now if you two marry, you can take over my *kopitiam* ...

YIN GUAN   *Towkay-pek*, this is exactly what I don't want. I don't want to have my wife bringing me property and money. That would give me a bad name. And it's no good for you and Yao Di also. Wait a few years more. I save some more money. I can also get some friends to make *hui*[19] and then open my own *kopitiam*, and then I marry her.

GRANDPA   I know you have good willpower. But you already have this *kopi* stall now and you have already realised your ambition!

YIN GUAN   Not the same, *Towkay-pek*. Before the war, I thought working in *kopitiam* was really hard. I envied people so much when I saw them go to school. I always thought how nice if my Father and Mother were still alive. Even when I worked in the machine shop I was not earning enough to go to school. But I really wanted to study, you know! And then, the Japanese came and I had to go to Johor, Endau, to open jungle. And then I knew what is really hard: cutting trees, digging up the stumps, cleaning up the burnt land, hot like hell, mosquito bites everywhere, and we had to drink ditch water. Not enough rice and later we can only eat *ubi kayu*,[20] and everybody got swollen feet ... No doctor, no medicine. People died like flies. When I was a small boy, *Baba* told us jungle life was very tough, jungle work very hard, and I never believed him. When I lived and worked there myself, then I knew. Just having money is not so

---

[18] Editor's note: The (Malayan) Emergency refers to a guerrilla war for independence fought between Great Britain and British Commonwealth armed forces and the military arm of the Malayan Communist Party from 1948 to 1960.

[19] Playwright's note: [*Minnan hua* or *minnan* language:] *hui*, tontine, [here referring to] a traditional Chinese way of group saving[s].

[20] Playwright's note: [Malay:] *ubi kayu*, edible root of a tropical plant. Editor's note: The specific tuber in question here is tapioca.

important. Knowing how to do hard work and live hard life is more important.

GRANDPA   I always wanted a son. That's why we called her Yao Di.[21] Now you two are not young anymore. Since you two like each other, why wait much longer?

Yin Guan's words are checked by customers calling 'Kopi!' *and Yin Guan responds and starts to make* kopi.

YIN GUAN   Water your own soil with your own sweat, and the rice you grow would also taste nicer. (*Takes* kopi *out to customer.*)

GRANDPA   Yin Guan had very good willpower. He managed his *kopi* stall all by himself. Night time, he'd pull down a big canvas cover, put two long benches together and slept inside. Rain or sun, he worked every day, all through the year. Finally he agreed to marry your Mother. But he insisted and worked another year. He saved altogether $333 for the engagement present. Like he was doing business with me.

Scene 2

Back to the present.

JIA CAI   *Baba* is a very capable man. He was unlucky to have been born in the wrong time. And he didn't get a chance to go to school. That's why he supported me to go study overseas. 'You must work hard. But most important of all is to study hard,' he used to say to me. If not for him, Mother would never have agreed to let me go. It was such a waste that he gave his entire life to this *kopitiam*.

GRANDPA   What's wrong with working in this *kopitiam*? You think running a *kopitiam* is easy? He bakes very fragrant *kopi* beans. His timing's just right. He used to say, 'You must never save on the ingredients. This is our name, our banner!' He grinds the *kopi* powder very finely. His *kopi* is more fragrant than other people's. And for every can of milk,[22] he would only make 15 cups of *kopi*. Other people can make more, but he doesn't want to make more. He wants to make them extra tasty ...

---

[21] Editor's note: The name Yao Di in Mandarin-Chinese means 'would like a younger brother'.
[22] Editor's note: The reference here is to canned condensed milk.

He was such a good man ... *Kopitiam*, yes, you can excel even by running a *kopitiam*!

JIA CAI   *Baba*'s problem is that he knew only how to look after other people but never knew how to look after himself.

GRANDPA   'Why do you come here every day?' He used to ask me. And yet he didn't know how to rest himself ... After the war, he became the only survivor in his family ...

JIA CAI   And so he worked day and night, day and night, until he got himself sick. This has got to stop. It's bad for your health. It's not even good economics.

GRANDPA   For parents, their children is everything ... But children don't always take their parents for anything! (*He remembers, pointing to another table —*) There, that's where your Mother pounded all the *haybee hiam*.[23] Right here. (*Sits down and starts caressing the table.*) Every time she pounded she would grumble, 'Why is he not back yet? ... Married now ... Got children even ...' And your Father would stop her and say, 'OK, enough *lah*.[24] If you want to grumble, why let him go and study in the first place? If he doesn't want to come back, let him be damned, why do you bother?' ... But, as always, after your Mother had packed the stuff for you, your Father would take it to the post office personally. They grumble every time, and they still send every time ... That's how it is. All parents live for their children. What else? All the hardship, for who, if not the children? What I don't understand is: Why would you want to stay overseas and not return for such a long time? ... Don't you miss home?

JIA CAI   Yes, at first. Then it got easier and easier. As you stay longer, your habits change. So would your thinking, your ideas.

GRANDPA   Change ... yes, things change, they do ... Many of the things you talk about I cannot understand ... You were not like that when you were young, you know ... You were always so obedient.

---

[23] Playwright's note: [*Minnan hua* or *minnan* language:] *haybee hiam*, shrimp chili paste.
[24] Editor's note: Malay: *lah*, '[A] particle emphasising the word to which it is appended' (*A Malay-English English-Malay Dictionary*, ed. A. E. Coope [revised edn.; London and Basingstoke: Macmillan Education, 1991]).

JIA CAI   Whether you change is not entirely up to you. Sometimes, when the reality changes, you have no choice but to go along. This is where I've had quite a few knockings. You know, traditionally, we Chinese have always been very humble. But you can't do it anymore in this day and age. In the past, when we Chinese talked, we always practised modesty; we always understate. When we know ten things, we say we only know eight; when we know eight, we say six. When opportunities come, we practise patience and deference, self-restraint and self-inhibition; we decline to bring focus to ourselves.

If you do that overseas, you may miss your university, or even risk not finding a job. You might even starve. If, for example, they ask you whether you are good at something, you must never say, 'Yes, a little.' Because no one would want to hire someone who knows only 'a little'. The way now is to 'grab whatever opportunity that comes to you and sell yourself in the best way you can'. In fact, this is more or less the general practice here already. Our traditional Oriental modesty is already out of fashion. Even the big government corporations are using smiles and beautiful girls to sell themselves.

GRANDPA   Our *kopitiam* is different, Eng Seng has never changed in all these years.

JIA CAI   But *Gong Gong*, ours is maybe the only one, and that's because you have refused to change. But if you go out and look around, look further than this neighbourhood, you'll see that everything has changed ... What's more, you'll find that no change may not be a good thing at all.

GRANDPA   Why must we change? So changed that we don't know anything anymore. We can't get used to all these changes. Nowadays I don't even know how to take a bus. The streets are all so different I can't find my way anymore ... So changed ... I can't even talk to your sister's children ... Your old teacher Mr Liu said the other day, 'Hey, I must go to night school to learn English, otherwise I won't know how to talk to my grandchildren.' You mustn't change too much, too fast ...

(*Remembering the past again.*) It's very difficult for us to understand ... Those of us who came from China ... So many decades ago ... The gap is so wide now ... Now you all know more about foreign countries than about your own country ... The hardships we suffered coming down here, we old people can only keep in our hearts.

Story-Teller from the past appears upstage.

Scene 3

Around a small wooden box set up by the Story-Teller, lit by a lamp, coolie listeners gather, some sitting, some lying down, some squatting, some standing.

STORY-TELLER   The rain continued for days. The flood level all over the county rose higher and higher. There was no indication that the situation would improve.

GRANDPA   Our farmland at home suffered natural disasters almost every two or three years.

STORY-TELLER   Things got worse in the north-western part of the county.[25] In some villages, the water rose to knee high; the worst hit villages had all their houses under water.

GRANDPA   My Father left home because there was a very bad flood. There was no harvest and he had to come over here to find a livelihood.

STORY-TELLER   Tens of thousand of victims walked along the railway line into the towns looking for food.

GRANDPA   Flood and famine, that was the year when my Grandfather fell sick and died, leaving behind my Mother and me, and Grandma ...

STORY-TELLER   War and natural disasters made life very hard for folks at home. Relief workers from Singapore witnessed all these and every one of them cried.

GRANDPA   My Mother's own village was even worse; they lived closer to the river and many people were swept away by the flood!

STORY-TELLER   The relief workers went to the worst hit areas with medical workers from the county. But they were attacked on several occasions by the bandits.

GRANDPA   I was told that my Mother even went begging in other villages ... I remember she used to go away for days.

STORY-TELLER   The county authorities presented two banners to the Singapore relief organisations. One for the drama club which organised the charity show, the other for the Rubber Association.

---

[25] Playwright's note: Probably in Fujian province [in China].

GRANDPA	My Mother was only 20 that year. But she was so thin and sick that she looked like a woman of over 50.
STORY-TELLER	According to those who managed to escape from the floods, the food shortage at home was very severe. No rice, oil, salt or sugar. Those who failed to get out were either seriously ill or died. On top of that, banditry was at its worst.
GRANDPA	I don't know how we got through those years. If my Father hadn't come over here and sent us money, we'd probably all have died ...
STORY-TELLER	Once the bandits discovered food, they would start killing everyone. So many people died in their hands. With flood and famine and banditry, that was the worst year this county has ever experienced.
GRANDPA	Later on, when they told us my Father had died over here, my Mother was so shocked that she couldn't cry ... In the end, she decided to send me over anyhow ...

The coolies begin to leave slowly, followed by the Story-Teller himself.

Scene 4

Back to the present.

GRANDPA	Sending me away was the only way to keep me alive. But my Mother didn't want to leave; she stayed behind to look after my grandmother, her Mother-in-law ... When I first came, I worked as a delivery boy, pulling a cart, getting up before dawn every morning. For some time, I rode to town in an old man's bullock cart. He loved telling stories, all the time teaching me the Confucian virtues. 'You know what's the difference between man and animals? Just eight characters: *Li Yi Lian Chi Xiao Di Zhong Xin*,' he said.[26] With him, it was like being at home. And that's what my Mother used to teach me ... I really don't know how you can go away so long and not miss home ...
JIA CAI	People are different today.
GRANDPA	Why different?

---

[26] Playwright's note: [Mandarin-Chinese:] *Li Yi Lian Chi Xiao Di Zhong Xin*, propriety, justice, honesty, sense of shame, filial piety, brotherhood, loyalty and trust.

JIA CAI

Why not? People can't ride carts forever, not even bullock carts! Like when I was young you bought me rubber balls to play, or *goli*,[27] or *layang*,[28] and when I got older, you bought me a bicycle. But kids now start playing video games before they even get to primary school. My kids started punching the computer before they entered kindergarten. And of course when you've got TV, film and radio you don't have any need for storytelling anymore, right? In the same way, many years ago you had earth floors, then you had cement floors, and now people want mosaic or marble. People today all want to go to a café or a fast-food centre. They don't want to go to a *kopitiam* anymore.

GRANDPA

But they're not the same! You have TV; yes, but I still want my stories. Café and fast-food centre are not the same as *kopitiam*. They use *kopi* essence, never as fragrant as our *kopi* powder. And they don't have *teh see*.[29] No they don't! We bake our own *kopi* beans, we grind our own powder, we make every cup special and they all taste special! *Kopi* essence nowadays can never compare with our home-made *kopi* mixed with 'Red-Headed Soldier' condensed milk!

After a prolonged detour, they finally arrive at the heart of the conflict. They are staring at each other, each knowing what the other is thinking — but neither will give in.

JIA CAI

(*Feeling it is time to lay bare the conflict.*) Grandpa, I can sympathise with everything you've said. But I know for sure your way has no future.

GRANDPA

No future?

JLA CAI

The way you operate is just too conservative, too old-fashioned!

GRANDPA

Old-fashioned? Conservative? No future? From 1936 ... almost 50 years now ... we saved from every cup, every cent, we have saved everything we have now! One generation, two generation, three genera-tion, we all lived on these one cup by one cup, one cent by one cent savings. The money we gave you to go to school, the money we used to send you abroad ... They may be old-fashioned but they all came from the one cup, one cent savings!

---

[27] Playwright's note: [Malay:] *goli* [or *guli*], marbles.
[28] Playwright's note: [Malay:] *layang*, kites. Editor's note: Usually *laying-layang*, 'a generic name for children's kites' (*A Malay-English English-Malay Dictionary*, ed. Coope).
[29] Playwright's note: [*Minnan hua* or *minnan* language:] *teh see*, tea with evaporated milk.

JIA CAI	Those with 60, 70, 80 years' history, some of them suffered even more! Grandpa, do you want to wait for this building to crash down before you wake up? Look, Grandpa, every up has its down and eventually fade away. Remember the shop you served as apprentice — Tai Heng? That's even older. So what? It disappeared well before us. But *Baba*'s good friend, Uncle Di Ge — now, that man's got a good head. He saw what was coming and decided to change as soon as he realised the need to change. He had one *kopitiam* turned into a coffeehouse and the other one into a fast-food café.

But he's OK only for now, because his children have all started bargaining with him. Unless he meets their conditions — each getting a house and a car — they would refuse to go on. And I know he's got to change again!

As for us? We don't even have the right kind of people, not to mention the way you manage and the way you do up this place. How can you cope with the change? Look, Grandpa, we must all change with the times. When you see a wall, and when you know the wall is hard, why do you want to run into it? Why can't turn away? Why can't you change?

GRANDPA	Turn away? Change course? Why are you young people all turning away and changing course so easily? You are only 30, why are you already so sophisticated?

When I first came down from China, I didn't have even one cent on me, so whatever I do I won't get worse! I'm not afraid. I don't care whether they are *ang mo*,[30] or Japanese devils, or whether it's natural disaster, I have tasted everything. I have not changed and will not change. But why are you, all of you who grew up in peace time and never tasted hardship, why are you all so easily turning away and changing courses? ... Your Great Grandmother, my Mother, I had wanted to bring her over every year since I came down here. But she never wanted to come. So, I can only buy her some land, and build her a house. Yes, she's satisfied ... She felt contented whether the harvest was good or

---

[30] Playwright's note: [*Minnan hua* or *minnan* language:] *ang mo*, Caucasian. Editor's note: The expression used here is a shortened version of the derogatory expression *ang mo kow*, literally 'red-haired monkey'.

bad. She never wanted to leave home, even when the flood water covered her waist!

JIA CAI   Yes, and she would rather fall sick, and eventually died there! Right? But is it worth it?

GRANDPA   Worth it? What do you mean, worth it? Everyone has a home, right? Everyone has to keep and protect his home, right? What's wrong with keeping your home? What's wrong with that? ... No, Jia Cai, we must never forsake our home, our origin! (*The grandson's disagreement hurts him.*) Oh, Jia Cai, don't you understand? Your Father ... your Mother, they all understand ... You know, during our most difficult times, when our *kopitiam* was nearly destroyed during our most prosperous days, we never gave up even then!

Grandpa enters into the realm of his memory again.

Scene 5

Almost instantly, the stage is overflowing with noisy customers patronising the kopitiam. *Presently, a string of bombing sounds hits the scene, followed by sirens. Then everyone freezes.*

GRANDPA   It was 1942, midnight on December 8th. The Japanese started bombing from the air. Two months later they marched into the city. Our business suffered badly and no one knew whether they would live to see tomorrow. Where could we run? If you were not a traitor, what choice have you got but to live under terror day after day!

A   That night, we had already gone to sleep. Then we were woken up in horror by the bombing. Everybody was shocked, we didn't know where to run. We were living in Boat Quay, the house next to ours was hit by the bomb. The first floor was blasted open, five people died in the front room. Half of our wall collapsed and we could see people running around in panic in the streets. Some crying for help, some running around helping others. The bombing made my Grandmother deaf and many of my relatives got injured. Then the ground floor caught fire and most of the merchandise there was destroyed. Later we moved to live on a farm in Changi. We thought that would get us out of trouble, but the Japanese continued bombing and my Father was hit and died there in Changi.

B

Around Christmas time, the Tanjong Pagar Wharf was hit by bombs and there was a big fire in the warehouse and nearly 500 people died. We rushed over to rescue the survivors and found so many people crying and yelling it was like a madhouse.

At the time, the Great World and Victoria Institution in Jalan Besar were all turned into first-aid stations. We drove the injured people into the General Hospital in Sepoy Lines[31] and then we drove the dead ones to the Atlantic Cinema in Great World to let people go and identify their relatives and friends.

From West Coast Road to Kim Seng Bridge in Havelock Road, the roads were all dripping with blood. People in the streets all stopped and talked nervously. In the cinema, all the seats were taken out, the entire cinema hall lined with dead bodies. Some lost limbs, some lost head, some only in parts. Blood everywhere. And wild cats, dogs and rats were feeding themselves everywhere. Then there were those who came looking for their dead relatives, and they were howling like mad, the place was a living hell.

C

Bloody hell, the *ang mo*s never got the heart to fight, because this was not their own country. And they didn't want to give us the guns because they were afraid we would rise against them. It was only on February 1st, only two weeks to their final surrender they decided to give us some weapon. All at once 3,000 of us joined the volunteers' force. I went to register with the son of the *kopitiam* owner in Cross Street and Yin Guan's elder brother. Jin Guan was only 16. We were given those old-fashioned double-barrel hunting guns and then we were sent to Jurong to guard the 18th Milestone area.

We had more than 100 people in the detachment, some from Chung Cheng High School, some also from Chinese High School. We fought for three days there. The Japanese planes were bombing us from the sky and the Japanese soldiers fighting us in the front. Finally, we retreated to Bukit Timah 6th Milestone ... Soon after that, we heard the British

[31] Editor's note: This is the present Singapore General Hospital at Outram Road.

soldiers had surrendered. So we dispersed in a hurry. Most of our comrades were captured by the Japanese and killed afterwards. Woodlands
was the worst. The Japanese met with stiff resistance there and they
were very angry and started a massacre there after the surrender. Even
women and children were not spared. Hundreds of people were killed
there for nothing.

D   My Mother, she took me and my three sisters to a farm in Tampines
waiting for my Father to return from China. One day, three Japanese
soldiers came to check our house. My Mother told us to go and feed the
pigs and chicken and stay away from the house and then she went to
deal with the Japanese soldiers ... She ... she ... We saw her body afterwards ... After the war, when Father returned, he told us Mother
hanged herself after she was ...

E   The worst came from the traitors who worked for the Japanese.
During the Great Cleaning-Up Campaign, we were rounded into
North Bridge Road and Victoria Street like cattle. The whole area
was fenced in by barbed wire. The traitors, some of them had their
faces covered, stood by the Japanese at the checkpoints. Once they
point at you, you are finished. They push you into a lorry, together
with the intellectuals and anti-Japanese people and those who refused
to co-operate with the Japanese, and drive you to Ponggol, Changi or
Pasir Panjang for mass execution. For those who were let off, the
Japanese would stamp a chop[32] on your shirt, or arm, or face, with
the characters 'Checked by the Great Japanese Military Police'. For
those who came through, the chop was like a life permit, some carried the chop for weeks and dared not take a shower or wash their
shirts. They were scared they would be dragged away if they lost the
stamp. Chop, chop, chop, we were treated no better than sheep and
cattle ...

The kopitiam *customers drift off.*

---

[32] Editor's note: 'chop' or in Malay '*cap* (noun), 1. Chinese printing: "chopping"; a Chinese chop
or seal for use with ink ...; a trade-mark; business name, "chop", of a Chinese firm' (*A Malay-
English English-Malay Dictionary*, ed. Coope).

Scene 6

GRANDPA   Your Uncle, your Father's elder brother, joined the People's Anti-Japanese Army[33] before the Japanese soldiers landed in Singapore. He was sent to defend the Bukit Timah area. Only 16. He never returned. Jin Guan is like your Father, hardworking, honest and cared a lot about friends ... Your Father, he was only 14, but he was a very tall boy. He was sent to Endau to open new land. Your grandmother ... this area where we lived, suffered a lot of bombing. Besides air bombing, the Japanese canons were also firing into the city centre ... One day, your grandmother was washing in the backyard, a bomb came down ... Jia Cai, do you understand what I'm saying?

Jia Cai understands, but disagrees, and he does not respond.

     Even if you don't want to take over the business, you would come home one day, wouldn't you? We Chinese have an old saying, 'Falling leaves return to their roots.' Although you're not that old, you would want to come home, wouldn't you?

JIA CAI   (*Feeling it is time to let out the truth.*) Well, Grandpa, actually I came back to settle some personal affairs, apart from attending *Baba*'s funeral.

Grandpa waits anxiously, holding his breath.

     Grandpa, Annie and I, we are planning to emigrate to Canada.

GRANDPA   (*Totally taken by surprise.*) Emigrate? ... Jia Cai, you mean you want to go away forever?

Jia Cai could only look at Grandpa, hoping to be understood although he knows it will not happen.

---

[33] Editor's note: This is a reference to the Malayan People's Anti-Japanese Army (MPAJA). The MPAJA was a guerrilla movement formed to oppose the Japanese occupation of Malaya (now West Malaysia, or peninsular Malaysia) during the Second World War. The British had trained small groups of Malayans as guerrilla troops, in anticipation of the Japanese invasion of Southeast Asia. These troops then became the MPAJA. Members of the MPAJA, who were mainly Chinese leftists, emerged as heroes from the war.

How can you go away forever? You are the only man of your generation. How can you go away? In peace time, or in war time, we braved natural disasters, we faced starvation, all for your generation. When you were first born, we feared you might not live. Then we feared you might not get to go to school. After school, we feared you might not get a job. And now, you've finished your studies, and you've got a job and you want to go away *forever?*

JIA CAI   Come on, Grandpa, you know I appreciate everything you all have done for me. You slaved all your life to give us a better life. But you must understand, when something gets better, other things also change. Things won't just change to where you want it and then stop.

GRANDPA   But why? What would your Father say if he were alive now? Have you told your Mother?

Jia Cai shakes his head.

You slave and slave all your life, day and night. For what? And why? Because you want to settle down, open a shop, make a home, so you can live more comfortably, and bury your roots. You want to buy a house so all the family can have a home. To go on and on, generation after generation in peace and tranquillity. Why? How come now we have come to this?

He remembers his daughter's wedding.

(*End of Part 1*)

Part 2
Scene 7

The wedding night of Yin Guan and Yao Di.

Roaring celebration music.

Excited guests usher in the newlywed couple, teasing them and trying to get them to perform intimate acts. Presently, they are all dispatched by the sophisticated matchmaker, leaving the couple who are now in front of the reflective Father [Grandpa] who is sitting by his marble-topped table.

On the day of great joy, he remembers his Mother and his wife, and the hard times he spent with them.

Yao Di understands her Father's feelings and is emotionally overcome. She kneels down and weeps on his lap. The Father turns his face away to hide his emotions but puts his hand over Yao Di's head.

Yin Guan is also deeply touched and he kneels beside Yao Di.

YIN GUAN   *Abah*,[34] please stop worrying, I will treat Yao Di well. I will try my best to make this *kopitiam* prosper. From now on, you have both me and Yao Di and you don't have to work so hard ... Peace time has returned, I will work very, very hard, to give you peace of mind, to look after the whole family, to make everyone happy ...

GRANDPA   I have no worries now. I am very happy now that you are married to each other. This is an auspicious day and I shouldn't say this. But now I can go away any time very happily, because I know Yao Di has you to look after her. I don't have very much to give you. This *kopitiam* is nothing much, but it's all I have collected all my life. Wealth is not permanent, it can come, it can go. To be a man, the most important thing is good character. Very soon, you will become parents and have your own children. You must teach them to be pious children, loyal friends, respect other people, be honest and faithful, don't rob, don't grab, be clean in everything you do ... You, and the next generation, and the next ...

He cannot go on, and waves them away.

---

[34] Editor's note: [*Minnan hua* or *minnan* language:] *Abah*, Father.

Scene 8

GRANDPA   (*Emotions turning to grief.*) Times are different now. I don't understand your generation, why ...

JIA CAI   *Baba* kept saying these things to me, even in his last letter.

GRANDPA   When people talk about tradition now, they think they are talking about old things in the past ... old things, useless things.

JIA CAI   Grandpa, I respect everything you've said. And I don't need to hide the fact that we don't see eye to eye on many things.

GRANDPA   I'm old, you are so young, of course we see things different. This I know. What I can't understand is why must you emigrate. You want to go away? Never to come back? You don't want this home anymore? Why are you thinking in this way?

JIA CAI   Did I ever say I was not going to come back? When did I say that?

But the issue is too big and he reckons he can only deal with it in a roundabout way.

Look, Grandpa, when I left home, I was very reluctant to go. *Mama* was a big pull. She said, 'Salaries, no matter how big, is only big enough to feed a family. But business, no matter how small, is enough to make a fortune.' She wanted me to see my future linked to the future of the *kopitiam*. The funny thing was, *Baba* saw it differently and I didn't think he objected to my leaving home. Anyway, what you and *Mama* and *Baba* think about the family influenced me a lot, and for a very long time — until something very serious happened after my graduation.

I've never told anyone of you about it because I knew our thinking was drifting apart. I was afraid this would cause more misunderstanding.

You know, Grandpa, I studied computer science and I did very well. After graduation, because I made some minor invention, I registered a patent and formed a company. It went very well, and very soon I hooked on to a very major buyer. My production expanded and my company began to show very good profits. But soon afterwards, this major customer told me he wanted to buy me over, the company together with patent rights. Of course, the company belonged to me, and so did the patent. It's up to me whether I wanted to sell. In theory, anyway. Because while I can hold on to my rights not to sell, he can decide not to buy anymore. And if he stopped buying, I would be stuck. So what's the point in holding on to your rights when they're going to be worth nothing?

I had to decide. So I looked at other people's experience and thought very hard about it. Eventually, I decided to sell it on condition that I would stay as the company's managing director. The day before I signed the contract, I was in a great depression. I felt as if I was forced to give up myself, as if I was selling a piece of my own flesh. But, you know, once the company left my ownership, the pain gradually went away. And when, a little later, a rival company invited me to join them on a much higher salary, I gladly accepted. Now I am competing with the company which I had first founded, and I am trying to develop a new product to compete with the one I developed earlier which launched my previous company. Grandpa, you'd imagine I would feel very painful about all this, right?

The fact is, no, I'm not. On the contrary, I feel a new sense of joy, because I am trying to compete and transcend myself. I'm feeling a new sense of freedom because I would never ever be inhibited by limits I set before. Because I won't stop at what I had previously started!

Realising he has gone over Grandpa's head.

Do you know what I'm saying, Grandpa? Somehow, I have a feeling that if *Baba*'s still alive, he would understand. Grandpa, you must understand, having reached where I am, there's no way I can get any further unless I go away.

GRANDPA   (*Jia Ca's views are completely beyond him. The Grandson has never looked more alien to him.*) But ... why? Give up your own invention ... Your own company ... If he doesn't want to buy your things, can't you sell to other people?

JIA CAI   (*Seeing the futility, he changes the subject.*) Grandpa, big business today just don't behave like that. But I want you to know, I understand how you feel. Grandpa, I know that elderly people become very attached to the past the older they get.

GRANDPA   What's wrong in keeping old things? They are all for the new generations, right? I worked all my life. Your Father worked all his life, all

	because we wanted to keep something for all of you. Your sister has married, she couldn't take over the business. Now you don't want it. Do you want me and your Mother to carry on?
JIA CAI	Grandpa, nothing in the world will ever remain unchanged. Many things were OK yesterday but not OK today and would be completely out tomorrow. Even in the *kopi* business, Grandpa, you started with *kopi* stalls, like what Father did at first. And then you opened a shop, a *kopitiam*. Then you make them bigger and bigger. Same here, you must continue to change. You must modernise, even apply automation. You have to change.
GRANDPA	Modernise. Automation. From one big container you make 80 cups. But the *kopi* goes sour before you sell half a container. How can we sell such bad *kopi*?
JIA CAI	But you have to expand the same time you modernise. And when you expand, 80 cups of *kopi* in one container will have no time to go sour. If you don't want to expand, why bother to modernise, why bother to buy automatic machines, why not go self-service? They're all geared to save labour and costs.
GRANDPA	Modernise? Expand? What for? Many customers are gone. And who wants self-service? It's so much better now: We make *kopi*, we serve *kopi*, we collect money, all by ourselves. You don't say it's trouble-some, this way you can chit-chat with your customers, and they all become your friends. After *kopi*, they stay; they play chess, they read newspapers, all free … When you go automatic, you only collect money, no time to talk, no newspapers and no tables and chairs to sit even. What's the joy in doing business like that? …

Remembers his friends, including an Indian, sitting around a kopi *stall.*

Scene 9

GRANDPA	This *kopitiam* belonged to an Indian man before. It was not in very good shape and I paid him $350. Then I changed all the tables and chairs, put up a big mirror on the wall, repaired the toilet and put in a big fan …

The Indian man wanted to go home ... Samy ... yah, Samy. Samy was selling curry rice here. At first he rented me this shop. Fifteen dollars a month ... including water and electricity ... Indian people are even more homesick then we Chinese, they must go home every three or five years ...

INDIAN

(*A bit tipsy.*) *Yah, balik rumah ... Lima tahun sudah guah belum balik lagi. Ibu bapak banyak tuah ... Sini bagus. Tapi mesti balik jumpa lah ...*

[Malay: Yes, go home. Five years have gone by since I last went home. Mother and Father are very old. ... It's good here. But I have to go home and see them.]

[GRANDPA'S]
FRIEND

Ini betul. Ibu bapak guah dan kawan itu saya punya pun semua di Cina lagi. Tapi kita tak senang balik rumah macam sama Samy. *Susah lah.*

[Malay: This is true. My Mother, Father and friend are all in China. But we have not time to go back, unlike Samy. It's difficult.]

GRANDPA

He wanted to go home to see his relatives. That's good! We also have old Mothers and Fathers at home but it's not so easy for us to go home ... (*To his friend.*) Di Ge, I can afford $300. I can buy this place for $300. You tell him he can go home very happy after selling this place to me. (*To Samy.*) *Yah, tiga ratus ringgit bagus* [Malay: Yes, $300 is good.].

INDIAN

Eh kawan, tempat ini bagus. Ada orang Cina, ada orang India, orang Melayu pun ada. Kawan ini pun tahu lah. Dia niaga sini sudah lama. Air api guna banyak, tiga ratus tak patut lah.

[Malay: Eh, friend, this place is good. It has Chinese people, Indian people and also Malay people. My friend knows this too. A lot of water and fire (i.e., electricity) are used, 300 is not fair.]

FRIEND

Tapi barang-barang sudah lama, pecah, kotor. Kawan guah mesti tukar beli banyak. Kerusi, meja, tanah, cermin, pasang kipas ... Tiga ratus cukup lah, Samy.

[Malay: But things are old, broken, dirty. My friend must change and buy much. Chair, table, land, mirror, fix the fan ... Three hundred is enough, Samy.]

INDIAN
: *Ibu bapak Samy sudah tuah. Kali ini saya balik mahu kahwin, mahu beli tanah bagi ibu bapak. Nanti Samy balik Singapore lagi, bini guah tinggal pelihara ibu bapak.*

: [Malay: Samy's Mother and Father are already old. This time I go back to get married, (and) will buy land for my Mother and Father. When Samy later returns to Singapore, my wife will remain behind to look after my Mother and Father.]

GRANDPA
: Oh, Samy wants to go back to get married? And to buy land to look after his parents? ... In that case, we must not take advantage of people ... Maybe, Di Ge, I can raise another *hui* to get some more money ...

FRIEND
: *Empat ratus banyak mahal lah. Kawan kerja kuat-kuat tapi duit tak cukup. Mesti pasang tontine.*

: [Malay: Four hundred is very expensive. (My) friend works very hard but there isn't enough money. Must resort to tontine.]

INDIAN
: *Guah tahu. Dulu guah pun kerja macam dia. Potong getah, pasang rumah, gaji sepuloh sen satu hari saja. Tapi orang Cina pasang tontin bagus. Interest murah. Guah pinjam duit, kawan pun ambil interest mahal tinggi. Barang-barang semua saya kasih dia, periuk, mangkok, cawan, semua. Guah mahu balik rumah jumpa ibu bapak guah!*

: [Malay: I know. Previously, I too worked like him. Tapping rubber, building houses, working for only ten cents a day. But Chinese people use tontine, which is good. Interest is cheap. I borrow money, (my) friend also gets high interest. I give him all the things, cooking pot, bowls, cups, all. I want to go home to meet my Mother and Father!]

He drinks and gradually fades away.

FRIEND
: Three hundred and fifty dollars is OK. You change the tables and chairs. Put another layer of cement on the floor. Get a new mirror. The rice stall you can rent out ... Raising another *hui* is no problem.

GRANDPA
: I can make at least $20 a month ... Must buy a daily newspaper. People can read and stay longer.

Scene 10

GRANDPA   ... Yah, buy a daily newspaper. And then a chess set. Later, we put in white tiles and made a new counter. Our customers increased very quickly. They come to drink *kopi*, read newspaper, play chess ... Most of them are single men, they had nowhere to go, like the Indian man ... Sometimes they stay until near midnight, drinking, sometimes gambling, even fighting ... That's what a *kopitiam* is like! ... Modernise, automatic machines. Yes, very clean, very tidy, but nobody wants to stay. They buy, they pay, they leave. What's the point of just earning money and people don't even stay and talk?

JIA CAI   But most of our neighbours have already moved away, Grandpa. Those who didn't have also switched to other work. They don't come to the *kopitiam* anymore. What's more, very few of the young people are interested in *kopitiam*. For those who do come, no one appreciates your home-made *kopi*.

GRANDPA   No, old customers still come back!

JLA CAI   But how many? Could they sustain your business? Most of them have moved away, or died altogether. How many are you left?

He realises he has said the wrong thing, but it's too late.

        Grandpa, things don't always turn out the way you want!

Grandpa senses he has something to say.

        Grandpa, tell me: Would you like to move to the New Town?

GRANDPA   Move?

JIA CAI   Yes. To the New Town.[35]

GRANDPA   New Town? Why move to the New Town?

JIA CAI   Urban renewal. That's going to affect us sooner or later. In two to three years' time, at the most five to eight, they would pull down all these.

---

[35] Editor's note: Jia Cai is suggesting that Grandpa move into a flat inside one of the public-housing estates — or New Towns — that the state's housing agency, the Housing and Development Board (HDB), has built outside the city core since the 1960s. The Grandson's fear is that the area Grandpa's *kopitiam* is in will be targeted for urban re-development.

	Unless we develop, all the houses will be taken over by the government. To carry on, you've got to move to the New Town.
GRANDPA	Move? Pull down? Take over? (*Panics.*) But we've been living and working here for over 40, nearly 50 years! ... No one said they are going to pull down all these houses ... Are they? ...
JIA CAI	It's a matter of time, Grandpa. Either you move to the New Town or you close down!
GRANDPA	Move, or close down? ... (*Helplessly looking at Jia Cai.*) I worked as a coolie for four years before I paid up the money I borrowed to come down from China. When I was an apprentice, I worked 14 hours a day, washing dishes, serving *kopi*, cleaning the floor, I was getting only $3 a month. From apprentice to chief assistant, I took eight years. I saved one more year, made another $100; then I raised a few *hui* with my clan folks and I bought this shop and started Eng Seng *Kopitiam*. Forty-eight years now! ... No one wants to continue. Now your Father's passed away and you want me to move away? Why are you so hard on us? ...
JIA CAI	Please keep your cool, and let's think and reason this out! Look, Grandpa, very few things in this world ever remain unchanged. People, places, business, everything changes. We can't live without changing. Grandpa, once you're stuck, you've got to change. That's the only way you can get out of the problem.
GRANDPA	*Change? ...*
JIA CAI	Look, Grandpa, if you really don't want to modernise your *kopitiam*; if you really don't want to go automatic, listen to this proposal I'm going to make to you.

Grandpa wants to hear it but he's also scared to hear it.

JIA CAI	(*He decides this is the right moment.*) Sell it.
GRANDPA	*... Sell it?*
JIA CAI	Yes. Sell it. And use the money to invest in other properties.
GRANDPA	Invest? ...
JIA CAI	Do it while the property market is good, but quick. The market is still OK for now but I'm not sure whether it's going to hold next year. There is someone interested.

GRANDPA	Someone interested?
JIA CAI	Actually, this person contacted me in Canada. He's a developer. He wants to take over 16 shophouses in this block to build a big shopping centre.
GRANDPA	How do you know? Nobody asked me?
JIA CAI	Grandpa, you forgot, Father had already transferred the property to my name a few years ago. They found my address and wrote to me direct.
GRANDPA	Sell it ... and then?
JIA CAI	There is an opinion that this region would go into relative stagnation in the next few years. By comparison, the North American and Australian economies look better. We should consider investing either in North America or Australia. Annie and I are emigrating to Canada. If you like, we can invest the money in Canada. Since I'm starting a new company soon, you could consider taking a share in it. The returns should be quite good at least for the next few years.
GRANDPA	What are you saying? Sell the *kopitiam*, take the money and go away?
JIA CAI	There's no need to worry, Grandpa, I'll take care of you and Mother. If you want to come with us, fine. If you want to stay back, fine, *Meimei* will look after you. Anyway, I'll take out a certain sum from the sales and set up a kind of old-age benefit for you and Mother; you can draw your expenses every month. The rest we'll invest in business. Your livelihood would not be affected at all and we'll make something out of the family savings instead of seeing it go down the drain.
GRANDPA	What we saved cup by cup, cent by cent over 50 years, all the savings we collected, you want to sell? Take everything to Canada and never come back anymore?
JIA CAI	Hey, Grandpa, please, don't get the two things confused. If you don't want to sell, if you don't want to invest overseas, that's OK. As for my own emigration, maybe this is not the best time to talk about it. All I'm trying to tell you is that, since I'm going to stay out there most of the time, it's better for me to live there. Look, Grandpa, all the sacrifices you and Father and Mother made for me, were they not to give me a better future? All the things I'm trying to achieve, aren't they what you wanted me to have?

GRANDPA   Yes, I want you to succeed! Yes, but I don't want you to ... emigrate, to go away to another country, to sell this place! You have stayed outside for so long already, isn't that long enough? Why do you have to uproot yourself? Why do you want to give up your homeland?

JIA CAI   But emigration has become such a common thing now, Grandpa. You haven't been around and you don't know. We in Singapore are also trying hard to draw professionals to come and live permanently here. As long as you live by the law and behave properly, as long as you work hard, it doesn't matter where you sink your roots. In this day and age, nobody's very serious anymore about things like homeland, nation, residency or even citizenship!

GRANDPA   Jia Cai, you mean all our relatives, this house, this home, this place where you lived for 20 years, you can just throw away and go away and feel nothing?

JIA CAI   But don't forget, Grandpa, you yourself had also forsaken your homeland and emigrated to a foreign land!

GRANDPA   No, it's not the same!

JIA CAI   I don't see any difference.

GRANDPA   Yes, we were different!

JIA CAI   In what way were you different?

GRANDPA   We ... we didn't choose to leave our homeland! ... We had to leave home and come down here because we couldn't get enough to eat. We didn't come here to look for a more comfortable life.

                   My Father, your Great Grandfather, he came down to work as a coolie. He was so overworked and sick he died within three years. Your Great Grandmother, my Mother, she didn't send me away the way we sent you off in the airport. No. The night before I left, she was still mending my clothes. She kept reminding me to take care of myself, don't overwork, don't fall sick, and she told me how to behave, how to treat other people ... Soon after that year, our village suffered a very bad flood ... Her body was carried away and I never saw her again ... Jia Cai, in those days, everyone left home with sad tears in their eyes. No one wanted to leave home, do you understand?

Yes, this is not where we were born, but we have already lived here so long. We have put down our roots here. Your Grandmother died here in the Japanese bombing. Your Uncle joined the People's Anti-Japanese Army and died fighting the Japanese. We didn't die like them, but we also gave our blood and sweat almost our whole life. We gave our everything, so why can't we stay here? In the fifties, we went to the rallies with everybody.[36] We signed petitions to demand citizenship, so we can live here forever.

We earned our living with hard work. Who doesn't want to live better and better every day? Above all, we wanted our children to have a better living, better education and better jobs. That is why we supported opening schools. We never went to school but we also supported building our own university. To collect donations for Nantah,[37] your Father, Mother, me and all the assistants, we sold kopi and gave all the day's income to Nantah. The trishaw riders were queuing up right in front of our *kopitiam* — stretching two streets long. In that one day, we collected more than $860. Who said we didn't want to improve our lives? Only that we never wanted to go and live somewhere else for the comfort!

JIA CAI   Look, Grandpa, I can understand your feelings. But don't be alarmed by our having different perceptions. You know, only a few decades ago people were still only walking, and you'd be lucky if you can ride a bullock cart. But now everybody rides a motorcar, at least a bus, and everybody wants to own a private car!

GRANDPA   No, not everybody! Not everybody wants to buy a car, not everybody wants to emigrate to another country!

JIA CAI   Grandpa, although I am going to emigrate, I'm not going to give up my citizenship here, so I can come back anytime. It doesn't mean that I'm gone for good. It's the same as we getting other people to come and live and work here. It's the same!

Their positions seem irreconcilable.

GRANDPA   No. No, you can't go.

---

[36] Editor's note: This refers to the political rallies that occurred during the unsettled years of the 1950s in Singapore leading to self-rule in 1959, and then to the city-state's joining the Federation in 1963, and finally to independence in 1965.

[37] Editor's note: This is a reference to Nanyang University, the only Chinese-language university in South-east Asia in its time. Classes started in 1956, but it was forced to merge with the University of Singapore in 1980; eventually, the National University of Singapore was formed out of this merger.

JIA CAI	Grandpa —
GRANDPA	You can't go. You can't sell.
JIA CAI	Grandpa —
GRANDPA	You can't sell. I forbid you to sell!
JIA CAI	Grandpa —
GRANDPA	I forbid you to sell, I forbid you to sell. This *kopitiam* was built with sweat and blood from two generations of our people. You cannot just sell off like that. You can't just take it away like that! You, you ungrateful ... (*Unable to articulate his feelings.*)
JIA CAI	Grandpa, if I were ungrateful, I would have sold the *kopitiam* without even telling you. And I would have taken the money out of the country without your knowledge. Grandpa, you know I have the legal power to do all that, but I didn't. You should know very well I would never do a nasty thing like that.

Grandpa is cooler but still fails to grasp Jia Cai's argument.

> Grandpa, if you want, I could transfer the ownership back to your name. That's easy, no problem for me. The reason I wanted you to change is because I hope in the end the family property would not be reduced to nothing. You and Mother put your whole life into this and you mustn't allow its value to depreciate. Don't you want to see this little shop turned into a big shop? A small business turned into a big business? ... Grandpa, if you don't trust me, I'll transfer the ownership back to you.

GRANDPA	No! I don't want it back. I want to give it to you! Everything we have we want to give to you! ... But ... not like this ... Not like this!

Scene 11

The old teachers have returned.

TEACHER	Aiya, *towkay*, you would never have guessed what children can come to nowadays. I've said this many times long ago, that Mr Li and his wife were pampering their children too much. So long as they could afford, they would give the children everything they wanted since their early

childhood. After secondary school, he sent the son to America immediately. And when he came back and got married, the Lis immediately transferred the ownership of their house to the son's name. They never expected the daughter-in-law to be so difficult to live with. In the end, the old couple were thrown out by the younger couple. And there's nothing the old folks can do. The house now belongs to the son and daughter-in-law. So the old ones had to move out. It was too much for Mr Li. A few days after he moved out, he returned to their old house, slashed himself many times with a knife right in the middle of the sitting room. And before he died, he used his own blood to write big characters on the wall: 'When I'm dead, I'll come back as a ghost to haunt you forever!' What a tragedy! Now the young couple dare not live there anymore ...

Settling themselves back again in the kopitiam.

This junior Li, he's actually quite nice when he was a boy. It's unbelievable how a person can change so much! Jia Cai, do you still remember him? I think he was in the same standard as you ... Ai ... children are most innocent and truthful when they were toddlers.

GRANDPA   Innocent and truthful ...

Now he remembers Jia Cai's childhood years.

Scene 12

GRANDPA   You were a very quiet boy, but very sharp. When everyone's busy, you always go over and help. You were very interested in watching us bake the *kopi* beans. Do you still remember? You were so small. You sat behind us — sometimes me, sometimes your Father — and watched the baking tin rolling over and over. If I were doing it, you would always ask me to let you hold the handle of the tumbler ... So close to the fire ... You were not even four then ... You wanted to go near the fire, but you couldn't even keep your eyes fully open because of the heat and smoke. But you would never want to leave. You'd stay on, holding the rolling handle of the tumbler close to my hand and roll and roll and roll ... Even when you started going to school, you still wanted to play with the baking roller ... And when I told you to go and do your homework, you'd always cry, 'I've finished my homework, I've finished my homework.' ... Do you still remember that, Jia Cai?

JIA CAI	Yes, I remember.
GRANDPA	You were good in studies from the very beginning. You never finished outside third place. Even in secondary school you never finished outside tenth place. Do you remember winning first place in a composition contest?

Only the two are in the spotlight.

JIA CAI	Yes. I was in Primary 2;[38] I won first place in the lower-primary section.
GRANDPA	Your Mother couldn't leave her work, so I went to the school with you to attend the ceremony. Do you remember?
JIA CAI	Yes, our new school building had just been completed and we had the ceremony in the new school hall.
GRANDPA	That's right! And do you remember what we did after the ceremony?
JIA CAI	(*Trying to remember.*) Yes. You took me to eat ice *kacang*.[39] Afterwards, you bought me an ice ball[40] to eat on the way home.
GRANDPA	You asked the Indian man to put more *kacang*, more syrup and more milk[41] ... But, Jia Cai, do you still remember what you wrote in the composition?
JIA CAI	... Something to do with home ...
GRANDPA	The title was 'My Home'.
JIA CAI	Yes, 'Our Home'!
GRANDPA	Yes, 'Our Home.' And do you still remember what you wrote in the composition?
JIA CAI	(*Thinks hard.*) ... No ... Sorry, I can't remember.

---

[38] Editor's note: That is to say, the second year of the primary schooling period.

[39] Playwright's note: ice *kacang* [Malay: literally iced beans, here referring to red beans], a local dessert made of crushed ice and sweet ingredients.

[40] Editor's note: Another local dessert, made of crushed ice and syrup.

[41] Editor's note: The 'milk' used here is evaporated milk.

GRANDPA   (*Very disappointed.*) ... I still remember. I remember the last paragraph very clearly: 'In future, I want to build a very big house with many rooms. There will be one for Grandfather, one for Father, one for Mother, one for *Meimei* and one for me. And a few more rooms so I can let my friends stay when they come to visit. And then I want to have a very big room so we can all play together and drink *kopi* together. I want to let all my friends taste our *kopi*. My Father bake the beans himself and they smell very nice. All my friends like my Father's *kopi* ...'

Overcome by emotions, he can't continue.

You ... don't remember at all? ...

Scene 13

JIA CAI   Grandpa, when the times want to change, there's nothing we can do to stop it. Things have been changing too fast. You can't stop at the *kopitiam* yesterday and I can't stop at the computer of today. If we don't read the newspapers for a few months we wouldn't know what's new flying over our heads, or what's new digging under our feet. We are too small, Grandpa, before the planes take off we're already out of the country. And very few things are made only for our own people.

Now, one press of a button and we can reach almost anybody anywhere in the world. All the *kopitiam*s are earmarked for change. Some will prosper, others will fold up and those in between are not the same anymore. Grandpa, people don't feel for each other the way they did yesterday, and you must understand that. Old things must either change, or fade away. Grandpa, please, be practical.

GRANDPA   You are all very practical now. As if you can throw everything away. I don't have your high knowledge, but I don't think it's right to throw away some of the things we have already lost. You can't get them back anymore. Never.

JIA CAI   Not entirely. With the kind of technology we have today, lots of things can be remade, if necessary. Look, they could even move the London Bridge to America, piece by piece. By comparison, our problem is so minor.

GRANDPA   No, they are different. That *Baba*[42] place in Orchard, I've been there. It's not right. They built that place to earn tourist money, it's different from the real ones. I have many *Baba* friends, I know. They only retained some superficial looks. Jia Cai, you don't know yet, some things can never be bought, cannot be counted in money terms. This house, this is what me and your Father and Mother have saved after working hard all our lives. We have always wanted to leave it to you. We all came with empty hands, we never had anything before. But I feel so sad that this is the only thing we can leave behind for you. There are so many, so many other things, but why can't we leave them behind? Why can't we leave them behind? Why can't we? ...

He remembers his Mother reminding him how to behave away from home as she mends his old clothes on the eve of his departure.

Scene 14

MOTHER   When you go away from home, you must be very careful not to fall sick. Going hungry is hard, but getting sick is worse. Going to a foreign land to work, you must give your best, you must be honest, you must not be greedy, you must never cheat people or bully people. You must remember, everyone has a Father and a Mother. As long as someone is a year older, then he is your senior and you must respect him ... Son, these are difficult times. Soldiers, bandits, flood, hunger, almost all the men have gone away. We don't have much of a family left now. *Mama* hopes you work very, very hard, and, one day, we may have a reunion. *Mama* hopes you will find a place to let our children and grandchildren rest their feet, somewhere to live in peace. A man can be poor, can be rich, can be bitter, can be sweet, the important thing is to be a good

---

[42] Playwright's note: [Malay:] *Baba*, Peranakan. Editor's note: ' "Peranakan", "Baba-Nyonya" and "Straits Chinese" (after the Straits of Malacca) are terms used for the descendants of the early Chinese immigrants to the *Nusantara* region, including both the British Straits Settlements of Singapore, Malacca and Penang and the Dutch-controlled island of Java among other places. The word *Peranakan* is also used to describe Indonesian Chinese. In both Malay and *Bahasa Indonesia* ["Indonesian language"]. "Peranakan" means "descendants". *Babas* refer to the male descendants and the *Nyonyas* the female' (*Wikipedia, the Free Encyclopedia*, http://en.wikipedia.org/wiki/Peranakan, accessed 3 June 2005). The 'place' that Grandpa refers to is Peranakan Place at 180 Orchard Road, now a complex with bars and some shops.

man of fine character. And most important of all, he must never throw away the old for the new, he must never forget his source. Remember, son, life is like the sugar cane, the sweetest is that part which is closest to the root.

She starts to hum the song 'Remembering'.

Grandpa hums with her. He picks up the bunch of keys and doesn't know what to do with them.

The 'sounds' of modernisation — as made by electronic machines, heavy machinery and pop songs — are heard, and they gradually build up into a chorus that drowns out the song 'Remembering', which also is played in the background. As the 'sounds' of modernisation get louder and louder, they exert an increasing pressure upon Grandpa.

Suddenly, as the sounds reach an intolerable level, they suddenly stop, causing Grandpa to jerk up. Grandpa holds on to the keys tightly, looking at Jia Cai with a complexity of emotions he is unable to articulate. He trembles, as if a critical nerve has just died.

Blackout.

(*End of Play*)

Day I Met the Prince

This play is not conceived for the conventional theatre. Designed for an audience of no more than 200, it plays best with the audience sitting on the floor around the players on three sides. This is so that the players can personally 'reach' every member of the audience.

The 'I' in the play can be played by one person or, as in its première performances, by several persons.

Prologue

The players come on. After introducing themselves, they invite the audience to join in to learn how to make a flower with the paper given on entering the theatre. The players should spread into the audience to ensure that every person has learnt how to make one, and that they have all actually made one on their own.

OPENING (*The players sing the theme song*)
Take a dot
Add a line
Then a circle

Flip them over
Turn them round
Anyway you like

La la la la la
He he he he he
Ha ha ha ha ha
Wo wo wo Ya ya ya
La la la Hu hu hu
Ho ho ho Ya ya ya

Pick a drop of water
Let's go row a boat

Blow a little bubble
And squeeze in for a probe

Crazy over a flower
Brings him 'across' the sky
Here I'm down on Earth, man
Yes, 'tis just as great as heaven.

At the end of the song, the players throw their flowers into the audience and invite the audience to throw theirs to them. The players then carefully collect each and every flower and keep them away in trays or boxes for later use.

Scene 1

I

Now I am going to tell you something from my childhood. But, as we are all gathered together, one moment we are talking, another we are singing, busying ourselves with this and that all the time, hurry here, hurry there ... Who has the time to think about our childhood days?

But, if I close my eyes, and forget about all the people around me, forget where I am, and start thinking quietly. Then, I will be able to remember ...

When I was six, I read a book. It was called *The Truth About Nature*. There was a picture in this book showing how a python — a big snake — swallows its prey. The book said, 'When the python swallows an animal, it takes a long, long time to digest. And after that, it would just lie there quietly, not moving an inch, for as long as six months!'

At the time, I was very fond of Nature: In my imagination, I was always making adventures into the great jungles.

So, I drew my first picture. See, this is my Picture No. 1.

I showed this, my Picture No. 1, to the grown-ups and I asked them whether they were scared or not.

They took a look at the picture, laughed, and said, 'Ha ha ha, why should anyone be scared by a hat!'

Aiyah, but I didn't draw a hat! It was a python swallowing an elephant!

Well, since the grown up couldn't understand, I just had to draw another picture. You know, grown-ups are always like that. They want to make everything very,

very plain. So I went on to add in the inside of the python so that they would he able to see everything very, very clearly. And that became my picture No. 2.

You know what the grown-ups told me this time? 'Stop drawing those pictures. The inside of the python or the outside of the python. You just stop drawing those funny pictures!'

Both pictures are torn up.

Well, those were the two pictures I drew when I was six. You know, if things turned out differently, who knows, I could have become a great artist now.

My guess is that you, all of you, have all done many things during your childhood which the grown-ups thought were ridiculous. But now that you are here together with so many people, one moment you're singing, another moment you're talking, and then you're making a flower from a piece of paper, where do you get time to think back about things in your childhood? Aaah, but if you close your eyes, if you forget all these people around you, forget where you are ... Yes, let's just try and close our eyes for one minute ... one minute ... and try and think of something which had happened when you were very young.

(*With closed eyes.*) You may remember a drawing you did when you were very young ... or a toy which you were especially fond of ... or the teacher you liked most in kindergarten, or someone you had a special fondness for ... Would you like to draw them out like I used to do? And show it to other people? But we haven't got any paper to do it with! Well, how about the flowers? I'll give you back the flowers. You can draw your pictures or write your thoughts on the petals of the flowers. How about that, eh?

All the flowers are distributed back to the audience. Make sure everybody gets one.

OK. Now while you draw and write, let me carry on with my story. As I said, after seeing my Pictures No. 1 and No. 2, the grown-ups advised me not to draw anymore — inside or outside of python — no more such drawings!

And they told me it was time to go to school. So I started going to school. And when it was the class of drawing and handicrafts, I couldn't help myself and drew my Picture No. 1 and gave it to the teacher.

(*As teacher.*) 'Class, isn't this a lovely hat? We should give her a Star for it, shouldn't we?' And my classmates became so envious of me!

'But, Sir, it's not a hat. It's ...'

Before I could explain, the teacher said, 'OK, now everyone draw another one. This time, draw "My School's Sports Day". OK? Start now!'

OK. Sports Day ... Sports Day ... What's most special about Sports Day? ... Aaah, I got it. It's the finishing line, the line that everyone tries to touch before everyone else. That's special. So, I submitted my Sports Day drawing to teacher — one straight line across the entire piece of my drawing paper. The teacher looked at my drawing this way and that way, scratched his head, frowned his face, and gave me a nought!

I decided never to draw again.

But I have to do something in the drawing classes. So I did another one. This time, to make it easier for the teacher to understand, I showed the inside of the python. And what did my teacher say?

(*Mimicking the teacher.*) 'What is this? Is this supposed to be the work of a sensible student? Now, you, go and do me a portrait — draw a person!'

This time, I didn't even think. Straightaway, I drew a big circle and submitted it to the teacher. I didn't expect him to give me good marks, but I never expected him to get angry over it. You know what he did?

(*Mimicking teacher.*) 'So you want to play the fool, uh? OK, go stand outside the classroom. Go!' So I went to stand outside the classroom ...

But what did I do wrong? I wasn't playing the fool! It was actually a very honest portrait. You know why? This teacher I drew, he was always scolding us. And when he did it, he would always open his mouth so big that we cannot see his face anymore but only the mouth. So what's wrong in drawing a big circle to represent him?

But he said I was playing the fool and so did everyone else, even the driver of my school bus. They all said I was trying to be funny with the teacher. They all didn't want to befriend me anymore ...

OK. If that's the way it's going to be, I don't want to see them anymore. And what's the point in going on like *this*?

I want to go away. *I want to go away!* I want to do somewhere where there's no one around. No one. Where there's no one but me. Yes, just me! So I ran away, far, far away from everyone I knew!

I came to a very tall building. Very tall. I ran towards the top. In one breath I made it. To the very top ... I walked to the edge, and looked down ... Wah, so scary! And then I looked up ... Wow! Up there, the sky was so dark, and so high. So far, far away ...

There were so many stars, twinkling in the sky. So vast! So free. So free! And I said to myself, 'I say, man, how nice if I could fly, if my spirit could get up there, far, far away into outer space!'

Song:
Stars, stars above me
Why are you blinking your eyes?
Dark, dark is the sky above
Are you feeling lonely like me?
This night
Next night
There will come a night
When I'll reach you and touch you
And keep you company.

Scene 2

As 'I' is looking into the sky ...

PRINCE   Hello. Do you grow flowers?

I   ...

PRINCE   Do you know how to look after the rose?

I   Shh ... Don't make noise.

PRINCE   Do you know how to draw?

I   Don't make noise! I'm trying to figure out how to get out there and fly free as a bird.

PRINCE   Do you know how to draw the rose?

I   I said don't make noise!

PRINCE   My little planet has a rose, if it gets eaten up by the goat ...

I   Who are you? Where are you?

PRINCE   I am here. Look, here.

I   Aaah, my friends, the Little Prince. Welcome, the hero of our story! Eh? But he doesn't look like a prince, *does he*? ... Sorry, it's all my fault. Since I didn't go on to study drawing, I couldn't draw out a good likeness of the Little Prince. So the director asked him/her to stand in for the real Prince. Don't mind him/her, he's/she's just an extra.

PRINCE   My planet has no other plant but the rose. If the rose gets eaten up by the goat, I will have no flower anymore. Can you tell me, do you know, how to protect the rose from being eaten up by the goat? (*He mimes to explain the problem, going into a complicated process. And after all that ...*) Do you know how to protect the rose from being eaten up by the goat?

I   OK, I help you. But you must help me, too. You must help me to go up the sky.

PRINCE   But why?

I   I want to get away from this place. Because nobody understands my drawings. (*The Little Prince goes over to examine the torn-up drawing.*) Hey, don't you underestimate this Little Prince. Although he's very tiny, he's very intelligent. He understands my drawings, every one of them. But do you know why he has travelled all the way across the Milky Way, all the way to Earth?

PRINCE   How to protect the rose from being eaten up by the goat?

I   Mmm ... Tie up the goat. Tie it up and keep it away from the rose so he can't reach the rose and that will do it.

PRINCE   Tie up the goat? Then it won't be able to move about freely, isn't it? No, I cannot do that.

I   Then make a fence for the rose and fence it in.

PRINCE   Make a fence and make the rose stay inside? Then the rose will be very isolated, isn't it? No, I cannot do that.

I   (*Thinking hard.*) Cannot tie up. Cannot fence in. Aaah, I know. If there's only you on the planet, and now that you are gone, and the rose is not tied up, and the rose is not fenced in, won't the rose be eaten up by the goat?

PRINCE   No, it won't. The goat is sleeping now. Night on my planet is only 35 minutes long according to Earth time. As long as I can return before the goat wakes up, everything will be all right. Which means (*Looks at watch*), I have to get back before ____. (*Here, the time to be indicated is that of 35 minutes after this moment in the performance.*) Please, will you all please remind me when the time is up? ... Now, how to protect the rose from being eaten up by the goat?

I   Cannot tie up ... Cannot fence in ... I don't know.

PRINCE   But you said you would help me!

I   I will. I will. I can go and look for people to help you.

PRINCE   OK. Let's go.

I   Wait. Where are we going?

PRINCE   We can try everywhere. I can take you to fly. Together with me. I can merge into your body. So you can take me as part of yourself. Then you can ask on my behalf.

I   You merging into my body? OK! Let's do it! Let's merge, merge, merge, merge into one!

They try all sorts of ways to become one but fail.

PRINCE   Why can't we merge?

I   Maybe it's better if you just make yourself disappear.

PRINCE   That's an idea! But, you can't look. Turn around ...OK, it's done.

I   (*Turns around and finds him still there.*) Come on, Little Prince, we have no time, do it fast. Disappear!

PRINCE   I have disappeared.

I   What do you mean? I can still see you!

PRINCE   Yes, but only you can. They can't see me. Ask them if you don't believe me ... Go ahead and ask *lah*![1]

I   Can you see him?

If the audience plays along and says they can't see, the show can proceed. If they say they can see, Little Prince has to cajole them into cooperating, persuading them to agree that the Prince has indeed disappeared.

---

[1] Editor's note: Malay: *lah*, '[A] particle emphasising the word to which it is appended' (*A Malay-English English-Malay Dictionary*, ed. A. E. Coope [revised edn.; London and Basingstoke: Macmillan Education, 1991]).

OK, let's go!

They take flight, with 'I' following the flying style of the Prince.

Music.

Scene 3

The Little Prince and 'I' arrive at the study of the Geographer. The Geographer comes in.

PRINCE   What is this place? (*Notices the big book carried by the Geographer.*) Wah! Such a big book. He must be a very learned scholar.

SCHOLAR   Aaah, here comes another adventurer. Hi ... (*The Little Prince comes over to shake the hand of the Scholar but Scholar can't see him. Instead, he goes over to shake hands with 'I'.*) How are you? And where are you from?

I   Grandpa, who are you? And what is this big book for?

SCHOLAR   I am a Geographer.

I   What does a Geographer do?

SCHOLAR   What does a Geographer do? Well, we specialise in the recording of the seas and oceans, the rivers and lakes, the cities and towns, the mountains and hills, the deserts and oases ...

I   Oh, is that so? ... Uuh, can you tell me what rivers we have here?

SCHOLAR   Here? (*Hurriedly refers to his big book.*) Umm, sorry, I don't know.

I   What mountains or hills do we have here?

SCHOLAR   (*Leaves through the big book again.*) Umm, sorry, I don't know.

I   What famous historical or scenic landmarks do we have here?

SCHOLAR   I don't know.

I   What? That even you don't know ah?

SCHOLAR   But why do you ask me all these trivial things? I am a Scholar, I'm not a tourist guide!

I   *Aiyah*, we are not tourist guides either, but we all know, don't we, eh? OK, let us tell him what rivers we have in Singapore. (*Asks the audience, and exhausts their knowledge.*)

Now, what mountains we have in Singapore? Now, what historic and scenic landmarks we have in Singapore? Nah, you see, although we don't have big books like yours, we all know these things. So why shouldn't you, if you are a learned scholar?

SCHOLAR (*Could not find any of those in his big book.*) How come no one ever told me there are these places in Singapore? But then I'm not an adventurer. I'm a Geographer. My job is to sit in my study and wait for the adventurers to come and tell me what they have found. So far, no one has told me these things about Singapore, so I shouldn't know. OK, now you tell me, where are you from?

PRINCE I'm the Little Prince from Planet BB 88.

SCHOLAR What did you say? (*The Scholar cannot see the Little Prince. Everything that is being said by the Little Prince must be 'articulated' by 'I'.*)

PRINCE

I I'm the Little Prince from Planet BB 88.

SCHOLAR What is there worth recording on this little planet?

PRINCE

I My planet has two active volcanoes, one I use for boiling water, the other one I use to cook rice. There is also an inactive volcano which I use for bathing. (*The Scholar starts to record somewhat reluctantly.*) There is no forest on my planet and there is no sea. But there is a rose plant and a small goat. (*The Scholar stops recording.*)

I Hey, why do you stop?

SCHOLAR No, no, no I don't record temporary things, things that pass away.

PRINCE What? You don't record things that are temporary? Things that pass away?

SCHOLAR I only record things that are permanent and lasting.

PRINCE Permanent? Lasting? ... Then I don't suppose you would either grow a rose plant or keep a goat?

SCHOLAR Grow a plant? Keep a goat? Why would you do things like that?

I Then I'm sure you wouldn't know how to protect the rose from being eaten up by the goat, do you?

SCHOLAR To protect the rose? From being eaten up by a goat? Ha ha ha ...!

I   Grandpa, do you realise that you look and sound very, very ridiculous?

SCHOLAR   (*Stops laughing abruptly.*) Now listen, you, all I'm trying to tell you is that there are so many very, very important things in this world waiting for you to do. Why would you waste your time growing rose plants and keeping goats?

I   Grandpa, how boring it would be if there were no flowers and trees on the hills and mountains.

PRINCE   How monotonous it would be if there were no cows and sheep on the plains.

I   How lonely it would be if there were no fish and prawns in the rivers.

PRINCE   How painful it would he if there were no oases in the deserts.

I   Grandpa, you see no value in things that are temporary; but just think: If there were no temporary scholars like yourself, there won't be big scholarship like your learned geography, isn't it?

SCHOLAR   (*At first taken aback, then expressing disdain.*) Hmm ... ignorant, uneducated good-for-nothing! (*And he walks away.*)

I   Don't worry, Little Prince, we'll look for someone else.

They fly away.

Music.

Scene 4

SELLER   (*A quack medicine seller doing a promotion to the audience like they do it in Chinatown.*) Come on, come on! Magic Pills, Magic Pills! Magical Long-Term Thirst-Quencher! Secret formula inherited from my great, great grandfather, integrated with the latest technological discovery, this Magic Pill is the most fantastic Long-Term Thirst-Quencher. Come on, come on, this is the greatest news for the time-hungry Modem Man!

ASSISTANT Wait a minute, wait a minute, can you tell us what the Magic Pill is for?

SELLER   You ask me what the Magic Pill is good for?! Well, let me tell you: It is the time-hungry Modem Man's best friend! Take one pill — one Magic Pill — and you can go on for a whole week without taking one drop of water!

ASSISTANT   What? Take one Magic Pill and you can go on for week without taking one drop of water?

SELLER   Yes, sir, that's exactly what I said. One Long-Term Magic Thirst-Quencher Pill can last you one whole week without taking one drop of water!

Now, ladies and gentlemen, I would like to ask you a very, very simple question. How much time do you take each day to drink water?

Asks the audience for answers.

No one knows? OK, let me tell you. Let me tell you how much time we take each day to drink water!

The answer is, according to reliable surveys conducted by the authoritative *Bukit Timah Times*, is eight minutes. Yes, eight minutes per day per person if you live in families with an average of two members!

You don't believe me? You don't know how it's computed? Well, of course you don't. But let me show you. Let my assistants and me show you!

Ready, folks? OK, here we go!

Starts the stopwatch as the assistant demonstrate the action as the Seller runs through the process.

You walk over, you take the kettle, you bring the kettle, you walk to the tap, you turn on the tap, you fill the kettle, you walk to the stove, you put down the kettle, you light the stove, you wait for the kettle to boil, you turn off the fire, you lift the kettle, you go over to the table, you take out the cup, you lift the kettle, you pour the water, you put down the kettle, you lift the glass, you open your mouth, you pour the water, you swallow the water, you lift the glass again, you open your mouth again, you pour the water again, you swallow again, until you finish the water, you bring back the kettle, you wash the glass, you place back the glass, and if you are in the habit of drinking cold water, there is the added chore of opening the fridge, taking out the flask, filling the flask, putting it back into the fridge and closing the fridge.

And see how much that has taken us, on average? Eight minutes exactly! (*Shows it on a stopwatch.*)

The words and action must be performed in an extremely fast and slick manner to achieve maximum effect, without losing clarity.

Now, if you live in a two-member family, your average time wasted on drinking water will be 56 minutes a week And if you are living alone, your daily time wasted will be 15 minutes which makes it 105 minutes, or one hour and 45 minutes a week!

Just think: What a waste it is! In this day and age of the Information Society, the Refined Society, how many better things we can do than to waste them on drinking water!

And if you work it out in terms of money, you will be even more stunned. Let's say you, the cream of our society, are earning a fair salary, of, say, $5,000 a month working 40 hours a week. Then, 56 minutes spent on drinking water will cost you no less than $30 per month. And that will be $360 a year. If you live alone, the money lost will be $600 a year! Well, well, if you add up everybody's loss together — 2.6 million of us in this country, the total money wasted every year by Singaporeans will come to $930 million! Will you believe it? Nearly one billion dollars a year wasted!

So, ladies and gentlemen, are we going to allow ourselves such a fantastic wastage? Why don't we all make it a habit to take the Long-Term Thirst-Quencher, the Magic Pill?

Just imagine: if all Singaporeans take the Magic Pill every day, if all the world's population takes the Magic Pill every day, I assure you, positively I assure you, within five years, yes five years, all the inflation problems will disappear, all the economic slowdowns will disappear, all the trade deficits will disappear, and the world will be a far better and richer place and we will have more water to use and we may even all have a swimming pool built in our home!

So, how about it, folks? Buy a packet of Magic Pills! Long-Term Thirst Quencher! Magic Pills! *Magic Pills!*

The seller and assistants try to sell them to the audience. Of course no one will actually buy them. So they give them away as free samples. Sweets can be used as the Magic Pills, and they should be given to every member of the audience.

I   Excuse me, do you grow flowers?

SELLER   (*Taken by surprise.*) What, flowers?

I   Yeah, roses.

SELLER   Roses?

I   Do you know how to protect the rose from being eaten up by the goat?

SELLER Goat? ... Eat ... the rose? (*Knowing not what is going on. Turns to the audience.*) Do you know what's wrong with this guy? We've just been talking about something of great importance, something which affects the welfare of the nation and the world, and this guy here talks about flowers, goat ... What's wrong with this guy, uh?

As they try to make each other understand, a very old woman appears. She's so old that she is unable to walk upright. But she is a picture of determination as she, with a bucket in hand, inches across the stage to scoop a bucket of water from a well. It is executed with the greatest concentration.

SELLER Ladies and gentlemen, look at this! This is a typical case of old-fashioned outdatedness. Just imagine, we have entered the computer age and our friend here is still using buckets to scoop water from the well. Not only for herself, but also carrying it all the way to her equally old-fashioned husband!

     How unhygienic, how uncivilised, how unmodern, how stupid! You are witnessing a chronic case of someone ignorantly resisting the glorious fruits of scientific discovery, slowly wasting her life away in completely meaningless occupations!

I   Granny, why don't you take his/her Magic Pill?

GRANNY Take? ... His/Her? ...

I   Why do you go to so much trouble to get water from the well?

GRANNY My ... Mine tastes nice!

SELLER Rubbish! What is so nice about water from a dirty well? Mine got better taste!

GRANNY Your? ... Yours? ... Yours has taste? ... No taste!

SELLER Mine no taste? Rubbish. I have any taste you want: Orange, apple, strawberry, vanilla, durian, rambutan, longan, lychee, mango, banana, watermelon. What taste has yours got?

GRANNY Your ... your taste ... stupid taste (*Turns to go.*)

I   Granny, since you are so old now, why don't you take his/her Thirst-Quencher Magic Pill and save your energy, and save your time.

GRANNY Save? ...

SELLER   Your energy.

GRANNY   Save? ...

SELLER   Your time.

GRANNY   Save ... energy? ... Save ... time? ...

SELLER

I   Yeah, yeah! Save energy, save time.

GRANNY   What for?

Totally surprised, neither has an answer.

GRANNY   (*With a naughty smile.*) Ahh ... save time, save energy to get water for my old man.

I   Granny, what is there so special about your water? Can I try a mouthful?

The old woman nods gladly, and 'I' tries a mouthful.

            I can't see what is so special about it!

GRANNY   You will know it when you get water for yourself.

Granny returns.

I   (*Looking at the old woman much puzzled. Suddenly realising ...*) Ah, yes, Granny, do you know how to protect the rose from being eaten up by a goat?

GRANNY   Flower? Flower?

I   Yes, a rose.

GRANNY   Go see the Old Gardener.

I   The Old Gardener? Granny, can you take me to him?

GRANNY   No time ... Got to take water to old man. (*She's gone.*)

I   (*To the invisible Little Prince.*) OK, Little Prince, do you know where the Old Gardener is? Let's go.

SELLER   Hey, Magic Pills, Magic Pills, Long-Term Thirsty Quencher, Long-Term Thirsty-Quencher Magic Pills ...

Music.

Scene 5

The Old Gardener's place. The Fox is hard at work watering the flowers. The Little Prince and 'I' arrive.

I	(*Looking around doubtfully.*) Is this the right place? (*Then looks at the Fox.*) How come this gardener has four legs? Excuse me, is this the Old Gardener's place?
FOX	Yes, it is.
I	May I ask if the Old Gardener is around?
FOX	Sorry, the Old Gardener is no more here.
I	You mean he has moved away?
FOX	Why do you want to see him?
PRINCE	I have a problem about flowers to ask him.
FOX	And who are you? (*Looking at the Prince head on.*)
PRINCE	Eh? How come you can see me?!
FOX	Because I'm a fox.
PRINCE	
I	Aahh ... He's not a man. And not a woman.
FOX	Who are you?
PRINCE	I am the Little Prince from Planet BB 88. I have come to look for the Old Gardener because my rose ...
FOX	I'm sorry, he's passed away.
PRINCE	
I	Ohhhh!
FOX	Well, tell me your problem.
PRINCE	My planet has the one and only rose. I have spent so much heart and energy to nurture it and now it is the most beautiful thing on my planet. Recently I have

	also been keeping a little goat. But the goat eats plants! So I'm worried that the goat will one day eat up my rose.
I	He doesn't want to tie up the goat, and he doesn't want to fence up the rose. He doesn't know what to do ...
PRINCE	I have asked many people and they all say there is no way. They say I must either tie up the goat, or I must fence up the rose.
I	We met this Old Granny by the well and she said the Old Gardener would know how to solve the problem.
PRINCE	But now he is dead. And nobody else can help me. What shall I do?
FOX	Oh, so that's your problem.
I	Would the Old Gardener really know how to solve the problem?
FOX	Yes. Don't believe me? OK, come I'll show you something.

Brings them to the audience, and invites all members of the audience to raise their paper flowers high above their heads.

PRINCE	(*Absolutely stunned by what he sees.*) What? So many? All roses?
FOX	A total of 200 roses. (*Or whatever the audience number may be.*)
I	All roses! (*The Little Prince turns away looking very sad.*) Little Prince, what's the matter with you?
PRINCE	I thought my rose is the only one in the world, the most precious thing on my planet. I gave everything I had to look after it. I watered it. I gave it vitamins to grow more healthy. I stood against the sun to give it shade when it became too hot. I put a blanket over it when it gets too cold. But now I know it is not unique at all. There are so many of them. Mine is just another ordinary rose!
FOX	What? Ordinary?
I	Yeah. Look at that. Two hundred roses, all same.
FOX	All same? No! (*To audience.*) Are you all the same? Of course not! Look, this one is long, that one is short. This one is plump, that one is slim. This one's got darker hair and that one's got a pony tail. This one giggles and that one smiles ...

First referring to the shape of the paper flowers, then gradually turning to the members of the audience themselves describing their peculiarities as if they were the flowers.

I   But they are still the same roses, aren't they?

FOX   Same? They may look alike from afar, but they all have different characters. And the Old Gardener gave them each a special name. If you don't believe me, just go out there and check the petals. You'll find they all have a different name. (*Signals the audience to quickly write their names on the petals, as the Fox brings along the Prince and 'I' to inspect some of the roses closely. The names of the various flowers are read out aloud. Indeed they would all have something different written on the petals.*) And what about your rose? What does your rose look like?

PRINCE   My rose became 1.56 metres tall this morning. It has 12 petals, five leaves and 13 thorns. It hates gusty winds because the stem is not very strong. So I cover it up every night to prevent it from catching cold. (*If there is a big piece of white paper somewhere on the set, the Little Prince can sketch out his special rose as he describes it.*)

FOX   And what's its name?

PRINCE   Rose.

I   OK, yours is called Rose. But no one else here is called Rose. (*If there is another 'Rose' in the audience, point out the distinctive characteristics of the person.*) See for yourself: This one is called Martha, this one is called Salim, this one is called Yueqing … this one is called Raja… (*And so forth, according to the names on the petals*) …

FOX   Take your time, Little Prince, take your time.

PRINCE   *Aiyah*, time! What's the time now, please? (*Gets the audience to tell him the time, which should be close to the deadline announced earlier by the Little Prince himself.*) I have to go now. Please, could anybody tell me how to protect the rose from being eaten up by the goat? Please, anyone?

All three of them approach the audience for answers. It is hoped that the audience is able to supply the full answer, or, if they can't, then part of the answer …

FOX   OK, I'll tell you. The answer is: You needn't bother!

I   What? Needn't bother? You mean you also think that the rose is not worth protecting?

FOX   No. I mean the rose doesn't need protection. You know why? Because the rose has thorns, it is capable of protecting itself. No animal dares to touch it. And as for the goat, you needn't worry about him either. The goat eats grass, yes, but it doesn't eat roses.

PRINCE   Really?

I   Which means, my friend, you never had a problem!

PRINCE   You mean I don't have to tie up the goat? You mean I don't have to fence up the rose? Hooray! Hooray! (*As he recovers from dancing and prancing around, he says:*) OK, now it's time to return to my planet. Let's go! We're ready to take off?

I   Little Prince, you have travelled billions of miles through space, across the Milky Way, it seems, all for nothing. And it does look like your rose is not that different from the others.

PRINCE   No, that's not true. What I have made myself will always be special ... OK, I'm ready to go now. Let's take off?

I   Wait, wait ... Little Prince, I don't think I'm going with you...

PRINCE   Why? Didn't you say you want to go away?

I   I ... I have changed my mind. Your little planet belongs to you alone. You have your rose, your goat, your volcanoes. But I also have things that belong to me. Here, on Earth. My home, my drawings. It doesn't matter if other people don't understand my drawings. As long as I know what I'm doing myself, then I'm happy. As long as I know what I am doing. Goodbye, Little Prince!

The Little Prince flies away. Following his trail, 'I' looks longingly into the vast, dark, endless sky ...

Song:
Stars, stars above

I can't see you in the day
Behind the clouds so high
But I know you are there
This night
Next night
There will come a night
When I'll get up there
And hug you, hug you tight

This night
Next night
There will come a night
When I'll reach you and touch you
And keep you company.

Scene 6

I   Well, that's my story. Oh, I forgot to tell you, before the Little Prince went away, he said to me, 'Everybody has a star. To some people, the star is only a spark of light; to the traveller, the star is the guiding tight; to the scholar, the star is a series of puzzles.' He said, 'Only for you (and that means me) the star means something very special. For you know that among all the glittering lights up there, there is one where the Little Prince lives, with a rose, and a goat. And they are all smiling at you. And you can smile back at them. And when your friends see you do that, they would say, "This guy must be crazy!" '

You know what? Perhaps I am!

Bye-bye!

When the cast takes the curtain call, it would be good to ask the audience to take good care of the flowers which they have taken some effort to make. If they do not wish to bring them home, or give them to someone they care about, ask them to leave them behind for the players. Very often, the flowers have on them memorable writing and unusual scribbling.

(*End of Play*)

Mama Looking for Her Cat

Darkness.

An overhead spot comes on centrestage. Mama walks slowly into the spot. Stops. Walks into, then out of the spot, and stops again.

Offstage, someone is heard singing 'The ABC Song'[1] softly. Then more voices are heard as ten young people are seen walking onto the stage from different directions. The lights become brighter. The actors cross the stage and pass each other in all directions, repeating the same song, singing louder as they walk faster. They finally form a circle enclosing the confused Mother in it. They move faster and close in on the Mother until they stop, trapping her firmly inside the circle.

There is a sudden silence and stillness in the air. Mother tries to move. The tight circle remains inflexible. She raises her hand, searching for something to grasp. When nothing is found, the hand is timidly withdrawn. Mother tries to move again. The tight circle refuses to budge.

She senses some leeway below waist level and moves to squat down. Exploring, she finds an opening in the wall of legs around her. Using all her strength, she forces two of the legs apart and squeezes through them with great difficulty. She is tired after the exertion and slumps to the floor. After a breather, she climbs up. Fatigued, she sits on a bamboo stool.

Silence and stillness.

A sudden burst of shouting and running and chasing see the group turning into children playing O Bei Som.[2] After the elimination process two are left. Then they resort to playing

---

[1] Editor's note: The reference is to the 'Alphabet Song'.
[2] Playwright's note: *O Bei Som*, a game [also see note 3].

Lom Cham Bas[3] *to decide who is to* pasang.[4] *When that person is chosen, they start playing the 'Hawker Game.' The children speak a mixture of Hokkien, Mandarin and English. They play 'Guessing the Hawker.' As they get into the second round, Mama turns up with a small bamboo stool in hand.*

CHILDREN   Oh, Mama's here! Mama's here! Mama!

The abandon the game and encircle Mother with great enthusiasm.

CHILDREN   Stories! Songs! What do we do tonight?

MAMA   I sing a song for you. (*She speaks in Hokkien*[5] *throughout.*)

CHILDREN   *Wah*,[6] new one, good, good!

MAMA   Let me tell you the words first:

                  Baby, baby, sleep
                  One night grow one inch

                  Baby, baby, dear
                  One night grow one foot

                  Minding baby till sun sets
                  Cuddling baby close to me

                  Baby, baby, you're my heart
                  Take care, take care, don't catch cold. [7]

                  Now I sing it once first, then all of you follow.

---

[3] Playwright's note: *Lom Cham Bas*, a game. Editor's note: Both *O Bei Som* (see note 2) and *Lom Cham Bas* are games analogous to 'Paper, Scissors, Stone'. The terms are in Hokkien-Chinese, or *minnan hua* or *minnan* language, a non-Mandarin Chinese language, but do not actually mean anything.
[4] Playwright's note: [Malay:] *pasang*, to play the banker. Editor's note: The playwright doesn't quite convey the full meaning in his note; the full expression here would be *kena pasang*, 'hitting a vital spot or hitting "full"' (*A Malay-English English-Malay Dictionary*, ed. A. E. Coope [revised edn.; London and Basingstoke: Macmillan Education, 1991]) — less literally, to pay the forfeit. In this case, the person who loses the 'Paper, Scissors, Stone' match pays the forfeit and ends up playing the banker for the next game, 'Guessing the Hawker'.
[5] Editor's note: Hokkien-Chinese, or *minnan hua* or *minnan* language, a non-Mandarin-Chinese language.
[6] Editor's note: Expression, here, of wonder; also used to indicate surprise, or a combination of both.
[7] Editor's note: This is a lullaby in *minnan hua* or *minnan* language, *tiam tiam koon, chi me tua chi chuni*, which the playwright translate as 'One Night Grow One Inch'; also see note 29.

She sings the song once through and the children are very impressed. They accompany her the second time round after which they sing on their own. As they go on, they get sleepy and the singing develops into humming, softer and softer, until one of them gets very impatient.

W	(*In Hokkien*) No good *lah*,[8] Mama. Look, everybody's going to sleep. Tell a story *lah*, Mama, tell a story!
CHILDREN	(*In Hokkien*) Yah, tell story! Tell story!
MAMA	All right. Which one?
W	(*In Hokkien*) Tell the one about little pigs.
CHILDREN	(*In Hokkien*) Don't want, don't want! That one told how many times already!
Y	(*In Hokkien*) Tell the Monkey King story, Mama, the Monkey one![9]
CHILDREN	(*In Hokkien*) No, no, no! That one also told don't know how many times already! No, tell new one. New one, Mama!
MAMA	All right. I'll tell a new one about the rabbit.[10]

After interruptions and explanations about what a rabbit is and what a tortoise is, she begins to tell the story.

MAMA   Once upon a time, long, long ago, there was a rabbit who runs very, very fast. One day, as he went walking in the woods, he met a very slow-moving tortoise. The naughty rabbit said, 'Hey, let's have a race. Let's have a running race!' The tortoise said, '*Aiyah*,[11] you must be joking. How can I race with you?' Rabbit felt very proud. He laughed, 'Ha, ha, ha,' and said boastfully, 'Aha, you no good, you no good! Sure lose, sure lose to me!'

---

[8] Editor's note: Malay: *lah*, '[A] particle emphasising the word to which it is appended' (*A Malay-English English-Malay Dictionary*, ed. Coope).

[9] Editor's note: The reference here is to the mythological novel, *Journey to the West* (*Xiyou ji*), by Wu Cheng'en (*ca.* 1500–1582), in which the irreverent Monkey accompanies the Buddhist monk Xuanzang in his journey west in search of Buddhist sutras.

[10] Editor's note: The tale here is 'The Hare and the Tortoise', from *Aesop's Fables*.

[11] Editor's note: Expression of annoyance.

Although the tortoise was a very patient person, he also got angry. As the Rabbit kept on saying, 'You sure lose, you sure lose!', he became more and more fed up until he said, 'OK, OK, I'll race you!'

They drew a line and both squatted down to get ready, and just as the tortoise counted to three, the rabbit flew off quick as an arrow! Before he took a second breath, the rabbit had already disappeared. The rabbit looked back and could hardly see the tortoise walking slowly one step at a time so far, far back.

Rabbit was a very proud fellow. He thought to himself, 'Ha, I am so fast and he is so slow, it will take him so very, very long to catch up on me. *Aiyah*, I should take a nap now before I go any further.' So he lay down by the roadside, and before he knew it, was snoring fast asleep.

Tortoise walked slowly step by step. When he could see the rabbit no more, he said to himself, '*Aiyah*, sure die this time; I'm going to lose — can't even see the rabbit now!' But as he walked on and on he came to where the rabbit was sleeping, then he knew what was happening. Very quietly, Tortoise walked past Rabbit and continued on his way.

When Tortoise was a long way away, he looked back and saw Rabbit still sleeping, so he felt happy and quickly walked on. After a little while, he looked back again and saw that Rabbit was still fast asleep. He began to feel very happy and excited. Although he was already very far away, he kept walking very quietly, on and on, on and on, until, until he finally, finally reached the finishing line!

CHILDREN	Hooray! Tortoise won, Tortoise won! (*There is great excitement among the children.*)
MAMA	So you see, it pays to work hard. Work very hard. And it pays to persevere. Persevere on and on.
CHILDREN	I like tortoise, Mama. I like tortoise. Mama, I know how to be tortoise. Look at how I walk. Look at me Mama, look like tortoise or not? I also can. Look Mama, slowly like this. Me also, Mama, slowly like this. Me also, Mama, slowly like this ...

Encouraged by Mama, they keep on imitating the tortoise on their fours. Gradually developing into a chorus:

Work very hard. Persevere on and on.

Work very hard. Persevere on and on.

Then one of the children began to imitate the rabbit! The others find her very queer ...

K   (*In Hokkien*) Mama, look, there is a crazy rabbit!

CHILDREN   Ha, ha, ha ... crazy rabbit, crazy rabbit!

V   No, I'm not crazy. But you all are stupid. You know what? I think it was the rabbit who won the race. And you know how he won?

CHILDREN   Ha, ha, ha ... crazy rabbit, crazy rabbit!

V   He won by bumping the tortoise and turning him upside down like this and left him roasting in the sun. (*Bumping one of them over — which all find very funny.*)

JH   (*In Hokkien*) Mama, Mama, she said it was the rabbit who won, not the tortoise. She said when the rabbit passed the tortoise he bumped him and left him baking in the sun upside down, like *panggang roti*.[12]

Everyone finds this proposition very funny and they all turn to imitating the Rabbit, jumping fiercely and bumping into each other aggressively. Mother tries to stop them but fails. In the end, she herself is bumped over. She seems to have been knocked unconscious.

Bumping into one another, they eventually all end up on their backs. Initially finding the upside-down position good fun, they gradually begin to struggle to turn over; but when they find they cannot, and as if the sun begins to shine hotter and hotter, their struggle becomes more and more anxious. Very quickly, all the fun has gone and utter desperation takes over.

One by one, as if fighting a life-and-death battle, they manage to turn over to regain their normal balance — totally cleansed of any boastfulness. Now they are all on their fours with their faces on the floor.

Mama wakes up, struggles to stand up, moves over to slump onto a low bamboo stool.

Then the children, one by one, begin to wake up, to discover Mama missing. They speak in either Mandarin or English.

---

[12] Playwright's note: [Malay:] *panggang roti*, toasting [or toasted] bread. Editor's note: The actual expression should be *roti panggang*; the inverted usage indicates a common bazaar-Malay usage.

SW   My mother's missing. We don't know where she's gone to. We've looked everywhere for her.

SS   You've got to help us, we don't know where to start, my mother's missing.

JH   (*In Mandarin*) Mama's missing. Don't know where she's gone to. Let's go and look for her. Quick! (*Followed by other similar exclamations.*)

POLICEMAN   When you find her missing?

CHILDREN   Last night.
                 Two weeks ago.
                 I think it was last X'mas.
                 Four hours' ago.
                 Yesterday afternoon ... (*And so on and so forth ...*)

POLICEMAN   Where you find her missing?

CHILDREN   At home *lah*. Of course at home. I last saw her at our apartment, must be at home. She never goes anywhere, so she must be at home.

POLICEMEN   How you know she was at home?

CHILDREN   She minds the house, she never goes out.
                 The home is all she has. Of course she's home.
                 That's her life-long habit, I just know it.
                 She never goes anywhere, so she must be at home ... (*And so on and so forth ...*)

POLICEMEN   (*In Mandarin*) How did you know she was always at home when you were not home?

CHILDREN   Mama minds the house and it takes a whole day to keep it clean and tidy. Since the place is always clean, she must have been home all the time. She never dares to go out, so always home. Every time I go home she's always there, no what time. So I presume she must be home when I'm not. My mother is a creature of habit. You can't teach an old dog new habits. The home is all she has. There's nowhere else she can go! (*And so on and so forth ...*)

TEOCHEW WOMAN   (*In Teochew*[13]) *Mata, mata*[14] *oi,*[15] I want to tell you something. You know that Ah Choo's mother? *Aiyoh,*[16] I think something is very wrong. You know what? She's been going out with the cat regularly recently. Very late at night, every time. The two of them, Ah Choo's mother and this black cat, they been going out every night. And the most worrying is what, you know? She cries to the cat, you know? Yeah, cry! Last night the third time I saw her cry, talking to the black cat as she bring her out again. Don't know where they go. But I tell you, very funny, very mysterious, very scary also!

POLICEMAN   (*In Teochew*) Is that so? OK, I'll make a report for you. Show me your IC.[17]

TEOCHEW WOMAN   What? Want IC, ah? No *lah*, no *lah*, I don't to want to report anymore.

As the woman leaves, all the children gather together as if watching a TV soap opera.

GIRL   (*In Cantonese*) And one night, Mama went away. All I could find was a letter she had left behind. It says she was going to commit suicide ... I was shocked. I didn't know what to do. I told Father. He said nothing and did nothing. So I dashed out of the house. I dashed to the street. I walked and walked and walked. But where could I find Mama? I looked up at the HDB flats,[18] dozens of them, in front of me. Could she be up there somewhere in this block? Or that block? Or that? Or that? ... I walked and walked and walked ... until I reached the *pasar*

---

[13] Editor's note: Teochew-Chinese, or *chauzhou hua* or *chauzhou* language, a non-Mandarin Chinese language.

[14] Editor's note: A Singapore-Chinese 'import' of a Malay-language term, *mata*, here meaning a policeman.

[15] Editor's note: Expression drawing another person's attention for the purpose to signal one's annoyance at some matter.

[16] Editor's note: Expression similar in meaning to '*aiyah*'; see note 11.

[17] Editor's note: IC, Identity Card, a shortened acronym for the National Registration Identity Card (NRIC) that citizens of the city-state of Singapore are required by law to have on their person at all times.

[18] Editor's note: HDB flats, i.e., subsidised public-housing flats or apartments built by the Housing and Development Board.

malam[19] where Mama used to go and buy her daily supplies. And it was already daybreak. But, as I was looking at the gathering crowd, suddenly Mama appeared before me, looking the same as she has been any other day. I thought I was dreaming until she came over to me and held out a hankie to wipe my tears, and I knew she was real. And then she told me she was really frustrated and had really wanted to take her own life. She said she had gone to the riverbank. But, she said, just as when she wanted to jump in, she saw our faces in the water. She said we were all waving at her, asking her to stay. So she changed her mind and slowly walked back to the *pasar*[20] ... I was so happy I didn't know what to say ...

The policeman goes over to the side of the girl to switch off the TV. And then he walks over to confront the children as if asking them: 'What do you say to that?'

CHILDREN	(*Some in English, some in Mandarin*) No, that can't be my mother. Yah *lah*, that's only TV what? My mother's never like that. Mama would never do a thing like that *lah*. How can that be my mother?
POLICEMAN	An old woman! Going out in the middle of the night?
CHILDREN	Midnight walk? Going out in the middle of the night? Without telling anyone? Every night? (*And so on and so forth ...*)
POLICEMAN	And with a cat!
CHILDREN	(*In English and Mandarin*) What cat? Ah! So that's what's been bothering her. See? I told you, that cat's a jinx. *Alamak*,[21] she's really too much now. I've told her how many times: No cats in HDB flats. And now she's gone crazy with this black cat! I knew there must be something to it!

---

[19] Playwright's note: [Malay:] *pasar malam*, night market.
[20] Editor's note: Malay: *pasar*, market.
[21] Editor's note: Malay: *alamak*, expression of surprise.

I think this cat's causing her to behave very strangely.

Yah, must get rid of the damn animal. First, it made people allergic, now it's inviting my mother to go out at night. Too much! Too much!

They go crazy with anger, looking everywhere for the cat which they believe is the cause of all the unhappiness. As they go 'crazy', Mother is alerted. She marches over to cut them short just before their frenzy reaches a climax.

MAMA   That's enough! Enough! I said that's *enough!*

They all stop at her severe command.

MAMA   So now you're very big already. Everyone's got wings now. Now you don't need me anymore, right? So I can't even have a cat for myself, right? Why can't I have even a cat? Is it so much to ask? Can't I have even a *cat?*

They all back off, not without embarrassment. As they withdraw to the rear, Mama begins to search for her lost cat intensely, at length. Disappointed, she sits down.

An old Indian man appears. He prays and then prostrates himself face down before the deity. Not moving at all, his stillness begins to worry the concerned mother. She goes over to look. Seeing no trace of life she becomes worried and touches him to see if he's OK. The old man jumps at her touch which gives her such fright. She apologises to the surprised old man and withdraws to her corner.

Mama continues looking for her cat, first by looking, then by 'meowing' around. This rouses intense interest from the old man who also begins to look for something. When he realises it is Mother who is making the sound, he breaks out laughing.

What follows is a scene between a Hokkien-speaking old woman and a Tamil-speaking old man trying anxiously to understand each other.

MAMA   What's the matter with you?

OLD MAN   Uh?

MAMA   I said what's the matter with you. I've lost my cat, what is so funny about that?

OLD MAN   Uh?

MAMA   I said what's the matter with you … *Aiyah*, you don't understand.

OLD MAN   Uh?

She, speaking in Hokkien, he, speaking Tamil, aided by the most expressive mime gestures, through a painfully but joyfully gruelling process, manage to communicate the following:

MAMA	I have a cat.
OLD MAN	I also have a cat.
MAMA	My cat is this big.
OLD MAN	My cat is this small.
MAMA	Ah, we all have cat.
OLD MAN	Your cat 'meow, meow'. My cat 'miu, miu'.
MAMA	My cat has black hair.
OLD MAN	My cat has brown hair.
MAMA	My cat has short tail.
OLD MAN	My cat also has short tail.
MAMA	Short-tail cats are beautiful.
OLD MAN	Very beautiful.
MAMA	My cat has been chased away by my children.
OLD MAN	My cat also chased out by my children. Bad people. Very bad. Very bad!
MAMA	Don't get excited. No need to pain yourself for what they have done. Cheer up. Cheer up.

As they comfort each other, Mama sees a cat not far away. It turns out to be the old man's kitten. Elated, he goes over to fondle the kitten and tries to get it to walk over to the old woman. It doesn't want to. So he guides the kitten to her, and Mother is very happy to meet the kitten. Then the old man walks back to beckon the kitten who quickly goes to him. He's very happy and proud and tries again to get the cat to go to the woman. No success; he again has to guide the kitten over. He walks away again and, at his beckoning, the kitten again quickly runs over to him. When he tries once more to get the kitten to go over to the woman voluntarily, he succeeds. Both he and Mama are elated that the kitten has recognised a new friend.

Then Mama says the kitten is very skinny and needs to eat. The old man agrees and he gets up to go to the market to get something for it. Very reluctantly, the old man bids the old woman goodbye and leaves.

Alone, Mama tries to look for her cat again.

No trace of it. She lies down, calling her cat while she gradually falls asleep. Light dims.

She hears kittens meowing in her dream. The children at the rear are transformed into kittens coming forward to caress her.

Then they retreat to form two groups and transform into little children, with one group practising their English vowels while the other group is practising Mandarin.

From now on, Mama, sitting at the centre with crossed legs, begins to beat the floor with her outstretched hands.

The groups then break into a kind of verbal competition.

SW	(*Playing word games with others in two languages.*) 'Bitter Batter' (*in English*).
SB	'Little stars twinkle bright' (*in Mandarin*).
V	'Peter Piper' (*in English*).
K	'Four is not Ten' (*in Mandarin*).
YH	'She sells seashells on the seashore' (*in English*).
YB	'One, two, three, four, five' (*in Mandarin*).
J	'The rain in Spain stays mainly on the plain' (*in English*).

Then the two groups begin to argue, one with 'Hereford' in English,[22] *the other with 'know is know', until they reach a state of utter confusion.*

W	Stop! Stop! This is not fun anymore. Let's change.
CHILDREN	Change what?
W	*Di xia tie!*[23]

---

[22] Editor's note: The references to 'the rain in Spain' and 'Hereford' are drawn from the musical version — written by Alan Jay Lerner and Frederick Lowe — of George Bernard Shaw's play *Pygmalion* (1916), *My Fair Lady* (1956): 'Henry Higgins: "In Hartford, Hereford and Hampshire ...?" / Eliza Dolittle: "Hurricanes hardly happen"...' (from the song 'The Rain in Spain').

[23] Playwright's note: *Di xia tie*, Mandarin for subway [or metro system]. Editor's note: The more usual expression now would be *di tie*.

CHILDREN   Ah!

They understand the new game is about translation and everyone happily joins in.

For every word mentioned by a player, the next appointed person has to give an equivalent in Mandarin, and then the next appointed person would have to give an equivalent in Hokkien. In every case, the players know both the English and Mandarin terms but fail to know the proper Hokkien rendition.

Terms chosen include:
MRT — underground railway.[24]
Library — where there are many books you can borrow.
Insurance — before you have an accident, you pay a little. After you have an accident, they pay you a lot.
Safety pin — a pin you can poke through and then press down.
Registry of Marriages — the place where you get your marriage licence.
They then end up in a quarrel. Mother is fed up and orders them to go and study.

MAMA   Go and study. Go, go and study now!

Most unwillingly, the children all go to the rear, line up and been to study — singing the 'I must learn my ABC' song.[25]

As they sing, they move slowly towards the front of the stage, while remaining in step with each other. They arrive after repeating the song three times.

They freeze. Then they go off in pairs, with one person riding piggyback on the other; they then start walking in a circle, with Mama at the centre, where she has been beating the floor with her hands.

They start 'writing' letters in English and Mandarin, simultaneously translating the texts into Hokkien. They share the letters and the translations by reading aloud, each taking a couple of sentences.

W   Dear Mama, I've just arrived at the airport. The winter is very cold here and I think I will find it a bit difficult to adapt myself.

The Hokkien version follows.

---

[24] Editor's note: MRT, Mass Rapid Transit — the metro rail system in Singapore.
[25] Editor's note: See note 1.

V   Mr and Mrs Leconte came to meet me at the airport. You know what?
           There was an accident at the airport. You packed too many things in
           my bag and it burst open at the customs and all the *sambal belacan*[26]
           and *haybee hiam*[27] came out.

The Hokkien version follows.

JH   I'm finding life in France very interesting. And I'm learning new things
           all the time. I'm even learning how to drink wine and eat cheese!

The Hokkien version follows.

J   Friends came to meet me and I'm now putting up in their apartment.
           When I get my own apartment, I'll write and inform you.

The Hokkien version follows.

K   Texas is such a big country that your eyes seem to reach no end. The
           scenery really makes you feel open and free.

The Hokkien version follows.

JH   I have already gone through the course catalogue and finalised my
           choice of subjects for this semester which I expect to be very exciting.
           I'm going to do anthropology, philosophy, economics, literature, psy-
           chology and history of rock and roll.

The Hokkien version follows.

YB   Mama, you are getting on in age, so please look after your diet care-
           fully. Try to stay away from things with high cholesterol content.

The Hokkien version follows.

MAMA   Write a letter for me. Tell him if he still want more *haybee hiam* or
           sambal belacan, or anything else, I can make for him. And tell him to
           be careful when he sleeps. Since the weather is very cold there, tell him
           to wear more than one shirt when he goes to sleep. Outside the pyja-
           mas, can put on the woollen top with long sleeves, the black one.
           Maybe also should wear socks if it gets colder. You come from hot
           place, must take special care. Better take the trouble to wear more now,
           otherwise you get sick and see doctor, worse.

---

[26] Playwright's note: [Malay:] *sambal belacan*, chilli paste made with dried prawns.
[27] Playwright's note: [*Minnan hua* or *minnan* language:] *haybee hiam*, dried shrimp with chilli.

J   (*Already impatient*) OK *lah*, Mama. 'Mother asks you if you want more of the *belachan* or *haybee hiam*. If do, she'll send some more. Keep warm. Wear woollen and socks when you sleep.' OK, Mama, written.

MAMA   Write me another one. Tell him to be careful when making friends. You know a person's face, you don't know his heart. Must be very careful not to trust people too easily. But you must also be nice to other people. I know honesty very often makes you lose out on things, but still you must try your best to be honest and courteous to other people. Specially when you are not in your own country, you need more friends more often.

JH   (*Already very impatient, in Hokkien*) OK, I know *lah*, Mama. I know *lah*. (*Now in English*) 'Mama ask you to make good friends but also beware of bad friends.' OK, finished.

MAMA   Write me another one. Tell him don't spend so much money. You know our money never come easy. Every cent is very hard-earned. But if he really needs to spend money on something important, like when you want to buy books or what, you just go ahead and spend. If that is the case, then you know I will try every means to send you more money still. The important thing is for you to understand the importance of thrift. You must also be very careful when you deal in money with friends ...

W   (*Already very irritated, in Hokkien*) OK *lah*, Mama, so big already, he knows what to do *lah*. (*Then in English*) 'Mama tell you to be thrifty and be careful with friends.' Finished!

MAMA   Tell him: Your big maternal uncle has gone to live in what's that place? ... Canada. Maybe I'll never see him again. I was so sad I didn't even want to go to the airport to see him off. I was scared I cannot control my tears ... And your maternal auntie also had problem lately. Very big problem. She fell one day and half her body cannot move anymore now. The right side. She can't even talk now, only cry. Every time I see her, she cries. Cannot say anything ...

SB   (*Already very impatient*) OK, OK, OK *lah*! (*In Mandarin*) 'Big maternal uncle immigrated to Canada. Maternal auntie paralysed by stroke.' OK, finished.

MAMA   Write and tell him ...

CHILDREN   (*Losing patience now, refusing to translate*)
                      Aiyah, Ma, you only wrote last week what!
                      Next week then write *lah*.
                      OK, OK. 'Mum sends her usual regards.'
                      'The usual reminders from Mum.'
                      'Same thing about your health, money and safety.'

As Mama carries on, the children become increasingly angry with her fussing and raise their voices higher and higher, and when they see that this does not work, they begin to sing the 'ABC Song', louder and louder, as they become tired of carrying each other pig-gyback. Finally their fatigue makes them abandon the piggyback game.

Mama senses the impatience of her children verging on hostility. She also becomes angry and shows it by beating the floor with her hands with increasing strength and sound. Eventually her anger is noticed by the children. Surprised, stunned, they slow down and eventually stop.

Mama's beating of the floor reaches a climax and abruptly stops. Her head is lowered.

The children are greatly disturbed. They squat down in a circle around her, studying her intensely. They feel regretful and somewhat guilty. After a moment, they exchange opinions with each other through eye contact. In agreement, all stand and begin singing the 'Birthday Song'.

Surprised, Mama slowly raises her head, sees them singing to her. Somewhat touched, she rises.

All the children, one by one, go forward to give their congratulations and express love. By the end of it, Mama is already transformed from her sadness. She attempts to approach them to return her love. But one by one, they turn away, as if to carry on their normal lives which have no place for Mama.

Sensing this, Mama plunges into an even deeper state of loneliness. Moving away from the sight of their backs, she looks for the cat. Finding it, she directs all her attention and love to the silent animal.

POLICEMAN   Yes, why does she go out every night in the middle of the night?

The children begin to realise the gravity of the matter. They turn to look inside the circle they have now formed, one by one, and look at the pathetic old woman lying on the floor fondling her cat.

CHILDREN   (*In English and Mandarin*)

I'd really like to do something for her, but I just haven't got the time.

What is she thinking, I wonder. But we must really do something for her now.

I could take her to my place for six months, but she couldn't understand what my children were talking about and they wouldn't understand her.

I'd very much like to have her around me, all the time, but how could I arrange my time?

I don't mind putting her up in my place, but I know she hates the apartment because there's no one there she could talk to.

POLICEMAN   And with a cat! In the middle of the night!

CHILDREN   *Cheh*![28] That cat again!

I told you, the cat's a jinx, you see what it's done to Mama? And the police are here too!

The cat, the damned cat. Mama would never be like that if not for the cat!
Where's the cat?
Where's the cat?
Let's find the cat!
Let's find the cat!
The cat!
The cat!

They start a frantic search for the cat. They rush in all directions, going faster and faster, until it becomes a crazy hunt. Finally one of them spots the cat and everyone joins the chase. Encircling it, they stalk the cat, each pounding on the animal with his or her body, piling on top of each other in a heap above the stricken cat.

Mama yells her disapproval above the horrible cries of the cat, kneeling in front of them.

MAMA   Don't do that! Don't do that! Don't do that!

But it is too late. Everything is quiet now.

---

[28] Editor's note: Expression of disgust.

Getting up, Mama goes to the pile of bodies. Pulling away the bodies one by one, she finally discovers the cat. Picking it up preciously, she begins to cuddle the animal as if it is her child.

As she walks off, she sings the 'One Night Grow One Inch' lullaby.[29] *And before she finally disappears into the darkness, she begins to tell the cat the story of 'The Rabbit and the Tortoise', reminding the animal in her lap to work hard, and to persevere on and on.*

Blackout.

(*End of Play*)

---

[29] Editor's note: See note 7.

The Silly Little Girl and the Funny Old Tree

1. Prologue

There is something on stage that has some resemblance to a tree but is not exactly a tree. Actors bring on a group of cloth puppets, one by one, lining them somewhere upstage.

The Little Girl sneaks in on stage, approaching the Old Tree. As she turns, she catches sight of the rows of puppets staring at her motionlessly. Shocked, the Girl runs off.

2. The Funny Old Tree

Where the Tree is, there is an actor with his back facing the audience. This is the personification of the Old Tree. He stands in silence, not moving.

The Girl comes again, looking around, making sure no one is there. She sits down facing the audience, with her back to the Tree but behaves as if she is looking up at the Tree.

GIRL   This tree. It's very old already. Old and funny.

       It's different from those we see along the streets.

       This one has never had its branches cut off.

       Branches, very long, very tall, stretching right into the sky.

       Skin all cracked, like the *tongkang*[1] drivers last time.

       Maybe it's too tall. Too tall you won't get the sun to cover you.

       This tree is really very funny. Old and funny.

       Other trees have leaves on top; this one has them at the bottom, near the ground.

---

[1] Playwright's note: [Malay:] *tongkang*, [a barge, a large open boat, a] rivercraft carrying people and goods.

Very unusual ... *Gong Gong*[2] said last time there were many trees like this ...

Now, it looks like the only one left.

I wonder if that's because it's very old so it's very funny ... Like *Gong Gong* last time.

Yeah ... I think trees are like people, the old ones are always the funny ones.

The Girl approaches the Tree to caress it. She freezes with her back to the audience.

3. The Silly Little Girl

The actor who has been still and silent now moves out of his character. He walks around the Girl for a moment, examining her, before starting to speak.

TREE   She comes here every day, to look at the tree. Many times. Once in the morning, once during recess when she purposely takes a detour into the carpark on her way to the canteen. On her way back, one more time. Then one more time after school before going home. And if she has ECA,[3] she would go and see it one more time before lunch and another time after lunch ... People call her the Silly Little Girl, not without some reason. Recently, she has grown more and more eager to see the Tree.

Why? No one has been able to find out why.

But, not anywhere in the school can you see the Funny Old Tree. In those classrooms closest to it you cannot see, because the place is too low.

In the block farthest away from it you also can't see, because the place is too high.

She doesn't like to go to the library anymore, you know why?

Because there the windows open the wrong way and you can't see the Tree either.

By comparison, the best place to look at the Tree is in the carpark.

You raise your head, looking up, the Tree is right there in front, up on the slope.

Very commanding! Very beautiful!

But, they are going to build houses there now. And the bulldozers are coming ...

Sudden outburst of bulldozer noises, closing in from afar, produced vocally by the actors themselves.

---

[2] Playwright's note: [*minnan hua* or *minnan* language, a non-Mandarin Chinese language:] *Gong Gong*, grandfather.

[3] Playwright's note: ECA, Extra-Curricular Activity.

The Tree and the Girl become very worried, reacting in slow motion. The Tree returns to its place while the Girl moves aside to see what happens.

The sound escalates to a climax, then suddenly ceases.

4. Voices from the Distant Past

The Tree is again standing with back to audience, motionless. Girl comes on and sits at the same old spot as in scene 2, which is her habitual spot.

GIRL   How are you? I had *tau suan*[4] for breakfast, curry rice for lunch and *beehoon goreng*[5] for dinner ...

Attempts to memorise some formula.

Mum takes the late shift tonight. Father also will be very late, overtime ...

Attempts to memorise something else.

Fatty bom bom[6] very cunning today. Test without notice. Don't you say she is kind because she is fat. Just the opposite! Her questions are worse than *Ah San*,[7] always trying to trick us into mistakes.

---

[4] Playwright's note: [*minnan hua* or *minnan* Chinese:] *tau suan*, yellow bean broth, a dessert.

[5] Playwright's note: *beehoon goreng*, fried vermicelli. Editor's note: The first term is *minnan hua* or *minnan* Chinese: 'vermicelli'; and the second term is Malay: 'frying in a pan'.

[6] Editor's note: The phrase "fatty fatty bom bom" may have been derived from a popular song (possibly American or Jamaican in origin) in the 1960s. It was certainly adopted quickly in Singapore as a kind of limerick. One common version of this is:

Fatty fatty bom bom
Curi curi jagung ([Malay:] stealing, stealing maize)
Mata mata tangkap (police, police capture)
Masuk dalam lokap (thrown into the lock-up)

Another variant was:

Fatty fatty bom bom
Makan makan jagung (eating, eating maize)
Balik balik kampung (going back, back to the village)
Jadi jadi King Kong (becomes, becomes King Kong).
(Kevin Y. L. Tan, e-mail communication to the editor, 3 January 2009.)

[7] Editor's note: *minnan hua* or *minnan* Chinese: 'the thin or skinny one'. The reference here is to one of half of the comedy duo popularly known as *Ah Pui* ('the fat one') and *Ah San* — Ya Fong (d. 1995) and Wang Sa (d. 1998) — who rose to fame in the 1960s in Singapore. They were dubbed as the Laurel and Hardy of Singapore, and performed in theatres and on television.

No wonder people call her: 'Fatty bom bom, Never *tolong*'.[8]

Attempts to memorise some more.

> You listen to me talk so much, ever get bored?
>
> If you can say, 'No, I'm not,' how nice!
>
> If you can talk, I'll let you talk.
>
> I'll shut up, and only listen to you talk.
>
> If you really can talk, I'll keep my mouth tightly shut like I do in school and at home.
>
> I'll keep quiet forever, only listen to you talk.
>
> You are so old, like *Gong Gong*, you must have so many stories you will never finish telling ...

After staring at the Tree for a moment, she puts her head down to her work. As she buries herself into her work, she hums 'Longing for the Spring Breeze.'

The Old Tree, frozen for ages, begins to stir. Struggling to move, it begins to turn around. Its eyes begin to open, with difficulty. Its mouth fights to breathe and articulate. After what seems to be a momentous struggle, it begins to emit sound — first breathing, then a sound, then, faintly, the first phrase of 'Longing for the Spring Breeze.'

The Girl seems to notice something is happening, and when she realises it is coming from the tree, she swings around to confront it in amazement.

GIRL   You ... you can sing? All I said ... for so long ... you heard everything?

TREE   I ... I ... have not heard this song for such a long, long time ...

GIRL   You can hear? ... You can sing? ... All I've said ... you can understand? ...

The Tree, with great difficulty, gives a nod. Then it begins to struggle on with the song, but with very little success.

GIRL   You forgot? ... I teach you, OK? ... I teach you, I teach you!

The little one teaches the old one to sing the song from the distant past. From what looks like a mummy, the Tree gradually revives its ability to move and sing. Stimulated by the

---

[8] Editor's note: Malay: *tolong*, a verb — to aid, show mercy, offer help.

Girl's unreserved eagerness, the vibrancy of the Old Tree is revived. The singing reaches a climax.

5. Island of the Abandoned Tree

The Old Tree is telling the Little Girl a story. It goes through a series of mimed actions tracing its own past before coming back to reality and telling her the story in words.

TREE   It was a very long time ago. Don't know why, but they cut it down and didn't want to use it. So they left it drying in the sun.

One year, there was a fantastic storm and the whole of heaven and earth shook in anger.

The river climbed over the banks, the smaller trees all went underwater and the fish occupied the nests of the birds.

Even this tree, although it was so big, began to flow over the water. It swam across long stretches of land, heading straight for the open sea.

But the sea was too far away. Before it reached the sea, the water had begun to go down.

After another long, long time, the abandoned tree felt its branches touching the bottom. Then it could no longer move on. Helplessly, the tree watched the water shrink, collecting the wide flow into the narrow meandering curves of the river course.

Soon afterwards, leaves and flowers covered the river banks once more, and the birds and butterflies returned to their homes. Within a few years, both sides of the river were once again covered by lush green forests.

The abandoned tree felt very sad. The branches of the trees on the river banks kept growing with increasing vibrancy, greening everything in sight. But the abandoned tree felt itself drying and shrinking with each passing day. Death was slowly approaching.

'Is this the end? Is this how I'm going to perish?'

Watching the withering branches around it, the abandoned tree felt so very reluctant to die off.

In great anger, it shook and made waves in the water.

Suddenly, the tree felt the earth under the river — it seemed the earth was still as rich as in the past. And, over the water, it also felt the warmth of the sun, fascinating as it had always been.

Gritting its teeth, the tree stretched its branches deeply into the river bed underneath. On top, it sprang out budding leaves once again, absorbing the eternal nourishment of the sun. Trying with all its might, the tree awakened the life forces within its body.

Very soon, the branches and leaves of this abandoned tree had become greener and lusher than those on the river banks. And the roots beneath the water had soon grown into a huge network, catching all the soil and refuse flown down from upstream. Then little fish and prawns began to gather there, just like there up above the water where birds and animals began to flock and breed by the tree.

So they went on, generation after generation, with the old ones burying themselves, turning into ashes and nourishment, feeding those who came after them. Finally, the abandoned floating tree had grown into a little island.

GIRL   Are you that abandoned tree?

TREE   No. That was a long, long time ago.

GIRL   Where is the tree now?

TREE   It's been cut down a long time ago.

GIRL   Why would they cut it down?

TREE   Too old. Doesn't match the young and green environment.

The thought brings both the Tree and the Girl to a freeze.

GIRL   How nice if you were my literature teacher. Then we'll get stories like this every day.

TREE   One 'every day', your hair will go white before I run out.

GIRL   But I wouldn't want you for geography, sure fail.

Reflecting, the Tree hums 'Longing for the Spring Breeze'.

GIRL   Who taught you this song?

TREE   ... Then, many people came ... They began working when the sun rose and stopped only when the sun went down. At night, they gathered under the trees, to chit chat, play chess, sing songs, tell stories ... What songs did your mother teach you?

GIRL   No, she never did ...

TREE   Then where did you learn the song?

GIRL   *Gong Gong* taught me, when I was very little.

TREE   Don't your mother and father sing?

GIRL   No ... Yes, they do. *Man in the Net*,[9] *King of Kings*.[10]

Girl starts humming 'Longing for the Spring Breeze' again, joined by the Tree. Then the sound of bulldozers comes on. They stop. The sound fades.

GIRL   The bulldozers, are they coming this way? Would ...would you ...

TREE   You coming tomorrow?

GIRL   Yes. And you ...

TREE   Sure I'll be here. Girl, trees are different from humans. Trees never move. Humans never stop.

GIRL   But is it always like that? Didn't your old tree swim a long way and then grow into an island? If trees, who are Supposed to be still, can move like that, why can't humans, who are supposed to be always moving, stop and be still ...

Looking out to where the bulldozer sounds come from.

6. Silly and Funny Games

The Girl is pacing around, reflecting on the things the Tree has said.

GIRL   ... The teachers, actually they do have good intentions, although they are very nasty sometimes ... Father and mother, they are also quite nice to me, although they always talk too much ...

TREE   Then why don't you talk to them?

---

[9] Editor's note: *Man in the Net* was a Hong Kong TVB-produced television series that ran from 1979–80, and starred Chow Yun Fat. The well-known theme song was sung by Theresa Cheung Tak Lan. The series was also popular in Singapore.

[10] Editor's note: This is probably the Hong Kong television series titled *The Shell Game* (1980) in English, but known as *Qian Wang Zhi Wang* (King among Thousand Kings) in Chinese, which starred Patrick Tse. The theme song was sung by Lisa Wang.

GIRL   I have! ... But no use ... They don't understand me ... And I don't understand them. They say I am silly, I say they are dumb. Like this story, my favourite, they all say it's stupid.

One day, a very hot day, a young man in shorts and slippers[11] walked into the air-conditioned library and he was stopped by the librarian at the door. 'I'm sorry,' she said, 'but you can't come in here wearing slippers.' And she turned him out. A few minutes later, the young man came back again. His slippers had gone and he was barefoot. The librarian stopped him again, 'I'm sorry,' she said, 'but you can't come in here wearing nothing on your feet.'

And she turned him out again. A few minutes later, the young man came back again. This time he wore a pair of heavy army boots.

Although he showed he was walking very carefully, his boots still made a lot of loud 'kik-kok', 'kik-kok' sound. The whole library was disturbed by the young man's walk, but the librarian never stopped him this time.

They all say my story is stupid, but I think it is very clever. Why are people so dumb, huh?

TREE   Do you like dancing?

GIRL   Yeah. But nobody likes to dance with me.

TREE   Do you like singing?

GIRL   Yeah. But they all think I'm silly and don't want to sing with me.

TREE   You want to sing and dance with me?

GIRL   I thought you can only sing and dance when there is wind?

TREE   That's what the wind says. Actually, it's only when we sing and dance is there wind; only when our leaves and branches swing is there wind. Wind mustn't be so proud.

GIRL   (*Reflecting*) Only when trees sing and dance is there wind; only when tree leaves and branches swing is there wind. Wind mustn't be so proud ...

TREE   OK, listen carefully: What plant has no root, no stem, no leaf, no flower, no fruit?

GIRL   Moss.

---

[11] Editor's note: In Singapore, 'slippers' refer to rubber flip-flops.

TREE   No, mushrooms. Why do plants have flowers?

GIRL   So they can bear fruit.

TREE   No, so the bees can have honey. Why are people scared at night?

GIRL   Because they are afraid of darkness.

TREE   No, because once night falls people forget the sun is still shining somewhere else.

GIRL   You are clever in asking questions.

TREE   How could a tree ask questions? Learnt from humans. Humans are the best askers. How come you don't know?

GIRL   Try me.

Why do people have to talk?
Why are tears not sweet?
Why is the tongue in the mouth?
Why is there wind?
Why doesn't the stone cry?
Why has the singlet no sleeves?
Why do people have to queue up?
Why don't the fish get tired of swimming?
Why do turtles walk so slow?
Why must people cut down trees? ...

By the time she has come this far, she is already very agitated.

After a pause:

TREE   A asks B, 'Why don't I ever reach the end?' B says to A, 'Because you are going in circles.' A then asks B, 'Why can't I reach the end even going straight?' Then B says to A, 'Because there is no end.'

GIRL   Why does he keep going if there is no end?

TREE   If there is an end, there won't be the need to go on.

GIRL   Don't understand.

TREE   If humans don't understand, what can trees do? You want to see me dance?

GIRL   Yes.

The Tree goes into a series of movements, turning and going around, shaking and wagging. Girl totally absorbed, but can't understand.

TREE   This is the dance of the bees. With this dance, the bee is telling its comrades: There, there is honey that way. In the direction such an angle to the sun, there is honey.

Girl finds it fascinating, and imitates the Tree. They are both amused. Then the bulldozer is heard coming closer and closer. The Tree returns to its position and the Girl hides away.

A group of people comes in worried, looking for something around the Tree which they cannot find. Apprehensively, they leave.

7. The Exorcism

Nightfall. The group of people comes on and performs an exorcism ritual facing the place where the girl usually comes on. They go away. The bulldozer sounds are heard off stage.

Girl comes on secretively.

TREE   You have come over?

GIRL   You saw me?

TREE   If you can see me, I can see you.

GIRL   Of course, you are a tree. Why can't humans see in the dark? Because human eyes are made to see only light. (*Reflecting for a moment.*) It was too far away. My feet are aching from standing too long.

TREE   They have seen shadows in the school building. Your presence creates shadows which are frightening to them. They reckon you are a ghost. You'll be found out if you do this too often.

GIRL   There are many holes in the wire fence, they won't catch me. Don't worry, I've done my survey ... They're coming very soon ...

Leaning against the old Tree, she begins to sing 'Little Stars'.

TREE   Very nice.

GIRL   You are very unusual. Why are you so funny? Why are you different from the ordinary trees? Why is there only one like you found?

TREE   The others have gone travelling.

GIRL   Trees can travel?

TREE   Some have disintegrated, travelling underneath the earth. Others have flown away, spreading seeds in other places.

GIRL   (*After a pause, with sudden impulse.*) I don't want you to go! I won't allow them to touch you!

TREE   (*Not responding to her agitation.*) You want to see my Tree Dance?

GIRL   Tree Dance?

TREE   Yes. It's a group dance. One tree joined to another tree, and to another tree, forming a row of trees; and one row of trees joined to another row of trees, forming ...

The bulldozer sound gets louder and closer. Fear begins to take hold of the Girl. She sees people coming. Before she can run away, they have already arrived. She runs and they chase after her. Eventually she is caught.

They order her to leave. Helpless, she complies.

Just as she goes, the bulldozer closes in on the Tree.

Screaming in horror, the Girl rushes to the Tree, shielding it from the encroaching machine.

She scuffles with them as the bulldozer runs towards the Tree.

Just as the machine is going to run down the Tree, the Girl struggles free and climbs up the Tree.

GIRL   I warn you. I warn you! You come another inch closer, I'll jump down!

There is panic in the group. They stop the bulldozer.

PEOPLE   Girl, come down, Girl, Mum and Dad are waiting for you!

Girl, come down, Girl, Teacher and Principal are expecting you!

Girl, come down, Girl, you have a bright future right ahead of you.

Girl, come down, Girl, come down, why waste your precious youth on nothing more than a funny old tree?

GIRL   Don't you dare call him funny old tree! He's not funny and he's not old. It's you who are funny and old. Do you know what has no root, no stem, no leaf, no flower and no seed?

Why do plants have flowers?
Why do people have to talk?
Why are tears not sweet?
Why is the tongue in the mouth?
Why doesn't the stone cry?
Why have singlets no sleeves?
Why is the world so dark?
Why don't fish get tired of swimming?
Why do turtles walk so slow?
Why are people afraid of darkness?
Why do people cut down trees?
Do you know trees can sing?
Do you know trees can dance? ...

She becomes terribly hysterical. Everyone is stunned by the Girl's outburst.

PEOPLE   Very bad. The girl is possessed by the devil. She is really silly and stupid now.

GIRL   Get the bulldozer out of here. Right now! Or I'll go down with the Tree!

PEOPLE   (*After some urgent consultation*): OK, we won't run down the tree. Come down now, Girl.

GIRL   You're lying, lying! You're just trying to con me down, and then you'll run it down all the same.

PEOPLE   No, girl, we really mean it. We really mean it!

GIRL   You lie. Lie! ... Swear. Swear if you really mean it. Swear!

PEOPLE   No lies. No lies ... OK. OK. We swear. We swear. If we break our promise and run down this tree, we will all die a violent death. Honest!

The Tree hums 'Longing for the Spring Breeze' as if giving comfort to and calming the Girl, as if persuading her to leave with peace of mind. She caresses the Tree fondly before finally agreeing to leave.

8. Dance of the Tree

The Girl convalesces in a resthouse. The conversation seems like telepathic communication.

GIRL   ... How are you? I had bread and butter for breakfast, fried fish for lunch and roast pork for dinner ...

It's very quiet here, most of them are old people. I'm the only young one. At first they thought I was mad. They said there was something wrong with my head. But they are beginning to change their mind. Now, they don't know what to think of me.

To make me believe everything is OK, Father goes to take a picture of you every day. The date printed on the picture tells me you are still there, and well. I can see everything around you has been cleared away. The ground is flattened, the trees are all gone and the buildings are going up every day. And now, they are beginning to plant new trees even. Can you do the tree dance with your new friends?

I am sorry I never remembered to ask you why you look the way you do. Why are your leaves not at the top but at the bottom near the ground? Other trees all have their leaves at the top, don't they? So they could catch more sunlight? Why are yours at the bottom?

Is it because you are afraid that 'Big Trees Invite Too Much Wind'?

The Tree, in its turn, begins to give her a vivid description of the Tree Dance.

TREE   Yes, yes, tree dance ... One tree joined to another tree, and then joined to another tree, forming a row of trees. One row of trees joined to another row of trees, and another row of trees, forming a forest of trees.

Facing the approaching storm, they begin to dance and sing. Girl, have you ever seen a forest of trees dancing in a thunderstorm? When the warning wind approaches, the trees eagerly bend forward as if in welcome, and as they touch the gusty wind, they gracefully bend backwards, caressing the wind as they arch. The trunk of the trees flex a little bit, gently swaying to and fro. The leaves, rows and rows, and patches upon patches, like shining scales of fish, receive the violent raindrops with choral delight, gently rubbing them before sending them down to the thirsty undergrowth. The storm crashes to the forest of trees with the violence of thunder and lightning. But the trees, in grace and gratitude receive them as their juice of life. Many bouts after, through bashing drenches and dancing responses, the sky is clear once more; the trees have become deeper-rooted, the branches have become tougher, the leaves have become greener and lusher.

So, Girl, don't be afraid of the thunderstorm. Since you like trees, why don't you learn the Tree Dance? It's ...

Suddenly the description stops ...

GIRL   How? How?

TREE   I'm sorry, I can't demonstrate it to you any longer ...

GIRL   Why? ... What? ... Have ... have they cut you down? They have cut you down! They have cut you *down!*

PEOPLE   No, we have not cut it down. We have not cut it down. We promised, we promised.

Girl runs out in panic.

9. Farewell, Tree

The Girl runs to where the Tree is. It is still there but doesn't look the same anymore. All its branches have been pruned, leaving only the bare trunk. Girl can't believe her own eyes.

PEOPLE   You see. We have kept our promise. We have not cut the tree down.

GIRL   But ... but ... but ...

PEOPLE   We have pruned its top. We have pruned its undergrowth. In this way, we expect the tree to branch out to a totally new shape. It was old and haggard and looked very funny. How could trees have leaves not at the top but at the *bottom?* We are confident you will also like its new form which will blend in perfectly with the new landscape design.

GIRL   No. No! No! ... (*Then to the Tree.*). Why. Why? *Why?*

TREE   (*Weakly*) I don't know. I don't know. I don't know.

GIRL   You know. You know! *You know!*

TREE   Why would I know?

GIRL   You know everything. You are old, you seem to know everything. Tell me why, tell me why!

TREE   Why would I know just because I am old? Why should I know everything just because I am old? Don't forget; I am tree, you are human.

GIRL   You know. You know! Why. Why? *Why?*

TREE   Yeah, continue asking. Ask yourself. Maybe that's where you will find the answers.

Hysterically, the Girl hits the Tree — on and on until she exhausts herself.

10. The Girl's Dance

In exhaustion, she stares at the tree, sinking into her deepest ever reflection.

GIRL   But you forgot to teach me the Tree Dance, the trees' group dance ... One tree joined to the next, and joined to the next, to form a row of trees ... One row joined to another row, and to another row, to form a forest of trees ... Now I can only do the Bee Dance ...

Then she tries to remember the Bee Dance. Painstakingly, she executes the Bee Dance in solemn seriousness. But when it comes to the last part, she is lost.

But where is the honey? Where is the sun? Where should I point? ... Where is the honey? Where is the sun? Where ...

In stark concentration, she searches her memory and the environment, humming the 'Little Stars' as she goes on. Behind, in cracking voice, is heard the Tree singing 'Longing for the Spring Breeze'.

The cloth dolls seen at the beginning appear again, staring at the Girl.

(*End of Play*)

The Eagle and the Cat (A Monodrama)

Once again I'm standing here. And once again nothing has happened. For more than a week now, nothing has happened.

But it's definitely here, right here where I'm standing now, that something had happened a week ago. Something ... Well, how should I put it? ... It has definitely happened although I've never told anyone about it. I didn't dare to. No one would have believed me. I wouldn't have believed it if I was not involved myself. It should have been a dream. Because something like that couldn't have happened in this world. And yet it was definitely not a dream. Because however hard I bit my hand, however painful the biting became, I did not wake up. So it couldn't have been a dream ...

I hung on to the eagle's steely claws with both my hands, gliding between patches of clouds. Gliding in the middle of an intense shaft of light between patches of clouds. One moment we were shooting upwards like an arrow, the next moment we were gliding downwards like a falling kite ... The wind around us was so cold it made me shiver. But the eagle's claws were hot like barbecue forks ... We glided. We glided in the clouds, and between the clouds. And we dived and swooped ... One moment upwards, another downwards ... How could this have been real?

And yet the whole process could not have been anything but real. It was ... it was the day I lost my way. By right, a person from China shouldn't have lost his way in Singapore. And I have personally never gotten lost here in your country. But I rather deserved getting lost that day, because I was in a really bad mood. I walked and walked and walked. Very fast. Although I didn't have the slightest idea where I was going. As a matter of fact, rather than to say I was going to some place, it's more accurate to say that I was running away from some place. Running away from something.

I felt really bad on that particular day. You see, I had just come out from the — OK, let's not mention names. To avoid more trouble, I won't mention names. Well, I just came out of an embassy, and I was feeling furious. Who did they think I was? Why did they have to look at a man with that kind of expression? I was just going to visit my friends, to do some sightseeing in those famous spots. I had shown them my letter of invitation, my return

115

ticket, my visa and my return permit ... I've got everything they needed for the documenta-tion so why were they still so bloody suspicious? What were the grounds for their suspi-cion? OK, we have special circumstances in our country, I grant you that. But is that reason enough for them to cut us down with that kind of stare?

Contradiction. Absurd contradiction. Every time I walk down Orchard Road, I get mistaken for a tourist from any other country but China. They would either speak to me in Japanese or they would ask me whether I was Korean. If they spoke to me in Mandarin, they would conclude that I come from Taiwan, or Hong Kong. Ha ha ha ...

Did I really look so well-fed and so well-dressed like those people from Taiwan and Hong Kong, I wondered! Because if I was, then why would this woman in the embassy stare at me with such a distasteful expression?

When I left the embassy, I was furious. I was mumbling madly as I walked away. I can't remember whether I was cursing the woman or cursing myself, or what. Anyway, as I walked faster and faster, I cursed louder and stronger. I didn't know how long I had walked or how far. But, suddenly, I had an instinct that something had gone wrong ... Hey, where was I? Hey, where have I got to? How come I couldn't recognise any of the buildings around me? Or any of the natural landmarks? Also, the people there were very curious. They wouldn't tell you anything. Whatever you asked, they would either say they didn't know, or they just wouldn't bother to answer you. It was really very un-Singaporean, you know! How come a people known the world over for their cour-tesy and hospitality had suddenly become so cold and uncaring? No, something must have gone wrong somewhere!

I looked up the sky. Yes, the sky's the same sky. And the road, nothing unusual either. Cars came and went, came and went. Maybe generally they were going faster, but there was nothing unusual about them, either. It was late afternoon on a Friday, nearing the end of the week; many people would have had a date of some kind, and were rushing home. But there was something wrong. For sure. I could tell from the expression on their faces. How come they all looked so cold? All rather like the woman behind the counter in the embassy. Well-mannered and courteous on the outside, cold and detached on the inside. And it was true not only for those walking along the streets. I could see the same expression worn by people riding in the cars. I could feel that through their windows. Even they were affected by that woman in the embassy, I said to myself. I tapped myself on the rear of my head several times, I slapped my face gently, and then not so gently, telling myself: Hey, stop that, stop that! You shouldn't let yourself be frustrated by one person who had decided to cut you down with her stare. Come on, do something to your old subjective habit. Hold yourself, hold yourself. Get out of this emotional rut, OK?

But however hard I tapped my head, however hard I slapped my face, nothing changed. Everyone around me looked cold, with absolutely no emotional expression on their faces. So I decided to close my eyes, hold my breath and try to make this condition disappear. Well, it's an old trick, an old habit I have cultivated since I was a kid. You see, I have a bad temper. Even as a kid I used to get very emotional very often. And nobody can cool it down for me but myself. I devised a method: Every time I realised I had gone too wild, I would find myself a corner, away from everyone, squat down and hold my breath. I would hold my breath for as long as I could stand it and then suddenly release the hold. No matter how upset I was, one long hold of my breath followed by a sudden release, and everything would return to normal. If you don't believe me, you can try it out yourself. No matter how upset you are, one long hold, one sudden release, you'll be OK instantly, even faster than instant coffee.

Now, as I was saying, because I wanted to purge my frustration, to stop feeling that everybody else was being rotten, I chose a little corner tucked between two shops on the main road, and squatted myself in that little recess. I squatted down, took a deep breath and held on, trying my utmost to turn myself back to a normal state. All around me there were all kinds of sounds: Car horns tooting, pedestrians talking, songs and music playing from the shops ... I tried to shut them out of my being. All of them. No listening, no hearing, no attention, all my focus concentrated on my heart-beat. But, gradually, very gradually, my concentration was drawn to a very peculiar sound. What is it? It's very muffled, but very complex. The lower register sounds like horses galloping, the higher register sounds like children crying or yelling. At first, I thought they were hallucinations caused by my holding my breath for too long. But it couldn't have been, because the sound came closer and closer, and it became clearer and clearer. That's right, that's right, it's people running, it's a whole group of people running. And the high-pitched crying and yelling, no it wasn't ... No, it wasn't from children ... It was ... yes, yes, it was ... yes, it was cats crying and yelling! Yes, cats. Not one, but a group ... a whole, big group of cats! What? Cats running? A cat race? No, no it couldn't have been. I have never heard of a cat race organised in Singapore. No, never. And it can't be, either. You see, cats are such nimble creatures, how could they make such loud, heavy stomping noises like horse-racing? No, no, no, it couldn't have been. But then, could it have been ... men chasing after cats? Yeah, yeah, it was. It was people chasing cats. Many, many people chasing many, many cats!

I couldn't hold my breath any longer. I gave up and relaxed and drew a long, deep breath. I stood up and stepped out from the little corner tucked between the two shop windows by the main road. I looked to my right. Well, everything seemed normal enough: The traffic of cars and people flowed normally, nothing unusual at all. And then I looked to my left and — *aiyah*, Mama help me! I've never seen such a grand cat-hunting scene in all my life! Dozens of uniformed men, some carrying nets, some carrying ropes, all chasing after a huge group of cats like a bunch of excited sprinters. As for the cats, there were at least a hundred of them with a stunning range of colours — black and white, yellow and brown, pure coloured ones and mixed coloured ones, some with dots and some with stripes ... And I'm sure there were male cats and female cats, old cats and young cats and middle-aged cats. They were at least 30 to 40 metres ahead of the group of pursuers, but none of them slowed down. They were not running as if they were in a race of some kind. They seemed as if they were really running for their lives! Crying and yelling while running for their lives.

I have always been a very devoted animal-lover since I was a little boy. Cats, dogs, chickens, ducks, goose, birds that fly and insects that sing, and silkworms and fishes and rabbits and ... you name it, I've kept them. All of them, and in many varieties, I've got them all. The thing I hated most was people ill-treating animals. I just can't stand that kind of thing. Even when I was visiting other countries I could not remain silent when I see people ill-treating animals. So, when I saw this cat chase scene, I decided to intervene. I took one step backward, thinking that I would let the cats run past, and as soon as the cats have run past I would move forward again to halt the group of uniformed pursuers. To try and talk them out of this vicious exercise. I thought to myself: Even if I couldn't make them listen to me, I would have at least slowed them down. And the cats would have had a much better chance of escaping.

But just as I was stepping back to allow the cats to run past me, the leading cat of the pack — a strong creature of mixed colours — suddenly stopped in front of me. It looked at me intensely for a fleeting moment and then it grabbed my right foot, tugging me towards the direction they were running to. My immediate reaction was: Hey, you stupid cat! How can you stop and play when the pursuers are chasing madly after you? Have you been scared crazy? But the cat kept on tugging my foot, it was so serious that I began to wonder. And then, as I glanced over, I realised the entire pack of cats had stopped. They were all there watching the leading cat tugging at my foot. In their huge variety of colours, they stared at me intensely, as if saying with their eyes: Why aren't you running? Come run with us! ... Come on, you! What are you talking about? You are cats, I am human. You are in fatal danger and I am comfortable and safe. Why should I run along with you? Come on, it's a bad joke. Run on, you stupid cats!

Right at this moment, as the leading cat tugged me again and again, I came to a position where I was squarely facing the shop window. I didn't quite look into the window, but suddenly a vague image caught the corner of my eyes and instinctively I shivered. And I couldn't resist staring straight at it. *Aiyah, aiyah*! How come there is no image of myself in the window? I ... I ... How come I can still see the cat tugging but I can't see myself being tugged? How come the cat was tugging ... was tugging ... a bigger, standing cat. Was that ... me? No, it can't be ... How could it be ... How could I be ...? Look, I am ...?

But as I looked down at my own feet ... *Aiyah*, how come my feet have all gone hairy? ... What followed were not thoughts anymore. They were reflexes. I turned and saw the group of uniformed pursuers. They were only about ten metres away now. As the cry of the pack of cats sounded, as they started to flee again, I instinctively followed. Before I knew it, I was sprinting furiously after the leading cat, and crying aloud together with them. My body became wet with sweat, and for some reason I began to weep uncontrollably. And I cried and yelled louder and louder as I followed the pack of cats as if I was also running for my life!

Everyone who has experienced nightmares would know this: When you come to the worst part of your horrible dream, there is a life-saving device. You could pinch yourself or bite yourself to wake up, and put an end to the nightmare. So, as I instinctively started running with the cats, trying desperately to shake off the pursuers waving their nets and ropes, this idea came to my mind: OK, enough. Enough is enough. Let's put this nightmare to an end. So I put my finger to my mouth and started biting myself. I bit my finger, then my wrist, then my lips, but nothing worked. However hard I bit myself, I couldn't wake up. I couldn't get myself out of this horrible nightmare. I became really desperate. And my tears kept coming, kept falling. And I could hear my cry become more and desperate and fierce.

I didn't know how far we had run, or where we had run to. Suddenly, the lead cat broke away from the road and jumped into a ditch. He made a few jumps and turns this way and that way and before I knew it, we were safely underground in the city's sewerage system. The entire pack of cats stopped running. So did I. We stopped running and started panting. Underneath, the light was dim. I couldn't see anybody's face clearly. I didn't know what their expressions were. I could only see their eyes, pairs and pairs of eyes shining in the semi-darkness of the underground. The chaotic rumbling of the pursuers above didn't bother them anymore. They were very sure they had escaped to safety.

When everybody had regained composure from the desperate run, my eyes had become adjusted to the dim light in the underground tunnel. I could see that the place was very wet. It was the meeting point of many ducts and drains, up and down and crossing in many directions. On the top, there were many types of piping and cables, beneath, there were the drains. Unexpectedly, they were dry at the moment. And, all over the place, shoulder to shoulder, paw to paw, it was filled with cats. But ... everyone was staring at me.

'Welcome to our pack!' I turned around to identify the speaker. It was the lead cat, the strong, mixed-colour one.

'... Me? ... Joining your pack? ... Hey, come on, I say, What's your problem? If you all want to run, by all means run. But why do you have to tug me along? By the way, how ... how did you manage to turn into this state? ... I mean, why? I don't understand. Why do I have to be dragged into this thing. You may not know this, but I really am up to here with my own problems. And I was planning to leave for another country, and to tell you the truth, I'm not even a permanent resident here. I'm an alien. I'm a Chinese national! Why, why did you have to make me into this?'

For a moment, there was no response. Absolutely no reaction. The shining pairs of cat eyes simply stared at me.

'Are you very *niao*[1] or not?'

'Eh? ... What do you mean, very *niao*?' I asked the lead cat who posed the question at me in the first place. 'I'm sorry, I don't know your name yet,' I added.

'Never mind. Just call me Big One will do, *lah*.'[2]

'OK, Big One, now tell me, what do you mean by *niao*?'

'*Niao* means you are very persistent, very particular, very insistent, very subjective, very idealistic, very stubborn! ...' Following the Big One, many others gave me their understanding of the word *niao*. It was quite overpowering, and I was for a moment lost for words.

'Well ... under certain circumstances, I have indeed shown some of these traits in my character ... But what has that got to do with what I was asking you?'

'You see, when a person is very *niao*, it is possible that he or she would actually turn into a cat when his *niao* character gets very strong. My guess is that you were under some kind of severe emotional excitement that was very *niao*, right?' The Big One was very serious in his delivery.

'... What do you mean? My stubbornness is nothing new. I have been very stubborn, very insistent, very particular, very persistent and subjective about many things for a very, very long time. I have never been silent with things I did not want to tolerate, and I have never turned into a cat. So you see, it cannot be my problem. It had never happened to me before you came into my life. Why did you stop? Why did you have to stop and stare at me? Why? ... Look, Big One, it's you, isn't it? You threw some magic over me, right? Through the stare you turned me into a cat, right? Well, I'm not going to ask you how you did it.

---

[1] Editor's note: Hokkien-Chinese, or *minnan hua* or *minnan* language: the meaning of *niao* will become apparent within the next four utterances in the text.
[2] Editor's note: Malay: *lah*, '[A] particle emphasising the word to which it is appended' (*A Malay-English English-Malay Dictionary*, ed. A. E. Coope [revised edn.; London and Basingstoke: Macmillan Education, 1991]).

Just undo it, OK? Just turn me back into my human form ... Please help me. Please help me, OK? ...'

'Under certain severe conditions, during some severe bouts of stubborn insistence! ... Tell me honestly, were you very excited today? Were you especially upset, or frustrated, or felt painful about something you firmly believed in? Were you thrown into a huge temper?' The Big One kept asking.

'I would be a bloody swine if I wasn't upset. I would be a good-for-nothing weakling if I didn't feel pain. OK, so I didn't have that much money in my pocket. And I haven't gone very far in my career. And my country has not been in the best of shape and we are not very rich, OK? ... But so what, you bloody swine, so what? Does that give you the privilege to look down on me? Does that qualify you to give me that shit of a face and humiliate my personal honour? ...'

'So you got into a big temper?'

'Only a big temper? I was furious! I was spitting fire! I quarrelled with the woman and I said, "To hell with your visa! I don't want it anymore!" And I cursed her. And I ran out of the embassy ...'

'And you have never blown your temper so high, right? You have never been so stubborn and so angry in your entire life, right?'

'And that ... You mean, that would make one turn into a ... cat?'

'Sometimes, yes.'

'... Ha ha ha ha ...Don't make me laugh, please. Ha ha ha ha ... Please, don't treat me like a three-year-old child. Stubbornness can turn a person into a cat? Look, Big One, I think this is all bullshit. However backward you think we are, I am not that gullible! Please, don't make a fool out of me just because you are economically more advanced than we are ... Ha ha ha ... You mean all of you were once humans, and because you were too stubborn, too idealistic, too persistent, too *niao* and so one day you all turned into cats? ... What? You mean ... you were all once humans? ... Really? You were all once humans? ...'

'That is precisely why collectors from allover the world are coming here to hunt for Singapura cats. You must admit, our cats are very, very different.' The Big One nodded his head, his clear and calm manner of speaking was never disturbed by my protestations.

To be honest, I still couldn't believe it. But neither could I doubt the seeming sincerity of the Big One. I did not detect one ounce of uncertainty in his eyes or any indication of deceit. Now, this mixed-colour cat was really some character. He had the expansive look of a leader with a big head, a thick neck, a robust physique, firm strong limbs and a tail seemingly trimmed by a severe cut. Its indescribable mixed-colour fur was spotted (they could be scars). The tip of his left ear drooped a little, his right eye slightly slanting — possibly the result of a major battle. There was possibly nothing on him that was not damaged in one way or another. But, somehow, none of that discounted his authoritative presence. There was an unusual charisma about him which exuded extraordinary power. He was the undisputed leader of the pack. If nothing else, the way he led the massive escape in the face of that army of uniformed pursuers was impressive enough, not to mention his benevolent attitude in picking up a perceived stray like me on the way in the face of imminent danger. Given all of these, it was quite impossible not to be impressed by what he had to say.

'You mean, all of you were once humans? ...'

It was really too much for me to stomach. Even though the Big One was so convincing! ... I turned around to look at the other cats, to look at their expressions, hoping that something on their faces would say to me that the Big One's story was not true ... Some of them looked firm, some looked happy, others sad, or angry, or unsatisfied ... But none of them encouraged me to think that I was being deceived ... Of course, these applied only to those dozens of cats in the front rows. I couldn't see how the others at the back looked.

'*Aiyah*!', I thought to myself, 'I really didn't know there are still so many stubborn idealistic people in Singapore today. My respects to you all, my friends!' But the thought didn't turn into words as something else of a more urgent nature came to my mind.

'But ... but can you ... all of you go back to your old self? ... I mean ... would I stay like this forever?'

'Now that depends. Once we shed our stubbornness and our idealistic persistence, it is possible that, under severe conditions, we could return to our human form,' the Big One confirmed.

'Under what circumstances?'

'Well, no one knows for sure. Because none of us here has ever experienced such a reverse transformation.'

'Haven't you asked those who have returned to the human form?'

'It's funny. Nobody who has returned to human form has been willing to talk to us about that experience.' The Big One wondered ...

'OK, Big One, stop this nonsense with the new guy and let's discuss the pressing issue we are confronted with, OK?' Some cats way behind started protesting. Their shouting created a strong reverberating echo in the tunnel system.

'Hey, Big One, we are absolutely with you whatever you say. We would do whatever you do. But, tell us why did we have to run away just now! I mean, we knew they were not from the Ministry of the Environment!'

'That's what I want to know also, Big One. You knew very well what they were carrying, didn't you? They were ropes and nets, not shot guns, right? You know they were not going to shoot us, didn't you, Big One?'

'Yeah, Big One, they were actually from the PR Unit[3] of the STPB,[4] weren't they? If I'm not wrong, they came to invite us to go overseas, right, Big One?'

I got more and more confused as they carried on. Maybe you all know your country better than I do. But I was really lost. I'm a visitor freshly arrived. How could I be expected to be so knowledgeable about your country? How was I to know that your Singapura Cat — this *Kucinta* — had become the international animal collector's favourite item?[5]

---

[3] Editor's note: PR Unit, Public Relations Unit.

[4] Playwright's note: STPB, Singapore Tourism Promotion Board, now known as [the] STB [Singapore Tourism Board]. Editor's note: The STPB was set up in 1964, when the city-state was still a part of the Federation of Malaysia. It was organised as a co-ordinating agency to promote Singapore's overall image. With the launch of a national tourism masterplan, *Tourism 21: Vision of a Tourism Capital*, in 1996, the STPB had its name changed to the STB. The Board mounts campaigns to market Singapore as not only a tourist destination, but also as a tourism 'hub', allowing visitors to use Singapore as a base to explore the region and as a headquarters for regional tourism business.

[5] Editor's note: ' "*Kucinta*, the Love Cat of Singapore", was introduced during 1991 as part of a tourist promotional campaign worldwide. "*Kucinta*", more familiar to Western cat fanciers as the Singapura cat, is known on the island as the Singapore River Cat, or less attractively as the Drain Cat since cats live in the huge, open monsoon drains during the drier seasons. ... By the end of 2002, the *Kucinta* emblem was fast slipping into obscurity as a tourist icon. The Singapore Tourist Board (STB) emphasised that it was never intended to be a mascot in the same way as the merlion [an STPB-created symbol in the early 1970s — a half-lion and half-fish]. *Kucinta* had been popularised by the STB in 1991, following the "discovery" of the Singapura cat by an American breeder. Its "discovery" was challenged and largely discredited in that same year. It was argued that its "discoverer" had created the breed from Abyssinian and Burmese type cats taken to Singapore with her (with documentary evidence to support this). By then the small ivory coloured cat had been accepted as a breed and the charming myth of the Singapore drain cat had circulated worldwide. Rare,

Anyway, the debate was very exciting. It was heated but courteous; it went on for the length of a meal. You would think that the underground tunnel must be an awful place to carry on a debate, wouldn't you, with all that squatting and everything? But actually it wasn't. Perhaps because I've had a lot of such types of experience as a child. Not hiding from the looting and killing of the Japanese soldiers. I was lucky I wasn't born yet then. My experience came from squatting in a cave I made for my pet animals when I was a kid living in our poor village. I remember it was a mud hole I made tucked behind the bushes just outside my village entrance. I raised rabbits, and dogs and cats in there. I brought them grass and food I saved from my meals every day, and I would climb into the tiny cave to play with them. That place was much, much smaller than this tunnel junction underground, so I had no problem with this place here. Of course, the most exciting thing was our mountain, to climb up the mountain to watch the eagles glide high above in the open sky. So expansive. So exhilarating. As if he could fly as high as he wanted, as far as he wanted. Once you leave the ground, there was no limit, there was no bound; the sky has all the freedom and space you could ever explore!

Of course, the ultimate beauty was watching the eagle flying, gliding ... with its wings fully stretched, as if not moving at all, cutting through the sky, playing to the wind ... up ... down ... turn ... and turn ... and turn ... up, up, up, shooting straight up as if going for the sun ... then suddenly swooping down like an arrow, his feathers shining, shimmering, reflecting the glare of the sun ... It was a really big one, this eagle. Brown coloured, white neck ... When fully stretched, the wings spread wider than what my hands could reach. He didn't live on ground level. He lived high up on a cliff, on top of a very, very tall tree. I'd tried climbing up the cliff, to reach the tree. Whenever I had the time, I would go

---

expensive and increasing in popularity, Singapura cats are bred in the USA and UK. Over the years, breeders seeking additional breeding cats from Singapore have found very few Singapura-type cats to import and according to the Singapore Cat Club, possibly 1 in 1000 cats (0.1%) resembles this pedigree breed. It is now generally considered that the cat is a man-made breed rather than being a type indigenous to Singapore. Despite the fact that the Singapura look is rare among native cats, the STB apparently selected *Kucinta* as an icon representative of cats commonly found at the Singapore River at the time. Cynics suggest that the growing popularity (and hype) of the Singapura breed in America simply made it a convenient icon at the time and Singapurabilia was highly marketable to tourists. No one can blame Singapore for taking advantage of a breed which claimed, rightly or wrongly, the island as its birthplace. The controversy surrounding the breed in America was simply additional publicity. ... Statues of *Kucinta* can be found on the banks of the Singapore river at Cavenagh Bridge where the cat supposedly originated' (Sarah Hartwell, 'Kucinta — The Love Cat of Singapore — and the Bobtails of Malaysia', <www.messybeast.com/kucinta.htm>, accessed 17 May 2005).

climbing to find the eagle. But I've never really reached the top of the tree. Only somewhere close to his nest. Close enough to actually see his nest. And when I got that far, I could also see his eyes ... Bright, shining, steely like a sharp ray of sunlight. They always say eagles are fierce, but this one sure was different, very different. He could see I was there, close to his nest, but he didn't show any trace of hostility ... *Aiyah*, the bright, steely glare of his eyes! ...

Eh? Glare? Where's that beam of light coming from? ... Is that? ...

It was an opening somewhere higher from where I was squatting. The glare seemed to have taken everyone by surprise. The cats close to the opening quickly moved away in a defensive rush, and created a moment of chaos. But curiosity and vigilance soon calmed them down. They all stared at the opening, watching carefully for the body that was going to emerge.

It was another cat. But it was a cat so different from all the rest. It had a walk different from ordinary cats: Tall and slim, shapely and strong, with fur that shone even in the dim lighting of the tunnel. The fur was evenly short, as if someone had manicured it. The cat's ears stood high and stiff. He was wearing a leather necklace, with a little bow tie in front swinging a little badge under its collar.

'Hi, I'm Spotty, don't you remember me?

'There's a chance to get away and you don't want to take it. Are you planning to stay in this filthy place for the rest of your lives? What's more, now the STPB people are all out searching for you, with every means they know. But you know that once they got their quota, or once the taste of the foreign market turns to something else and they are no longer interested in Singapura cats, the chase would go back to the officials of the Ministry of the Environment! Like what they used to say: He is a hero who knows when to change colour. What better time to jump if you wish to get out of this rut of an uncertain life?'

Spotty sounded very enthusiastic in his persuasion. I must say, I thought he was a she at first. His dressing and his makeup misled me. Only when he started to talk that I realised he was a male. Yes, although he sounded somewhat sissy, he was definitely a male.

The position of the great majority, led by the Big One, was very clear: No, they would not go. No, they wouldn't get out!

'Now we are standing next to the wall separating us and the food storage of the big hotel above us. There's no danger of any of us starving for at least six months. So there's no need to worry about any mass rounding-up campaign. Since we have gone through so many crises in the past, there's no reason why we can't get over any new ones that may come upon us.'

The Big One said it with such confidence and style that really got me feeling very good. After that, a number of other cats also spoke, and some had very strong things to say. Gradually, a funny feeling came creeping up from the bottom of my stomach. How familiar were those words, some of which I had said myself almost word for word. But somehow it didn't sound right anymore. Big, high sounding stuff, but not very convincing. So many things said, so few things done. So beautifully said, so difficult to reach. It was like binding our own selves up ... The more I listened, the more uncomfortable I became. My tucked out bosom softened down. My eyes became misty, wet ... Yes, I was persistent, stubborn, ide-alistic ... my personal position, my collective principles, my national pride, my ... I held on to my ideals, stubbornly, persistently for so long, so sincerely. But for what? What would we lose if we were to give and take as pragmatically as Spotty? Would we have lost any-thing at all? Well, I didn't have to put on that stupid necklace with a ribbon like his if I didn't like it. But should we give up the chance of totally transforming our lives for the better just because of a stupid little thing like a ribbon necklace?

Strange. As if Spotty saw through me and understood exactly what was running through my mind. For he pushed away all the cats blocking his way and headed straight to where I was. He stared at me sharply for a moment before he spoke.

'This is a new friend, right? OK, since you are new here, you should be the most un-subjective one around here. Now, why don't you come and do a field study with me and give them an objective report when you get back. My mistress lives on the 65th level of the hotel above us. Come, you. Come and see for yourself whether what I have is wor-thy of your most serious consideration.'

'Since you have already gone overseas, why should you bother with our future?' Someone at the back shouted out a very sensitive question.[6]

'Simple. I get a commission out of this, according to the number of cats I can pull over. Is that clear enough? It's got nothing to do with loyalty to the feline clan. No. And it's got nothing to do with longing for my old flame. No. Let me tell you this: When you are out there in another country, you are free to jump over to any other owner who could offer you a better deal, OK? The owner can choose the cat, and the cat can also choose the owner! All right, you, come with me upstairs!'

---

[6] Editor's note: The island-state's small land area — a matter that became particularly apparent after it left the Federation of Malaysia in 1965, losing what had formerly been a hinterland — has tended to create, in some of its citizens, a desire to seek experiences and oftentimes tertiary education outside the island's small confines. Those who gain such experiences are then considered privileged.

I don't know what power it was that got over me. At the call of Spotty, I just picked up my feet and started to follow him out.

You can imagine, I must have been damned messy and ugly at the time. I didn't look very pretty from the very beginning, and then there was this desperate run for our lives, across so many streets, and then through the underground drainage system. You can imagine. Well, you must give it to this Spotty cat. He really knew what he was doing. Turn this way, turn that way, and then up and down, up and down and then you're out of the underground, right there into the lobby of the hotel! We passed through side doors and windows, passages and corridors, and finally came upon a beauty salon for pets. He must have been a frequent customer there, for the ladies in waiting there immediately greeted him with enthusiastic welcome. They saw me but weren't surprised although I looked so different. They didn't ask anything and straightaway took me into the inner room. I protested out of instinct although I didn't mean it. Spotty reacted immediately by saying: 'Look, if you don't clean up and make up, do you think anyone would allow you to go upstairs? You wouldn't clear the first level!' I dropped my resistance and subjected myself to the caring hands of the girl attendant.

Fortunately, they didn't do anything radical. They only gave me a bath, dried my fur with a warm drier and sprinkled my body with talcum power. And then we were on our way upstairs.

To tell you the truth, the way up, although it didn't take all that long, was a most impactful journey. Quietly and carefully, I followed the steps of Spotty. We passed by the shopping area, the café, the restaurant for Western food, the restaurant for Chinese food, the bar, the ballroom area and the grand lobby. Numerous people passed by us and contributed their share of compliments. I wasn't sure whether I felt more happiness or more sadness. Everything just seemed to be floating past me like a dream. But I distinctly remembered that when I followed Spotty into the lift, an attendant hurried over, made sure we entered the lift safely and pressed level 65 before the doors closed, bowing gently and smiling.

The room Spotty lived in was not bolted. He gave it a nudge and the door opened slightly, just wide enough for us to squeeze in. His owner was not there and he led me round for a quick tour. Luxury was everywhere but most impressive was what Spotty had for himself: His own little cot, his own eating bowl and his own drinking bowl. He had more than a dozen toys and he had his own comb, his own soap, shampoo, talcum powder and his own drier.

'Overseas, we live in a much bigger place. Much, much bigger than this. Look over here, some pictures to show you my home there.'

His home was really big. The garden of the house was like an open field. The interior of the house seemed like the lobby of a hotel.

'You have to make some adjustments. And they don't have to be anything constraining. In return, you get a whole new world. Now, how about that? Is that worth pursuing or not? You tell me!'

I was really confused. My heart was feeling a kind of pain. I didn't dare to look at him. I walked out, on to the balcony. I felt as if I was panting and I wanted to have an extra breath of oxygen. I breathed heavily, but I didn't dare to turn around to look at Spotty. Because I didn't want him to see my tears dripping down my face. Above all, I didn't want him to ask me anything at this moment of time.

Then, something way up in the sky caught my attention. Black spots, dropping, floating down from the sky. One of them floated towards the balcony. I stretched out my hand and grabbed at it. What do you know, it's a feather! A bird's feather. Eh? ... Is it? ... I felt a sting in my stomach and looked up, searching, hoping to find something in reply to an urgent question. It was already dusk, and the sun was nearly down. But because the sky was overcast and the clouds were low, you couldn't really see the sun. But, in the dusk of daylight, there was a huge, bright column of light coming through the sky, throwing down a very privileged thrust of ray towards the ground. And, yes, high, high up in the distant sky, I can detect a dark shadow floating, gliding, flying. Oh, it was so familiar ... The smooth glide, the relaxed feel, the free flow ... Could this be? But how could it be? ... How could it be here? ... Now, there it shot upwards again, thrusting high into the sky, aiming straight at the shaft of light. Up and up, and up ... And then, abruptly, it dived as if it hit something and lost control, dropping down rapidly, accompanied by a number of tiny shadows floating in the air. As they became clearer, I could see these were his feathers.

Was it really him? If it was, then what was happening to him? Almost instinctively I started whistling like a mad man. I blew and blew through my thumb and forefinger in my mouth. I blew so madly until I felt dizzy! I knew that if it was really him, he would surely come to me.

Yes, it was. It was him! Yes, he was flying over. With his big wings stretched fully, he was flashing towards me, cutting through the air like a razor. In no time, he came into my full view and in no time he had gracefully landed on the balustrade in my balcony 65 levels up in this posh hotel.

'How come you're here? What's been happening? What are you doing here? And what's happened to your feathers?'

The eagle's eyes were as piercing as before. And as sharp and bright. Except that, added to his natural majesty, there was now a feeling of sadness. Then I noticed his head was balding; the feathers were thinning. But, no, it was not from ageing. It wasn't a natural thinning. There were traces of blood. And there were traces of missing feathers even on his body.

'What's the matter with you? What were you hitting at shooting upwards like that? There were no hostile birds up there, right?'

The eagle had never looked so dejected in my memory. Is it ...? 'What's up there? Why did you leave your native land, fly all the way here and keep bumping at something up there in the sky?'

'OK, take me up there, will you? Will you please take me up there? ... Now, I'll hang on to your claws. And you grab me. Hard. It won't hurt. Yes, grab my hand! That's right ... Hand ... Hand? My hand? ... Hey, how come I've got hands again now? Didn't I have only paws? Like the other cats? ... And my feet. Hey, I've got my feet back also! Hey, hey! ... Everything's gone back to normal now. And ... hey, where's Spotty? Spotty! ... Spotty's gone, too. But, what's happening now? ... Oh, never mind that. Let's go up first, eagle. Let's go up and see what's up there in the sky. Let's go! There's no point in staying here anyway. Come, let's go up into the sky!'

So I hung on to the eagle's claws, and the eagle gently but firmly grabbed my hands. He then stretched out his wings, lunged forward and off we went out of the balcony of the hotel, shooting fast towards the column of light. The wind, getting cooler and cooler, swept past me, caressing my whole body. It was an exultingly beautiful feeling! The next moment, we were into the column of light, and a warmth came upon me, contrasting sharply with the air, now getting cold, around me. The eagle floated round and round and round in the column of light, as if looking for something. Then, as if he had found the target, the eagle started beating its wings hard and we started to accelerate towards the light, towards the sun. He worked hard, his powerful wings flapped and flapped as we rose and rose in increasing speed. Thrusting up directly towards the source of light. As we flew higher and higher, the air became colder and colder. The higher, the colder. Until we reached beyond the clouds above. Oh, it was a marvellous sight! Way up above the clouds, the sun, fading away, was still there, sharing its infinite brilliance. But, as the transcending feeling was exciting, the cold of the higher reaches of the sky became increasingly unbearable. I was as ecstatically happy as I was horribly scared ...

Then, out of nowhere, as we kept on ascending, there appeared a shadow. It never became very clear, but somehow I felt it was a net. I couldn't quite see it, but I could clearly feel it. A net. Before I could make any more sense out of this oncoming shadow, the eagle had crashed into it. There was no sound, but the impact was very heavy. I didn't see the impact but I felt the bump. And, instantly, I saw blood dripping down from the top of the head of the eagle. And some feathers fell off. From his head as well as his body. The impact was so strong that I was nearly thrown off his hold. But we held on, my cold hands and his hot claws held on tight.

The impact made us fall, descending rapidly in the column of light. But, very quickly, the eagle regained his balance, glided for a brief moment, and then, as he summoned enough reserve energy, began to flap his wings once more, accelerating and shooting upwards. And again the shadow, the impact, the blood, the feathers … the fall … and the recharge, and the … He just kept on repeating it, unrelenting … But it was clear the net showed no give, no damage. The sun was fading away, but the net seemed as invincible as ever. I started shivering. As the eagle went on, my shivering got worse and worse. Until it became quite unbearable. But I couldn't get myself to tell him to stop and go down. I didn't have the courage to say it. As he crashed the net again and again, I was convinced that he would never make any headway; there was no way he could penetrate the net. But I knew he would never give up. … He would never relent … As for me, I just kept quiet. I gritted my teeth, shivering all over, passively holding the hot claws of his grasp!

I lost count how many times the eagle shot up and was then put down. I was so cold and fatigued that I had become almost unconscious. I so desired to tell him that I wanted to come down, but the words were swallowed down every time. Then, for some reason, he stopped flapping hard, stopped going up, relaxed his wings and gradually glided downwards. After many circles in the sky, we finally landed on solid ground. You couldn't imagine how grateful I was. I felt I could live again. And I was very gratified that the eagle had also chosen to live again. As the saying goes: 'Preserve the forest when it's green and you'll have timber for firewood.' I was really happy that the eagle had finally understood the wisdom of preservation.

But I was wrong. The moment I loosened my hold on his claws, and his grasp of me, the eagle gave me one intense look, then spread its wings, and in no time he was up in the sky again, charging single mindedly into the shaft of light. Up and up, and up, and up … As the light started to fade away altogether …

It was getting dark. I gathered all my strength and kept whistling to the eagle. There was no response. As darkness enveloped the sky, I could see no trace of either the eagle or the shaft of light anymore. There was darkness all over the sky.

It's been a week now. I have been coming here every day. But I have never seen the eagle again. What the Big One had predicted saw its realisation in me. I returned to my original form. For what reason, I did not know. But one thing I was certain: On my way up with

Spotty, from the underground drainage system to level 65 high up in that posh hotel, something had happened. Something so radical had happened there and then that I was enabled to break out of the cat form to regain my human form. But the Big One is nowhere to be found ... That powerful, majestic, mixed-colour cat ...

But I keep coming here every day. In the hope of seeing the Big One, Spotty and all the rest. Most of all, I long to see the eagle again. But what would I say to him if he were really here again? Yes, if the eagle were to appear in front of me once more, what could I say to him?

(*End of Play*)

0Zero01

1

Darkness. Silence.

Cindy walks in. Makes up and dresses up as she narrates The Salmon Saga.

2

CINDY   They hatch in freshwater upstream in the creeks. The small fry are often eaten by bigger fishes and birds. Those who survive swim downstream into the river, and then towards the sea. On the way, many more perish.

They move easily from the freshwater of the river to the salty water of the sea. Actually, they spend more time in the open sea. There, they swarm towards the vast ocean, looking for the rich feeding grounds.

They swim for tens of thousands of kilometres, and get bigger and bigger on the way. They roam the ocean for up to two years and grow up to 20 kilograms. They then respond to a signal, from somewhere. A signal calling them, beckoning them, pulling them to return. To return to their origin. Thereupon, in their hundreds of thousands, they head for the land. And that's when they become valuable prey for the fishermen from many continents. Hundreds of thousands of them perish on the way.

In spite of all the hazards, they single-mindedly trace their journey home. By some means, they are able to find the land, find the river, find the creek, find the nook where they were given life. Once they hit the freshwater again, they stop feeding. Against the current, they battle upstream. Against the current, they struggle to return home. To birds, and animals, and men, many more thousands perish again.

After countless days of hard travel, they finally reach their fated destiny, by which time their battered bodies have turned intensely red. Instead of resting, the survivors begin to search for hatching nests. The female, using her own body, beats the pebbles, the sand and the mud to create a nest, protected by the male who by now has battled and defeated all his competitors.

Then, at the climax of their homing saga, she spawns the eggs as he sprays them with sperm. Then, with the last ounce of their energy, they beat the pebbles, the sand and the mud to cover up the fertilised eggs. Finally, at the very place where they received life, the last surviving salmon die away, littering their mutilated carcasses upstream along the creek.

3

After finishing the story and dressing up, she puts on a pair of dark glasses, picks up her handbag, proceeds to a prepared table across the room.

4

Zai walks in with a serving tray, prepared to serve food.

He crosses the room to serve Cindy dinner.

Cindy begins to eat the dinner.

5

After a few moments, she stops, turns to Zai, stares at him hard and then:

CINDY   Who are you?

ZAI   My name is Zai ... Zai Kuning.

Cindy gazes at him, waiting. Then:

CINDY   Who are you?

ZAI   ... I live in Yishun[1] ... I have three brothers and four sisters ... My parents are still living ... I am 27... I studied art ... I have one pair of jeans, one pair of slippers, one t-shirt.

––––––––––––––––––––

[1] Editor's note: A public-housing estate in the north of the city-state.

But Cindy is not satisfied. She keeps on asking, 'And then?'

Zai, after much struggle, starts to develop his answer further and further.

ZAI   … Yesterday … I am ten. I laugh during national anthem. Later my headmaster ask me to go to his office. He bring out three canes and ask me to choose one. I say, 'Use all, *lah*!'[2] … Whack whack whack … Next morning he take me to school hall, on the stage. He say to everyone, 'This boy very brave. Laugh during national anthem and not afraid of caning! I show you what you get for being so brave.' Whack whack whack whack …

Zai climbs up a rope.

ZAI   I love climbing trees, coconut trees, in my *kampong*.[3] When I hate school, I run to Jardine Steps.[4] Smoke cigarette. Smoke *ganja*. And my brother always come look for me. 'Go home *lah*, *Mak*[5] waiting far you …'

Now I am five, *Mak* bring me to school first time. '*Jangan jahat-jahat, ya?*[6] *Nanti Mak ambil Nani balik, ya?*'[7] School finish, *Mak* no come. I cry. *Kakak*[8] come. '*Mak* give birth to baby girl. Little sister is called …' We laugh …

Now I am … on the beach … water very warm … wave not big … silent … no sound … *I am from Sulawesi*,[9] *I sail the seas of Nusantara!*[10] … Sail! … Sail! … Sail! …

He is already lying, crawling on the ground.

---

[2] Editor's note: Malay: *lah*, '[A] particle emphasising the word to which it is appended' (*A Malay-English English-Malay Dictionary*, ed. A. E. Coope [revised edn.; London and Basingstoke: Macmillan Education, 1991]).

[3] Editor's note: Malay: *kampong*, village.

[4] Editor's note: The Jardine Steps are at the southern coastline of the island-state; the World Trade Centre is located at the Jardine Steps.

[5] Editor's note: Malay: *Mak*, mother.

[6] Playwright's note: [Malay:] *Jangan jahat-jahat*, 'Don't be naughty.'

[7] Playwright's note: [Malay:] *Nanti Mak ambil Nani balik*, 'I will take you [Nani] home later.'

[8] Playwright's note: [Malay:] *Kakak*, sister.

[9] Editor's note: The island of Sulawesi, formerly known as Celebes, is part of the Indonesian archipelago. South Sulawesi is home to several ethnic groups. The Makassarese, the Buginese and the Mandarese live in the southern part. These three peoples are known for their skills as seafarers and are said to be very fine sailors.

[10] Editor's note: *Nusantara*, 'Indonesian, archipelago, especially the Indonesian archipelago' (*A Malay-English English-Malay Dictionary*, ed. Coope).

6

After a while Zai suddenly stops. He gets up, reaches into his pocket for a pair of dark glasses, puts them on, goes to the table and roars at Cindy.

ZAI   *Who are you?*

Cindy is startled but does not answer.

Zai takes off Cindy's glasses and roars at her again.

ZAI   *And who are you?*

After a pause, Cindy begins to answer ...

CINDY   I am Cindy. I used to teach English ... Now I am a performer ... I am married ... live in Bukit Timah ...[11]

ZAI   And then?

CINDY   Yesterday ... I am seven ... I have three white mice ... in a cage. Mother feed me to eat, I don't want. Father gets angry. Eat or not? Eat or not? If you don't, I'll smack your mice in the cage. *One ... Two ... Three! Whack! Bang! Ahhh! Chi bai!*[12] ... I run I run I run, in the forest, night in Sabah[13] ... Like a cat ... I shit in the grass ... Like a cat, I climb up the tree, I find the nest of the sparrow, I pounce! *Ahgg!* I scratch! I tear! I bite! I eat! ... I kill ... I die ...

The sky ... very high ... very dark ... I can see ... the mice, the cat, the sparrow floating in the air ... all dead! ... Uu-u-u-u ... I run into the river ... to swim ... there's a wolf ... there's a pony ... I suckle the wolf ... the pony suckles me ...

Umm ... The water ... warm ... soft ... like *Lao Ma*[14] holding me ... *Lao Ma!* ... I am *Lao-Ma* ... (*Transforms into the lady.*) ... I bring my granddaughter to the

---

[11] Editor's note: A middle-/upper-middle-class residential area in the south-central part of Singapore.

[12] Playwright's note: Hokkien[-Chinese or *minnan hua* or *minnan* language, a non-Mandarin-Chinese language] expletive. Editor's note: female genitalia.

[13] Editor's note: A state in East Malaysia.

[14] Editor's note: Possibly Mandarin-Chinese: old mother.

wayang[15] ... *Mung ka chek chang lai*[16] (*Sings*) ... (*Using an imagined whip representing a horse.*) chiang-chiang-chiang ... My grandfather play two-string violin ... (*Transforms into grandfather*) E-e-eee. I also make these things ... E-e-eee (*Also sounds like mice squeaking*) ...

Realises Zai is watching, and stops. Zai gives her back the dark glasses. They hug.

7

Lut enters.

Zai and Cindy confront him.

ZAI

CINDY   Who are you?

LUT   I am Lut Ali.

ZAI

CINDY   And then?

LUT   I am 36, married, have one child, I am actor, director ... I live in Ang Mo Kio[17] flat ... No, in *kampong* ... plenty coconuts, *ayam, itek, kucing, anjing, rumah kayu*[18] ... I peep at girls *mandi*[19] ... splash! splash! *Oi oi oi, run!* ... My father my mother my uncle beat me. I run I run I run ...

Yesterday, I am ten, I sell *roti prata*[20] at PUB[21] canteen. Fifty cents and two prata. One for sister, one for me ... Run run run ...

---

[15] Editor's note: Malay: *wayang*, a general term, relating to 'theatre' or 'show', but here used to refer to traditional Chinese opera.

[16] Editor's note: Teochew or *chauzhou hua* or *chauzhou* Chinese: *Mang Ka Chek Chang Lai*, 'outside the doorway stands a pear tree' — a sort of operatic limerick. The next line would be: *Sng Lai Sng Ker Sah Peh Kai*, 'counting it up and down, there are 300 of them'.

[17] Editor's note: A public-housing estate in the north-east of the city-state.

[18] Playwright's note: [Malay:] *ayam, itek, kucing, anjing, rumah kayu*, chickens, ducks, cats, dogs, wooden huts.

[19] Playwright's note: [Malay:] *mandi*, bathing.

[20] Editor's note: *Roti prata* or *prantha* is a form of South-Asian bread.

[21] Editor's note: PUB, Public Utilities Board.

Yesterday, I am ... my uncle. Run run run ... Japanese soldiers! Run run run! ... *Henti henti henti!*[22] Japanese soldier make me say *banzai!*[23] I say *bangsai!*[24] They kick me, kick me, kick me! until I become so weak ... and I can only say *Banzai!*

Datuk[25] say I died when I was six, swimming on the beach. They carry me to the house, and *datuk* put oil on my body, and I lived again ... But *datuk* say I must never go into water again ...

I very sad ... very sad ... because my ancestors come from sea ... From Pulau Boyan[26] ... Boyanese ship cross the seas ... Ummm ... (*Sings and dances, like sailors, like creatures roaming free.*)

(*Then, realises*) ... I am ... Lut ... Lut bin Ali ... Ali bin Bakar ... Bakar bin Yusof ... Yusof bin Ahmad ... Ahmad bin ... bin ...

Unable to continue.

Zai and Cindy sympathise, give him back the dark glasses and they hug.

8

Gey Pin enters. Talks fluently, almost in one breath.

GEY PIN   Who am I? I am Ang Gey Pin, 27. Ethnic Chinese. I speak Mandarin, Hokkien,[27] Cantonese, English ... I go to work by MRT[28] go to play by car ... I like noodles and barley water ... I exercise in the morning and perform at night ... I weigh 40 kilograms and I measure five feet one ... I live with my sister and brothers and parents and the maid and the dog and there is scaffolding outside because they are renovating the apartments ...

---

[22] Playwright's note: [Malay:] *henti,* stop.
[23] Playwright's note: [Japanese:] *banzai,* long live!
[24] Playwright's note: [*minnan hua* or *minnan* Chinese:] *bangsai,* defecate.
[25] Playwright's note: [Malay:] *Datuk,* grandfather.
[26] Editor's note: Pulau Boyan, or the isle of Bawean, is located between Java and Borneo.
[27] Editor's note: Or *minnan hua* or *minnan* language.
[28] Editor's note: MRT, Mass Rapid Transit — the metro rail system in Singapore.

ZAI
CINDY
LUT And then?

GEY PIN I ...

ZAI
CINDY
LUT And then?

GEY PIN I ...

ZAI
CINDY
LUT And then?

GEY PIN (*Looks at fingers trying very hard to remember.*) ... One 'whirl' is ... Two 'whirls' is ... (*first in Hokkien, then in English*) ... My mother says, one 'whirl' is poor, two 'whirls' is rich, I have three 'whirls', I bang-bang-bang sell soya-bean cake ... (*She counts up to 10, then begins to sing the counting to 10.*)

Yesterday, I am five. *Baba* and *Mama* take me to kindergarten ... *Ahhh!* Cheat, cheat! *Ba* gone without telling me. *Cheat!* ... (*Hums*) Oo-oo-oo, yesterday I am just leaving the boat. One small bag, move to *O Gio Tao*[29] ... (*Sings immigrant song*) ... Then, *Ah Gong*[30] gone ... His bag he carried from boat. Stories about big trees ... Tall ... plenty leaves ... keeps the rain away, the sun ... but the moon comes through ...

At this suggestion, the lighting transforms into moonlight and, as if all their animal instincts are drawn out, they try to access animal sensitivities — each searching for an animal movement/posture and sound.

---

[29] Editor's note: *chauzhou hua* or *chauzhou* Chinese: the 'head of the black bridge'. This refers to the Ord Bridge at Clarke Quay, which spans the Singapore River behind what is now the Liang Court/Hotel New Otani complex. During the colonial period of Singapore's history, the Clarke Quay was an area with many warehouses, or 'godowns', where migrant Chinese workers would have worked; they would also have lived close-by, in the neighbouring tenements. The warehouses have since been converted into a shopping and entertainment area.

[30] Editor's note: *minnan hua* or *minnan* Chinese: *Ah Gong*, grandfather.

Eventually, they all face and howl at the moon like wolves.

At the climax, they freeze, looking as if magnetically drawn towards the moon.

9

Running water is heard.

They are drawn into an organismic existence. Moving into each other like amoeba.

They gradually gather enough energy to attempt a group 'rising'.

After an extended attempt, they manage to rise and howl in victory.

But at this very moment they are shocked by a loud sound of a bell and they drop to the floor, moaning, as if in agony.

10

Reminded of their mundane existence, they struggle to resume their normal behaviour. They dress up and proceed with their routine duties, walking faster and faster in circles. Until the sound of the bell suddenly stops, and everyone falls down.

11

The didgeridoo inspires the memory recall of the salmon homing saga.

At first, drawn by some mystical power, they gradually rise in response to a call from somewhere distant, then from within themselves.

They crawl irresistibly towards a common destination. Then they gradually rise, and walk on all fours. Then they gradually rise onto their hind limbs, and begin running.

As they develop this frenzy in relation to their common destination, they begin to undress, to free themselves from all that is external.

As they run faster and faster, their excitement grows. And they become more and more excited. And they begin shouting. Yelling. Howling. Hopping. Jumping.

Then they reach their destination. In pairs, they pound the ground, like salmon beating the river bed into nests with their own bodies.

Then they mate. She has the eggs; he has the milt.

Then they struggle to beat the ground to cover the nest. With great effort, they complete their destined life mission.

As they expend their last ounce of energy, exhausted and exhilarated, they gasp their last breath.

With the disappearing sound of the didgeridoo, everything falls silent.

(*End of Play*)

The Evening Climb

Prologue

Darkness. There is in motion an intense excitement of a primitive kind. Like thunder and lightning, but not as violent; like animals crying in a valley, but not as fierce; like winds sweeping through the forest, but much more masculine; like tremors of the spirit, but much more powerful.

Everything is in a state of flux, unformed, as in a dream. The forest is calling. A soul-arresting, piercing sound suddenly cuts across the sky, followed immediately by the appearance, seemingly from nowhere, of a great big bird. Its full appearance is never exposed, but it definitely has shiny feathers of stunning green, though its size and features are never clear and certain; flying one moment here, another moment there, its movement displays an astonishing freedom and grace.

A single, brilliant spark charges in from afar, accompanied by the peel of the innocent laughter of a child; as it rendezvous with the mysterious bird, a magical dance ensues.

For a moment, the whole world is dedicated to the child and the bird. They plunge into the joy of play, the brilliant spark and the shadowy green enjoying each other's company to their hearts' content. One moment they seem to be fiercely wrestling each other like animals; another moment, they are intimately caressing each other like parent and child.

At the height of their joy and pleasure, an explosion splits the sky like a thunderbolt. As suddenly as they appeared, the big green shadow and the brilliant innocent spark disappear, leaving behind a sense of solitude and emptiness.

Part 1: The Evening

Sounds of the wild. Music without a consistent melody. Those who are familiar know they are the sounds of the wind, of stone, of the earth, of water, of trees; they are the sounds of animals with feet and animals without feet, sounds of birds with wings and birds without wings; they are sounds of space without start and end, and of time without beginning and end.

Upon the hills, it is twilight; dusk has created a heaven of brilliant colours. Down on earth, green has enveloped the living hills; the wilderness shimmers in tranquility. But the sounds of the wild remind all that the irresistible impulse of life continues to create excitement, despite the peace the hills project.

The only trace of humans in this whole scenario is the distant chant of warden Mat, which is sometimes heard clearly, other times not so clearly. The chant is part of an ongoing dialogue between the protector of the forest and his trees.

Old Chen moves slightly, indicating that there is indeed someone in the foreground. He seems to have been experiencing the sense of being part of this whole natural being. He also seems to be leafing through his memory book, looking for something which has not yet been located. He looks far and near, high and low; he looks in different directions, taking different vantage points. He raises his heels, he crouches to the ground, he narrows his eyes, he shakes his head, all the time muttering some children's nursery rhymes, none of which he is able to complete. He is trying to remember what he had done a long, long time ago, the games he played, the dreams he dreamed. He tries to do the somersaults, the headstands, the games of goli,[1] *the flights he took, the yells he gave ... He fails in each and every attempt.*

Without his knowledge, Old Wang has unwittingly walked in, curiously observing Old Chen's stupid display. Old Chen gets such a fright when he suddenly discovers Old Wang watching him.

WANG	Are you crazy?
CHEN	Hey, why didn't you make some noise before coming so close to me?
WANG	I asked you whether you are crazy. What lousy standard!
CHEN	OK, you show me. Come on! If you think you are so good, you show me.
WANG	I never said I was good.
CHEN	'What lousy standard!' You come and try. Come, you try!
WANG	Hey, I didn't come up here to play circus with you!
CHEN	Come on, I'm giving you a chance, man. Look, nobody is interested in you anymore. Not like my Grandson, when even his leak of water on

---

[1] Playwright's note: [Malay:] *goli* [or *guli*], marbles.

the floor would make everybody so excited: '*Aiyah*, look you all, look, his water is still hot, you know! Look, not yellow, not smelly, but steaming hot still!' Consider yourself not so fortunate anymore, OK? And when I give you an opportunity to perform, you better grab it.

Come on, I'll beat the gong for you! 'Come on, come on! Come and see mature-aged acrobat Mr Candlestick in person! Come and see: Old as a turtle, young as a baby, white-haired complexion, supple as a monkey. The miracle of Southeast Asia, Mr Candlestick, making his first public appearance after 20 years of mysterious retirement. Come on, come and see! ...'

Hey, what's the matter? You don't want to perform? Look, if you don't want to do it now, I'll never look at you again. Never! Not even if you give me money! ... Come on, Old Wang, try!

After all the encouragement by Old Chen, Old Wang reluctantly comes forward to perform, very impressively for an old man of his age, some fantastic falls, turns, cartwheels and somersaults. They are both immensely amused and are laughing their heads off when a mysterious sound suddenly appears cutting across the sky, drawing old Chen impulsively up to the top of a mound.

He searches the sky for something but finds nothing.

WANG   Are you sure? ... Is this the right place?

CHEN   Yes. Except the trees are fewer, the stones are dirtier, the mountains are lower.

Old Chen contemplates for a while. Coming down from the mound, he begins to quietly unpack their camping gear, laying the groundsheet, etc. Old Wang comes over to partner him spontaneously.

CHEN   (*Suddenly remembers something.*) Yes, it came back again, this dream, the one where I went walking all naked.

WANG   Oh, that one! You running around all over the place wearing nothing, right? Bloody pervert, you're getting wet dreams again, right?

CHEN   Bloody pervert yourself! No, this time very different: I was holding a big bunch of keys in my hand.

WANG   A bunch of keys? What were you doing?

CHEN   Going home *lah*![2] ... But I just couldn't find my home. There were houses everywhere. Apartments, semi-detached, bungalows, they all looked like my home. I tried with my keys on every door but I couldn't open anyone. I knocked on the doors but nobody answered. I got so frightened I started to sweat all over. I can't do anything but keep on trying. Trying to open up with my keys and knocking to get some response. Just then, I carelessly turned back and — *wah*! — the whole street was packed with people, staring fiercely at me. Some were carrying sticks, some were carrying knives, some were carrying brooms and all kinds of rackets — all walking towards me with a fierce look on their face, and muttering something under their breath.

I couldn't hear anything they were saying but somehow I knew they were swearing at me. For knocking on their doors. They were even accusing me of trying to eat their cats and dogs. I got so scared I started to run, throwing away all the keys I was holding. I ran through narrow back lanes, jumping over wide ditches, desperately heading for the park nearby. Before I reached the park, I saw a taxi nearby and I started to shout at the taxi at the top of my voice. But before I reached the taxi, I heard a strange voice over my head. I looked up, there's nothing there but the voice is still over me, and the voice was telling me not to take the taxi but to head straight for the forest on this side of the park. So I turned and started running towards the forest. Behind me, the noises of cats and dogs and footsteps of people came closer and closer until I got so scared that I summoned all my energy and jumped into a flower bush thinking that once I got into the bush I'll be able to hide myself better from all my pursuers. But the bush turned out to be bougainvillaeas. The pricks cut me so badly I started to scream my head off. And I woke myself up.

WANG   Your dream is bad. My dream is good.

CHEN   A big bunch of keys and no one can open any door. Even the dogs and cats were chasing after me.

WANG   I always get something to eat in my dreams.

---

[2] Editor's note: Malay: *lah*, '[A] particle emphasising the word to which it is appended' (*A Malay-English English-Malay Dictionary*, ed. A. E. Coope [revised edn.; London and Basingstoke: Macmillan Education, 1991]).

CHEN	You bloody hungry pervert. You eat in the morning, you eat in the evening and you eat even in your dream. And what do you get? Forever skinny like a candlestick. What a waste you are!
WANG	You know what I dreamed this time? Fish-head curry!
CHEN	Eh, aren't you a vegetarian?
WANG	Vegetarian fish-head curry.
CHEN	Come on, man, vegetarian fish head curry!
WANG	Of course! They even have vegetarian pig's head and vegetarian pig's brain.
CHEN	(*Looking at his head.*) Yes, I can believe that.
WANG	I dreamed eating fish-head curry treated by my children and my grand-children. My youngest Grandson carried a toy koala bear and a kanga-roo, and can remember he said: '*Gong Gong*,[3] happy birthday.' And then they gave me a long red paper with seven big Chinese characters. You know what they were?
CHEN	*Fu ru Donghai, shou bi Nanshan.*[4]
WANG	Not eight, seven, seven characters.
CHEN	*Gonggong zui ai chi yutou.*[5]
WANG	Hey, don't play the fool. It's my birthday party, OK?
CHEN	Ah, I know! *Yi jiang chunshui xiang dong liu.*[6]
WANG	*Choi!* Don't spoil my luck!
CHEN	OK, then what's on the paper?

---

[3] Editor's note: Either Mandarin-Chinese, or *minnan hua* or *minnan* language: *Gong Gong*, Grandpa.

[4] Editor's note: Mandarin-Chinese. Chinese proverb: Good fortune like the eastern ocean, longevity like the southern mountain.

[5] Editor's note: Mandarin-Chinese: 'Gong Gong loves to eat fish-head best.'

[6] Editor's note: Mandarin-Chinese. A famous line from a poem by the late Tang poet, Li Yu. This line is now commonly used as an idiomatic expression. The literal meaning is: 'A river flows towards the east', which suggests: 'All good things are gone forever.'

WANG   *Rensheng qishi gu lai xi.*[7]

              How about that? Good, uh? They raised the paper very high, waving and waving, and everybody started to sing happy birthday and we all had fish-head curry and Brandy XO.[8] So happy!

CHEN   Do you know what that means? They were all wondering why you're not dead already.

WANG   *Choi, choi, choi*! Just because you are treated badly by people in your dream — chased by everybody, so you are jealous I had fish-head curry in my dream, right? You are jealous I had all my children celebrating my birthday and you got chased by all those people and cats and dogs. Well, too bad. That's my dream!

CHEN   Let me ask you. Do you know the meaning of the character *xi*?[9] Well, *xi* means rare, difficult to come by; it also means special and odd. Which means you are a rare and odd animal. Which means, if you are normal and not rare, you should have died long ago.

WANG   *Aiyah*, you are also 70. Are you also a rare animal?

CHEN   Of course I am! And, instead of eating your damned vegetarian fish-head curry, I would rather run along the street and let everybody chase after me. That's more fun! ... Eh? Where is your old woman?

WANG   She's still down there somewhere, looking for temples. She said people told her there's a temple around here.

CHEN   A temple?

WANG   Don't know who told her that. She said she saw many burnt candles on the way up here.

CHEN   They could have been left behind by secret society gangsters from their sacrificial rites. If she's not careful, they might use her to make sacrifices. Then we'll be in the news.

WANG   Eh, what if the wild pigs eat her up?

---

[7] Editor's note: Mandarin-Chinese. A Chinese idiom: 'Since antiquity, living up to the age of 70 is usually rare.'
[8] Editor's note: Brandy XO, that is, extra-old brandy.
[9] Editor's note: Mandarin-Chinese.

CHEN	Then we kill and eat up the wild pigs.
WANG	No good. She's too old, after eating her, the wild pig's meat will get too tough.
CHEN	Why do you bring along this horrible woman?
WANG	She wants to learn Mandarin from us.
CHEN	Maybe this is the reason why the big bird is not coming — because there is a horrible woman here ... Eh, you better go and find her. When it gets dark she might really be eaten up by the wild pigs.
WANG	Do you think there are ghosts here?
CHEN	Of course, all kinds of ghosts and devils come here: secret society devils, *ang mo*[10] devils, Japanese devils. You name it, they've been here. They say the Japanese killed many people here. They say every plant, every stone, every bird and animal has a ghost. Look around you, there are ghosts everywhere!
WANG	Enough, enough! (*He goes away.*)

Old Chen looks around, searching in deep earnest. Now dusk is fading into night, a juncture where day and night are inseparable. The mountain and its forest have become even more blurred, hazy and mysterious, evoking an increasingly charismatic presence ... Old Li comes in singing a song with her voice and body obviously highly charged with enthusiasm.

LI	Hi, Mr Chen, how are you? (*Climbing up a mound.*) I know he's been here before, I know.
CHEN	How come you know?
LI	I guessed.
CHEN	You don't have to guess. He's definitely been here.
LI	You know?
CHEN	Who would, if I don't? Didn't I tell you? I have seen him before.
LI	What? You have seen him? What did he look like?

---

[10] Playwright's note: [*Minnan hua* or *minnan* language:] *ang mo* [literally 'red hair'], Caucasian.

CHEN	Didn't I tell you? Very big. Very green. Very majestic and very kind.
LI	What is 'majestic'?
CHEN	Majestic is *weiwu*.[11] You know, very powerful looking, very fierce. No, not fierce, very strong, very impressive.
LI	And what do you mean 'very kind'?
CHEN	Very kind means he's very *wenrou*, very friendly, makes you feel very comfortable. Good tempered.
LI	Eh? That's not what I saw. What I saw was a small small, black black fellow, sitting on the top of the table in the temple.
CHEN	What? Big bird's in the temple?
LI	No, no, no, not bird. I'm talking about Sam Poh Kong![12]
CHEN	I'm talking about the big bird. Bird, bird!
LI	No, no, no, bird means girl. Sam Poh Kong doesn't have that thing, but he's not a girl. You know, that thing? That ... (*Gesticulating with her hand.*) Aiyah, *lampa*,[13] *lah*! How do you say it in Mandarin? *Lampa*.
CHEN	... *Niao.*
LI	Eh?
CHEN	*Niao, niao!*
LI	*Niao.* That thing you call 'bird'?
CHEN	Yes, *niao*, bird.
LI	Eh? Sam Poh Kong had no *niao*. No bird. Ha ha ha, Sam Poh Kong had no bird. Sam Poh Kong had no bird, Ha ha ha ...

---

[11] Editor's note: Mandarin-Chinese.

[12] Editor's note: This is a reference to the famous Ming Dynasty admiral Cheng Ho, or Zheng He (1371–1435), who was a eunuch — hence the wordplay on that idea through the Mandarin-Chinese term for bird, *niao*, that will follow in the play. Between 1405 and 1433, the Ming government sponsored a series of seven naval expeditions. Zheng He was the admiral in control of the huge fleet and the armed forces that undertook these expeditions. The eunuch admiral is honoured in some Chinese temples.

[13] Editor's note: *Minnan hua* or *minnan* language: *lampa*, testicles.

CHEN	No, no, no, that's wrong. Sam Poh Kong had a bird.
LI: EH?	But my mother told me Sam Poh Kong had no bird; his bird had been cut.
CHEN	Tell me, do you know the story of the durian?
LI	Story of the durian?
CHEN	You see, Sam Poh Kong came to Nanyang[14] and one day he was very thirsty and they got him a coconut. But after he drank the water he got a stomach ache. So he went to shit and buried his shit wrapped in the coconut shell. Soon after, a plant grew out of the ground. But it's not a coconut, it's …
LI	Durian! I know that one. My mother told me so many times, I know.
CHEN	Oh, your mother told you many times, uh? OK, but did your mother ever tell you that Sam Poh Kong had with him a big bird which followed him everywhere he went? She didn't tell you right? OK, I'll tell you. Now, when Sam Poh Kong was drinking his coconut water down there, the big bird was drinking its coconut water up there. When he was having his stomach ache down here, the big bird also had a stomach ache up there. And when he shitted down here, the big bird shitted up there. And when Sam Poh Kong's shit turned to durian, do you know what the big bird's shit turned to?
LI	What?
CHEN	Another fruit. Do you know what fruit?
LI	What?
CHEN	*Lingkim.*[15]
LI	*Lingkim?* … Ya, ya, ya, *lingkim* is lumpy lumpy outside and it's got seeds inside. Black black, small small … Ya, they really look like bird shit!

---

[14] Editor's note: Mandarin Chinese: *Nanyang* means 'south of the ocean' or 'south seas', a reference to the Southeast Asian region.

[15] Editor's note: *Minnan hua* or *minnan* language: *Lingkim*, sweetsop, sugar-apple or custard-apple.

CHEN   And do you know why they are called *lingkim*? Because, you know — of course you don't know — because *lingkim* in Chinese means 'spiritual bird' — *ling qin*[16] — a holy bird. Because Sam Poh Kong was a holy man, so his bird also became a holy bird. That's why I say although Sam Poh Kong had lost his small bird, he still had the big bird. Also, Sam Poh Kong had never been here, but his big bird was here. And when Sam Poh Kong went back to China, he left his big bird behind. You see here, the trees are all very tall, and that's what the big bird likes — tall big trees.

LI   Ya, ya, ya, that's even better! Many trees, all very tall, very tall! Hey, I tell you, this is what I really like. I can sing, I can play, I can shout. Mr Chen, I tell you, I am very happy! I can sing and make very loud noises. You know, when I was a little girl I liked singing very, very much but my mother won't let me. And then, when I was bigger, I used to go down and play in the playground. Plenty of people came to see me play. But the police also came. They told me I cannot sing because they said I made too much noise. Afterward, when everybody's gone to bed, I went to the playground again. Eh, police also came again. 'Hey, what are you doing here three o'clock in the morning, Miss?' I said to them, 'Sing *lah*, what else?' Then they said, 'But you are disturbing everybody's sleep, you know, Miss?' And I said, 'Where got? You look, everybody's standing in the corridor watching me sing, who's sleeping?' Anyway, they say cannot cannot, cannot. So I changed and I went to this ... what do you call this in Chinese? One piece of wood, two ropes and I swing on it?

CHEN   *Dang qiuqian.*[17]

LI   Ya, ya, ya, *dang qiuqian.* I swing! I swing! I swing! Eh? Police come again. What's wrong? 'This is three o'clock in the morning. I'm not singing. I'm just swinging. See, swinging only!' And then they said, 'Please, you might fall down. Miss, please come down.' 'OK, OK, cannot sing, cannot swing, OK, then I go swimming!' So I went swimming, and swimming and swimming. *Alamak,*[18] police come again. 'And what are you doing this time, Miss?', the police asked me again. I said,

---

[16] Editor's note: Mandarin-Chinese.
[17] Editor's note: Mandarin-Chinese: *Dang qiuqian*, swing.
[18] Editor's note: Malay: *alamak*, expression of surprise.

'Swimming *lah*. Now it's only twelve o'clock, why can't I swim?' Then he asked me, 'Tell me, Miss, what is this?' I said, 'It's sand, officer, sand.' And he said, 'And how can you swim in the sand, Miss? Why don't you go and swim in the water?' And I said, '*Aiyah*, how can you be so stupid! I don't know how to swim. How can I go swim in the water. I'll drown, you know?' And then they said, 'But, Miss, please *lah*, how can you swim in the sandpit. Why don't you go and swim in the pool?' And I said, '*Aiyah*, you want me to drown, ah? I don't know how to swim, how can I swim in the pool?' But they still say I cannot swim in the sandpit because it is not a swimming pool. OK, OK, can't swim can't swim *lah* ... But here is really good. You can sing, you can swing, you can swim also. *Shiok sekali!*[19]

Old Li is being carried away by her own story and starts to 'swim'. Old Chen was at first very fed up, but gradually became more and more interested in the innocence of the old woman. He begins to 'swim' with her.

LI   Mr Chen, do you like singing, swinging and swimming? (*Old Chen shakes his head to all of them.*) Then what do you like?

CHEN   I like climbing trees. I like catching birds. I like stealing bird eggs. I like stealing fruits from other people's trees and I like fighting and cheating!

LI   *Aiyah*, you bad boy. Aren't you a bad boy?

CHEN   Very, very bad boy.

LI   How old are you?

CHEN   What?

LI   Mr Wang said this is your birthday. So how old are you?

CHEN   You guess

LI   Sixty.

CHEN   Ha ha ha ... I'm 70!

LI   Don't bluff me!

CHEN   No bluffing. Exactly 70. And you? How old are you?

---

[19] Playwright's note: *Shiok sekali*, Malay for 'very enjoyable'.

LI   You guess.

CHEN   Forty-five.

LI   *Aiyah*, you really naughty boy, you. (*But very happy.*) But are you
            really 70 already?

CHEN   Because I was 69 last year, I must be seventy this year. In 10 years time
            I'll be 80. Another 10 years, 90. Another 10 years, 100 — a 100-year-
            old turtle.

LI   I'm 66.

CHEN   Really?

LI   No *lah*, I'm bluffing you. I'm only 45.

CHEN   Oh, then I'm 40.

LI   Then I'm 30

CHEN   Then I'm 28.

LI   I am 18.

CHEN   I am 17.

LI   I am 16. Sweet 16! (*Sings*) 'One day when we were young one wonder-
            ful morning in May. You told me you loved me when we were young
            one day.'[20] Yes, I'm 10 years old.

---

[20] Editor's note: These lines are part of the opening from the song 'One Day When We were Young',
lyrics by Oscar Hammerstein II, with music from Johann Strauss II's *Gypsy Baron* (1885), adapted by
Dmitri Tiomkin. The song was featured in the 1938 Metro-Goldwyn-Mayer film, *The Great Waltz*:

One day when we were young,
One wonderful morning in May,
You told me you loved me,
When we were young one day.

Sweet songs of spring were sung,
And music was never so gay,
You told me you loved me,
When we were young one day.

You told me you loved me,
And held me close to you heart,

CHEN I am eight.

LI I am seven.

CHEN I am six.

LI *Aiyah*, six is too small *lah*. No fun, small fart don't know anything.

CHEN No, six is already very good fun. I first saw the big bird when I was six. (*Mimicking the big bird.*)

LI *Aiyah*, six years old you already looking at girls ah? You *chikopei*![21] Sam Poh Kong sure get angry with you!

CHEN Sam Poh Kong himself raised a big bird. And so he doesn't mind other people looking at birds.

LI What?

CHEN (*Mimicking more energetically.*) Bird. Big bird. Sam Poh Kong's big bird!

LI (*Gets excited, starts singing.*) Bird? ... Bird! ... '*Burung Kaka Tua* ...'[22]

We laughed then, We cried then,
Then came the time to part.

When songs of spring are sung,
Remember that morning in May,
Remember, you loved me,
When we were young one day.

[21] Playwright's note: [*Minnan hua* or *minnan* language:] *chikopei*, lecher.

[22] Playwright's note: [Malay:] *Burung Kaka Tua*, old parrot. Editor's note: The bird in reference here is probably the *Burung Kakatua* [Indonesian], 'cockatoo'. Li sings an Indonesian (or possibly Malaysian) children's song that was popularised in the region by Dutch-Indonesian singer Anneke Grönloh in the early 1960s as '*Boeroeng Kaka*':

Burung kakatua [The cockatoo]
hinggap di jendela [Sits on the window sill]
nenek sudah tua [My grandmother is already old]
giginya tinggal dua. [And she only has two teeth]

(Refrain:)
Letrum, letrum [sound of a drum], *letrum oolala*
Letrum, letrum, letrum oolala
Letrum, letrum, letrum oolala
Burung kakak tua. [The cockatoo]

Li gets Chen equally excited and sings along with her which they enjoy immensely. Then Wang is heard calling out from afar, as he approaches.

WANG   *Oi! Oi!* Ah Chen, have you seen that old woman somewhere? I can't find her. Maybe she really got eaten up by wild pigs, you know, Ah Chen!

CHEN   Hey, this is no good. I cannot let Ah Wang see me dancing like this. He would die of laughter, unless you also make him dance. Now I give you a chance to make him dance. If he dances, I'll dance. Go, you make him dance!

Chen leaves and Li starts pretending to practise Taiji.[23]

WANG   Ah, here you are. I thought you were eaten up by the wild pigs.

LI   I have Sam Poh Kong looking after me. Sure safe. Is this correct, Master Wang?

WANG   Not exactly. Now, *fangsong,* ... *hanxiong,* ... *shoufu,* ... *babei,* ... *tigang* ...[24]

LI   (*Repeats after him.*) Relax, ... round in the chest, ... tuck in the tummy, ... straight in the back, ... backside open ...

WANG   No, backside close!

LI   Open, open, then you can have Sam Poh Kong's durian.

WANG   Heh, don't talk about durian, I'm hungry already. When are we eating?

Giginya tinggal dua [She only has two teeth left]
Nenek sudah tua [Grandma is already old]
Hinggap di jendela [She sits on the window sill]
Seperti kakatua! [Like the cockatoo!]

[23] Editor's note: *Taiji* is a Chinese martial art, typically practised for health reasons. A variety of training forms exist, both traditional and modern. The training forms that Chen probably goes into are the well-known slow-motion routines that groups of people practise together in the mornings in parks around the world — particularly in China, but also in Singapore.

[24] Editor's note: Mandarin-Chinese: The translation immediately follows and is given by Li.

LI   Anytime *lah*. I got curry chicken. All cooked and ready. And *nasi lemak*[25] we have for breakfast tomorrow.

WANG   This place is really good for *Taiji* exercise. Good weather, good position. Good company.

LI   Hey, Master Wang, disco is better for slimming than *Taiji* you know?

She starts to disco dance to the song 'Burung Kaka Tua', slowly drawing Wang into it. He declines at first but as he looks around and is certain there is no one around, he begins to respond and join in.

WANG   Where is Ah Chen?

LI   Gone to look for his bird *lah*.

WANG   *He is already into the sing-song. But as he swings around, he finds Chen there staring at him. Shocked, he stops dancing and starts to shout —*

                  Stop, stop, stop making noises! You're going to frighten the big bird away! (*Li is puzzled.*)

CHEN   *Staring at Wang for a while as if very angry. But then he suddenly begins to shout at Wang.*

                  I think the big bird might have become hard in seeing and hearing. I think we need to shout and yell to draw his attention and bring him over. (*So he gets Wang to join Li in an even more rousing song and dance.*)

LI   (*Simply ecstatic.*) Today is Mr Chen's birthday. Last week is Mr Wang's birthday. Next week is my birthday. *Shiok sekali*, let's celebrate!

They go into a mad dance singing 'Burung Kakak Tua', calling loudly at the big bird.

Starting with mimicking the big bird, they go on to a game of 'Eagle Catching the Chicken'.[26] *Dancing and singing in a circle, they finally lose their balance and all fall to*

---

[25] Editor's note: Malay: *nasi lemak*, 'rice cooked in coconut milk, usually with fish and chilli paste' (*A Malay-English English-Malay Dictionary*, ed. Coope).

[26] Editor's note: 'Eagle Catching the Chicken', a young children's game in which a child taking the role of a 'big chicken' will move around to protect 'little chicks' behind him/her from being caught by a marauding 'eagle'.

*the ground. They laugh so much as if they are all going to die. All of a sudden, a fantastic
sound cuts across the sky, chasing all their laughter away.*

CHEN	Big bird! Big bird!
LI	Big bird? Where?
WANG	Big bird! Big bird!
LI	Are you sure there is a big bird?
WANG	A big bird of 70? What bird can live until so old?
LI	How can you say 70 is old? My mother says some birds grow until they get to be 1,000 years.
WANG	That's the crane they tell in the fairy stories. Stories only!
CHEN	*(He hangs up a camping lantern to serve as a beacon for the big bird. And then he lights up a candle, holding it up high as if to guide the big bird. As he goes through all this, he is drawn into a spiritual state of being which opens up his mind and heart.)*

I was six when I first met the big bird. My *Baba*,[27] Grandma and
Grandpa — my mother's father and mother had all died. Then *Mama*
brought another man into the house. Then my friends and neighbours
all started to make fun of me. I never cried before other people. Even
when *Baba* and Grandpa and Grandma died I didn't cry. But when this
man moved into my house, I cannot stand anymore. I ran up the hill
all by myself and I started to cry and shout, and I cried very loud. I was
so upset I sat by the edge of the cliff over there and I nearly jumped
over the cliff.

Later, I fell asleep, but I had nightmares all night. When I woke up, the
sky was very dark. No moonlight. I raised my head, and there it was,
so green, so shiny, so masculine, so stylish ... Very powerful but not a
bit aggressive. At first, I was very scared. But slowly, as I looked at it,
I felt it was actually very, very friendly in the eyes. Then it raised its
head and let out a loud call. Very loud, but not piercing to the ears. The
call was very clear and pleasant. Then it opened its wings and before I
knew it, it was already in front of me. It was taller than me. The eyes

---

[27] Editor's note: Mandarin-Chinese: *Baba*, Father.

were clear, and deep and very loving, like my *Baba*'s, Grandpa's, Grandma's. For some reason, I felt a compulsion and I just rushed over, held its neck tightly and started to howl. Its feathers were soft and smooth, its shoulders were broad and strong. I didn't know how long I cried because I became so tired that I simply fell asleep.

When I woke up, it was almost daylight and I couldn't see the big bird anymore. Was it a dream? The next evening, I went up the hill again. Earlier than the day before. No, it was not a dream. The big bird came again, don't know from where. One moment, there was nothing. Next moment, it was right there in front of you. This time I didn't cry. I just told him everything about *Baba*, and Grandma and Grandpa. And how I ran away from school, how I fought with other boys, how I stole things from other people, how I lied and I cheated. Big bird played with me, allowed me to hug, to pull, to ride and all that. I sang, I told stories, I performed *kung fu* and everything. And from that day on, I went up the hill every night and played and played and played. Nobody knew. But the funny thing was, although I played all night, I didn't feel tired in the day. It was the happiest time in my life.

And then, we moved from our small town to the big city. Before I went, I cried all night as I played for the last time with big bird. I said I would come back. I promised to come back to visit it or else I would die a tragic death. And when I first got to the big city, I missed big bird very badly. I wanted so much to steal back to the hills to see it again. Then, gradually, life got busier and busier and I became less frustrated. And then I became very occupied. With work, with women, with kids, and gradually I forgot all about it. Not really forgetting, but the memory was slowly getting thinner and thinner. And later on, I even began to ask myself whether what I remembered had actually happened, or was it just a fantasy which I had created for myself.

WANG   I say you are just kidding yourself with all these funny stories. What big bird? And now Sam Poh Kong even!

LI   Hey, you, Sam Poh Kong is real, you know. You don't play the fool with Sam Poh Kong, OK?

CHEN   But they are all true. The trees, the rocks, the evening scenery, I remember everything very clearly.

LI	Hey, old birds, do they celebrate birthday or not, uh? Let's celebrate for them, OK? Happy birthday to the big bird, how about that?
CHEN	Good idea! So we should! Let's light up the candles. In my bag, I brought white candles.
LI	White ones no good, I've got yellow ones here I brought for Sam Poh Kong.
WANG	Light up how many sticks? One big big one, or many small small ones?
LI	Of course big big ones *lah*. One for Mr Chen, one for Miss Li.
CHEN	Light as many big ones as you can. Big bird is old now, its eyesight must have gone bad. So, light as many as you can.
LI	No, holy birds never get old.
CHEN	No, that's not enough. Seven candles for each one of us. And seven more for big bird. Four times seven is 28. Altogether 28 candles.
WANG	Why not make it 70. Let's all celebrate our 70th birthday.
LI	Hey, I'm 66 only, not 70 yet.
CHEN	Never mind, just light everything we have. Light them all up.

As their joy escalates, they get into a spirited song and dance as the candle-lighting action develops into a ceremony. As more candles are lit, Li and Wang begin to spread out into the other parts of the hill beyond the stage. As they light the candles, they loudly call upon the big bird to come to them.

LI/WANG/CHEN	Come on, big bird, come back. Come and see your friends. Your little friend has come back. He's come back to see you. He's come back to celebrate your birthday. Happy birthday!
	We sing for you. We dance for you. We bring you chicken curry, and *nasi lemak*. We also bring you durian. Come on, big bird, come back. Once you come back, Sam Poh Kong will follow also.
	Come on, big bird ...

At last, only Chen is left on stage. By now, he has developed a condition close to a trance, highly charged. Unnoticed by Chen, two men approach. As they sneak in, they begin to put off the candles one by one, and then they start to attack Chen, by which time Wang and Li have both returned and they help Chen to defend himself against the attackers. The two men are too strong for them.

Suddenly, there is a mysterious noise cutting across the sky. Everyone is awed, including the attackers. Then a chant is heard nearby. As they search for the source, a bearded man appears. He is warden Mat, the source of the chant. There is no doubt he is approaching the two men. Awed by the mysterious sight and sound, the two men let go of the old folks and run away.

Grateful for the rescue, the old folks move over to thank the bearded Mat. Just at this moment, they hear faraway shouts from Chen's children searching for his whereabouts.

A thunderbolt strikes and Li is shocked by a shadow she sees appearing in the lightning. She shrieks and Chen and Wang rush over to discover a shadowy figure up the slope.

CHEN	Ah, big bird, you are here at last! You are here at last!
SHADOW	I'm sorry you have suffered on my behalf.
LI/WANG/CHEN	You ... you're not the big bird?
SHADOW	You want to look for the big bird? Follow me.

In great thunder and lightning, amidst the greatly excited forests in the hills, the three old folks are overjoyed.

Part 2: The Old Man

In a cave. Mat is chanting. The Old Man guides Chen, Wang and Li into the cave. They are immediately awed by the mysteriousness of the place. They recognise Mat and go over to say hello. Mat does not respond and keeps chanting as he walks out of sight.

CHEN	Who is he?
OLD MAN	Mat is the protector of the natural forest reserve.
CHEN	He saved us.
OLD MAN	He also saved me.

CHEN	Why doesn't he say anything?
OLD MAN	He has lived in the forest all his life. Now he only chants. He doesn't talk much anymore.
WANG	How long have you been staying here?
OLD MAN	Forty years.
THREE	*Wah*, 40 years?
CHEN	Old Uncle how should we address you?
OLD MAN	As you please. After so many years here, name has lost its meaning. (*Thunder is heard.*) You have suffered on my behalf and I have no means to repay you. All I can offer you is a place to keep away from the storm. But I must plead with you not to reveal this place to anyone. Otherwise, my refuge for 40 years would come to an end.
LI	Refuge? You mean you have been running away from something? What from?
WANG	Those two men who attacked us, are they policemen or gangsters?
OLD MAN	I think they are both looking for me.
LI	Everyone looking for you. You some kind of big shot?
CHEN	Old Uncle, please tell me, where is the big bird?
OLD MAN	It's so late now, why are you still on the hill?
LI/WANG	Looking for the big bird *lah*.
CHEN	Very big and very tall, with feathers that are very soft and very green.
OLD MAN	Who told you you can find such a big bird up here on the hill?
LI	He has seen it.
OLD MAN	You? You have seen it?
CHEN	Long, long ago.
OLD MAN	How long ago?
CHEN	More than 60 years.
OLD MAN	More than 60 years. Where can you find birds that could live so long.

LI	Eh, Sam Poh Kong's bird lived many hundred of years!
WANG	Holy cranes can live a thousand years.
OLD MAN	If there is such a bird, why have you not seen it again for so many years?
CHEN	I'm sure there is. I know there is! I can still remember its feathers — so warm and smooth, its eyes so deep and bright, like a deep, deep pond of water. Looking into it, as if I could see the eyes of my *Baba*, Grandma and Grandpa.
LI	He danced with the big bird, sang with the big bird, without anybody disturbing them. They cried, they yelled and they were very, very happy.
WANG	They played every night throughout the night and he never felt tired in the day.
CHEN	When I was with the big bird, I felt as if I was floating on air. When I laughed, it seemed big bird also laughed with me. When I cried, big bird remained very patient, always listening to me without interrupting. They cannot be illusions, Old Uncle!
OLD MAN	When you cried, it always remained very patient? Always listening to you without interrupting?
CHEN	Yes, as patient as my Grandma.
OLD MAN	With eyes very, very deep and very, very bright?
CHEN	As if it can look into the very depth of your heart.
OLD MAN	And when you are frustrated and drifting away, it seemed like a rock, peaceful and steady. And when you are going through the greatest of pains, it was like a clear little stream, flowing gently and softly. Helping you to calm down, to stay on your feet, helping you to quieten down, to relax and remain balanced.
CHEN	Yes, yes, yes! You have ... seen it?
LI/WANG	You have seen the big bird?
OLD MAN	It's like a dream when it comes, and it's like a dream when it goes. Have you really seen the big bird?

CHEN	Yes, yes I have I really have seen the big bird! ... Old Uncle, have you also seen it?
LI/WANG	Yes! Yes! Say yes! Say you have seen it! Say you have!
OLD MAN	Yes, I have.
CHEN	Yes! Yes! He has seen it! He has seen it! You see! I told you I wasn't bluffing you! (*They are so excited.*)
CHEN	Please, Old Uncle, where did you see the big bird. And when did you see it? And where is it now?
OLD MAN	If it was real, it was more than 40 years ago ...
CHEN	Where?
OLD MAN	Here.
CHEN	Here? Right here on this hill?
OLD MAN	Right here in this cave.
WANG	In this cave?
LI	This cave? Where? Where in this cave?
CHEN	Old Uncle, why did the big bird come to you?
OLD MAN	Why did the big bird come to me? ... I don't know. Maybe, because I was suffering in the depth of my misery.
CHEN	In the depth of your misery?
LI	Someone very close died?
WANG	Who died?
OLD MAN	It was many, many times more painful than having someone close dying ... Forty years ago, I was involved in a gang fight between secret societies. Both sides put in many fighters and the casualty was very high. I personally hacked three people to death. But at the end I was captured by the leader of the other gang, and I faced a cruel, certain death. It turned out that death was too easy for me. What they gave me was many, many times worse than death. No, they did not cut off my hands or my feet. They did not even want to kill me as I expected. Instead, they castrated me and threw me into the hills. Then they left.

I thought that was the end of me. But I was lucky, or maybe unlucky. Mat came upon me and saved me. He hid me in this secret cave, nursed my wounds and taught me a way of keeping healthy. And the castrated man survived.

LI (*Following the story partly by Wang's assistance.*) Ah, he is Sam Poh Kong! Sam Poh Kong! (*Jumping up in great excitement but held back by Wang.*)

OLD MAN Sam Poh Kong? It would have been a blessing if I was Sam Poh Kong ... At first, the pain in my body was intolerable. And everything around me seemed to be adding to my misery. The sound of the birds in the day, the flight of the bats in the night. The ants on the ground, the spiders on the wall. Everything bothered me. But because they were bothering me, the days went by easily as I was occupied with all these frustrations. Indeed, the most painful time came to me after my wound had healed. By then, the many layers of my tragic sadness precipitated in full force. I felt as if everything around me was laughing at me impetuously — every grass, every tree, every piece of rock, every grain of sand. They were laughing at me because I have lost not only my power, my weapon but also the very organs which made up the nature of my manhood. I became mentally confused and emotionally depressed. I was nearing the point of a complete breakdown. One night, as I walked out of this hill and approached the edge of the cliff, I had the urge to jump down, putting an end to my miserable life. But I finally backed down. Not that I was afraid of dying. I was just not satisfied with ending my life in this way. Because I asked myself: I've lived my life so aimlessly for so long, am I going to end it so aimlessly too? ... So I wandered back to the cave again. And I started crying, very very loudly. I have never felt so wrongfully condemned in my life. My crying shocked the bats in the cave as well as the birds homed outside the cave. Shocked by my crying, they were flying all around me. And then, I don't know how much time had passed, eh? How come? Why is everything so quiet, so calm? ... Then I heard a most unusual sound approaching from afar, reverberating in the cave. I felt curious and lifted my head And there, up on that stone column, high above at its top, a very big, very green bird which I have never seen or heard before was sitting there looking at me. Intensely looking at me ... The next moment, it was by my side. Yes, its feathers are —

CHEN   Very, very green —

OLD MAN   Its eyes are —

CHEN   Very, very deep and very, very bright

OLD MAN   As if it was piercing right into the depth of your heart (*Approaching the highest part of the slope in the cave.*) From that day on, my entire life changed. I don't know what the big bird did, but I became relaxed and free. I started to run, to jump, to yell and to sing and dance. All my self-pity, all my frustrations, all the dark shadows in my heart, disappeared. Completely disappeared. But, underneath all my new gained happiness, I knew there was still buried there my deepest untold sorrow.

                One day, the big bird came again. After having great fun for a while, for some reason, I just stopped. I looked at it, I didn't cry, but somehow my tears started to fall. I knew I couldn't hide anymore. So I asked, 'Big bird, you are so masculine and so tender, so strong and so loving; are you male or female?' It understood me but did not reply. Instead, it just looked at me, intensely, for a very, very long time. And then it turned its attention to the things around it — the sand and the stones, the grass and the trees, the sunlight and the running water. I followed its eyes and looked at all these things, intensely. Then it turned to look at me, as if asking: What do you think? These sand and stones, grass and trees, sunlight and running water, do you think they are male, or female? ... And me, do you think I am male, or female?

CHEN   How did you reply?

OLD MAN   I had no reply. I only looked at big bird. And all the things around it. Intensely. But as I looked, intensely, after I don't know for how long, I gradually felt the sand and stones were not sand and stones anymore, and the grass and trees and the sunlight and running water were not the grass and trees and sunlight and running water anymore. They have all become, as it were, clouds of colour, clouds of air. They were all alive and moving, dancing, chanting, flowing and merging. In my body, I felt a tremor, and everything in front of me turned fuzzy and vague. I felt as if I was floating in the air, as if I was transforming into something else — I was completely wrapped in a kind of ecstasy I have never experienced in my life. I was as excited as I was afraid. I called out at the big bird: 'Big bird, what do you think, what is male and what is female?'

CHEN   And what did big bird say?

OLD MAN   Big bird didn't say anything. Its eyes were shining as brightly as ever, piercing right into the very depths of my heart, into the very soul of my being. And then, suddenly, big bird lifted into the air, started to fly all over the cave. Up and down, to and fro, all over the cave, at the same time making tremendously loud whistling calls. The flight and the calls became so frantic and crazy and loud and powerful as if the whole world was being brought to the edge of explosion. Then, at the climax of all this, big bird gave out an ear-piercing shrill, shot right up the top of the cave, heading straight towards the sky-hole at the top and flew away! ... And then, everything returned to silence. I was panting, but my heart had become very quiet I had completely calmed down.

CHEN   And the big bird?

OLD MAN   Gone.

CHEN   Gone?

OLD MAN   For some days after that, I could occasionally hear its call, coming from I don't know where. And then, later, even the calls did not come anymore.

WANG   Gone?

LI   Gone?

CHEN   *Disappeared?*

OLD MAN   Perhaps.

CHEN   Then where is it now?

OLD MAN   Perhaps in this cave. Perhaps somewhere outside the cave ... Perhaps, in my body ... Sometimes, I felt as if I was the big bird. Like the sand and the stones, the grass and the trees, the sunlight and the running water ... Sometimes I felt as if I was that sexless big bird.

The three old folks are stunned. The thing they had most urgently sought after seemingly ended in disillusion.

WANG   You mean there is no more big bird?

LI   Gone forever?

LI/WANG/CHEN   Disappeared forever? But we have waited for so long ... It is not coming anymore?

Chen is in hysterics, crying and yelling in desperation.

Mat is heard chanting and walking into the cave.

Lost and disillusioned, the three old folks' emotions are highly charged, nearing a complete mental breakdown. The accumulated uncertainties, fears and anger buried deep down in them begin to surface in an increasingly unchecked manner. The free, honest and excited deluge and outpouring soon reach a trance-like sublimation, producing a kind of ritualistic display of their inner selves.

CHEN   *Rensheng qishi gu lai xi.*

People of 70 are a rarity.

Big bird, I'm already 70! You should come back now. We promised each other, remember? It's time you come back now.

LI/WANG/CHEN   (*As in a chorus, using an assortment of English, Mandarin and their respective Chinese dialects, and highly agitated, they call upon the big bird to appear.*)

I'm 70 already!
Big bird, Sam Poh Kong! *Lingkim*!
Rare species. I'm a rare species.
I'm 80, but I managed to climb up here. I'm 70, but I managed to climb up here.
I was running, carrying a bunch of keys. Running, carrying a bunch of keys.
Why won't you open the door! Why won't you open the door?
Mummy, I can cook, I can wash. Mummy, I can clean, I can sing. The door won't open. The door won't open.
Why are the cats and dogs chasing after me? Why are they chasing after me?
My health is OK, give me a chance, please. Please, give me a chance. Please *lah*, Mummy, give me a chance. Please *lah*, Mummy, give me a chance.

I'll do it. I won't talk. I'll do it, I won't talk.
Don't lock the door. Don't lock the door.
Mummy's a widow. Sorry, I can't. Mummy's a widow. Sorry, I can't.
You have taken all the keys. You have taken all the keys.
This is no good. I've stripped. This is no good. I've stripped.

After a series of mind shattering noises, the three old folks gradually sink into hyper excitement.

Please, don't, Mummy. Please, don't, Mummy. A-a-ahh!
Don't, don't cut it. Don't, don't cut it. Don't, don't cut it.
Don't, don't cut it. Don't, don't cut it. A-a-ahh!
Take away the knife. Take away the knife. Take away the knife.
Take away the knife!

As their arousal reaches a peak, the Old Man and Mat guide them into articulating as loudly as they could, leading them to vent all the frustrations accumulated within themselves in their many years of ups and downs.

And then, the Old Man and Mat resume chanting which develops into a declamation, alternating line by line —

MAT
(*In Malay.*)
Langit-nya, jauh jauh
Bumi-nya, tebal tebal
Air-nya, jemeh jemeh
Hutan-nya, hening hening
Hati-nya, hati-nya, terang terang[28]

OLD MAN
The sky is distant, very, very distant
The Earth is thick, very, very thick
The water is clear, very very clear
The trees are calm, very, very calm
The heart is clean, very, very clean

The light and shadows in the cave begin to go fuzzy, as if the entire universe is thrown into flux, into some form of transformation. In the end, all three old folks calm down.

---

[28] Editor's note: The Old Man gives the translation in the lines that follow what Mat has just said.

From somewhere is vaguely heard the sound of running water and the laughter of playful children. As if going to take a bath, the three of them slowly, gently and freely take off all their clothes. Without a care in the world, they walk slowly back into their childhood. They speak in English, Mandarin and Chinese dialects.

CHEN   (*Singing*) Yueguang guang, zhao ditang ...[29]

Bright moonlight shines upon the floor.

WANG   (*Chanting*) Ren zhi chu, xing ben shan; xing xiang jin, xi xiang yuan ...

LI   (*Translates the Chinese into English.*) In the beginning, humans are good-natured. Nature brings them together, teaching sets them apart ...

WANG   (*Singing*) Yueguang guang, zhao ditang ...[30]

CHEN   Mama, lala shou, buyao nanguo le. Women dao shanshang qu zouzou. Men shi kezhe de, mao zai shuijiao, gou zai shai taiyang.

LI   (*Translates sentence by sentence.*) Mama, let's hold hands. Don't be sad anymore. Let's go and take a walk up the hill. The door's open. The cat's asleep. The dog's enjoying the sun.

CHEN   Mama, wo yao dao yu li qu zouzou. Rang shui ba wo quanshen linshi. Ni zhidao ma, wohai meiyou gen ren haoguo.

LI   Mummy, I'm going into the rain. I'm going to take off my clothes. And let the water run through my body. Do you know Mama? I've ... still ... not ... had a man?

WANG   Yueguang guang, zhao ditang ...[31]

CHEN   Mama, shuye shang de luzhu jingying de faliang. Shitou shang de yecao kaihua le. Women dao shuili qu zouzou ba ...

LI   Mama, the dew drops on the leaves are sparkling. The flowers on the rock have bloomed. Let's walk into the stream ...

---

[29] Editor's note: Mandarin–Chinese: 'Bright moonlight shines upon the floor ...'
[30] Editor's note: Mandarin–Chinese: 'Bright moonlight shines upon the floor ...'
[31] Editor's note: Mandarin–Chinese: 'Bright moonlight shines upon the floor ...'

The speaking has stopped. The singing has stopped. The laughter has stopped. Everything has stopped. In order to allow the old folks to savour a rare moment they had either never tasted before or one that they had sadly missed, the entire universe has stopped. Silence. Silence.

Then, the sound of running water is heard, very softly. It comes so fresh as if it is happening for the first time. It is not the sound of running water. It is the sound of life flowing. Clearly, bubbly ...

From afar, there is a murmur of thunder and lightning, followed by a mysterious sound cutting boldly across the sky. It is so dynamic as if the big bird is indeed coming.

OLD MAN   The big bird? Is it here *again?*

LI/WANG/CHEN   (*Calling and yelling in great excitement.*) Big bird. Big bird. Big bird!

Shadows dance in great excitement and mystery in the cave. Multi-colours dance in the air. People are investing the greatest of hopes for the re-appearance of the big bird.

Suddenly Mat rises, realising something is wrong. He puts his ear to the floor and listens intensely for a moment. Certain that something is indeed wrong, he moves immediately over to escort the Old Man away into the deeper recess of the cave.

Presently, a number of secret society gang members burst in. They are overjoyed to find people inside. But, as they realise who the three old folks are, they are greatly disappointed and continue in pursuit, following in the direction that Mat had taken.

Then several policemen appear, followed by members of the Chen family. They are deeply satisfied to find Mr Chen, but awed by the trance-like condition they are in.

Part 3: The Climb

A hospital ward, clean, quiet and comfortable, but also somewhat hazy and dreamy.

The three old folks are lying in bed, totally motionless. If not for the comings and goings of nurses and relatives looking over them, they could easily be taken as having already passed on.

Chen's eldest son arrives.

DAUGHTER-IN-LAW   Why are you so late?

GRANDSON   *Baba*, the doctor just came.

A police inspector arrives.

POLICE   Mr Chen, I'm Inspector Goh. I'm here under orders from DSP Wong,[32] commander of the assault task force. Have they woken up?

SON   Not yet. None of them has spoken to anyone.

POLICE   Not even the nurses and doctors?

SON   Not to anybody.

INSPECTOR   Has the doctor discovered anything?

SON   No. One doctor just came round and said nothing. At first we thought they were suffering from shock. But doctor said not so. Doctor cannot understand why they have all refused to respond. Any news from your side?

POLICE   We've told you everything we know. You followed us into the cave. You know the gangsters never harmed them in any way. You see, we tailed them very closely. According to our information, they have been looking for an old enemy for many, many years. They discovered the cave before us but we went in close on their heels and made sure they didn't harm the old folks.

SON   When we got in, my father was still in a trance, yelling some fantastic things nobody can understand.

POLICE   The cave has a lot to do with the old gangster. We are quite sure he's the gangster leader who had disappeared from the scene about 40 years ago. We all believed he had already been killed by his rival gang in a big showdown. In fact, one of his enemies was charged and convicted and subsequently hanged for his alleged murder. But his enemies didn't believe that because nobody ever found his body. So, for 40 years they never gave up looking for him. That's why we are not in a hurry to attack the cave. We hope we can persuade the

---

[32] Editor's note: DSP Wong, Deputy Superintendent Wong.

old man to walk out, to help us solve the mystery of the case. We've captured his partner, the man with the beard. But he's a mute, can't talk.

A policeman approaches Inspector Goh, talking to him in confidence.

POLICE Sorry, Mr Chen, I have to report to DSP Wong. Please wait for me, I have a feeling DSP Wong might have something for me to relay to you.

SON (*To his son and wife.*) Don't go away. When the doctor comes back, I want you to tell him what you told me about *Gong Gong*. Diana, have you done what I told you to prepare?

GRANDDAUGHTER Yes, *Baba*. Auntie made chicken soup for *Gong Gong* but he won't take any.

DAUGHTER-IN-LAW *Gong Gong* seems to be able to see us and recognise us. But he just won't talk. Uncle Wang also the same.

GRANDSON That old Granny seems to want to say something. But when we talk to her, she doesn't reply.

SON Nobody came to see them?

DAUGHTER-IN-LAW Only us. You want to make a long distance call to Uncle Wang's family?

SON I'll do it later.

GRANDSON *Baba*, are they possessed by evil spirits?

SON Don't talk nonsense. Everybody be more patient. And don't make stupid guesses.

DAUGHTER-IN-LAW If they can't find the problem, do we take him home?

SON Of course *lah*, if they can't find any problem.

DAUGHTER-IN-LAW But how to look after him?

SON Take turns *lah*.

GRANDSON Easy to say, *Baba*. Even Diana is going to school now. Who can look after him daytime? What if he goes out? We can't follow him everywhere he goes. Who is going to look after Grandpa Wang? And the other Granny?

SON   OK, let's not talk now.

Doctor comes in.

DOCTOR   Could you all wait outside for a while. Mr Chen, may I have a word with you.

All leave except Mr Chen and his wife and son.

SON   You discovered anything, doctor?

DOCTOR   Earlier symptoms indicated shock. But their heartbeats were all quite normal and that dismissed the shock diagnosis. Physiologically, they all seemed quite healthy. I have all along felt that they are actually quite normal and conscious and that they were purposely not responding to our treatment and questions. But I haven't found out why they are behaving like this.

SON   Doctor, I've asked my wife and my son to stay and talk to you. I think you may be interested in what they are going to tell you. May be helpful in understanding my father's condition.

DAUGHTER-IN-LAW *Baba* became very funny these last few years. More and more he doesn't want to talk to us anymore. Once he goes out, he doesn't come back until late at night. At first, he kept making very long phone calls. And, lately, when he's home, he would lock himself up in his room and not talk to anybody. Last time, he used to be very fond of Diana. Take her to play very often. Now no more.

SON   Diana is my youngest daughter, his favourite Grandchild.

DAUGHTER-IN-LAW Lately he's not even interested in Diana. Actually the family was planning to give him a big birthday party when he turned 70, the day before yesterday. He first said he's not interested, then he disappeared.

DOCTOR   Did anything unusual happen lately?

SON   Tell the doctor what happened when I was away that time.

DAUGHTER-IN-LAW It's like this. Last month, one morning, about three o'clock, we were woken up by the phone. It was the police. They say *Baba* was detained in Woodlands Checkpoint.[33] They asked us to go and take him back.

---

[33] Editor's note: Woodlands Checkpoint, the customs point on the Singapore side of the Causeway that links the island-state to the southern West Malaysian state of Johor.

I was so frightened because my husband was not home. When I drove to Woodlands, *alamak*, I was so embarrassed. He and Uncle Wang together, they were both still wearing pyjamas, with a jacket on top. Uncle Wang even had his *kung fu* belt on; he looked so funny. The police said they were trying to cross to Johor but they never carried their passport or their IC.[34] Of course the immigration people stopped them. At first the police thought they were drunk. But after they tested, they found no alcohol. On the way back, they didn't want to say anything. So we thought maybe they were sleepwalking.

SON   How can both of them sleepwalk together?

DOCTOR   Did you bring them to a doctor?

DAUGHTER-IN-LAW We wanted to take them but they didn't want to go. Afterwards, everybody just forgot about it.

SON   OK, you, tell doctor your story.

GRANDSON One day, by accident, I overheard his phone talk with Grandpa Wang. They were talking about another old lady, I think it's this one here. Not that I want to eavesdrop, you know, our house phone got extensions.

SON   OK, go on, go on!

GRANDSON You know what *Gong Gong* was talking about? Going to see strip show in Johor! And the most fantastic thing was that it seemed as if this Granny was the one who suggested they go and see this strip show! Grandpa Wang sounded like he knew the strip shows in Johor so well. What theatre, what strip star, what price is the ticket, he knew everything by heart. And then Grandpa Wang said this: Granny had no passport. *Gong Gong* said no passport no passport *lah*, we can swim over to Johor in the night. And then they both laughed very loudly over the phone. They sounded very, very happy, and not like they were joking. And yet you know, *Gong Gong* used to be a very serious old man. Everybody's very scared of him. Nobody dared to tell dirty jokes in front of him. And now he's going to see strip show in Johor. When I told the other people in my family, nobody believed me!

---

[34] Editor's note: IC, Identity Card, a shortened acronym for the National Registration Identity Card (NRIC) that citizens of the city-state of Singapore are required by law to have on their person at all times.

SON   *Baba* has been very successful in business and in family life. We're not
                  very rich but we're quite well off. Mother passed away a few years ago,
                  but the family remained quite close. We all respected and even feared
                  him a lot. He usually doesn't talk very much. But we've never had any
                  trouble at home. Why a person like him can suddenly become so
                  strange in old age, doctor?

DOCTOR   Come and talk to my colleagues tomorrow. There's a psychologist and
                  a psychiatrist in the team. They may have some answers.

SON   Yes, doctor. The day before yesterday was my father's 70th birthday;
                  now we'd like to make up with a little celebration, if you don't mind.
                  Maybe this would stimulate some response from him.

DOCTOR   Wouldn't do any harm.

Diana takes out a birthday cake with lit candles, helped by other relatives.

DIANA   *Gong Gong*, please wake up, please. You wake up and I'll sing you a
                  birthday song.

*Gong Gong doesn't wake up but she sings all the same. It is a Cantonese song, accompa-
nied by the whole family. When it is over, everyone looks at him anxiously. To everyone's
great surprise, Chen opens his eyes. He looks around for a moment and, again to everyone's great surprise, he closes his eyes again. No amount of pleading could change his
mind. The other two old folk remain motionless throughout.*

The inspector returns. After conferring with the doctor, he approaches Mr Chen's son.

POLICE   Mr Chen, we know your father's condition is still uncertain. But, with
                  your permission, we'd like to say something to your father. It is very
                  important to our task at hand.

*Chen junior has no objection and so the inspector walks over to the beds of the three old
folks and starts his appeal.*

                  Old Uncles and Auntie, may I have your attention, please. The counter-
                  gangster operation on the hill is in its last phase. We were very pleased
                  to be able to rescue the three of you from the cave yesterday. Several
                  of the gangsters in the cave have been arrested, including the bearded
                  mute old man. But the mysterious long-haired old man is still at large,
                  somewhere in the cave. We are quite certain now that he is the secret
                  society gang leader who went missing and was thought murdered 40

years ago. We were told that you all knew him. So we are hoping that perhaps you could help us persuade him to walk out peacefully. Would you all, or anyone of you, care to help us please?

The old folks do not respond.

We prefer not to allow this situation develop into a bloody and tragic ending. We sincerely hope that at least one of you would come forward to help us, OK? Let me play a recording of the news broadcast to convince you of the urgency of the situation.

The inspector signals the policeman to play the tape.

TAPED NEWSCAST   The operation to drive out the gangsters occupying the mysterious cave in the nature reserve has come to its final phase. According to the police spokesman, most of the gangsters on the run have been captured except one old gangster leader who is still holed up in the cave resisting arrest. Reliable sources say the cave has been a secret hideout for many years and no one knows how deep it is. Reports say the inside of the cave is well lit. The air inside is extremely refreshing and there is a clean and clear stream running through it. Someone even said it's like a paradise in miniature ...

POLICE   (*Detecting no response from the old folks.*) OK, thank you very much. (*He takes his leave.*)

The news broadcast now comes from offstage.

NEWSCAST   And we learned that something very unusual had happened during the initial police raid. Members of the raiding party said they saw many long, green feathers, seemingly from some kind of very big birds, strewn about on the floor of the cave, and they ... Now, wait a minute ... Something's happening. Now, ladies and gentlemen, it looks like the police are preparing to make the final assault on the cave. Yes, this has been expected for some time, because the police have made a number of appeals to the old gang leader to come out. But the response has been a constant dead silence. I believe there are 60 fully armed police commandos participating in this operation and they include the best sharp shooters in the police force. According to DSP Wong, the commander of this operation, once they unleash the final assault, the end would come very soon. According to the captured members, the old gangster could be very well armed. And so we can expect a full force lightning strike. The irony is, the imminent bloody operation is taking place against a background of the most fascinating sunset. The twilight is amazingly beautiful, the brilliance of the setting sun, the hazy air in the valley and tens of thousand of birds chirping and flying all over the sky as they return to their nests — making the mystery and irony all that much more tragic and epic. Despite all this extraordinary beauty, the bloodshed seems unavoidable.

By now, the three old folks, drawn by the newscast, have opened their eyes, sat up, got off their beds and, overcoming all efforts by members of the family, the doctors and nurses and the policemen to stop them, managed to come together and start to get out of the hospital.

LI/WANG/CHEN   Green feathers? ... Why did the feathers of big bird fall off? ... Big bird cannot die. Big bird ... big bird ... Old uncle ... No, no, no, you people cannot do this to him ... No, he's not a bad person, he's not a gangster. Let him go. Let him go. Let me go. Let me go. I want to get to the hill ... I want to get to the hill ...

The three old folks' resistance to the blockade by people around them becomes stronger and stronger. They try to escape in all directions, pushing along their beds madly around the ward trying to find a way out.

By now, the people and the hospital scene have receded. The hills and the forests in twilight have appeared in the background and the hospital scene has disappeared along with the people around them. And the chanting of Mat is heard again, seemingly serving as a strong source of energy leading the three forward — singularly aiming for the hills. At the same time, a mysterious sound is heard gradually cutting across the sky, and the sound of children's laughter and the appearance of countless lit candles all over the twilight hills.

Like birds escaping their cage, the three old folks savour their newfound freedom in sheer exhilaration. Each tugging a bed sheet from the hospital beds, they run along like big birds in flight, with unbelievable youthfulness and joy, madly all over the open stage. The laughter of old folks is heard together with the laughter of young children.

Vaguely, in the flux of twilight, gradually, they are seen and heard as being accompanied by what might be perceived as another level of being — a brilliant spark dancing with them together with the shadow of a great big bird in flight. The spark, the feathers, the three old folks, amidst the sounds of cries, shrieks, laughter, the song of the forest, the hills, the water, the sky, the sun and the moon ... It is life itself, it is fulfilment itself, dancing and singing.

Suddenly a round of fierce gunshots bursts out, shocking them out of their trance-like excitement. All the lit candles are killed by the gunshots. So are Mat's chanting, the children's laughter, the mysterious noises, the chirping of the birds, the sparks and the shadows — all gone. The three old folks freeze, feeling as if they themselves have been shot. As if they themselves have been killed.

Another round of gun shots bursts out. As if going straight into their own hearts. Agony prevails upon them, in shadowy darkness where, if anything, it seems there is an endless falling down of green feathers.

All that is left is for them to emit a deathly cry, at which time they begin to desperately run towards the hills. The hills!

The cry is really a howl, a sound beyond normal human capabilities. They sound more like the howl of animals, a sound so primitive that they are more harmonious with the sound of running water and the rustling of trees and the tremor of valley winds ... Reverberating endlessly amidst the evening hills ...

(*End of Play*)

Lao Jiu — The Ninth Born

The Puppet Master is performing Lan Tian Yu [Lam Tian Geok].[1]

Lan Tian Yu, on his way to the capital to take the imperial examinations, encounters Han Ke Yun, a fellow scholar, as the latter is attacked by a tiger. Lan overcomes the tiger and saves Han and his family. In gratitude, Han invites Lan to become blood brothers. They take the oath and together resume their journey to the imperial capital.

Before the Master can complete the act, however, he starts to cough so seriously that he has to stop the show. The lean and gaunt old man, aged 70, reluctantly pushes his theatre-on-cart out of view.

As the Master performs, Lao Jiu, hidden in the background behind a gauze-like layer of cloth, imitates the Master with his hands while his body develops the pleasurable sensation which the puppetry is obviously giving him. After the Master's exit, Lao Jiu's play with puppetry goes far beyond the Master's original. The boy freely uses the old man's technique to amuse his youthful and contemporary fancies. He seems to be making discoveries and derives immense amusement from all this.

Mother is heard calling 'Gao gia'ng'.[2] Lao Jiu immediately resumes reciting his poem — 'Ku teng, lao shu, hun ya, xiao qiao, liu shui, ren jia ...'[3] *— and exits.*

Against the background of shadow play on the backdrop/cyclorama, Lao Jiu's voice is heard —

---

[1] Editor's note: We have not been able to establish the provenance of this puppet play or opera.

[2] Editor's note: *Minnan hua* or *minnan* language: ninth child.

[3] Playwright's note: [Mandarin-Chinese:] *Ku teng, lao shu, hun ya, xiao qiao, liu shiu, ren jia ...,* Dried rattan, aged trees, crows at dusk; little bridge, running stream, and a homestead. Editor's note: The text that is recited is derived from the poem 'Yearning in Autumn', written by Ma Zhiyuan (1250–1321) during the Yuan dynasty (1279–1368). See <http://baike.baidu.com/view/188620. htm#7>. *Ku teng* might be translated as 'withered vines' instead of 'dried rattan'. Thanks to Chan Cheow Thia.

LAO JIU

I am Lao Jiu — the Ninth Born. In *Hokkien*,[4] they call me *gao gia'ng*, or *lao gao*, which also sounds like 'old monkey';[5] some deliberately pronounce wrongly and it becomes like Old Dog. So, although I was born a pig, I'm sometimes also a monkey and a dog. That's why my school friends say I'm extra or super 'animalistic'.[6]

My proper name was given by Master Tan. It sounds very civilised: Youwei, meaning 'got achievement'.[7] You know why? Because my Father is a labourer — a manual worker; he wants his son to achieve great things. He even wants me to emulate that famous Chinese reformer-scholar Kang Youwei.[8] But there is a problem. Because my surname is Chng, or Zhuang in Mandarin,[9] and Zhuang also can mean 'act', 'pretend'. Which means I sound like someone who act like, or pretend to be like, the great Kang Youwei. Basket,[10] my school friends all make fun of me. They say my Father *aksi borak*,[11] want me to act like great man.

Anyway, I think Lao Jiu sounds good. Because I am my Father's ninth born. In *Hokkien* we call ninth son *gao gia'ng, gao gia'ng*!

---

[4] Editor's note: *Hokkien* in Mandarin-Chinese is known as *minnan hua* or *minnan* language.

[5] Editor's note: *Minnan hua* or *minnan* language: Literally, old ninth. 'Ninth' (or 'nine') and 'monkey' are homophones, so with a change in character, the same phrase will then sound like it means 'Old Monkey', as Lao Jiu notes.

[6] Editor's note: Lao Jiu makes references here to the animal signs in the Chinese 'zodiac', or *shengxiao*. Each animal in the astrological system represents different personality types.

[7] Editor's note: This is the meaning in Mandarin-Chinese.

[8] Editor's note: Kang Youwei (1858–1927) was a Chinese scholar and a leader of the Reform Movement of 1898. He was a key figure in the intellectual development of modern China. Kang was a believer in constitutional monarchy and, controversially, wanted to re-model the country after Meiji-era Japan. During the last years of the Qing Dynasty and the early years of the Republic of China, he promoted Confucianism as an antidote against 'moral degeneration' and indiscriminate Westernisation.

[9] Editor's note: 'Ch'ng' is the *Hokkien*-Chinese pronunciation of the Chinese character that is pronounced 'Zhuang' in Mandarin-Chinese.

[10] Editor's note: Basket, this is a mild (and now dated) swear term in Singapore English.

[11] Playwright's note: [Malay:] *aksi borak*, proud, show-off. Editor's note: Equivalent to the English expression, 'acts big'.

Scene 1: The War Horse

Lao Jiu's parents come on, calling 'gao gia'ng' as they look for him. Father is wearing only a singlet and pyjama trousers.

MOTHER   *Gao gia'ng*! Guest coming already. Go meet him outside, you, OK?

Lao Jiu comes in one way and then dashes out the other way.

FATHER   *Gao gia'ng! Gao gia'ng!*

MOTHER   *Aiyah.* You go and change. How can you meet guest in pyjama singlet? (*Pushes Father out.*) Oi! *Zabougia'ng*,[12] you go and call out all your sisters and their *dabougia'ng*.[13] Cannot ask our guest to wait, you know!

ZABOUGIA'NG   O *lailo*![14] *Ma*, you better go and comb your hair a bit. Go! (*Then, calling offstage —*) Hey, all you *zabougia'ng*, call your men out. Guest coming already!

GIRLS (INSIDE)   O! *Lailo*!

All eight sisters come out like a Chinese opera parade entrance, paired with their respective man, who carry a chair for their woman, with extras for Father, Mother and the Guest. They all line up.

LAO JIU   (*Comes in and, as Father and Mother enter, announces:*) The Representative for East Asia of the International War Horse Foundation, Mr Kim!

A grand entrance fanfare. As the lights dim down to a mysterious level, we behold the entrance of Senior Horse accompanied by Junior Horse. In a grand sweep, Senior Horse 'inspects' each and every member of the family before settling into a commanding position.

SENIOR HORSE   Please be seated.

They all sit.

---

[12] Playwright's note: [*Minnan hua* or *minnan* language:] *Zabougia'ng*, daughters.
[13] Playwright's note: [*Minnan hua* or *minnan* language:] *dabougia'ng*, husbands/men.
[14] Playwright's note: [*Minnan hua* or *minnan* language:] *lailo*, coming.

SENIOR HORSE	Candidate Zhuang Youwei, please introduce.
LAO JIU	Father, 60, retired harbour worker.
	Mother, 56, housewife.
	1st sister, 37, private dressmaker.
	1st Brother-in-Law, 40, contractor.
	2nd Sister, 36, housewife, also make cake — *kueh*.[15]
	2nd Brother-in-Law, 38, insurance salesman.
	3rd Sister, 35, baby-sitter, at home.
	3rd Brother-in-Law, 36, primary school teacher.
	4th Sister, 34, hawker, selling soyabean milk.
	4th Brother-in-Law, 36, also sell soyabean milk.
	5th Sister, 31, production operator, electronics factory.
	5th Brother-in-Law, 33, taxi driver.
	6th Sister, 29, salesgirl.
	6th Sister Fiancé, 30, sales representative.
	7th Sister, 25, clerk.
	7th Sister's Boyfriend, 26, library assistant.
	8th Sister, 21, Poly student.[16]
	8th Sister's Boyfriend, 23, also Poly student.

SENIOR HORSE   Thank you, Mr Zhuang and distinguished members of your family, for extending to me this warm welcome. Before I begin, please accept my heartiest congratulations for candidate Zhuang Youwei's success in having been selected by the War Horse Foundation to participate in the World Top Achievers Contest.

As you may well know, the War Horse Foundation is an eminent institution dedicated to the nurture of the very top achievers of the world. Every year, we select 350 brilliant young men and women from seven regions over the five continents to participate in an extraordinary contest. They will be tested, over four full days, by the most sophisticated examination discipline ever developed. Out of this, 35 will be selected. And they, the cream of the world's top talents, elite among the elites, shall be given unlimited and uncompromised education to the limit of their

---

[15] Editor's note: Malay: *kueh* (or *kuih*), general name for cakes or puddings.
[16] Editor's note: A shortened reference for 'Polytechnic', here probably referring to the Singapore Polytechnic, as that was the main polytechnic institution in Singapore when the play was written.

potential — undergraduate, postgraduate, post-doctoral and further research and study. The Foundation would stop at nothing to nurture them so they would inevitably become the pride of the human race, the protégés of heaven and, eventually, become the humble servants of the world.

I am pleased to note that, in addition to candidate Zhuang Youwei's dedicated interest, his conscientious effort, his disciplined conduct, you, the family, have given him warm, unwavering support. In my opinion, you have given him the most reliable assurance for success. If I were to describe him as a pony of immense potential, then, I would have no doubt that he will grow up to become an aggressive, dynamic war horse! It is absolutely necessary for all of us to understand that gifted stallions are not born to draw a cart or a plow. Gifted horses are fated to undergo rigorous training, disciplined nurture, to serve great leaders of their times — such as Alexander the Great, Genghis Khan or Napoleon Bonaparte — great leaders who are destined to lead the human race, to change the face of the world.

My friends, you have all along toiled hard, labouring in an ordinary, mundane life. You are fully aware of the importance of paving a smoother path so as to lead our young ones into a brighter, affluent future. As such, I have no doubt you are all gloriously happy and proud of candidate Zhuang Youwei's selection. And you would all give your utmost support to ensure that he performs well during the Top Achievers Contest. The pride and glory he earns is also the pride and glory of your distinguished family!

Candidate Zhuang Youwei, I wish you the highest success!

Mr Zhuang and members of the Zhuang family, I wish you great prosperity and the best of luck!

With your permission, I will now take my leave.

Father does not understand.

LAO JIU   *Ba,*[17] he's going.

---

[17] Editor's note: *Minnan hua* or *minnan* language, *Ba*, Father.

FATHER	Oh! Thank you.
FAMILY MEMBERS	Thank you.
FATHER	Come again.
FAMILY MEMBERS	Come again.

Senior Horse, accompanied by Junior Horse, exits to another grand fanfare, accompanied by Lao Jiu. The Family, in tense politeness, sees them off. The grip sustains until Father breaks the tension.

FATHER   *Gan ni ni'ang e!*[18]

The young ones yell for joy, the older ones chat with great excitement. Utter confusion.

FATHER   (*With a grand sweep of his hand, the Family's attention is arrested.*) You all got good sons and daughters. But this *gao gia'ng* is different. You all hear what he said. All the world 350 and he is one! *Gan ni nia'ng e!* After contest he can be one of 35 in all the world! I never dream our family have anyone so special, clever, *li hai!*[19] You all must help him. Everybody. Our ancestors, so many generations, never one read so many books, never one succeed so high. You all must help him!

1ST BROTHER-IN-LAW   Ah *Ba*, *gao gia'ng*'s room, I make air-con for him today. Also soundproof the wall. Cut all outside noise. Everyone talk very loud also cannot disturb him!

2ND SISTER   *Ma*, from tomorrow, I take over cooking for *gao gia'ng*. Your cooking taste good, but you don't know what food got more vitamin. Now he use more brain, must get more vitamin.

4TH SISTER   Yah, *Li ji*,[20] we bring him soyabean milk every day. They say soyabean got high protein, best for brain.

3RD SISTER   Best for brain is eating pig's brain. Ma, I cook pig's brain for *gao gia'ng*.

---

[18] Playwright's note: *Gan-ni-nia'ng-e*, a *Hokkien* expletive. Editor's note: Literally, 'screw your mother's …!'

[19] Playwright's note: [Mandarin-Chinese:] *li hai*, fantastic. Editor's note: Literally, 'dangerous'.

[20] Playwright's note: [*Minnan hua* or *minnan* language:] *Li ji*, 2nd Sister.

3RD BROTHER-IN LAW	Since this is about examination, I think the most important thing to do now is to get him a good, private tutor.
FATHER	You *lah*.[21] You teacher, also relative.
7TH SISTER	Cannot *lah*, *gao gia'ng* 'A' Level,[22] *Sa ji hu*[23] teach primary school only. He doesn't know *gao gia'ng*'s studies.
3RD BROTHER-IN-LAW	But I can help in getting a good one for him.
7TH SISTER'S BOYFRIEND	That's not easy, you know. I mean, he's too brilliant to get a tutor for. Maybe the best thing is to give him the best of library support. I mean, I work in the library, I can help him get all the reference books and materials he needs.
8TH SISTER	That's a good point. Stephen and I can help him gather the most difficult questions from past exams to test his limits.
5TH SISTER	OK, *gao gia'ng* can go in Ah Beng's taxi. Save time and energy.
6TH SISTER	(*To Boyfriend.*) Eh, can you lend *gao gia'ng* your computer or not?
6TH SISTER'S BOYFRIEND	Eh, my one is for demonstration, you know!
6TH SISTER	For a little while only what. Give you back after exam *lah*.
6TH SISTER'S BOYFRIEND	OK *lah*. Mine very powerful one, you know.
8TH SISTER	OK *lah*. Skip the promotions, please.
2ND BROTHER-IN-LAW	*Ba*, I go and buy an insurance policy for him.
2ND SISTER	Choi! This kind of time you go and talk about accident. *Tolong*[24] *lah*!

---

[21] Editor's note: Malay: *lah*, '[A] particle emphasising the word to which it is appended' (*A Malay-English English-Malay Dictionary*, ed. A. E. Coope [revised edn.; London and Basingstoke: Macmillan Education, 1991]).

[22] Editor's note: A reference to the Singapore-Cambridge General Certificate of Education 'Advanced' ('A') Levels.

[23] Playwright's note: [*Minnan hua* or *minnan* language:] *Sa ji hu*, 3rd elder brother-in-law.

[24] Editor's note: Malay: *Tolong*, help me, or please.

2ND BROTHER-IN-LAW   I'm just saying in case something happen —

He is noisily shouted down.

Lao Jiu returns.

FATHER   Wah, *gao gia'ng*, Tan *Shifu's*[25] 'Lam Tian Geok' winning, Number One place in the imperial exam also not so *lawak*[26] like you, ah!

Lao Jiu is rather embarrassed at all this love and attention showered on him.

MOTHER   *Hola, hola,*[27] you all go prepare what you want to do. You, *gao gia'ng*, go and study!

FATHER   Wait!

Father turns attention to the ancestral shrine placed right in the middle of the area upstage. With utmost respect and dedication, Father takes Lao Jiu's hand, goes to the shrine, solemnly faces his imagined ancestors, kneels in front of the shrine and starts kowtowing. The others follow, some most obediently, others reluctantly. Yet others step aside and bow instead.

Scene 2: To the Examinations

Lao Jiu is left alone. The thought of having won the candidacy to the Top Achievers Contest thrills him. The gravity of the challenge worries him. To alleviate all this pressure, Lao Jiu tries to relax himself with a series of loosening up exercises. As he does that, his mind gradually drifts into the immediate subjects of study [the sciences], and formulas, and 'questions and answers' come out of Lao Jiu one after another ...

LAO JIU   Science!

Head exercise.

Heat, Pressure, Light, Optics, Sound, Magnetism, Electricity, Quantum Physics, Waves and Particles. Mechanics!

---

[25] Editor's note: Mandarin-Chinese: *Shifu*, master – here used as an honorific, 'Master Tan'.
[26] Editor's note: [Malay:] *lawak*, in this context, not so grand.
[27] Playwright's note: [*Minnan hua* or *minnan* language:] *Hola*, all right.

Goes into kung fu exercise.

> Force, Power, Energy, Potential Energy, Motion, Motion, Motion,
> Motion Picture ... Superman,[28] Mutant Ninja Turtle,[29] Monkey
> King,[30] *Xiaoao Jianghu*,[31] My Left Foot,[32] Uh-uh, Rain Man,[33]
> ET[34] ...

The light and sound gradually transports Lao Jiu into a fantastic-mysterious world. A number of puppets appear, pushing Lao Jiu on towards exam preparation. They begin by sharing with him a Q & A session. Then the tempo develops into a song and dance routine. Finally, the screen transforms into a militaristic drilling session.

PUPPETS   Force, Power, Energy. What is Force?

Lao Jiu answers by repeating a TV commercial.[35] After that, Lao Jiu relaxes a bit.

---

[28] Editor's note: There have been many film versions of the DC Comics *Superman* hero, but this reference is probably to the 1978 version. Richard Donner directed that version, and it starred Christopher Reeve as Superman.

[29] Editor's note: The animated cartoon *Teenage Mutant Ninja Turtles* was made into a film in 1990; it was directed by Steve Barron.

[30] Editor's note: The Monkey King is also known as Sun Wukong, a main character in the epic classical Chinese novel *Journey to the West*. This was published anonymously in the 1590s, during the Ming Dynasty, and its authorship has been ascribed to the scholar Wu Cheng'en. Monkey accompanies the monk Xuanzang on a journey to gain Buddhist sutras from India. The novel has had numerous film and television adaptations made of it.

[31] Editor's note: Mandarin-Chinese: *Xiaoao Jianghu*, literally 'Laughing proudly in the pugilistic world'. This was a martial arts or *wuxia* novel by Jin Yong, first published in 1967. Film adaptations of the novel were made in 1978 (Shaw Brothers, Hong Kong), 1991, 1992 and 1993 (all by Film Workshop, Hong Kong). Various TV adaptations have also been made by studios in Hong Kong, Taiwan, Singapore and mainland China.

[32] Editor's note: *My Left Foot: The Story of Christy Brown* (1989) is the Irish film directed by Jim Sheridan. It starred Daniel Day-Lewis.

[33] Editor's note: *Rain Man* is a 1988 American film drama directed by Barry Levinson. It tells the story of a self-centred yuppie, Charlie Babbitt (Tom Cruise), who discovers that his estranged father has bequeathed his multimillion-dollar estate to his other son, the autistic Raymond (Dustin Hoffman).

[34] Editor's note: *ET* or the *Extra-Terrestrial* is the 1982 American science-fiction film directed by Steven Spielberg.

[35] Editor's note: The reference to the TV commercial in question is not clear.

PUPPETS   Organic Chemistry, Inorganic Chemistry, Physical Chemistry, Salts, Acids, Elements, Carbon, Ammonia ...

Lao Jiu, as he descends to the floor, weakens the kungfu drill, and gradually deviates into his own playful fancies.

LAO JIU   Organic, inorganic, salt and pepper. Acid, vinegar, chilli, ketchup, *belachan*,[36] soya sauce, ammonia, dirty toilet, $150 fine.

Lao Jiu lies on the floor. Forced up by the Puppets, they return to the study track.

PUPPETS   Atomic Theory, Valency, Hydrogen, Nitrogen, Oxygen, Carbohydrates, Amino Acids, DNA ...

LAO JIU   DNA, Deoxyribonucleic acid are the strands on the genetic chain. From the single cell to the homo sapiens, they govern the forms and behaviours of all living things. From the Monkey King to Miss Piggy, no one could escape their dictation and command ...

PUPPETS   (*The Puppets release a barrage of questions revolving around physics, chemistry and biology as they surround and confront him.*)

LAO JIU   (*The confrontation builds up to a rhythmic climax when Lao Jiu, as if tightly cornered, breaks out by yelling at the top of his voice.*) $E = mc^2$! Einstein in heaven, help me come through the first round with flying colours please!

5TH BROTHER-IN-LAW   *Gao gia'ng*, taxi *lailo*!

Time's up. Accompanied by a grand fanfare, Lao Jiu majestically marches out, as if towards the Hall of Fame.

Against the background of shadow play appearing on the cyclorama/backdrop, Lao Jiu's voice is heard —

LAO JIU   Since I am Lao Jiu, the Ninth Born, you can imagine my Mother must be a great bearer of children. That's very true. In my Father's words, 'This woman give children easier than *lao gueh bu*[37] shit eggs. Boot, boot, boot, no stop one ...'

---

[36] Editor's note: Malay: *belachan*, a hot paste made with prawn paste; now spelt as *belacan*.
[37] Playwright's note: [*Minnan hua* or *minnan* language:] *lao gueh bu*, old hen.

But, it's very strange, you know. When it came to my turn, my Mother had a lot of trouble. I was told that, when my birth was due, everybody in the family went along. To help my Mother give birth to me, my *shifu*, Master Tan, came with his monkey and tiger also!

Scene 3: The Beginning of Lao Jiu

About 17 years ago, in a maternity hospital ward. Two nurses come in.

NURSE A	Come and see. You come and see *lah*. Mother and daughter pregnant and give birth same time. I work in maternity ward 20 years, never seen funny thing like this one.
NURSE B	*Wah*, this old Mother really romantic, so many kids already still want to do it.
NURSE A	Not so old *lah*, 40 only. But got eight kids already. She must really like it so much.
NURSE B	*Alamak*,[38] eight already still not enough, ah?
NURSE A	All girls *lah, tak boleh tahan*[39] what!
NURSE B	*Alamak*, eight already still want to bet ah? *Susah*,[40] man, if come another girl?
NURSE A	That's why she so nervous *lah*. Don't know whether she afraid or shy. *Mati*[41] also refuse to come in. You listen, her husband and all her children trying to get her in. This is her ninth baby. Her daughter's first one. But she's ten times more nervous than her daughter — really *tak boleh tahan* her. Look, look, coming now. Come and see, come and see.
FATHER	(*Leading the rest.*) *Tolong lah* you. Heh, *ginna*,[42] all shut up! Come in here first, OK? OK, OK, *zabougia'ng*, come in first.

[38] Playwright's note: [Malay:] *Alamak*, expression of surprise.
[39] Playwright's note: [Malay:] *tak boleh tahan*, can't take it.
[40] Playwright's note: [Malay:] *Susah*, difficult.
[41] Playwright's note: [Malay:] *Mati*, die.
[42] Playwright's note: [*Minnan hua* or *minnan* language:] *ginna*, children.

(*Leading his pregnant first daughter.*) OK, sit here first, sit. Eh? How come Ah Leng not here? *Gan ni nia'ng e*, he think becoming Father so easy, ah! Wife give birth also, don't want to come. Ah *Si*, Ah *Gor*,[43] come help your big Sister! (*In come seven girls wearing pyjamas, aged five to 20.*) Eh, all you *ginna* get out. Small, small ones get out. Out! Get your *Ma* to come in *lah*! *All little ones chased out.*

Come on Ah Lian,[44] come in *lah*. No problem *lah*. I tell you! Eight come out already, why you scared this one! Like you say what boot, boot, boot — like shitting eggs, simple like that. Five years no baby now you nervous, ah? Hey, you *ginna* all get out! Ah *Li*, Ah *Sa*,[45] go help your big Sister, *tolong lah*! Come on Ah Lian. Come, come. (*At last, the Mother is persuaded into the room.*)

MOTHER	I don't want, I don't want. Sure another girl. I don't want. Take me home. I want to go home!
FIRST DAUGHTER	*Aiyah*, *Ma*, don't be like that *lah*. This is my first time you know. You like that make me so nervous! *Alamak*, why Ah Leng[46] still not here. *Aiyah*, painful, *Ba*, painful! ...
FATHER	Call missy. Eh, call doctor! You, one of you go and call doctor! *Aiyah*, *ginna* get out!
MOTHER	Don't want, don't want. I know this another girl one. They all say another girl. They all say my stomach round one. *Tolong lah*. Ah *Ba*, go *tolong* doctor take my baby out. Don't want to give birth *lah*! Sure another girl one!

Nurses A and B come in to help get first daughter into the inner room. Then they wheel in another bed to try and get Mother in. Mother gets hysterical. Between persuading Mother to go in and shouting at the children to get out, Father is in near hysterics.

---

[43] Editor's note: *Minnan hua* or *minnan* language: Ah *Si*, Ah *Gor*, Number four, number five. This refers to Father's fourth and fifth daughters.

[44] Editor's note: Ah Lian. The given name of one of the daughters.

[45] Editor's note: *Minnan hua* or *minnan* language: Ah *Li*, Ah *Sa*, Number two and number three. This refers to Father's second and third daughters.

[46] Editor's note: Ah Leng. The given name of one of the daughters.

FATHER   *Aiyah*, Ah Lian, *lu*[47] *gila*,[48] *lu*! How can take out now! Hey, you *ginna* get out ...

Suddenly, framed behind a hospital blanket, a puppet performance appears. Accompanied by exciting percussion music, the Monkey King beats back the Tiger chasing after a pregnant woman, warning it that expecting mothers must never be offended.

The children are very amused. As they cheer and applaud, Master Tan comes out of the improvised stage.

FATHER   *Ginna* get out! Kong Nam *hia'ng*.[49] So good you are here this time. Some more longer like this, I take her to Woodbridge Hospital[50] also.

Mother still crying.

MASTER   Eh, this time you are finally going to get a boy. You know, in the Tang Dynasty, this great General Guo Ziyi,[51] he had seven sons and eight daughters. In the end, he had a fantastic reunion of the whole family before he died happily, laughing 'Hahaha' as he swallowed his last breath. Now, you have already got eight daughters, so you are sure to get eight sons-in-law. This time, I guarantee you'll have a son. So you should be very happy. Hahaha. Why so nervous? I tell you, you keen on working very, very hard. In six years, you will also get seven sons. Then you can also laugh like the great General Guo Ziyi, 'Ha ha ha' very lucky! Of course you don't have to die like him.

MOTHER   This round one ... again stomach round one ... they all say girl again.

---

[47] Editor's note: [*Minnan hua* or *minnan* language:] *lu*, you.
[48] Playwright's note: [Malay:] *gila*, mad.
[49] Playwright's note: [*Minnan hua* or *minnan* language:] *hia'ng*, brother.
[50] Editor's note: In 1951, during the colonial era in Singapore, the Mental Hospital was renamed Woodbridge Hospital. The hospital still exists, as part of a larger institution called the Institute for Mental Health.
[51] Editor's note: Guo Ziyi (697–781) was formally Prince Zhongwu of Fenyang. He was immortalised posthumously as the God of Wealth and Happiness.

MASTER   Who said it's a round one? I've told you already so many times. Your stomach this time is definitely a pointed one. But this one is not the usual pointed one. This rounded one is also a bit pointed. You don't believe? OK, let me ask you. Remember Ah Lim's wife end of the street? Remember her? Everyone was saying her stomach was pointed one; sure give birth to boy. And remember what I said? I said No, I said that woman's stomach was a pointed one. But not the usual pointed one, pointed but also a bit rounded. And what happened? She got a girl! She gave birth to a girl, right or not?

Also, let me remind you, you have given birth to eight girls already. Did I ever say you were going to have a boy? Never! I never said one. Why? Because I knew you were going to get a girl every time. But this time different. This time I know for sure it's a boy. Take my word for it. Not only the shape of your stomach say so, but also your hand. It's written in your palm. Look here, eight girls and then a boy! Both your hands say the same thing. This is going to be a boy, I guarantee!

MOTHER   Ah, ah ...

Labour pains begin. Father gets help from the nurses and his family to get Mother into the inner room.

Children are chased out. Mother is taken into the labour ward. The two men wait.

MASTER   Look, Ah Chng, look at your hand. Eight daughters, one son, all written here. Mm, I think your son is going to be very clever, very successful. *Wah*, Ah Chng, ah, you're like that demigod Lord Li who carries a pagoda in his hand — his son, Nezha, people call the wonder boy Third Prince Nezha — his son was also born when Lord Li was quite old.[52]

FATHER   You know *lah*, Kong Nam *hia'ng*, of course I want a boy. But if god give me girl again I also happy. Eh, you better not make me

[52] Editor's note: The Third Prince Nezha is a child-divinity who also is known by other names such as the Jade Emperor's Princely Lord. In popular legend, Nezha was one of the generals who attended the Jade Emperor, and who later descended to earth as the third son of Li Jing, the Celestial King Tuota. Nezha later became a martial deity relied upon to exorcise demonic forces.

very happy now and then another girl come I *kena*[53] lose, *jin cham*![54]

Sounds of new born baby.

MASTER   Listen. *Wah*, your son cries so loud, good voice!

FATHER   *Alamak* so quick one. Like I say *lah*, easy like old hen shitting eggs.

Nurse comes in.

FATHER   Missy, that one boy or girl? Boy or girl?

NURSE   Girl, six pounds three.

Father so shocked he nearly cried.

MASTER   (*Stunned, immediately starts calculating with his fingers.*) Cannot be, cannot be.

FATHER   (*Affected by Master.*) Cannot be. Cannot be.

NURSE   What you mean cannot be?

FATHER   (*Only now the truth has registered.*) Alamak. I lose, *jin cham*!

NURSE B   (*As she enters.*) The Father here?

NURSE A   This one *lah*.

NURSE B   You sure? So old one.

NURSE A   *Aiyah*, mind your own business. Young or old also Father what!

MASTER   (*Notices something in the nurses' conversation.*) Hey, excuse me. Can you tell us again: Who gave birth just now? Who is the Mother?

NURSE A   That one lor, that Mrs ...

NURSE B   That one Mrs Tan *lah*, Tan Ah Lam.

_____

[53] Editor's note: [Malay:] *kena*, in this context, to suffer or to incur.
[54] Playwright's note: [*Minnan hua* or *minnan* language:] *jin cham*, very sorrowful.

FATHER   *Alamak*, that one my daughter's baby. That one my daughter's
                            girl, not my wife one. My daughter's girl. Wah, I'm Grandfather
                            now, Kong Nam *hia'ng*. I'm Grandfather now! Eh, eh, eh. How
                            about my wife? Her baby already come out or not? My wife, the
                            old woman one?

NURSE A   *Aiyah*, you keep quiet *lah*. So old already still so impatient. Wait *lah*.

Both nurses go back to inner room.

*Both men wait nervously outside. More so than before. Master Tan's confidence, although
salvaged, is somewhat suppressed. Presently, again a new born baby's cry is heard. This
time neither man dares to respond promptly. Staring at the door, both approach it cau-
tiously, anticipating the nurses to appear with good news.*

NURSE A   (*Out, at long last.*) You Mr Chng? Eight pound one. Boy.

*Father first jumps with joy, then calms down, then falls onto his knees, kowtows, sobs
silently. Master Tan also overcome with emotions.*

MASTER   See, what did I tell you? What did I tell you?

FATHER   (*Suddenly jumps up to grab Master's hand.*) I won, I won! Kong
                            Nam *hia'ng* I won!

MASTER   Yah, I know you won, you've finally got a son.

FATHER   Not that *lah*. I bet $200 with my friends if my wife give me a son.
                            I won, I won! (*Remembering the children outside, rushes out.*)
                            Eh, you *zabouginna*, your *Ma* got a son. You got a brother now!

The girls all rush in shouting and jumping with joy with their Father. Pandemonium.

NURSE A   Eh, eh, eh! Go out, out. Your wife we will take to the ward. You
                            all go and wait there.

Master Tan herds the children out.

FATHER   *Gan ni nia'ng e*, how come *zabougia'ng* husband still not here. He
                            think becoming Father so simple, ah, *gan ni nia'ng e*!

*As Father leaves, Nurse A also returns to the inner room. The telephone rings and there is
a series of enquiries all directed at Mother Chng's outcome — in various languages.*

NURSE A   Who? Mrs Chng, ah? Gave birth already. Eight pounds one. Boy.
                            (*Another call.*) Eh? Yah, gave birth already. Eight pounds one. Boy.
                            (*Another call.*) Yah, boy, eight pounds one. Yah, yah, boy — yah.

Then, impatiently, she rings up the operator.

> *Oi*, operator, *apa macam ini*,[55] ring, ring, ring, this Mrs Chng got friends ring ring ring never stop. How to work like that? Eh, why don't you go and ring up Radio Singapore[56] and get Lee Dai Soh, Ong Toh or Ng Chia Keng to tell everyone the story. Tell them that woman after giving birth to eight girls now finally got a boy. Yah, boy! One pound eight!

As she slams down the phone, the finale of Tchaikovsky's '1812 Overture' is heard. The grand celebration.

Lao Jiu's voice, against the shadow play.

LAO JIU   My Father once said, before I came to this world, he was like a lonely rooster, locked in a cage filled with old and young hens. Gok-gok-geh, gok-gok-geh, *beh tahan*[57] man!

And according to my Mother, after I was born, the lone cockerel in the family all of a sudden became a family man. Every day, after work, he would immediately come home, pick me up then start parading me around the neighbourhood, showing off the new prize he had won with $200.

Scene 4A: Into Good Form

Members of the Chng Family parade onto the stage. They then seat themselves down, waiting in solemn anticipation.

2ND BROTHER-IN-LAW   Of course you want everything to go well. But what if they don't? You collect water on rainy day, then you'll get water when the dry days arrive.

---

[55] Playwright's note: [Malay:] *apa macam*, what's the matter?
[56] Editor's note: Television broadcasting only began in Singapore in 1961, and was organised separately from Radio Singapore until 1965, when Radio Television Singapore was formed.
[57] Playwright's note: [Combination of *minnan hua* or *minnan* language and Malay:] *beh tahan*, can't take it.

2ND SISTER	*Aiyah*, you, good things also turn bad because you always talk about bad things happening.
2ND BROTHER-IN-LAW	That's what insurance is for what! You prepare for the worst, then you can enjoy the best. If you want to enjoy longevity, you must first prepare to die young!
2ND SISTER	Choi, choi, choi, enough *lah* you! Ah *Ma*, this basket of *kueh* you keep *lah*. Some *dao sa*,[58] some peanut, some coconut and some lotus seed one. You give *gao gia'ng* in turns so he doesn't get fed up.
4TH BROTHER-IN-LAW	Today I put in some almond flavour. This *hengjin*[59] flavour I only give to restaurant orders. You cannot get in hawker centre.

Fanfare, Lao Jiu returns. Very exhausted, slumps into a seat. He is immediately subject to everyone's queries about how he did in the first round.

7TH SISTER	Wah, nine to five, how many papers did you do altogether?
8TH SISTER	There's only one paper. Five hundred questions? He completed 487.
7TH SISTER	*Wah*! Five hundred questions ah?
4TH SISTER	Why not finish all 500?
6TH SISTER	Are you crazy or what? You think doing those questions like you grind the soyabean, any amount also can go in ah? Got to do one by one, you know!
3RD BROTHER-IN-LAW	On the record, no one had ever finished all 500. It's considered quite good if you could complete 400.
5TH BROTHER-IN-LAW	Eh, anyone finished more than you?
LAO JIU	The next highest is 486.

---

[58] Playwright's note: [Cantonese-Chinese:] *dao sa*, Cantonese bean paste.
[59] Editor's note: *Minnan hua* or *minnan* language: *hengjin*, almond. Thanks to Chan Cheow Thia and Jeff Chen.

5TH SISTER	*Wah, gao gia'ng* Number One!
3RD SISTER	Eh, first day only, don't be so proud. Come, *gao gia'ng* go and eat. Food all warm already.
8TH SISTER	Tomorrow maths. Steven, we go and get more tricky questions for him, want or not?
1ST SISTER	Don't *lah*. I say let him go and sleep. Don't *kachau*[60] him, all of you.
1ST BROTHER-IN-LAW	Don't worry, you. The soundproofing I did for him very good. *Kachau* louder also cannot go in.

Scene 4B: To the Examinations Again

Lao Jiu is at the formulas again.

'Ring ...' The alarm clock sounds.

FATHER	(*Offstage*) *Gao gia'ng*, get up and study *lah*!
MOTHER	(*Offstage*) Let him rest some more *lah*.
FATHER	(*Offstage*) Lam Tian Geok going to the imperial capital already.[61] Wake up, study!

Lao Jiu makes himself alert. Shakes his head, takes some snacks, drinks the soyabean milk, swallows some vitamins.

LAO JIU	Mathematics.
	Algebraic Equations and Topics, Functions, Coordinate Geometry, Trigonometry, Integration, Differentiation, Vectors, Series, Permutations, Combinations, Probability, Distribution, Random Variables, Estimation ...

He begins to jog fast, hips swinging.

---

[60] Playwright's note: [Malay:] *kachau*, disturb.
[61] Editor's note: A reference to the puppet play performed at the very start of this play.

P(1) is true. P(n) is true. P(1 + 1) is true.

$f(a) = R$

$f(x) = x^2 - 2x + 6$

Starts to gesticulate.

the increase in the y coordinate
the increase in the x coordinate

$$\frac{y_2 - y_1}{x_2 - x_1} = \tan O$$

$y = f(x)$

$y > f(x)$ and $y < f(x)$ defines regions of the plane

Puppetry and opera gestures begin to seep in.

The gradient of curve at any given point is defined as the gradient of the tangent to the curve at that point and measures the rate of the increase of *y* with respect to *x*.

a higher, *b* lower, *x* bigger, *y* smaller, the more you beget, the less you share. Boys should study more, girls should beget more.

Pizza Hut Delivery Service, the more you bake, the more you make, the motor cycle more faster, the profit curve shoot higher. 2-3-5-3-5-3-5 ... (*He does a take on a Pizza Hut commercial.*[62])

The Puppets appear. They both partner and push him into a recitative mode, a Q & A dialogue mode, a verbal 'reggae' mode, a song and dance mode, gymnastics movements, kung fu movements, militaristic drilling exercises, tortuous punishments. He is pushed to his physical limit.

PUPPETS   There are four couples and eight seats in a row. How many ways can the couples sit, if:

1. The women and the men must sit alternately:
2. Every couple must be separated;

---

[62] Editor's note: Drawn from a TV advertisement current at the point of the play's first presentation.

3. Couples A and B must sit together;
4. Couple A must sit in the first two seats;
5. Couples A and B must be separated;
6. Each couple must sit together;
7. The man of couple A must sit with couple B;
8. All the women must sit together;
9. The couples must sit in the order of ABCD ...

LAO JIU   ... could A sit a bit this way?

B and C are not very friendly, do they have to sit together?

Why do you have to separate them?

Why do they have to be next to each other?

This is going to encourage extra marital relations.

You sure you want all the women together? You're asking for trouble.

In the end, the puppets push Lao Jiu to the limits.

LAO JIU   (*Yelling out the answer.*) Yes! There are 1,234 ways of sitting! But! The best way to sit is — *anyway they like*!

5TH BROTHER-IN LAW   (*Offstage*) Gao gia'ng! Taxi ready!

Fanfare. Lao Jiu marches away as Mother and 1st Sister come on.

1ST SISTER   Ah Ba leh?

MOTHER   Gone to pray to Buddha.

1ST SISTER   So early in the morning?

MOTHER   He promise Buddha; one hundred days, every morning every night he go and worship. And every first day and 15th day of month he take no meat. He said, 'I must do more good. Ask Buddha to help *gao gia'ng* pass examination.' He said ancestors also happy. You know he never study. Every time he talks about study, he feel sorry. You all cannot go up, you know *lah*, so every day he pray for *gao gia'ng*.

Scene 5: The Fighters

Chng, in his youth, leading groups of fighters through a pugilistic exercise. They are strong and well-disciplined, and evoke much power and strong commitment. Before they can complete the exercise, a member rushes onto the stage, whispers to Chng, reporting the approach of hostile forces.

Chng orders a halt to the exercise. But before they can move off with their weapons and equipment, the rival gang arrives. Forced into combat, Chng's buddies struggle to hold their ground. Finally they cave in and his friends begin to run away. Chng is left confronting three rivals as Master Tan comes to his rescue. Tan's superior kung fu readily frightens the offenders off.

The police whistles are heard. Policemen arrive. Seeing no one seriously hurt, they go away.

FATHER	*Gan ni nia'ng e*! How come you know they attack us?
MASTER	I was reading newspapers in the clan *huiguan*.[63] Ah Sum ran over to tell me.
FATHER	*Gan ni nia'ng e.* He call *mata*.[64]
MASTER	No, the *huiguan* secretary.
FATHER	*Huiguan* secretary? Why lose face like that? We can beat them back! All the time they are so proud we are strong enough …
MASTER	Don't let them cheat you *lah*. They are going to disband the self-defence group, I tell you.
FATHER	What, disband? Then who come and protect us?
MASTER	Call *mata-mata* lo! Eh, Ah Chng, ah, times have changed, don't you see? Everybody's thinking of changing their ways. You cannot live on this being a fighter anymore, you understand?
FATHER	True ah?
MASTER	True.

---

[63] Playwright's note: [Mandarin-Chinese:] *huiguan*, association [or guildhalls].
[64] Playwright's note: [Malay:] *mata*, police.

FATHER	Really true?
MASTER	Why should I lie to you?
FATHER	*Gan ni nia'ng e* ... Then ... What can I do? Last year only clan secretary say we get kung fu teacher from China. And buy more weapon ... and now disband ... Lose face *lah*, *gan ni nia'ng e*! Clan leader all lose face!
MASTER	*Aiyah*, Ah Chng, don't you worry about the leaders. They all know how to change with the time. Except you. You think too simple. You give your life for other people. Now they get other protection and you still don't understand.
FATHER	After disband, what happen to all my friends?
MASTER	There are many ways out.
FATHER	*Gan ni nia'ng e* ... What can I do? Fourteen I come out fight to the clan!

Bares his top, revealing his tattoos.

MASTER	Yah, seven streets up, eight streets down, who doesn't know Ah Chng is the best fighter here!
FATHER	*Gan ni nia'ng e*, don't joke *lah* now. If not fighting, what can I do?
MASTER	Iron fist, iron arm, iron shoulder, can you lift up a 100 *kati*[65] bag of rice?
FATHER	100 *kati*? *Aiyah*, one hand only up my shoulder!
MASTER	Or, if you like, you can come and play puppets with me. I play Lam Tian Geok, you play ...
FATHER	*Tolong-tolong*, my fist beaten like iron already, how to play small puppets like that, I cannot read and sing also.
MASTER	Come on *lah*, don't see yourself so bad.
FATHER	OK, if no more fighting, I go carry rice bags.

---

[65] Editor's note: Malay: one *kati* is equivalent to 1⅓ pounds.

MASTER	OK. Now go and change.
FATHER	What for?
MASTER	Great World.[66]
FATHER	You treat me *makan*[67] and drinks ah?
MASTER	I take you to see someone.
FATHER	Who?
MASTER	A woman.
FATHER	A woman? You play the fool with me?
MASTER	No. A woman to give you for a wife.
FATHER	*Gan ni nia'ng e.* What woman want to marry me.
MASTER	It's your Father's order! Come, let's go!

They dash out.

Scene 6A: Transformation

Master and Father are seen behind a gauze-like sheet, the latter in underpants, his entire body covered with tattoos. Master is doing a body cleansing for him. And then he helps the young man with a set of new clothes, piece by piece, almost like going through a solemn ceremony. As this happens, Grandfather's voice is heard offstage.

GRANDFATHER	*Gan ni nia'ng e*, this bloody fool only know fighting. He can do nothing else. Now defence force go to disband, what can he do? *Gan ni nia'ng e*, give him a woman and see how. People say wife can change a man. Try try *lah*. That pig *degia'ng* end of the street is like that. Wild like mountain pig, once married, all changed.

---

[66] Editor's note: The Great World (early 1930s–1978) was one of three amusement parks built in Singapore before the Second World War. The other two were the Gay World and the New World. The park had an eclectic mix of entertainment options, including cabaret, Chinese operas, cinema film, gaming, sport matches and shopping.

[67] Playwright's note: [Malay:] *makan*, food[, to eat].

But this bloody fool, *gan ni nia'ng*, who wants to marry him? Every time he open mouth, bad language only. Talk three sentence only he ask you to fight. And his tattoo, all over whole body. Old woman see also scared. Young girl sure faint on wedding night. I'm shy even in asking people to introduce him to girls.

Ah Kong Nam, you give him a hand. You move around a lot. Go some place far — Sio Poh, Augang, Geylang, Basi Banjang, Zulong, Lim Zugang, Wulen,[68] even *kampung*[69] also can, go find him a girl.

Anyone is OK as long as she's good and proper, as long as she agree to marry out here. Can't speak our dialect also never mind. Can learn after coming to our family. His Mother is also not *Hokkien* ... Oh, got one in Ang Sa Li[70] ah. Can Ah Kong Nam, you go and see, terms can negotiate. Hot temper also can. Hot temper girl good for him, as long there's no murder on wedding night. But she must know how to cook and do housework. Beautiful or not never mind. Can get ugly wife also lucky for him, *gan ni nia'ng e* this hopeless son.

Scene 7: Father and Son

Lao Jiu, all by himself.

LAO JIU   Ah, third and last day. Thank goodness this will be the last day.

Takes a deep breath, begins to attack the studies.

> *Gu dao, xi feng, shou ma, xi yang xi xia, duan chang ren, zai tian ya ...*[71]

---

[68] Editor's note: *Hokkien* versions or transliterations of or other versions of names of these areas, respectively, in Singapore: Tekka, Hougang, Geylang (this is the same), Pasir Panjang, Jurong, Lim Chu Kang, Woodlands.

[69] Editor's note: Malay: *kampung*, village.

[70] Editor's note: Otherwise known as Serangoon Gardens.

[71] Playwright's note: [Mandarin-Chinese:] *Gu dao, xi feng, shou ma, xi yang xi xia, duan chang ren, zai tian ya ...*, Tang poem, literally meaning: Ancient pathways, West wind, Skinny horses, The setting sun, Heart-broken people, On the edge of the world. Editor's note: See footnote 3. This is probably the text that completes the poem that is recited at the start of the play by Lao Jiu. As pointed out in the earlier note, this is most likely a poem from the Yuan Dynasty, rather than from the Tang Dynasty, as indicated by the playwright. Thanks to Chan Cheow Thia.

Father steals in to observe his precious son at work. It takes a while for Lao Jiu to notice him. Lao Jiu stands up. Both nod, embarrassed silence.

FATHER	Study?
LAO JIU	Yah, study.
FATHER	Hard work?
LAO JIU	OK *lah*.
FATHER	Eat already?
LAO JIU	Yah, plenty.
FATHER	Want any drinks? Ah *Si* brought *dao hueh zui*.[72]
LAO JIU	I had already.
FATHER	Ah *Sa e*?[73]
LAO JIU	The pig brain also ate already.
FATHER	Oh ... Like that you sure get very good marks. (*He picks up a textbook.*) Wah, so heavy.
LAO JIU	This one not so bad. There are heavier ones still.
FATHER	For me, this is heavier than my 100 kati rice bag.
LAO JIU	Once you get used to it, they are not so bad *lah*.
FATHER	(*Timidly flipping a few pages.*) Wah, all *angmo zi*?[74]
LAO JIU	(*Quickly gives him a Chinese text.*) This one's in Chinese.
FATHER	Chinese also I cannot understand many.
LAO JIU	Some are not too difficult. You read the Chinese papers!
FATHER	I read pictures and comics only. The big words I also cannot understand much.
LAO JIU	Never mind, you can listen to the radio news!

---

[72] Playwright's note: [*Minnan hua* or *minnan* language:] *dao hueh zui*, soybean milk.

[73] Editor's note: Father is asking, 'Then, what about what 3rd Sister brought?'

[74] Playwright's note: [*Minnan hua* or *minnan* language:] *angmo zhi*, English words. Editor's note: Literally, red-hair words.

FATHER	Now also very difficult. You know now their *huayu*[75] always *zhi chi shi*,[76] like eating *gana*,[77] sometimes also cannot understand.
LAO JIU	Yah, sometimes they are like that ...
FATHER	... Yah, you can study, that's very good. You know, our family, my side or your Mother side, we never got anybody who can study well. Before never got scholar, now never got anyone go to university. Your Ah *Bui ji*[78] go to Poly, highest one. Can pass or not still don't know ... But you ... you ... everyone hope you can go university! ...

Tan *Shifu*, you know, Ah Kong Nam *beh*[79] (*manipulating his fingers in the way the fortune teller does*). He's very good in this. He say you got good fortune, good future, how to say? ... '*Dayou zuowei*'[80] is it? Big success! He know it before you are born: And in your Mother stomach already he know you are boy.

Last time, very young, I admire your Kong Nam *beh*. Good puppet technique, can read and write, can talk and play. Then he got many shows. Wife and son in *Deng Sua*,[81] he spend everything himself. Very *shiok*.[82] I say, 'Wah, Kong Nam ah, you very smart, everything in your hand ah? Can live like that can do *lah*!' But he said, 'Useless *lah*. You want real success, you really want "*you zuowei*"? Must study!' He say success belong to scholars only! The world all in scholar hands! (*Sings a few lines from* |

[75] Playwright's note: [Mandarin-Chinese:] *huayu*, Mandarin [language].

[76] Editor's note: '*Zhi chi shi* here is used as a shorthand form to describe standard Mandarin pronunciation, which may be difficult to understand for people who hail from the southern parts of China, as Mandarin was adapted from the Beijing dialect in the north, which has a fair amount of retroflexed sounds (卷舌音), as represented by the group of sounds *zhi chi shi*. Hence Lao Jiu's father, who probably is of southern Chinese extract, cannot quite follow the news, as the northern accent of standard Mandarin might sound to him like slurred speech, and is thus alienating for him' (Chan Theow Chia).

[77] Playwright's note: [*Minnan hua* or *minnan* language:] *gana*, dried olive.

[78] Playwright's note: [*Minnan hua* or *minnan* language:] Ah *Bui ji*, 8th Sister.

[79] Editor's note: Mandarin-Chinese: *beh*, an honorific address for male relatives and friends of one's father's generation. Thaks to Chan Theow Chia.

[80] Playwright's note: [Mandarin-Chinese:] *Dayou zuowei*, having excellent potential to succeed.

[81] Playwright's note: *Deng Sua*, [a place in] China.

[82] Editor's note: Malay: *shiok*, or *syok*, pleasant, entrancing.

Lan Tian Yu.) He said, 'If you and I are again born brothers like this, we must go and take examinations like Lam Tian Geok and his blood brother, OK? No more kung fu, no more hand puppet. OK?'

What can I do now? Kung fu cannot feed stomach. He cannot do much also. No one want puppet show nowadays ... Maybe next life *lah* ... Maybe ... *Mai*[83] *kachau lah* ... you study ... I go and sleep ... You study ... um ...

Father leaves.

Scene 7B: Third Exam Offensive

Lao Jiu begins to study again.

LAO JIU   Humanities.

Tries to do some head exercise to relax.

History. Geography. Literature.

(*Tries again.*) Culture. Arts. Ecology.

Still can't get the exercise right. Knocks his own head, strolls a bit. Starts to do feet exercise.

Homer ... Shakespeare ... Du Fu[84]
Dickens ... Li Bai[85] ... Hemingway
Ku teng, lao shu, hun ya, xiao qiao, liu shui, ren jia[86]
Stamford Raffles,[87] Zheng He,[88] Melaka

---

[83] Editor's note: *Minnan hua* or *minnan* language: *Mai*, do not.
[84] Editor's note: Du Fu (712–770) was a major Chinese poet of the Tang Dynasty, which is often considered China's golden age of poetry.
[85] Editor's note: Li Bai, or Li Bo (701–762), also previously known by the transliteration Li Po, was a major Chinese poet, and is regarded as one of the greatest poets during the Tang Dynasty.
[86] Editor's note: Mandarin-Chinese: 'Dried rattan (or withered vines), aged trees, crows at dusk, little bridge, running stream, homestead'; from the poem 'Yearning in Autumn' – see footnote 3.
[87] Editor's note: Sir Thomas Stamford Bingley Raffles (1781–1826), the British statesman who in Singapore is regarded as the official founder, in 1819, of the city-state.
[88] Editor's note: Zheng He (1371–1435), also known as Cheng Ho, is the Hui Chinese admiral who, during the Ming Dynesty, famously commanded voyages to Southeast Asia, South Asia and East Africa.

Shakespeare, Dickens, *Xi feng, shou ma*
xi yang xi xia, duan chang ren,[89] Sang Nila Utama[90]
Environment, birth control, Catch the elephants on Tekong[91] is a must;
Rain forest, pollution, ballerina playing *pipa*;[92]
Hero of the Condors,[93] Julius Caesar's spilling blood;
Big Hole in the ozone layer, come Little Prince
Protect the rose, don't go far;[94]
Lan Tian Yu looking for Shakespeare
Chase the tiger, call me to the Bar;
Old Man gone fishing with Ernest[95]
Marcos is gone,[96] Berlin Wall falling apart;
May so hot, June so rainy, Mooncake festival changed to Christmas.

Lao Jiu gradually finds this game absurdly interesting. Having gotten rid of his inhibitions, Lao Jiu just goes on and on ...

At the height of his enjoyment, the puppet figures drilling him in the study exercises again appear. They direct him into gruelling exercise, drawing out his reserve energy. Finally, he is once again brought into a positive, disciplined frame of mind, ready for another round of exam battles.

PUPPETS   (*Getting him on to the right track.*) History, Geography, Literature, Art, Ecology, Culture.

LAO JIU   New York, Beijing, Jakarta
                   We have the most tranquility by far.

---

[89] Editor's note: Mandarin-Chinese: *Xi feng, shou ma, xi yang xi xia, duan chang ren*, West wind, skinny horses, the setting sun, heart-broken people; a partial continuation of the poem 'Yearning in Autumn' – see footnotes 3 and 76.

[90] Editor's note: Sang Nila Utama was a Srivijayan prince who in 1324 founded the kingdom of Singapura.

[91] Editor's note: Pulau Tekong is one of Singapore's larger outlying islands.

[92] Editor's note: The *pipa* is a four-stringed, lute-like Chinese musical instrument.

[93] Editor's note: A reference to Jin Yong's *wuxia* (or martial arts) novel, *The Legend of Condor Heroes*, first serialised in 1957 in the *Hong Kong Commercial Daily*.

[94] Editor's note: A reference to Antoine de Saint-Exupéry's novella, *The Little Prince* (1943).

[95] Editor's note: A reference to Ernest Hemingway's novel, *The Old Man and the Sea* (1952).

[96] Editor's note: A reference to the former Philippine president, Ferdinand Marcos (1917–1989).

PUPPETS   History, Geography, Literature, Art, Ecology, Culture.

LAO JIU   *Mee siam,*[97] *hei mee,*[98] *rojak,*[99] Bugis Street, *roti perata.*[100]

PUPPETS   Question answer, question answer, question answer.

LAO JIU   You question I answer? I question you answer better *lah*.

PUPPETS   What is energy crisis?

LAO JIU   Energy crisis is petrol price go up. Energy crisis is when exam paper make you gaga.

PUPPETS   What is environment protection?

LAO JIU   Environment protection is sweeter air for the earth; no chopping trees and no smoking car. Also, before you go swimming in the pool, piss everything in the toilet.

PUPPETS   What is women's lib?

LAO JIU   Women's lib is to nurture house husbands. Women's lib is girls no need to wear skirts in office. Women's lib is finding shorter husbands for the wife.

PUPPETS   What is birth control?

LAO JIU   Birth control is the contest between the pill and the condom. Birth control is whether one should hire Filipina maid. Birth control is the SDU part 2.[101] Birth control is yesterday two today one tomorrow don't know.

PUPPETS   What is love?

LAO JIU   Love is patience. Love cannot be explained. Love is pimples. Love is buying flowers on Valentine's Day. Love is lending you study notes.

PUPPETS   What is history?

---

[97] Playwright's note: [Malay:] *mee siam*, vermicelli in spicy sauce.
[98] Playwright's note: [*Minnan hua* or *minnan* language:] *hei mee*, prawn noodles.
[99] Playwright's note: [Malay:] *rojak*, vegetables, dried tofu and pineapple salad.
[100] Playwright's note: [Malay, and Malay derived from Hindustani:] *roti perata*, Indian pancake.
[101] Editor's note: The SDU (Social Development Unit) was a government agency, started in 1984, which worked to create opportunities for single men and women to interact in social settings.

LAO JIU	History is time. History is war. History is the Yellow River. History is big guns. History is Raffles. History is woman's binding cloth. History is a scar. History is *Niucheshui*.[102] History is Tiananmen. History is atom bomb.
PUPPETS	What is art?
LAO JIU	Art is civil and affluent. Art is poetry and painting. Art is frustration venting. Art is getting funny ideas. Art is making something from nothing. Art is 1999. Art is starting from zero. Art is going into the unknown. Art is the innocent child's heart and soul. Art is going hungry sometime.

Lao Jiu falls to the ground.

PUPPETS	Get up. Get up. Get up. Get up.

Lao Jiu struggles to get up. Bombarded by relentless questioning, Lao Jiu is driven into a confused state of mind. The answers become totally muddled. As percussion music helps indicate that the frustration is reaching a climax, Lao Jiu is on the verge of exhaustion.

5TH BROTHER-IN-LAW	*Gao gia'ng*! Taxi *lailo*!

Scene 8: Lao Jiu Is Missing

The entire family is preparing for a feast to mark the end of the examination saga. It is also a relaxation exercise to prepare Lao Jiu for the day-long interview.

FATHER	Hey, *lu xiao*,[103] ah? Cook so much, how can we finish all this?
MOTHER	Cannot finish, take home lo. Everybody happy good enough.
1ST SISTER	*Ba*, all our eight lives, plus you and Ma's two lives, all ten lives we never have so much good luck. Celebrate *lah*! This will make *gao gia'ng* also happy.

---

[102] Playwright's note: [Mandarin-Chinese:] *Niucheshui* [literally, 'bullock cart water'], also known as Telok Ayer [Malay: literally, 'bay water']. Editor's note: This is a reference to Singapore's historic Chinatown district.

[103] Playwright's note: [*Minnan hua* or *minnan* language:] *lu xiao*, are you crazy?

7TH SISTER	*Ba*, you don't know how difficult this exam is. Afterwards like having gone through serious sickness.
FATHER	I know *lah*. Every time I see him study so *gik sim*,[104] I rather go carry rice bags any time.
2ND BROTHER-IN-LAW	But his pay packet in future also very heavy you know?
8TH SISTER'S BOYFRIEND	Not necessary *lah* nowadays. They do computer account transfer, you never see the cash. How heavy also you have to worry.
FATHER	Exam already finish. How come tomorrow more test?
3RD BROTHER-IN-LAW	It's the interview tomorrow. Face to face. Just talking. And there is no way you can prepare for it. I hear that they have as many as ten members on the interview panel. Nine to five, a long day of chit chats. Nothing in particular, but very very wide-ranging. You're not expected to give any stock answers. Very free and casual in format. What they look for is a good feel of the candidate's intellectual strength and breadth of knowledge. They want to test the candidate's manner of response under pressure, his style of conduct, personality and sense of vision.

5th Brother-in-Law, the taxi driver, dashes in.

> *Aiyah*, back already?

But then, he realises that Lao Jiu is not with him. They all then notice 5th Brother-in-Law is in a state of panic.

2ND SISTER	Where *gao gia'ng*?

5th Brother-in-Law shakes his head and hands.

FATHER	*Gao gia'ng* not back with you?
5TH SISTER	You didn't go pick him up?
5TH BROTHER-IN-LAW	No, I did. But cannot find him.
	Everyone is confused. Then 8th Sister and her boyfriend dash in.
8TH SISTER	*Ba, Ma, Ji*,[105] *gao gia'ng* disappeared! *Everyone is shocked.*

---

[104] Playwright's note: [*Minnan hua* or *minnan* language:] *gik sim*, heartache.
[105] Editor's note: [*Minnan hua* or *minnan* language:] *Ji*, Sister.

FATHER	*Lu gila*,[106] *lu*. How can he disappear?
8TH SISTER'S BOYFRIEND	He left the examination hall before completing his paper.
8TH SISTER	First they thought he was going to the toilet. But he never returned.
8TH SISTER'S BOYFRIEND	He finished 42 out of the total 50 questions. He left the paper on the desk, never submitted.
MOTHER	Then where is he? Go and look. You all go and look for him! Go!
FATHER	No head no tail, where to go and find him? Think where he will go?

In the middle of this confusion, Junior War Horse enters.

JUNIOR HORSE	Members of the Zhuang family. It is with deep regret that we have found candidate Zhuang Youwei has deserted the examination without a proper excuse. Though he has completed 42 of the 50 questions, this remains a very serious breach of the rules, highly disadvantageous to his selection. On behalf of the War Horse Foundation, I hereby give you notice that should he breach further rules, such as arriving late for or absenting himself from tomorrow's grand interview, he would then be disqualified from the contest altogether. It is hoped that the Zhuang family takes this seriously.

He turns to go.

FATHER	Mr Junior Horse, please, do you know where Youwei has gone to?
JUNIOR HORSE	Would I have come to you if we knew where he's gone to? No, we don't. But according to people who, saw him leave, he had walked into the hills ... Did you, anyone of you, give him any pressure? ... We were told he was muttering something as he walked away. Like as if he was singing, some funny tune. We suggest you act immediately to save the situation.

Junior Horse leaves. Everyone is at a loss. They look to Father for decision. The old man sinks into deep thought. Suddenly, he realises something —

FATHER	*Aiyah*! ... Yah! ... I go, look for him.

Exits.

---

[106] Playwright's note: [Malay:] *gila*, mad.

Scene 9: Master and Father

Father and Master Tan are both doing a kung fu routine. Master Tan excels in the school of 'internal-soft formed kung fu'. Father excels in the school of 'external-hard formed kung fu'. They complete their routines almost at the same time.

FATHER	Long time no practice.
MASTER	Should practise regularly. Don't wait for age to catch up on you, like me, when your body does not obey your head anymore.
FATHER	Funny, so long no exercise, can still remember.
MASTER	Things you put in lots of practice never really get lost.
FATHER	... Kong Nam *hia'ng*. You tell him, go back with me.
MASTER	You know the boy's temper very well. Do you think he would listen to me?
FATHER	But you know, this is so good an opportunity. Must not miss! We can try and try and try, another 18 lives also cannot get another chance like this.
MASTER	Yes. He is even more clever than Lam Tian Geok. Lam Tian Geok captured first place in all-China. *Gao gia'ng* may become the best in the world.
FATHER	Yah *lah*. We cannot allow him to run away.
MASTER	But I didn't get him to come here, you know.
FATHER	Yah, you also don't ask him to go back!
MASTER	He has been here half a day, but he hasn't said one word to me. Not one word. When he talked to you just now, it was the first time he said anything.
FATHER	What he did all day?
MASTER	... He watched me playing music. He played with the puppets. He slept. In his sleep he cried, and talked, and sang ... He slept without much peace ...
FATHER	You go and tell him to go home. He always listen to you from very young.

MASTER	He liked me because he like the puppets. He liked it since he was very very little ... Pity there is no time left ...
FATHER	Just now he said he's not going back to exam. He said he wants to stay here, live here for a few days. You know?
MASTER	No, I don't know. He hasn't told me.
FATHER	What's happened to him, uhh? Chance so good, people can't get in 18 lives, how come he can give up just like that?
MASTER	He's very disturbed in the heart.
FATHER	All the family run in run out every day. This foundation spend so much money and time to give him chance, why is he so unreasonable and crazy, uhh?
MASTER	*Gao gia'ng* is a very perceptive boy. If only I had a pupil like him.

Father senses something in the Master's words.

MASTER	What he sees he remembers. What he practises, he does well. Other kids play with it because they thought it's fun. He's different. He puts his heart and soul into it.
FATHER	In your heart you want him to do that, right?
MASTER	We had not spoken one word to each other before you came over.
FATHER	Hmm! I remember a long time ago you ask him to learn your act. Yah, you also want him to be your foster son, take over your kung fu, pass on your act.
MASTER	That was a joke we shared when he was a little boy.
FATHER	This is a joke you are doing, now. Make him come here middle of his big exam.
MASTER	*Aiyah*! I am almost out of work, how can I drag him into this hopeless business?
FATHER	That's what I say. You are almost out of work. Why do you pull him down to sink with you together?
MASTER	(*Deeply provoked.*) Yes, I had wanted to have a son here.
FATHER	But I have only one son myself, you know?

MASTER	Yes, I had wanted to get a talented pupil.
FATHER	You want pupil to carry on your act. We don't want son to carry on our family line?
MASTER	But my act will not be passed on!
FATHER	How much longer can we live? Your act, pass on or not, what so important? How can you gamble with the boy's future?
MASTER	But my act will not be passed on even if I want to!
FATHER	Who want to see your act nowadays? Pass on for what? My Chng family has only this one scholar, why do you try to take him away from us?
MASTER	I have at the most ...
FATHER	I am fated to be a *pai gia'ng*[107] ...
MASTER	At the most ...
FATHER	Even if everything go well ...
MASTER	Two years at the most ...
FATHER	(*Beginning to hear the Master's words.*) ... What?
MASTER	How can you think I want to pull the boy into the water and sink with me!
FATHER	Kong Nam *hia'ng*, you say again! ...
MASTER	You are right. Nobody want to see this kind of act anymore.
FATHER	What you mean ... two years! ...
MASTER	My throat ... the doctor say ...
FATHER	Two years! ...
MASTER	... Enough *lah* ...
FATHER	You! ...

---

[107] Playwright's note: [*Minnan hua* or *minnan* language:] *pai gia'ng*, gangster. Editor's note: Literally, 'bad child'.

MASTER	Earlier or later, not much different, isn't it! Nobody want to see anymore ... (*Firmly recovering.*) OK, now we come back to *gao gia'ng*!
FATHER	... What I mean is ... don't spoil his future.
MASTER	Of course, cannot spoil his future. But, do you know why he is here! ... You have seen, right! Did you notice there was dark cloud between his eyebrows! The boy is still very young. I have not seen him for only a few months, why is he so unhappy!
FATHER	I also feel very funny. Everything going so nicely, why he run away from examination halfway and come here!
MASTER	Many things in this world are funny. Don't think we can understand everything. This afternoon I had another round of severe pain. I sat down to meditate. Somehow, I had a feeling something was going to happen, someone was coming. I started to play my flute. And then, during the worst moment of my pain, suddenly, I saw *gao gia'ng* walk in. Ah! I said to myself, my best friend's son had come to save me!
FATHER	What? *Gao gia'ng* can cure people?
MASTER	He didn't say anything. He started to play with the puppets. He was really enjoying himself. And I was so happy. And my pain started to go away. He was so deeply immersed in the puppets, so much feelings he put in ...
FATHER	You still want him to stay ... right?
MASTER	You must not think he had come over because of me. No. I don't think he was even seeing me. He had come for the puppets, the music. The puppets came alive in his eyes. I don't know. I don't know myself, why he had to come. You must see, the boy's dark cloud between the eyes are too heavy. You must allow him to let go a bit. As for me, don't worry, I knew this boy would go very far a long, long time ago. He's so good, what good is there for him to come and sacrifice for me? ... Nobody want to see anymore ... What's the use of learning it ...

Lao Jiu's shadow is cast on the rear screen, playing with hand puppets. Mysterious music expresses the nature of his wondering heart. The old men are fascinated.

Scene 10: The Kin

The couples parade on, speaking as they enter.

1ST SISTER	You don't shout to him. *Gao gia'ng* don't like tough talk.
1ST BROTHER-IN-LAW	Talk about him and I want to spit fire! Everybody spend so much money, so much time. And he say stop he stop! If he's my son, slap, slap, slap also cannot kill my anger!
1ST SISTER	Don't be funny, I tell you!
2ND SISTER	Cook, cook, cook, everything was for nothing now!
2ND BROTHER-IN-LAW	I told you all of you should buy accident insurance. No one want to listen. Now everything lost, and no compensation
2ND SISTER	Compensation your head. All because you always talk about bad things. I tell you, wait you talk about good things. Don't talk insurance or compensation, hear or not?
3RD SISTER	All my pig brains wasted. And you, if you want to talk, don't be so long-winded.
3RD BROTHER-IN-LAW	The boy is too smart. Don't imagine anyone could win him over in talking. I don't think anyone, except me, could even carry on an argument with him.
4TH BROTHER-IN-LAW	Talking with him like this is wasting time. He's very stubborn. When he want to do something, very difficult to change his mind.
4TH SISTER	Don't talk if you don't have important thing to say. We just give *Ba* and *Ma* support *lah*.
5TH BROTHER-IN-LAW	Morning drive over, afternoon drive back, now night also go and talk, talk, talk. Like this when I go make money?
5TH SISTER	*Aiyah*, long long time once only, why you grumble so much? I also take off from factory what!
5TH BROTHER-IN-LAW	That's the trouble. You off, I also off, how to make money?
5TH SISTER	Long long time only what. How many family got clever boy like my Brother, hmm?

6TH SISTER'S FIANCE	This Brother of yours really too much, man. Today this, tomorrow that. If he carries on like this any longer, my whole sales schedule is going to be upset.
6TH SISTER	You want to get a lot of course you have to give a lot. You don't complain about him like that. In future you will have many things you need his help. I tell you!
6TH SISTER'S FIANCE	You don't say first. If he goes on like this, most likely he would need my help.
6TH SISTER	That's why we must go and persuade him, lor!
7TH SISTER	If you don't want to go it's OK.
7TH SISTER'S FIANCE	The thing is, why does everyone want to get him to change his mind?
7TH SISTER	But do you know how much is at stake for the family? Especially for Father. It's not just his own personal problem any longer.
7TH SISTER'S FIANCE	You Chinese people are really funny.
7TH SISTER	Don't talk nonsense. Keep going!
8TH SISTER'S BOYFRIEND	Every time he's like that. Do, not-do, do, not-do. Fed up!
8TH SISTER	But he's never been like this. And exam has never been a problem for him, you know!
8TH SISTER'S BOYFRIEND	But he's never struggled so hard before.
8TH SISTER	Yah, and he's never been expected to perform well before!

Scene 11: Master and Pupil

Night. Lao Jiu is playing with the Monkey King puppet, accompanied by animated music. He is deeply engrossed in performance. His shadow is cast on the rear screen.

Master Tan, by a table at the front of the stage, is packing up a number of puppets. Lao Jiu's behaviour puts him into a reflective mood.

Lao Jiu comes on to talk to the Master. Seeing him in such a state, Lao Jiu hesitates.

MASTER	*Gao gia'ng*, these heads and these tape recordings, you keep them well. I made them all. I painted them all. Maybe you can make an exhibition one day.

Lao Jiu is overcome with great joy in being given the puppets. He brings them out, admires them, plays with them.

LAO JIU	*Shifu*, which do you like best?
MASTER	Lam Tian Geok.
LAO JIU	Why Lam Tian Geok?
MASTER	Because he studied very hard; he has great determination; he is a very honourable man. And you?
LAO JIU	The Monkey King.
MASTER	Why the Monkey King?
LAO JIU	Because he could transform into many different things. Forever changing into new things.
MASTER	Do you think he is really that great?
LAO JIU	Why not? He could fly into the clouds; he could transform into just about anything he wants to; in each somersault he could travel across 108,000 miles.
MASTER	He could transform into just about anything? Actually, he has only 72 transformations. And sometimes he couldn't even hide his tail nicely. And even when he somersaults 108,000 miles he still cannot transcend the palm of the Buddha.
LAO JIU	(*Sensing something serious the Master's voice.*) *Shifu*, is there something you want to tell me?
MASTER	Yes, my child, go home.
LAO JIU	*Shifu ...*
MASTER	It's all right for young people to have dreams. But you must wake up quickly.
LAO JIU	If that's the way you think, why did you let me stay?
MASTER	Because I saw heavy clouds between your eyebrows. Because you have serious frustrations needing resolution.

LAO JIU	Do I still have them now?
MASTER	Yes.
LAOJIU	Would it get better if I go home and return to the exams?
MASTER	Not necessarily.
LAO JIU	Then please allow me to stay a while longer.
MASTER	... OK, you stay.
LAO JIU	Thank you, *Shifu*.
MASTER	I'll go.
LAO JIU	*Shifu*, *Shifu*! This art you have practised all your life, don't you want to pass it on?

Lao Jiu's question comes so suddenly that both are stunned.

	Shifu, I really want to learn it.
MASTER	... Why do you want to learn it?
LAO JIU	Because I like it. Because ... because ... *Shifu*, why did you want to learn it when you were young?
MASTER	Because our family was very poor; we have to find food ... I was only 12 then.
LAO JIU	Just to find food?
MASTER	Of course, all kids like to play. But the master wouldn't teach me anything in the beginning. You want to learn, you steal it. The glove puppets are very good fun. The fighting is fantastic. Not only with weapons, but they can change costumes as they fight on ... Kids can only see the fun in the fighting, very exciting, but they don't understand the *qiankun* universe behind it ...[108]
LAO JIU	The *qiankun* universe behind it?

[108] Editor's note: The *qiankun* is usually translated as 'heaven and earth', and are taken as a binary pairing. *Qiankun* are often associated (and seem synonymous) with the the *yin* and *yang* trigram symbols of the *ba gua* (literally meaning 'eight symbols', and are eight diagrams used in Taoist cosmology to represent the fundamental principles of reality), an ancient divination system known as *Yiching*.

MASTER   A tiny little glove puppet allows endless transformations: You move the hands, you roll up the sleeves, you tidy up the head-dress, you strike a posture. When you walk, you distinguish between the young man *xiaosheng*, the old man *laosheng*, the young lady *huadan*, the old woman *laodan*.[109] You stand, you sit, you swing around, you lie down. You drink tea, you write, you play kung fu ... endless changes bang, bang, bang. When you've learnt all the secrets, you would then understand that what is fantastic is not the puppets, but the hand behind the puppets. Whatever greatness you show, it comes from the hand, behind the puppet. Hand puppets mean just that-puppets handled by hand; the whole *qiankun* universe in my hand! What is so great about the Monkey King with all his fantastic transformations? When I withdraw my hand, he becomes a helpless puppet.

LAO JIU   Everything's in your hand ...

MASTER   (*Beginning to fantasise.*) Dozens of puppets lined up in a row. When the music comes to a crescendo I stretch out my hand, I open my throat, the entire world comes to my command. I can make them cry. I can make them laugh. I can make this character the winner. I can make the other character the loser. Behind the veiled curtain, I control all the players on stage, and all the spectators in the theatre. They laugh when I make them laugh; they cry when I make them cry. In the '40s and '50s, I can make four, even five, performances every day. It was a wonderful time!

                      And then, the world started to change. People became more interested in seeing films, and television. And they even begin to use recordings for their worships and rituals. My glove puppets began to stop moving. And then I begin to understand there are other hands behind my hand. I play the puppets, they play me; I laugh when they want to make me laugh, I cry when they want to make me cry ...

LAO JIU   Have you ever taken pupils?

MASTER   Not one of them made any good. In our days, we must learn and work very hard for three to four years before we graduate. Now,

---

[109] Editor's note: These are four role types in traditional Chinese theatre.

people think this is too long, can't be bothered ... At first I can't be bothered also: you don't want to learn, OK, go away, don't waste my time! But as I get older, as I perform less and less, I long more and more for a good, serious pupil ... I have been living in it for over 50 years, you know! ... The last few years, my hands started trembling ... my throat has got ... sometimes, late at night, maybe in my dreams, I see people coming to learn from me, and all the puppets begin to come alive again. They dance, they sing, they fight, they somersault ...

LAO JIU

Shifu, I feel as if I am in all this ...

MASTER

To tell you the truth, I have always wanted to take you up as my pupil since you were a child. You have good hands, good head, good heart ... But you are also the only son of the family. And you study so well. What's the use in learning this — something which people don't even want to see for free in the streets ... No harm if you just play it for fun. Very bad if you take it seriously.

LAO JIU

Why very bad?

MASTER

Your parents, your whole family, don't you know what high hopes they have for you?

LAO JIU

I know.

MASTER

Then, how can you just say you don't care? Do you know what you are giving up?

LAO JIU

I know.

MASTER

Do you know how this would disappoint your parents and your whole family?

LAO JIU

I know.

MASTER

Do you know that this is the kind of opportunity which thousands of people dream of but can never get?

LAO JIU

I know.

MASTER

Then why do you still do it?

LAO JIU

I don't know.

MASTER

What?

LAO JIU	All I want to do now is to come and learn glove puppetry from you.
MASTER	My puppets are not working anymore. *Gao gia'ng!* Your *qiankun* universe is in your own hands. 'Everything in this world is lowly. Learning is the only lofty pursuit.' I am lowly, you are lofty!
LAO JIU	*Shifu,* I don't understand.
MASTER	'There are golden houses in the books and scholarship leads you to bureaucracy', *gao gia'ng.* In the olden time it was true for Lam Tian Geok; in the modern time it is still true for you.
LAO JIU	I can learn any time I want to. But the point is learning for what?
MASTER	*Aiyah, gao gia'ng,* you are surrounded by blessings and you don't know what blessings are!
LAO JIU	What do you mean?
MASTER	After primary school, you go to high school; after high school, you go to university. If you win the War Horse Foundation contest, you can go on studying — everything is all laid out for you. Isn't that a blessing?
LAO JIU	Like keeping a pet; morning feed and then afternoon feed, and then evening feed!
MASTER	Eh, how can you talk like that?
LAO JIU	Everything is prepared for you, isn't it like keeping pets? *Shifu,* let's face it: Compare yourself and me — you are more fortunate than I am. You know what you're doing ...
MASTER	Yes, I know, I know I am walking step by step into the coffin! *Gao gia'ng,* come on, why don't you wake up?
LAO JIU	*Shifu,* you don't understand ... You know, there is a young man in Japan. He avoids the proper highway to walk on dirty road; he avoids the staircase to climb walls; he's always looking for difficult mountains to scale, swims across rivers which are considered wild. Finally, he decided to cross the North Pole alone on sledge. He never made it and no one has seen him again ... Must be dead by now ... But, *Shifu,* in a way he is like you — you hold your own world in your own hands.

MASTER   It is very easy for kids who have never tasted defeat to fall into all kinds of fanciful daydreams. *Gao gia'ng*, why can't you appreciate all the hopes and sacrifices your parents and relatives have for you?

LAO JIU   I do, I do appreciate! I have known my family's hopes for me ever since I was a little child. *Ba* and *Ma* have never been to school. 1st, 2nd and 3rd Sisters never finished primary school; 4th, 5th, 6th and 7th Sisters never finished their 'A' Levels. 8th Sister is in Poly but there is no guarantee she would graduate. I know all that, I have heard them hundreds and thousands of times before. Can I think about something else now? Please?

The Sisters and Brothers-in-Law and Sisters' Boyfriends are heard yelling at Lao Jiu as they parade on stage.

ALL   (*Offstage.*) *Gao gia'ng*, Don't-do-it!

Scene 12: Persuasion

All the Sisters and their men rush out in procession.

ALL   Don't do it! *Gao gia'ng*, you mustn't give up! You cannot give up this golden opportunity!

1ST SISTER   *Gao gia'ng*, you know *Dua ji*[110] cannot speak nicely. But I am also a Mother. My Ah Kiau was born same year same month same day and five minutes before you. Every Father and Mother want their children to come out better than other's children. No Father and Mother will see their son give up chance like this and keep quiet ... (*To husband.*) You talk *lah* now!

1ST BROTHER-IN-LAW I also like playing the fool when I was a boy — *layang*, *goli*, *tikam*, *kasing*, fighting fish, polka, mahjong, everything. Now I work as contractor. I tell you all those playthings never any use for my job. They don't earn you any money. Now emergency time for exam, why you want to fool around with these useless puppets? If you are my son, I tell you — (*Stopped by 1st Sister.*)

---

[110] Playwright's note: *Dua ji*, elder sister.

2ND BROTHER-IN-LAW	*Gao gia'ng*, do you know why insurance companies never like to sell policies to people over 55? Because they normally only live another 20 years or so. And why do they prefer young people? Because they will live a long long time. Now this is simple statistics, right? Same thing: If you get scholarship from War Horse Foundation, your success rate would be 99.9 per cent. If you play puppets, your success rate would be 0.01 per cent. See, this the same as insurance law —
2ND SISTER	OK *lah*, OK *lah*, your insurance! *Gao gia'ng*, whatever you say, *Li ji*[111] and *Li ji hu*[112] only have one meaning to tell you: You must get opportunity to study hard. Study hard, right?
ALL	*Right!*
3RD BROTHER-IN-LAW	*Gao gia'ng*, let me tell you something very private today. Frankly, I really envy you. I am even a bit jealous of you. Well, among all of us here I can be considered well educated although I have never been to a university. But I've finished my TTC[113] — I'm tertiary educated! But although I am a teacher, and I can talk loudly in front of my students, I tell you: I'm just another employee; I teach strictly according to the planned curriculum. I don't have much choice, you know. To study for a degree? In theory yes. But where to get the money? And my English may not be good enough. To change career? Easy to talk, but what can I do? Contractor? Insurance? Hawker? Drive a taxi? Marketing? Computers? Or what? You know, *gao gia'ng*, when you make the right choice, you will be more freer than I am — many many opportunities. How can you give up like this?
ALL	Yes, *gao gia'ng*, don't give up! Don't give up!
LAO JIU	*Sa ji hu*,[114] this is not a choice. Ever since I was a child, everything was decided for me. I was just led to them step by step. What is

---

[111] Playwright's note: *Li ji*, 2nd sister

[112] Playwright's note: *Li ji hu*, 2nd Brother-in-Law.

[113] Editor's note: Teachers' Training College. The TTC was established in 1950. In 1973, the TTC was turned into the Institute of Education, and in 1991, the Institute and the College for Physical Education merged to form the National Institute of Education, which became an institute of the Nanyang Technological University in 1991.

[114] Playwright's note: *Sa ji hu*, 3rd Brother-in-Law.

so clever or intelligent about me? It's to do everything according to your wishes, to realise all the plans that you have laid out for me. More and more, I am feeling like the puppets that Chen *Shifu* has been playing. Everybody says how bright and clever I am as they look at me from out there in front of the stage. But in actual fact, it was your hands that are bright and clever. The War Horse Foundation opportunity is just a step to put me on to a larger stage, together with similar other puppets, to be played by more sophisticated hands behind us ... That's why I think the freest and most fantastic thing is Chen *Shifu*'s art of puppetry, his ability to create a world of his own-with his very own hands!

MASTER
Me? Free? *Gao gia'ng*, do you know that I can hardly fill my stomach nowadays?

LAO JIU
Shifu, don't degrade yourself. I am sure your difficulties are only temporary. If you don't believe me, I am prepared to join you and try and create a new situation ...

FATHER
(*Rushes in together with Mother.*) Enough! Enough! You want to play, I let you play. Everything Chen *Shifu* got: hand puppet, string puppet, shadow puppet. You can play as long as you like. But, first, finish your exam!

LAO JIU
But, *Ba* ...

FATHER
Now don't talk anything to me now. You go back to exam and win that scholarship for me!

LAO JIU
Ba, please listen to me —

FATHER
I don't want to listen! You already talk too much. *Gan ni ni'ang e*, if you are anyone of your Brother-in-Law, I would have punched you long ago!

LAO JIU
But this scholarship is not important to me —

FATHER
Lu diam![115] Your life has been too good, you never know what is good what is bad. *Gan ni ni'ang e*, you think everything can come and go anytime you want, ah?

---

[115] Playwright's note: *Lu diam*, shut up. Editor's note: *Lu* ('you') is derived from *Hokkien-Chinese*; *diam* (Malay) means 'to be silent'.

LAO JIU   *Ba*, I know you all are very concerned about me —

FATHER   No more talk! Now go back with me. Go back to exam tomorrow! Go!

MOTHER   (*Intervenes to defuse what she sees as a dangerously explosive situation.*) Aiyah, *gao gia'ng*. What are you going to do? You always very obedient. Why make your Father so angry today? You loved exam since a young boy, right? They all afraid but you always like exams. Why this time so funny? I think you are tired. Let's go home, OK? *Li ji*'s pig brain already cold now, let's go home, I warm up again for you. Come ...

FATHER   Go home. Go! Go or not? *Gan ni ni'ang e*, I'll kill you if I have to!

Father resorts to violence, Mother shields Lao Jiu and is knocked down. The Master comes to intervene, so do all the Sisters and In-Laws. There is utter confusion. Finally, the men managed to pull Father to one side and also rescued Mother to a seat.

MOTHER   (*Braving Father's fury.*) *Ba*, he's your son, *Ba*! You really want to kill him? (*Father stops.*)

                     (*Then turns to Lao Jiu.*) Gao gia'ng, what is the matter with you? Uh, son?

LAO JIU   ... You all say I'm very clever, very intelligent, fantastic ... But today, in the examination hall, I suddenly got the shivers. I trembled like mad. I sweated non-stop. I felt dizzy. I don't know what happened, but I was totally blanked out ... Finally, I cannot stand it anymore. I ran out of the hall. I ran to the lake side, to catch my breath. But, it's so strange. Somehow, I could see the fish in the water. They were smiling at me. And the clouds up in the sky, they were waving at me, as if telling me I should walk towards the other side of the hill. So I walked and walked. Not very far from there, I heard the sound of a flute. So I walked towards the source of the music, and I came to an *atap* house. I pushed open the door and walked in. It was Chen *Shifu*. He sat there, crossing his legs, with incense burning in front of him, he was peacefully blowing the flute. He saw me but he didn't stop. He carried on blowing. I think he was crying. I saw tear-drops on his cheeks. I sat down. I listened to his music. And I noticed his puppets. Then, I don't know when, I started playing with them. I kept on playing and playing and playing. It's strange: I was so good; things I didn't know before, now I knew. As if some strange power was assisting me. It was wonderful. But, suddenly, I noticed all the puppets have got a face exactly like mine. And they were all smiling. Whatever I did to them, they just kept on smiling, their faces never changed. I became very frightened. I shouted, I yelled, but they kept smiling at me. There was no change in their expression. Then I think I cried and I slowly fell asleep. When I woke up, *Shifu* was already gone. The sun was already gone. It was very quiet in the house. I could barely see the puppet heads lying there, every one was still wearing my smile and staring at me. I became so frightened ... all my hair stood on end ...

And that's your beloved wonder boy ... tender, polite, intelligent, hardworking, who does everything according to schedule ... just like *Shifu*'s puppets ... never knowing himself what was happening ...

(Lao Jiu's honesty touches the Master.)

MOTHER   *Gao gia'ng*, what are you thinking now, boy?

LAO JIU   I don't know! *Ba, Ma*, let me stay, please. I am not going to spend more of your money from now on. You all should stop bothering with this useless bit anymore ... I can look for a job. After work, I'll just stay here, learn, and play, and try and understand what lies behind the puppets ... Chen *Shifu*, I don't have very much time left, please let me stay, OK? ...

His parents and the Master can feel for Lao Jiu's honesty and the depth of his frustration. Though they cannot agree with him, they also do not have the heart to pressurise him any further.

Scene 13: The Battle of the Puppets

Senior War Horse calls from offstage.

SENIOR HORSE   Zhuang Youwei, ah, why are you so stupid? Why are you so stupid?

He enters and strikes a tableau, as the entire Zhuang family exits. What follows is played in the manner of the Chinese opera battles.

You have been blessed with war horse substance, and yet you fail to understand your god-given duty — this is your first stupidity. While others are trying their utmost to propel you into greatness, you have chosen to decline — this is your second stupidity. After repeated counselling and advice, you not only have refused to repent but have gone on to question the very historical role which the war horse talents have firmly built over the years. Zhuang Youwei, you have shown a stupidity beyond our understanding!

LAO JIU
(*He stands challenged, bravely countering the onslaught.*) Mr War Horse, please leave now. There is no market in our house for your promotions.

Accompanied by dynamic cymbal and drum percussion music, the warring camps are clearly defined.

SENIOR HORSE
Zhuang Youwei, ah Zhuang Youwei
You should carve it in your heart that
We are the favourite sons of heaven
We are the elites of the human species.

LAO JIU
War Horse, my War Horse
You can keep on weaving your fancy dreams
But don't decide anything on my behalf
Go on with your favourite son's dream
Only leave me entirely out of it.

SENIOR HORSE
Come on, Zhuang Youwei ...
Take a good look at the world:
May we call upon His Royal Highness:
Alexander the Great!

The Alexander puppet enters.

Zhuang Youwei, ah Zhuang Youwei:
Don't you want to be saddled with Alexander the Great
To share all the splendours of His Euro-Asian conquest.
To live in greatness when you're alive
And to be long remembered after death?

LAO JIU
Mr War Horse, my friend, take a good look at the world from another's eye: May we call upon our dear old friend: Sun Wukong, the Monkey King!

(The Monkey King puppet enters.)

My dear Mr War Horse:
Some people prefer to live like a monkey
To roam the forests and it's not funny
And if he should meet a sacred monk indeed
A journey to the West I'd gladly embark in good speed.

(The two puppets battle each other. Neither wins.)

SENIOR HORSE   May we call upon His Majesty Genghis Khan!

(The Genghis Khan puppet enters.)

Zhuang Youwei:
Don't you want to be the great Khan's companion
Battle half the world to usher in a new era
Life is so short, my friend
Don't you want to carve a career which would
Be remembered in all eternity

LAO JIU   May we call upon the venerable hero: Master Guo Jing!

(The Guo Jing puppet enters.)

Dear Mr War Horse:
No one has known a life as wondrous as Master Guo Jing.
Great eagles fly him to the heavens with Huang Rong
What career is there with Genghis Khan
Death on the grassland seems the best a soldier could hope for
Never hope to return to one's homeland

(The two puppets battle each other. Neither wins.)

SENIOR HORSE   May we call upon His Royal Majesty Prince Rama!

(The Prince Rama puppet enters.)

Zhuang Youwei:
Don't you want to inherit the great tradition of Rama
A curse of Evil, a blessing to Goodness
Lofty in character, noble in Culture
Make Justice your business, Truth your creed.

LAO JIU   May we call upon Nezha the Playful Prince!

(The Nezha puppet enters.)

Dear Mr War Horse:
Some people would rather be the simple-hearted Nezha
Brave deeds by spontaneity, to hell with perpetuity
Saints and gods are what men worship
Justice and truth is nobody's private domain

(The two puppets battle each other. Neither wins.)

SENIOR HORSE   May we call upon His Majesty Napoleon Bonaparte!

(The Napoleon puppet enters.)

A fine pony needs nurture to become a war horse
A hero defines greatness by his great enterprise
Super human traits are not for ordinary consumption
Brilliant elites are born to create history.

LAO JIU   May we call upon The Little Prince!

(The Little Prince puppet enters.)

The war horse is known by the lord who saddles it
Whatever choices it has are defined by its master
The Little Prince's planet has only one rose plant
And he doesn't boast any great enterprise
But he would travel the Milky Way to protect that flower
He holds his fate in his own little hands.

The two puppets battle each other. Neither wins.

Senior Horse has exhausted his resources. He summons all his puppets into battle once again. But again he couldn't produce a victory.

SENIOR HORSE   Ai! Zhuang Youwei, ah Zhuang Youwei, god-given talents you have wasted, Heaven-bestowed missions you have declined. What a pitiful short-sighted boy you are, in awesome stupidity you have wasted a golden opportunity others could only dream of. From now on, you are out of the realm of wealth and fame, your family's lowly life will perpetuate. You have destroyed an opportunity which millions would have given their life for.

In rage, he exits, followed by all the puppets — as the Zhuang Family re-enters in procession.

MASTER   (*Stops the Father from attempting to persuade Lao Jiu again.*) He doesn't want to be another Lam Tian Geok. He want to hold his *qiankun* universe in his own hands. Us, let us go on our own way.

Father looks desperately at Lao Jiu, beginning to appreciate the boy's honesty and firmness of character, although the boy's decision is still beyond his understanding. The Master understands but is unsure if the boy has made the right choice. Reluctantly the two elderly men exit following the others — accompanied by the Lan Tian Yu *music.*

Epilogue

Facing the audience, against the background of the shadow play performed to the mysterious flute music, Lao Jiu reflects …

LAO JIU   Three months later, Master Chen died. We were all very sad because he had always been like a member of our family. And, of all people, Father felt the loss more heavily than anybody else. He cried and howled like a little boy. I've never seen him cry like that before.

But, deep down, I know, that his death mattered more for me than even for Father. Because I know that, from now on, there would not be another place like his where I can go, to while away my frustrations. A place where I can fantasise my worries away, in any crazy way I need to. I was so sad I couldn't even cry.

The day after his funeral, I went to pack his things. Looking at those puppets, I felt a sense of loss so intense that I shivered inside. I knew that, in losing his hands, all these puppets have also lost their mysterious powers.

Sitting in that little hut of Master Chen's, I suddenly remembered an old tale. About a little boy, his Father, a bird and their *qiankun.* The story goes something like this:

Long, long ago, there lived a little boy. One day, the boy found a singing bird in the forest and brought it home. He showed it to his Father and asked his Father to feed the bird. His Father refused, saying, 'Why should I feed a mere bird!' Not only that, he killed the bird.

But, with the bird, he killed the song; and with the song, he also killed himself. He was dead, completely dead, and was dead forever ...

But the story didn't say what happened to the little boy.

(*End of Play*)

Descendants of the Eunuch Admiral[1]

1

I have come to realise of late that dreaming has become the centre of my life.

Yes, dreaming. Dreaming all by myself. Alone, painfully alone, and floating away.

But this loneliness is a potent one; it is an inviting loneliness. There is a vast space all around me. Endless. Haunting. Unknown. But promising. And seemingly reachable.

I have a fear of this unknown. And yet this fear is also part of the yearning to depart, to leave the place I'm so used to — even when I know what I am going away from is a terrible insanity. Yes. Everyday. Everyday, I long to return to my nightly unknown.

Was he also like this? Was he also like this when he was sailing across the vast ocean in the dark of the night, looking into the eerie distance, alone at sea, forgetting at least for the moment the insanity forced upon him, forgetting the pain created in him by the removal of his manhood?

In these dreams, the days were no more just fun, no more just cheerful and full of hope.

In these dreams, being alone, I was able to look at myself, look inside myself and look through myself. And as I dived deeper and deeper into the stark loneliness of myself, I felt I had become closer and closer to him, closer to this 600-year-old legend of a molested and incarcerated man.

Yes, each night, through my own fear and uncertainty, I discover more agony in him, more respect for him, and more suspicion of him. And the more I discover — longing for him in the day and taunting him in the night — the more I discover, the more I am convinced that we were related, closely related — so closely related that I had to be a descendant of the eunuch admiral.

---

[1] The English-language version of *Descendents of the Eunuch Admiral* is co-edited by C. J. W.-L. Wee and Lee Chee Keng.

235

2

With divine command from the Ming Emperor in 1405
He brought the imperial influence to distant nations

Over the treacherous straits and thunderous seas
He braved savage waters to explore the Western lands

For three decades Zheng He's armada ruled the ocean
Exploring the exotic from Tenggara, India to Arabia

When he returned to the splendours of the Imperial Court
Peace and friendship had stretched as far as Africa

3

There are 999 rooms in the Imperial Palace in Beijing — big ones and small ones, a total of 999. Among the 999 rooms, so they say, there is this very special chamber in the Palace where, in the olden days, all the cut and dried penises of the eunuchs were kept ... Yes, penises, all cut, fried and dried. The most interesting thing about this chamber is that all the boxes of penises, or 'treasure' or '*baobei*', as they called it, were not stacked or stored in the chamber. No, they were not stacked on any racks or locked in any cupboards. No. Instead, they were all hung, or suspended, in the air from the ceiling!

Now, when they first enter the Imperial Palace to join the eunuch service, they begin at the bottom. Which means the most junior, new eunuchs get their boxes suspended on the ground level. Then, as they are promoted, their positions go higher, and so their penis boxes, commensurate with their new status, also will be raised to higher levels.

Of course, every time they get a promotion, they have to go and show their treasures again. You know, as when every time we get a promotion or a new job we have to show our certificates, diplomas, degrees and testimonial letters. For the eunuchs, they have to show their *baobei*s because, you see, for the eunuchs, this is their single most important document or article of qualification. In fact, it is their only qualification. Therefore, as they get promoted higher and higher, their boxes also go higher and higher, higher and higher. Until they reach the very top, near the ceiling, when they have become the leading grand eunuchs, like Liu Jin[2] and Wei Zhongxian[3] in the Ming Dynasty. Or An

---

[2] Liu Jin (died 1510).
[3] Wei Zhongxian (1568–1627).

Dehai[4] in the Qing Dynasty — you know, the favourite eunuch of the Empress Dowager.

Fancy, having this chamber in the Imperial Palace filled with many, many boxes each containing a carefully preserved, dried, deep-fried penis. According to one record, there was at one time as many as 10,000 eunuchs behind the walls of the Forbidden City. Fancy, hanging 10,000 penises packed in boxes, suspended in this chamber, or maybe the big hall, in the Imperial Palace. What a sight! What an interesting network?

Now, I'd like to share a funny thought with you. Now, you look at us: Together like this, don't you think it looks like the organisational chart of our companies or departments?

What I mean is, don't we look like a network of pricks?

4

But, hey! Listen! I think I've made an academic discovery! ...

As you know, when a eunuch dies, his family or colleagues are obliged to re-unite his treasure with his dead body. They must put it back exactly where it belonged. And I mean exactly, physically touching the cut-off base as if it was a re-connection.

'Is it in the exact position? Is it touching the body?' These are very, very serious concerns.

It was a crucial post-mortem operation for the deceased eunuch because if it was not done, or not done properly, then they believe that, in the next life, this guy can never come back to the world as a man anymore.

As we were talking, I just remembered that there were records saying Zheng He died in Calicut in India, or on the ship on the way back from his seventh and last expedition to the Western Ocean. Now if that was true, then how could he possibly have had his treasure put back in place? So, my discovery is this: The great admiral, Grand Eunuch Zheng He, despite his very high status, was not buried with his full body!

Why not? Just because he was out there at sea?

Of course! ... You mean, he could have taken his treasure on board?

Why not?

---

[4] An Dehai (1844–1869).

Come on, *lah*,[5] be practical, there were maybe a hundred eunuchs in the armada with Zheng He, how can they all —

Why not? The armada was huge; there were maybe a hundred ships carrying anything and everything needed for almost 30,000 people — food, drinks, medicine, laundry, cooks, tailors, even hairdressers, not to mention soldiers and officials, and all their required weapons, tools and sundry supplements. So, why can't the eunuchs all have brought their *baobei*s with them on board the ships? Unless you really believe they had this chamber in Beijing where they kept all their *baobei*s.

In theory, yes, they could all have carried their treasures everywhere they went, but you must understand that these were not only personal treasures; in a way, they were something of national treasures.

Just think, senior grand eunuchs were in positions of high authority and carried the same superior esteem as our ministers and permanent secretaries, or chiefs of staff and chief executives. Therefore, they were the most important national assets. And by extension of that argument, are not parts of their body as highly valued as national treasures?

You mean if they had come to Longyamen, Singapore, all the eunuchs would have carried their treasures ashore?

Seriously, this discovery makes me feel so sad. I mean, we have always looked upon people occupying high positions as very strong men — and women. We have never — at least I haven't — doubted their authority and responsibility. This discovery about Zheng He who may have been buried without a full body ... Suddenly suspicion arises as to how fragile all these big men and women are — and how temporary and transient the power, status and authority of these people occupying high positions really are — when we found that a supremely powerful grand eunuch like Zheng He could end up so pathetically.

5

It was my own decision to want to become a eunuch, because our family was very poor. No money, no status, no education — we were fated to be poor and downtrodden forever. So, I decided that going into the imperial court to serve as a eunuch was the only way to get us out of our condemned poverty.

---

[5] Malay: *lah*, '[A] particle emphasising the word to which it is appended' (*A Malay-English English-Malay Dictionary*, ed. A. E. Coope [revised edn.; London and Basingstoke: Macmillan Education, 1991]).

I was at peace with my ancestors as my elder brother had already married and borne my father two sons, so my becoming a eunuch would not have caused a discontinuity in our family line.

On the day of the operation, Father had to get drunk before he could come into the room holding a razor he had sharpened many times throughout the day.

By then, I had already taken off my pants and sat on the *kang*.[6] As I saw Father, I started to tremble. But I managed to keep my voice calm and I said, 'Come, Father, let's begin.' And I flipped over the blanket covering my underparts, revealing my genitals. Then I spread my legs and laid back.

Father walked towards me very slowly. With tears flowing down his cheeks and with his teeth tightly clenched, he asked me, 'Doggie (my nickname was "Doggie"), you won't regret?'

I said, 'Father, I won't regret.'

Again, Father asked me, 'Doggie, you won't regret?'

Again, I said, 'Father, I won't regret.'

Father again asked me, this time crying and trembling, 'Doggie, you really won't regret?', as if he was begging me to say, 'Yes, I would.'

But again I said to him, this time also trembling but not crying because I knew if I had cried Father would never have been able to do it — and I said, 'Father, I promise I won't regret. Please come and do it.' And I clenched my teeth and turned my head away.

Then I heard Father, drawing a heavy breath, rush over to my *kang*, violently grabbing my genitals; he gave out a desperate cry and a shattering pain stung my underparts, and I passed out immediately.

When I woke up, I felt a stinging pain in my underparts. And I could hear all my relatives around me congratulating me and saw them embracing each other because I was urinating. And then I remembered: once you start urinating, you are OK; you will survive.

Then Father, red in the eyes from crying and probably from going days without sleeping, brought a box before me and opened it carefully. The content was covered in dry husk. He shuffled the surface layer and uncovered a packet wrapped in heavily oiled paper. Unwrapping the paper, I saw before me a piece of something, which was evidently deep-fried in oil to keep it dry and antiseptic. Instinctively I knew: this was my severed penis.

---

[6] A heatable brick bed, common in northern China.

It was then that the reality hit home, that I had really done it. And from then on, I knew I would have this treasure of an article to serve as evidence of my dedication and loyalty to the Emperor and to the imperial family — a licence to enter the imperial palace, to hold privileged positions in the imperial household, to scale higher positions, to attain wealth and status. I was on my way to becoming a eunuch.

But of course Zheng He didn't choose like this. He was summarily cut and cleansed by his masters when he was barely a teenager — because there was a need, a huge need for eunuchs. You see, eunuchs seem to have started fulfilling a very important aristocratic need since many thousands of years ago.

The word 'eunuch' in Greek originally meant the 'bed attendant'. By attending to the bed-pleasures of emperors and princes, of noblemen and noblewomen, eunuchs were fated to sacrifice their own bed pleasures. More than that, they also attended to the nobility's personal affairs such as eating, drinking, dressing, cleaning, pissing, shitting and, of course, copulating. As well as more stately affairs such as writing, building, worshipping, warring and sailing — sailing great armadas of tens with thousands of men, representing the great empire in the capacity of a great admiral!

6

'Imperial Decree for Chief Eunuch Zheng He!'

'Zheng He humbly receives the Imperial Decree. Ten thousand years of longevity to Your Gracious Majesty!'

'Now that the Ming Dynasty has firmly entrenched its majestic authority with heavenly blessings, with peace and prosperity prevailing upon the entire *Zhong Hua* Nation, our attention should now turn to the coastal regions and our farther neighbours. The pirates from Japan and other lands have been bothering my loyal subjects and our friendly aliens in the East and South East. Furthermore, for decades now we have not extended our imperial presence and goodwill to the Western Ocean. It is therefore now my explicit wish that the power, prestige and splendour of the Imperial Court be extended once more to the farther shores.

'To expedite this historic mission, I appoint Grand Eunuch Zheng He Commander-in-Chief of the Imperial Expedition. Details of the mission are herein listed. Go in power, authority and peace. Do justice to the grandeur and splendour of my Dynasty!'

'Zheng He obediently accepts Your Gracious Majesty's Decree with great honour and gratitude. Ten Thousand Years of longevity to Your Gracious Majesty!'

'Now, come and take your orders.'

'Grand Eunuch Wang Jinghong,[7] listen carefully: you are tasked with organising the Staff Command of the Expedition and recruiting diplomats, interpreters and guides who are familiar with the Western Ocean. Expedite this immediately!

'Commanding Officer of the Long Jing Dockyard, listen carefully: you are tasked to commandeer or to build — or do both if required — the necessary ships to make up the armada. I am envisaging a fleet of at least 60 ships, including two command ships measuring 440 feet long, 180 feet wide, carrying staff, troops, weapons, equipment and supplies for up to 30,000 men for as long as two years. Expedite this immediately!

'Governor of Zhejiang, listen carefully: you are tasked to gather general and specialist supplies for up to 30,000 men for the entire expedition, which might last as long as two whole years. Expedite this immediately!'

'Fellow servants of His Gracious Majesty: our historic mission shall take us to Campa, Ceylon, Cochin and Calicut, possibly even to Tianfang Mekka!

'Be clearly warned: this is a historic mission conceived by the wisdom of His Gracious Majesty the Emperor, and it must be nothing less than an absolute success!

'I want everything to be totally ready by the First Day of the Sixth Month of the Third Year of Yong Le Era for final inspection! We shall set sail precisely on the Fifteenth Day of the Sixth Month. This is a military command: The punishment for whoever fails to expedite his duties as commanded is no less than summary execution!

'Dismissed!'

7

Expedition One: 1405
Expedition Two: 1407
Expedition Three: 1409
Expedition Four: 1413
Expedition Five: 1417
Expedition Six: 1421
Expedition Seven: 1431

---

[7] Wang Jinghong (died *ca.* 1434).

In almost 30 years, Zheng He and his imperial armada visited Campa, Panduranga, Cape Varella, Pulo Condore, Gelam Island, Siam, Palembang, Melaka, Pulo Sembilan, Sumudra, Battak, Lenkasuka, Bras Island, Nicobar Islands, Silan, Quilon, Cochin, Calicut, Ormuz, al-Ahsa, Bangala, Camboja, Pulo Aor, Tamiang, Governador Strait (Longyamen), Langkawi, Gili Timor, Pahang, Mindoro, Karimata, Jangala Surabaya, Brunei, Solot, Aden, Zufar, Jobo, Mogadishu, Maldives Islands, Brawa, Mecca, Harwa Aru, Litai and Lambri.

8

Last night I dreamt a dark dream. The sky above me was covered with thick clouds. Not greyish or black but it looked moody and broody, like something cooking in a stew pot.

All around me, sounds were straining to press upon my entire body, like the steaming hot air one gets in a sauna. I couldn't make out what they were. One moment they sounded like a record playing on an old gramophone, but when the speed is not right. The next moment they seemed more like a thousand animals howling at the same time, all trying to get at me.

Then I realised I was on a ship. A very big ship with many masts and many sails. But there was no one around me, anywhere. I was the lone sailor on the deck of this big ship floating on an ocean of water that was unusually calm, in spite of the cloudy sky above me and the intimidating sounds around me. And yet the calm water produced no tranquillity. It was vast, seemingly endless, and all the more eerie because there was no one around, and there was no sign of a control room. I panicked. What was happening? Where was it going? I looked around frantically searching for a hole or a door, to reach somewhere to find the controls. But there was no access to the lower decks of this huge ship that was sailing over the ocean with such commanding authority and firm sense of purpose. I had no idea what was happening.

For some reason, it began to dawn upon me that I may have gone back in time as the sci-fi books say we can, and that actually one of my former lives was none other than the great Admiral Zheng He himself. For a moment, I felt very 'high'. I mean, fancy yourself having been the legendary great sailor who had sailed from the China Sea to the Indian Ocean seven times, and had reached as far as the Coast of Kenya in Africa more than a century before Magellan saw the Philippines!

But the next moment I got frightened, so frightened that I immediately began to sweat. Because I suddenly realised that if I was Zheng He, I would have been a eunuch. And if I was a eunuch, I would have been ... Oh, my god! My hands instinctively reached down.

Oh, my god! It was real. There was nothing there! I was so shocked I started to jump and run and scream, and I woke up.

When I caught my breath, I froze, and I reached down again ... Oh, my god, it was all still there, everything ... And I was glad that I wasn't Zheng He ...

But somehow, the ship in the dream stuck in my mind. Big, forceful and sure. I was right there on the deck, as if I was the commander. Yet I didn't have a clue where I was going ... The water was calm and inviting, but the brooding sky and the strained sounds created such an eerie feeling of uncertainty ... It was an exciting dream but I was glad to wake up. And eternally grateful that I still had what I have! ...

9

I sometimes wonder whether we really understood this grand eunuch. As you know very well, of all the famous eunuchs in China, Zheng He's history is the cleanest and the most respectable. After he passed away, the Ming Emperor decided to close up China and subsequently all of Zheng He's records were destroyed. We know so little of him. Had he really done nothing evil or untoward as a trusted lieutenant of a powerful emperor well-known for his cruel and scheming nature?

If we do believe this, then are we not presuming too much to Admiral Zheng He's discredit?

But with good reasons. We know for sure he was a totally loyal lieutenant of Zhu Di — also known as Ming Chengzu, the Yongle Emperor[8] — even in the days when the Prince staged the coup to oust his nephew in order to ascend the throne. Zheng He was one of his bravest warriors and most trusted lieutenants. We also know that it was Ming Chengzu who created the *Dong Chang*, or the Eastern Institution, China's most notorious secret police. Personally reporting only to the Emperor himself, the *Dong Chang* was always commanded by a trusted grand eunuch.

There is a debate among scholars on whether Zheng He had actually played a part in the Emperor's draconian scheme set out for the *Dong Chang*. Yes, even today the debate is still alive on whether he was actually sent to sea by the Emperor to trace the deposed emperor who was supposed to have been burnt to death. This speculation about Zheng He's mission, although never proven, was never dismissed either. And it would tally well with his suspected role of being one of the Emperor's top secret manhunters. He might well have been a senior officer of or advisor to the *Dong Chang*.

---

[8] Yongle Emperor (1360–1424).

If all the eunuchs were acting as informers, what reasons do we have to believe that Grand Eunuch Zheng He could be different, bearing in mind that he was after all one of Emperor Yongle's most trusted lieutenants? Could he have refrained from suppressing the dissidents inside and outside of the Imperial Court when he was so intimately subjected to the personal whims and fancies of that supreme emperor?

Don't forget, the emperor who sent Zheng He to Melaka, Ceylon, India, Mekka and Mogadishu was the same sovereign who allowed his secret police chiefs — all of them grand eunuchs — to devise horrendous punishments such as club-whipping, skin-peeling, fingernail-tearing, spine-breaking and heart-piercing treatments for the emperor's less obedient subjects.

He was out of the country precisely to avoid getting involved!

Possible? Yes. Maybe. Except that between 1422 and 1430, a period of about eight years, Zheng He was not travelling at sea. And the *Dong Chang* was created in 1420, which means Zheng He was in China during the pioneering years of the *Dong Chang*'s operations!

What was he doing then? Did he play a role in the secret police at all? Or did he try very hard to stay away from the *Dong Chang* by getting another commission to go to the Western Ocean in 1430? ... And eventually die on the ship at sea ...

I have often wondered what Zheng He was thinking when he was alone on deck in the South Seas, in the Indian Ocean, sailing away to the distant lands, in the middle of nowhere ... In his loneliest moments, which probably were also his freest moments ... Was he more than the eunuch that we have generally imagined him to be, or less than the hero which the historians and legends have portrayed him to be?

Maybe he was feeling what we would be thinking when we travel out of the country. In a state of limbo, but free from constraints and controls ... There is no doubt that if there was really a chamber in the Forbidden City storing the eunuch's treasures, Zheng He's box would be very high up near the ceiling. But the climb must have involved plenty of hard work — and often going against his own good conscience – which had to be pleasing to the Emperor.

There was a folk story saying that the Emperor Jianwen,[9] the one that Zheng He's master deposed, had actually fled the palace and that the charred body found was actually one of his loyal servants. The story says this Emperor had fled to Quanzhou in Fujian Province.

---

[9] Jianwen Emperor (1377–1402).

Then, on his way to the Western Ocean, Zheng He, while passing through the area met the deposed Emperor who was hiding in the temple as a monk. When Emperor Jianwen asked Zheng He to use his powerful armada to support his attempt to regain the throne, Zheng He at once knelt down, sobbed and was unable to speak ...

'Pray, do not draw me into these palace struggles again, I beg you, Your Gracious Majesty. I belong to no party, no clique, no clan; I was not even born a member of the Han people. I am just a humble alien, a wandering slave, a worthless servant to all and sundry. *Insya Allah*, I am still alive ... I serve everyone ... every emperor and every prince, every minister and every commander ... Please spare me the pain and torture of this imperial rivalry ...'

To Zheng He's credit, the story never said anything about him turning into an informer against the deposed Emperor ...

10

To keep my head
I must accept losing my tail
To keep my faith
I must learn to worship others' gods

To please my lord
I must eliminate his enemy
To serve his pleasure
I must purge my own

Allah knows my bitterness
Buddha has mercy upon my soul
Sea Goddess protects my fleet
Voyages to the West fulfil my life

Alone, I can stand up to any man
Freed, I can scale any height
'Cleansed', I cling to but one thought
My master's will is my survival

11

Oh, what a beautiful morning on the auspicious First Day of the New Year of the Pig. I hear firecrackers distant in the imperial city. With snow gracefully dancing in the winter breeze, the polar bears are playfully amusing themselves in the imperial garden lake now richly covered with ice.

Presently, Zheng He enters with a group of eunuchs. They all kow-tow to the Emperor and start presenting their New Year greetings dedicated to the Emperor.

But before Zheng He began, the Emperor stopped him and said, 'Ah, how can we have a horse running in the Imperial Court!' Everyone was shocked and started to look around for the culprit who dared to ride a horse into the imperial court. But they found no one on the horse anywhere. And then the Emperor started to laugh, 'Hahaha ...' and looked in amusement at Zheng He. As you know, Zheng He was a very clever eunuch, so he immediately understood what the Emperor was talking about, and got very frightened. He kowtowed energetically and appealed to the Emperor, 'Oh, Your Gracious Majesty, please pardon me. My crime deserves death but please pardon me, Your Gracious Majesty! Pardon me, please! ...'

By this time, all the eunuchs, although they were not as clever as Zheng He, also realised what was wrong, and they also prostrated before the Emperor to plead on behalf of Zheng He.

But why? Do you know what was happening? Although Zheng He was walking, not riding a horse, why was he behaving as if he was the culprit the Emperor was accusing of riding a horse in the Imperial Court?

Ah! Because at that time Zheng He was not yet Zheng He. Actually his name then was Ma He and *ma*, of course, as you know, also means 'horse' in Chinese, and so when he went to pay respects to the Emperor, you could, arguably, say that a horse had gone to court.

For the superstitious, this can be seen as a very serious crime because it was said that when horses are let free in court, there would be war and rebellion in the land — because only rebel soldiers dare to ride their horses into the Imperial Court. So Zheng He was very, very frightened.

'Bring me ink, brush and paper!' the Emperor ordered. Wah, everybody became very scared. What's happened? Was he going to decree death for Zheng He — no, Ma He — ? Indeed, Zheng He, no Ma He, was trembling all over. But when the writing desk was brought in with all the writing instruments, the Emperor walked over and, in the grand orthodox or *kai* style of calligraphy,[10] he wrote the character *zheng*. And he asked the junior eunuchs to present it to Ma He.

---

[10] Or, alternatively, in the 'standard' style of calligraphy.

'From now on,' said the Emperor, 'You shall be surnamed Zheng!' And so, from then on, Ma He became Zheng He ...

'Thank you, your Gracious Majesty! Thank you Your Gracious Majesty!' Zheng He was so relieved and became so happy that he lived happily ever after ...

'At 12, I was taken prisoner from my parents, my hometown and my people in Yunnan. I had to love my master who cleansed me and enslaved me. I had to learn the ways of the Hans. Their Buddha became my second protector, their Sea Goddess my other guardian angel. To live, I had to die; to act, I must submit. My life and fortune has been nothing more than that of a rootless wanderer's.

'I am exceedingly grateful to my elder brother who gave me his son to be my adopted heir, so that something of me, or at least something of my fore-parents, is passed on ... Under another name ... away from my ancestral graves.'

12

Removing the genitals? But of course there were many better ways of doing it: as scientific development continued, less painful methods were discovered. Historic records show that, to get the same effects, the courts and temples found more humane ways, which removed many of the cruelties associated with cutting and cleansing.

One improved method took away much of the pain. It works like this:

You take a piece of string, tie it at the base of the scrotum when the boy is still young and small. Tie it tight enough but short of causing pain to him, and leave it there permanently. As the boy's body grows bigger, the tightness of the string remains. Gradually, in time, the base of the testicles will break off. Just like what some people do to cut off the tails of cats and dogs.

You start them early enough and they won't feel the pain much. They may not even experience trauma if you do it carefully. However, even with this method, a significant part — the life-giving part — of the organs is taken away. But, for the users, what is left is much treasured. Because what is left is not only still functional, but that by removing the life-giving power of the eunuch, the enjoyment of the pleasure-seeking noblewomen becomes more enhanced and more safe.

Another improved method, although still somewhat painful, retains much of the physical exterior:

Take a needle
A silver needle
Poke the balls with the needle
With loving care
Again and again, again and again
You poke the balls, until they're destroyed

Take a spoon
A silver spoon
Nurse the man with the spoon
With loving care
Year after year, stage by stage
You nurse the man, until he is usable

It doesn't matter the pain is unbearable
It doesn't matter the results are still visible
Because this thing the loyal creature
Has always been, and still is, highly marketable

13

Early in the morning before sunrise, the emissaries from Zheng He's armada are getting ready to bring their goods ashore for the great trading festival — silk, brocade, china of many varieties such as vases, plates, bowls. The grand eunuchs, the junior eunuchs, the generals, the officials and officers and errand boys and soldiers ... a flotilla of people and goods began their joyous journey to the marketplace.

On land, the king and his lieutenants, the wealthy traders and their assistants, the soldiers and the helpers, the *Chettiars*[11] who hold the money, the slaves and servants who man the carts and horses all started to stir well before the cockerel begins to sound the morning call.

The powerful and the wealthy bathed, and then applied on themselves a paste mixed with the most exquisite of cosmetics: a fine grey powder of baked cow dung — three times over on their foreheads and on significant parts of their body including the inside of their crotch.

---

[11] Tamil: *Chettiars* are a successful and prominent trading community in the South Indian state of Tamil Nadu.

Zheng He's armada and the festivals and markets and gatherings brought together all sorts of people: There were Buddhists, Muslims, Hindus and Taoists — children of parents of a great description of people ... They brought fabrics made of jute, of cotton, of silk; they brought metalwork made of gold, of silver, of bronze, copper, iron and steel; they brought seeds, coral, pearls, fish bones, turtle shells, birds' feathers, stones and earth. All of these were priced beforehand and the gentlemanly exchange which takes place now becomes more a festival, a celebration, a meeting of friends thirsting for each other's goods and each other's company and the great coming together.

Soon after the exchange, the festivities began. Food galore, of all colours, tastes and descriptions. But there was neither beef nor pork and a great amount of vegetarian food — a show of mutual respect between the Muslims, the Hindus and the Buddhists.

And then the circus began. There are bulls that charge not at red but anything that is blue in colour. There are acrobatic goats with green fleece; fighting bulls the size of elephants; magic shows with black tigers, which are said to have the power of masquerading as humans at night; dancing chickens as tiny and exquisite as pearls; formation flights of bats as large as eagles; the marching feats of dozen of turtle dragons and *giris*, or *chilin*, which would now be described as crawling crocodiles and stomping giraffes.

At the end of this great market festival, Zheng He and the king exchanged gifts of gold and silver, silk and ivory, jewels and porcelain. As the setting sun displayed the most brilliant of its colours, they parted in passionate sorrow. The king and his attendants hold on to their treasured silk, porcelain and jewels while the Grand Eunuch leads away the rare animals and birds given to his mission as reciprocal gifts. Even when they were sailing down the river back to the armada, the music from instruments made of shells and reeds could still be heard from land. And the departing visitors knew that their hosts were still on shore listening to the drums and flutes coming from their boats.

Grand Eunuch Zheng He, faithful servant of the Ming Emperor, was sent to the Western Ocean as an imperial emissary to blaze a trail of glory for the Middle Kingdom. Never did he expect to leave a path of amazing splendour that would seep into the lives of so many people in so many places, through so many ways over so long a time ...

That evening, Zheng He failed to sleep all night. And his soldiers and officials softly talked and sang all night long.

14

For almost 30 years, Zheng He ploughed the South China Sea and the Indian Ocean. He wandered the wilderness at sea and on land, tens of thousands of miles away from his home, his nation, his emperor and lord. An outcast almost for life, exiled on the vast, open sea, he — apart from serving the emperor's imperial interest — also must have been looking, deep in his heart, for his own paradise.

There is story told like this in folklore:

One day, some way after the great armada entered the Indian Ocean north-west of Sumatra, a terrifying storm came upon his ships. Despite the immensity of his 440-foot command ship, they were thrown into the air like a toy and everyone seemed destined for the bottom of the sea.

'Ah, let us learn from Sang Nila Utama the Prince of Temasek!' And they started to throw everything into the sea including their valuable personal apparel. But no use, the storm persisted, even after the grand eunuchs had also thrown their various headgears into the water.

Usually a very calm leader, Zheng He also began to panic.

'*Insya* Allah, save us!' he cried out, remembering how he and his family and relatives prayed in his childhood days.

'Ah, Buddha, save us!' he appealed, remembering the monk in Xian who enlightened him as to the holy scriptures.

'Ah, Sea Goddess, rescue us!' he prayed, clearly remembering the stone tablets he erected in Tai Cang and in Chang Le.

Then a miracle happened. The storm subsided. Not only that, drums and cymbals and chanting were heard from high up in the sky and, as an invigorating fragrance filled the air. Suddenly, there appeared on the top of the highest mast an angel-like young lady with a graceful face and a youthful body. Her costume and long hair were floating in the air where the storm had altogether lost its trace. And the next moment the lady was gone. People say this was the Sea Goddess herself appearing to calm the hearts and minds of Zheng He and his armada of men.

Soon afterwards, land was sighted and the intimation of tragedy became memory.

'Hey! Hoi! Good people there. Where have we come to? What do you call this beautiful land of yours here?'

'Oh, this is the land where the Buddha walked, where the Buddha bathed, where the Buddha slept. This is the jewel of the world, the jewel formed by a drop of the Buddha's tear.'

Zheng He and members of his fleet were overcome with joy. Is this the promised land of abundance and tolerance where men are free to work and live, the land where there is only justice and no reign of terror?

Maybe, because they said this was the place where Adam made a mountain and Adam is the brother of Pan Gu, and both Adam and Pan Gu are ancestors of men.

Soon, they were overjoyed because they found that this place not only had very just laws, it also had a most enlightened ruler. The good people said their *raja*[12] had ruled for 20 years and then voluntarily stepped down and forbade his children and relatives from succeeding him. Furthermore, he not only refrained from intervening with the ruling of the land, he withdrew from society completely. In fact, he wandered away and became a hermit in the mountains, exposing himself to the wilds of rain and wind, of animals and birds, of plants and insects. He vowed that he would not even defend himself against any creature but would rather succumb to their beastly desires.

But because the *karma* he had accumulated was so massive, none of the creatures in the wild would harm him. Instead, all of them — those with wings and those without wings, those with sharp teeth and those with sharp claws — all came to pay their respect to him. After three years exposing himself to the elements in the mountains, the former ruler became a holy man. And when he was asked to return to the throne, he ruled the country in such a wise manner that oppression and injustice completely disappeared, this time permanently, never again to be found. People say this time he had become a deity, an eternal spiritual protector of the land.

And because of his teaching and his example, the people became very enlightened, too. They needed no policemen to control their lives and they needed no courts to arbitrate their quarrels. When there was a dispute, they would let nature reveal the truth: the contending parties would both walk through a pond filled with crocodiles. The guilty one will be eaten by the beasts while the innocent one will wade through without any harm coming upon him.

From then on, the country became known as a country without rulers. But some people also called it the country of rulers — *negara*[13] *raja-raja*,[14] because all the people became their own rulers — *negara raja-raja*.

---

[12] Malay, of Sanskritic derivation: *raja*, an Indian or Malay prince or chief.
[13] Malay: *negara*, state.
[14] Malay: *raja-raja*, the plural form of *raja*.

15

Of course, the story of *negara raja-raja* could only come to Zheng He in a dream. But it was a good, satisfying dream.

Unfortunately, the good dream was followed by a not-so-good dream — a dream where he found that even the wise ruler had kept eunuchs.

Indeed, life had not been too kind to Zheng He. Perhaps the greatest of all ancient eunuchs, he was subjected to the most savage form of mutilation.

Had Zheng He lived much later, or had he lived in more civilised lands, he could have suffered only the minimal trauma through the experience of a more modern and, by far, the most sophisticated method of cutting and cleansing that is the least painful and the least traumatic man has ever known. Some say it was even comforting and pleasurable. It goes like this:

You need highly trained specialists to do this, and again you have to do it when they were very young.

The operation is usually handled by specially trained nannies, applied to the boys when they are still very young children.

When a nanny has won the confidence of the little boy, she would begin to massage his testicles — perhaps after a bath, during playtime or before bedtime. Massaging softly, very softly at the beginning, so that there is not only no pain but is actually comforting and pleasurable.

As the boy gets used to it, the nanny would gradually increase then pressure of the massage — again, always making sure it is done below the pain-tolerance level of the child.

As time goes by, the nanny would have increased the pressure of her massage to such a degree that although the boy still finds it pleasurable, she would have actually started to crush the testicles so hard that the impact begins to damage the inside of the organ. Of course the child, by which time his pain tolerance level would also have risen so high, would continue to perceive the massage as not only benign but also pleasurable.

Very soon, the function of the testicles is completely destroyed and the job is done.

Apart from the absence of any perceived pain, and the advantage of retaining all the organs intact — nothing is cut off, all the parts are preserved — the greatest merit is that it is received by the subject as comforting, enjoyable and even highly desirable.

Externally, everything looks exactly the same. Nothing is missing; everything looks normal and untouched. The only difference is that life will come to an end after he has lived his own; there will be no afterlife ...

16

It looks as if, however well-meaning one is, however hard one tries, the fate of the cut and dried, cleansed and uprooted eunuch is all but decided ...

But the eunuch admiral seemed never to have given up the hope of finding an alternate life. On board his drifting vessels, in the loneliness of the vast ocean, in the limbo between departing and arriving, between being a man and a non-man, he kept on dreaming, hoping, searching, struggling:

> Home? I have no home
> My home is across the ocean, on the seas
> Home? I have no home
> My home is in alien countries, on faraway waters
>
> I have no name
> I have no sex
> Departing is my arriving
> Wandering is my residence
>
> Stop asking, stop
> Ma He, Zheng He, Sampoh Gong
> Cut and dried, plugged and exiled
> Orphan, wanderer, eunuch, admiral
> Yesterday, from Liu Jia He to the Western Ocean
> Today, from Longyamen to the Suzhou Park
> Tomorrow, the Earth, the Moon, Mars, and the Sun
>
> Nameless, sexless, rootless, homeless
> Everyone's a parent to the orphan
> Every god's a protector to the wanderer
> Every land and sky and water is home
> It's forever *Zaijian, Selamat Datang, Vanakkam*,[15] Farewell

---

[15] 'Farewell' in Mandarin-Chinese, Malay and Tamil.

I cannot tarry
I must hurry
The sea, the land, the sky is waiting
The Market is calling me!

(*End of Play*)

Geylang People in the Net

1. Prologue

The cast casually walk onto the stage with their life-sized puppets, which are a sort of human dummy. They look into the auditorium, recognise friends and wave to them, showing off their puppets.

The durians begin to come down via the fly system and the cast acknowledges the durians to the audience.

As the music begins, they all leave their puppets on stage and go to get ready in the wings.

In full costume, the cast then performs a welcome dance, presented enthusiastically and directly to the audience as if they are offering a present to their friends.

Dance One.

After the dance, they catch their breath and pick up their puppets again. One after the other, they begin to speak, each finding the best form of personal expression. They seriously make an effort and respond to each other, and eventually build up to speaking in an integrated, full and intense 'group' voice.

They stop abruptly as they achieve an intense group resonance. Silence.

Then, sensing something, they all put on their puppets in front of them, and all move sideways to give way to two figures — both blind and mute. The two — slowly and intensely — move from upstage centre down to centre stage, pulling a long stage cloth downstage until it is fully stretched, and then disappear. No one can quite understand what the pair are saying, despite their — unperceived — effort to be articulate.

2. Geylang Lost

YATI and ONI remain upstage. They begin to sing 'Ikan Kekek' [1] *as they walk downstage to both sides of the river that is suggested by the cloth.*

When they are finished, a rumbling sound made by the cast brings in everyone from the wings; they gravitate and gather upstage centre with their dolls in front of them. They freeze as ONI and YATI begin to tell a story.

ONI   *Tujoh haribulan Juli, pukul 7.07 menit pagi, Geylang telah dijilat api. Bukan saja punca kebakaran itu sebuah misteri, kawasan yang terkena api lebih menakjubkan. Pertama, kawasan yang terkena api ...*[2]

YATI   *Tidak tinggi dan tidak rendah. Tidak terlalu kekiri dan tidak terlalu kekanan. Kesan kebakaran merangkumi kawasan Lorong*[3] *1 dan Gay World*[4] *di sebelah bawah, Geylang Serai dan Haig Road di sebelah atas, Sims Avenue di sebelah kiri dan Guillemard Road di sebelah kanan. Menjadikan kawasan itu hampir empat persegi.*[5]

ONI   *Dan sekarang, punca kebakaran itu. Menurut seorang pemandu teksi di Geylang Serai, inilah yang dilihatnya.*[6]

---

[1] There are several versions of this Malay folk song for children, and the following is one of them:

Ikan kekek mak iloi, iloi,
Ikan gelama mak iloi, iloi,
Mari adik mak iloi, iloi,
Menyanyi sama mak iloi, iloi.
Ada satu si ikan parang,
Badannya banyak berbelang,
Isi sikit, banyak tulang,
Sedap di makan, masak panggang.

[2] Malay: On the 7th of July, at 7.07 am, Geylang was on fire. Not only was the origin of the fire a mystery, but the way the area caught fire was shocking. Firstly, the area that caught fire ...

[3] Malay: *Lorong*, corridor, passage. Here it refers to a small road — or a lane — that has been numbered; hence Lorong 1.

[4] Gay World — originally Happy World — was one of three amusement parks built in Singapore before the Second World War. It opened in 1936. The other two were the Great World and New World. The Gay World was located between Mountbatten Road and Geylang Road.

[5] Malay: It is neither high nor low. Not to the left nor to the right. The effect of the fire included the area around Lorong 1 and Gay World further down, Geylang Serai and Haig Road at the top. Sims Avenue was on the left and Guillemard Road on the right. The area is like a square.

[6] Malay: And the origin of the fire. According to a taxi-driver, this is what he saw.

JOHN　已经7点钟了, 奇怪, 天还那样黑, 我吃了*roti prata*,[7] 刚要开车下坡, 忽然听到碰碰的声音。我想, 嘿, 奇怪, 什么声音? 我掉过头去一看, 哇唠! 是榴梿啊, 榴梿啊! 咦, 这个时候什么人丢榴梿? 联邦罗厘没有这么早来的。

我左右看看, 嘿, 没有人啊。难道是天上掉下来的! 碰碰碰! 哇! 一直掉一直掉, 满地都是, 吓到满街的野猫野狗都呱里呱叫。

天上掉下来的免费榴梿, 好啊! 你知道我最喜欢榴梿! 当然要吃!

可是我走近一看, 啊, 不对啊! 什么东西在爬? 我再看, 哇唠! 是虫啊! 从那榴梿爬出来, 而且爬得满街满地都是!

那些猫啊狗啊, 本来都想来吃榴梿, 可是, 你绝对想不到, 那些虫一下子就爬上那些猫狗的身体, 拼命咬啊咬啊, 咬到那些猫狗惨叫, 而且, 不懂为什么, 那些猫狗给那些虫子咬到全身是血, 血流到满地都是。而且突然间就起火了。*Alamak*,[8] 我怕到要死, 我赶快跑进 taxi, 开引擎, 油门踏到完, 死命冲向 Geylang Road。我看一看望后镜, 哎呀! 那个火不懂为什么它拼命追向我的车, 张牙舞爪好象要把我吞掉。我想完了完了, 我就拼命冲向 Kallang 桥。

很奇怪嘞, 我一冲过 Lorong 1, 火就没有追来了。过了 Kallang 桥, 整个 Geylang 就这样没有了, Geylang 以外却一点都没有烧到。你说奇怪不奇怪?

后来, 报纸和电视台还放了我的相片, 而且还有, 他们也用了我讲的话作标题, 叫它做 '芽笼的超级榴梿大火'![9]

---

[7] *Roti prata* is flour-based flatbread that is cooked on a grill. In Singapore, it is usually served with a vegetable or meat-based curry. *Roti prata* is an adaptation of a traditional North Indian food known as *paratha*.

[8] Malay: *Alamak*, expression of surprise.

[9] Chinese: It's already seven o'clock. Strange, the sky was still so dark, I ate some *roti prata* and was about to drive into the city, when I suddenly heard a thud. I thought, hey, how strange, what sound was that? I turned around to look. Oh my! They're durians, durians! Who would be throwing durians at this hour? The lorries from Malaysia don't come [in] so early.

I looked to my left and right, there wasn't anyone. Can it be that they dropped from the sky? Thud, thud, thud! Wow! The fruits just kept coming down, and were all over the place. The stray dogs and stray cats in the streets were so frightened that they made a din.

Free durians from the sky, wasn't it great? You know I love durians best. Of course I wanted to eat them.

However, I walked closer to take a look, and oh, something was wrong. What were those crawling things? I looked again, oh my, they are worms! They crawled out from the durians, and crawled all over the place!

Johnny goes back to the group centre upstage. They all have their puppets in front and gaze at them in an intense manner — for a moment.

TIAN   Geylang.

ALL   Gone.

WEE   Geylang.

ALL   (*In Hokkien-Chinese.*) Bo liao loh.[10]

3. Remembering Geylang

They break up, and become children, all vying for a chance to tell story about Geylang — as dolls. They do this as if they are taking part in a primary school story-telling competition.

ONI   I tell my story in Chinese. 我的公公说芽笼有三个*naga*,[11] 对不对啊?[12]

KAMAL   不对啦, 三条龙。[13]

ONI   OK, OK, I tell in English. My grandpa say, Geylang burn down never mind, sure get rebuilt better because, my grandpa say, Geylang always treasure island, because Geylang got dragon. My grandpa say, Singapore very lucky, altogether

---

Those cats and the dogs originally intended to eat the durians as well, but you would never imagine, those worms swiftly climbed onto the bodies of the cats and the dogs, and started biting them hard, in fact so hard that the cats and the dogs screamed in pain. Moreover, inexplicably, those cats and dogs were bathed in blood from the bites and the blood was everywhere; and suddenly, a fire broke out. *Alamak*, dismayed and extremely scared, I ran to a taxi, got in and started the engine, stepped on the accelerator all the way down and desperately sped towards Geylang Road. I looked into the rear-view mirror. Oh dear, the fire for some unknown reason was hot on my trail, pursuing my car threateningly as if it wanted to gobble me up. I thought, it's all over, and I charged towards the Kallang Bridge for dear life. It was extremely strange, the moment I charged past Lorong 1, the fire stopped the chase. After crossing the Kallang Bridge, all of Geylang was gone, just like that, but the areas beyond Geylang were completely unaffected; don't you say that's very strange?

Later on, the newspapers and television stations all used my picture and what's more, they also used my words as the headline and called it 'The Great Durian Fire of Geylang'.

(The translations from Chinese into English in the notes are by Chan Cheow Thia.)

[10] *Minnan hua*, or *minnan* language: *Bo liao loh*, Nothing better to do.

[11] Javanese: *naga*, snake or dragon.

[12] Chinese: My grandfather said that Geylang had three *naga*, is that correct?

[13] Chinese: No, it should be three dragons.

got three dragon. Big Brother Dragon like eating, Second Brother Dragon like girls, Third Brother Dragon like shopping.

My Grandpa say: Big Brother Dragon who like eating live in Geylang; Second Brother Dragon who like girls also live in Geylang. That's why my grandpa say Geylang is treasure island and it's always good living there!

She bows and starts to go off.

ALL   Eh, eh, eh! ... Where's the Third Brother Dragon living?

ONI   *Aiya*, Third Dragon like shopping, lives in Orchard Road *lah*![14] You stupid or what?

YANG   我讲, 我讲, 轮到我讲。我的家住在Lorong 32。可是现在fire, *habis*[15] 咯! 我爸爸讲, 我们一定要 Geylang, 因为Geylang 一定发![16]

You know, my father told me that his father told him. Many many years ago, there was a construction site at Geylang. They dig dig dig ... *Alamak!* Finally they discovered a very deep *lobang*.[17] I tell you, nobody dare to go down to see how deep it was. 真的是很深的*lobang* 哦。没人敢下去呢。[18]

ENG   Hey, if the *lobang* so big until 没有人敢下去,[19] then who make the *lobang*?

YANG   唉呀。[20] *Mestilah datuk aku nampak. Kalau tidak, mana boleh bapa aku tahu? Engkau bodoh atau apa?*[21] 他讲哦, 后来他们敢敢下去看, 到了那个*lobang* 洞口, 刚刚要进去看, 哦~~! 哇! 一个东西飞出来, 快到谁都看不见,[22] o~~ and it is gone! Flew so quick that nobody saw what it was.

---

[14] Malay: *lah*, '[A] particle emphasising the word to which it is appended' (*A Malay-English English-Malay Dictionary*, ed. A. E. Coope [revised edn.; London and Basingstoke: Macmillan Education, 1991]).

[15] Malay: *habis*, finished or ended.

[16] Chinese: Let me talk, it's my turn. I live in Lorong 32. But because of the fire, all was gone! My father said, we must have Geylang, because Geylang will definitely prosper.

[17] Malay: *lobang*, hole.

[18] Chinese: It was really a very deep hole, nobody dared to go down.

[19] Chinese: ... nobody dared to go down, ...

[20] Chinese: *Aiya*. Note: An expression of annoyance.

[21] Malay: Must be my grandfather who saw it. Otherwise how can my grandfather have known about it? If my grandfather didn't know how can my father have known? Are you stupid or what?

[22] Chinese: He said, in the end they plucked up the courage, but when they reached the edge of the hole and was about to go down for a survey, oh wow! Something flew out, it was so fast that nobody could see what it was, ...

DICK　Hey, you bullshit again. If the thing fly so fast nobody can see, how can your *Ah Gong*[23] see, huh? You tell me.

YANG　唉呀。*Mestilah datuk aku Nampak. Kalau tidak, mana boleh datuk aku tahu? Jika datuk aku tak tahu, mana boleh bapa aku tahu? Engkau bodoh atau apa?*[24]

DICK　*Alamak*, go ahead and tell, *lah*. Quick, quick!

YANG　OK, 那个东西哦~~一下飞走了, 我的阿公就进去看。*Alamak!* 好象有人住过哩! 可是又好象不是人住过窝! 因为啊, 他们发现那个住在里面的东西, 他的大便有这样大粒哩!![25] You see, how can a human has shit this big? My grandpa thought, must be a giant creature lived there!

KAMAL　Hey, hey, how come your grandpa know those big things are shit?

DOREEN　He tasted it *lah*, of course!

　　　　What happened after your grandpa found the big shit?

YANG　他们看到*lobang*里面的墙上有一些很奇怪的图案, 弯来弯去, 没有人会看, 很多年以后, 我的阿公第一次搭MRT,[26] 他一进MRT 就差一点心脏病爆发, 因为他发现那个MRT 的地图和那个*lobang* 里面的图案是一模一样的哩。[27] You don't believe it. The map of the MRT is exactly the same as the picture on the wall of the *lobang*.

KHALID　What? The sign in the *lobang* same as our MRT route map? Fantastic — bullshit!

YANG　你们觉得很奇怪啊? 因为, 我的爸爸讲我的公公讲, 那个 '呼' 一下子飞出来的东西, 原来就是新加坡的 dragon![28]

---

[23] Mandarin-Chinese: *Ah Gong*, grandfather.
[24] Malay: Must be my grandfather who saw it. Otherwise how can my grandfather have known about it? If my grandfather didn't know how can my father have known? Are you stupid or what?
[25] Chinese: That thing flew away in a flash. My grandfather went into the hole to take a look. Oh my, somebody seemed to have lived there, but it didn't look as if it was the den of a human being. Because they discovered that the thing that lived inside, its excrement was as big as this!
[26] MRT, Mass Rapid Transit — a reference to Singapore's metro train system.
[27] Chinese: They saw that there were some strange pictures on the walls inside the hole, twisting and turning, nobody understood them. Many years later, my grandfather took the MRT train for the first time and almost got a heart attack when he entered the station, for he discovered that the MRT map was identical with the pictures inside that hole.
[28] Chinese: Do you guys find it strange? Because, according to what my father and grandfather said, what flew in a flash then was actually Singapore's dragon!

YATI   I also got *naga* story.

LIAN   I never used to believe in this kind of folklore. Until last year, not long before Great Geylang Durian Fire.

I went to watch a friend competing in water-skiing in Kallang River. I was standing on Kallang Bridge, cheering her from there. Then, when I turned my head to look at Geylang Road, *alamak*, so incredible, the whole of Geylang Road was like a glittering river, shining so bright I cannot keep my eyes open, And then, this river started to flow, to float, like it was going to fly away. I stared hard, I rubbed my eyes and stared hard. And then it was gone!

I was shivering all over. Excited, or scared. What was happening? *What?*

Then, I remembered. I remembered an old fortune teller once told me: Geylang would always be a lucky place, because there is a dragon living underneath Geylang Road. But only those with a third eye can see it.

WEE   哇, 你有第三只眼啊?[29]

LIAN   大概只开了几秒就关了，所以我只看到了住在芽笼地下那条龙亮亮的龙麟。真是神龙见首不见尾啊![30] You know, I didn't even see which way was the head of the dragon and which way was the tail of the dragon.

DOREEN   *Naga* head must be in Geylang Serai side *lah*.

KAMAL   Maybe, but I think also maybe the *naga* head is in Gay World. See, the Indoor Stadium[31] round round one, looks like *naga* head.

Now the two blind-mutes walk by again.

DOREEN moves over to wave before them to test if they would respond. Khalid stops her by telling her in mime that the two were made blind, deaf and dumb by the fire.

As they walk off, a more sombre mood sets in.

Seeing people coming, TECK LIAN motions them to leave.

---

[29] Chinese: Wow, have you got a third eye?

[30] Chinese: It probably opened only for a few seconds before shutting again, and thus I merely saw the shiny scales of the dragon that lived in subterranean Geylang. It was amazingly elusive!

[31] A reference to the Singapore Indoor Stadium, an indoor sports arena, located in Kallang, Singapore, that was completed in 1989.

LIAN　　Hey, kids, better go away. Grown-up people doing business. We better get out of the way!

The kids go to the side areas of the stage.

A platform with scaffolding on it is wheeled out with a woman upon it, with her back to audience. Then the two stage hands — DICK and KAMAL — play the roles of two men.

DICK　　(*In Hokkien-Chinese.*) Oi ... Psst ... Oi......弟啊[32]...... *siao eh?*[33]

KAMAL　　(*Points to himself to seek clarification.*)

DICK　　(*He gestures to Kamal to come closer.*) 有鸡吗?[34]

KAMAL　　*Kueh apa?*[35]

DICK　　鸡啦![36]

KAMAL　　*Kueh tutu, kueh lapis, kueh paiti, kueh sugi ...*[37]

DICK　　我不知道你在讲什么啦?[38]

KAMAL　　*Kueh.* (*Puts hand to his mouth.*)

DICK　　哎呀, 不是吃的*kueh*啦, 鸡啊, 鸡啊![39] (*Pretends to be a chicken*)

KAMAL　　Oh! *Pasar ...*[40]

DICK　　哎呀, 我不是讲巴刹的鸡啦! 我是讲这种鸡啊![41]

KAMAL　　*Perempuan ... pasar ...*[42]

---

[32] Chinese: Young man ...
[33] *Minnan hua* or *minnan* language: *siao*, mad.
[34] Chinese: Do you have 'chicks'? Dick is using a pun, where 'chicks' in Chinese is a slang term for 'prostitute'.
[35] Malay: *Kueh apa?* What [sort of] cake?
[36] Chinese: 'Chicks'!
[37] Malay: *Kueh tutu, kueh lapis, kueh paiti, kueh sugi ...*, Tutu cake, layered cake, paiti cake, semolina cake ...
[38] Chinese: I don't know what you are talking about?
[39] Chinese: *Aiya,* I don't mean cakes to be eaten, I mean 'chicks', 'chicks'!
[40] Malay: *Pasar,* market.
[41] Chinese: *Aiya,* I am not talking about chicks in the market, I am talking about this kind of 'chicks'!
[42] Malay: *Perempuan ... pasar ...*, Women ... market ...

DICK   *Wah piang eh!*[43] 弟呀! 鸡啦。(*Mimics a prostitute posing against railings.*) 这种鸡啦![44]

KAMAL   Oooh ...

DICK   Oooh ... 在哪里?[45]

KAMAL   *Apam?*[46]

DICK   *Wah lau!*[47] *Kek sim*[48] ah! 在哪里? 鸡在哪里?[49]

KAMAL   Oh ... *mana*[50] ... Gay World ... Lorong ...

DICK   我不懂你在讲什么啦![51]

KAMSAL   *Ini*[52] Gay World.

DICK   我知道! 打球那里?[53]

KAMAL   Lorong 2.

DICK   二巷![54]

KAMAL   Lorong 4.

---

[43] *Minnan hua* or *minnan* language: *Wah piang* eh! The Talking Cock website defines this expression as being a more 'polite' version of the expression *Wah lan* or *Wah lan eh*: 'Hokkien[-Chinese] term which can be loosely translated as "Oh Penis". Probably the most common Singlish [i.e., colloquial Singapore English] expression of all, it is used in much the same way as "oh my goodness", "wow", or "damn!", depending on the tone used, and the context. More polite variants include "*Wah Lau*" and "*Wah Piang*".' Available from: http://www.talkingcock.com/html/lexec.php?op=LexLink&lexicon=lexicon&keyword=Wah Lan&page=1, accessed 7 March 2012.
[44] Chinese: Young man! 'Chicks' (*Mimics a prostitute posing against railings.*) This kind of 'chicks'.
[45] Chinese: Where?
[46] Malay: *Apam*, name of a cake, but also an indirect reference to a woman's private part.
[47] See note 43.
[48] *Minnan hua* or *minnan* language: *Kek sim*, literally frustrated hard; thus, very frustrating.
[49] Chinese: Where? Where are the 'chicks'?
[50] Malay: *mana*, where.
[51] Chinese: I don't know what you are talking about!
[52] Malay: *Ini*, This is.
[53] Chinese: I know! The place where people play ball games?
[54] Chinese: Lane 2.

DICK 　　四巷![55]

KAMAL brings DICK upstage describing the Lorongs.

DICK 　　*Wah!* 这么多啊![56]

Both shake hands. They walk back to the platform with the scaffolding.

JUDY 　　We very clean. You very welcome. Our sitting room clean, corridor clean. My room small but also very clean. And we very, very clean because we wash after every serving. And customers also very clean because we shower them before they do. When we do it, we do it very clean. Law say man must always wear condom — many colour, you choose. Oh, no eat no drink and no smoke in our place before or after service. Your law very good.

I start three o'clock sharp. Every job 30 minutes; if you slow slow, my boss ring bell. Over 30 minutes, overtime charge. Advance booking can do. I stop work 1 am, midnight. But we also have special overnight service.

Where I stay? I stay where I work, I work where I stay. Very good.

What? Oh no, sorry, no home delivery. But my friend say you can get delivery service in the upper Lorongs. There, local service, I think, you can use phone or fax also, very fast.

My boss say very nice, he say we must offer our services with our unique spirit of excellence — clean, courteous, comprehensive. The three Cs of Geylang S!

'S' for what? 'S' for sex lor!

All come on stage with their puppets, singing 'Geylang Sipaku Geylang'.[57]

---

[55] Lane 4.
[56] So many [places]!
[57] 'Geylang Sipaku Geylang'
Chorus
Geylang sipaku Geylang,
Geylang si rama rama,
Pulang, marilah pulang, marilah pulang bersama-sama. (2x)

Jangan memegang arang,
Letak di dalam raga.
Jangan mengata orang,
Diri sendiri baik dijaga.

SAM   My mother's favourite has always been the Geylang Serai *Pasar*.[58]

As JUDY's platform is moved away, another platform with scaffolding is wheeled in, followed by two old women chatting. They climb up onto what is supposed to be a verandah.

All the others sit at both sides of the stage and lower their puppets.

BT   你知道吗? 芽笼的巴刹样样有, 样样有。[59]

Jangan masuk ke kota,
Jikalau membawa pandan.
Jangan suka mengata,
Akibat nanti binasa badan.

Mari pergi menjala,
Jala di tengah kuala.
Tikus maharajalela,
Melihat kucing pening kepala.

(Lyrics from Aisha Akbar [compiler], *Thirty-Six Best Loved Songs of Malaysia and Singapore* [Singapore: Eastern University Press, 1966]).

'Geylang Sipaku Geylang' (translation)

Chorus
Geylang full of ferns,
Geylang full of butterflies,
Come let's go home, let's go home together. (2x)

Do not carry the charcoal,
Just put it in a basket.
Do not be quick to criticize others,
Better to watch your own behavior.

Do not go into town,
If you are carrying *pandan*.
Do not be gossipy,
Lest you damage yourself.

Let us go fishing,
In the middle of the river mouth.
The mouse went crazy,
Sees the cat and gets a headache.

(Translation by Lai Ah Eng, Available from: http://www.myjoochiat.com/, accessed 7 March 2012.)
[58] Malay: *Pasar*, Market.
[59] Chinese: Do you know? There's everything at the Geylang wet market, everything.

YATI   Ah … *Pasat*.[60]

BT   有肉啊, 有菜啊, 统统便宜到拉屎。朋友也很多啊, 有他 '吉灵'、你、'番仔'、我'唐人', 统统都在巴刹里面。[61]

YATI   Ya, *pasat* … *kacang*[62] …

BT   *Kacang*! 是啊, 是啊, 巴刹里面那摊 *cendol*[63] 的 *kacang* 好吃啊。[64]

YATI   Ah … *cendol* … ah tat chee[65] …

BT   亚达籽! 哎哟好吃啊。我的孩子最喜欢吃了。我看了也流口水。[66]

TAM enters.

TAM   Ma!

YATI/BT   Aye!

TAM   Auntie!

YATI/BT   Aye!

TAM   I'm so angry.

BT   什么事?[67]

TAM   This teacher of mine, bad woman, bad mouth, she said, 'Very good, very good, Geylang burn down very good. All the evil brothels and all the dirty hawkers I don't have to tolerate any more. Now can build big big building, supermarket, fast-food centre.' Terrible, this woman!

---

[60] Singapore-Malaysian Hokkien-Chinese adaptation of the Malay term *pasar*, market.

[61] Chinese: There's meat, there's vegetables, all dirt cheap. There are also plenty chances to make friends, there are Indians like him, you, the foreigners, the Malays, the Chinese like me, all in the wet market.

[62] Malay: *kacang*, nut.

[63] Malay: *cendol*, a dessert that can be found in Indonesia, Malaysia, Singapore and even Burma. The main ingredients consist of coconut milk, little worm-like slivers of jelly made from rice flour (coloured green with food colouring often derived from the *pandan* leaf), shaved ice and palm sugar.

[64] Chinese: Right, the *kacang* of that *cendol* stall in the market is delicious.

[65] Yati's attempt to say *attap chee* (*minnan hua* or *minnan* language), the seed of the Nipa palm that is used in *cendol*.

[66] Chinese: *Attap chee*! They are delicious. My children love them as their favourite food. I also salivate in expected delight when I see them.

[67] Chinese: What is it?

YATI   *Bodoh lah, cikgu-tu!*[68]

BT   喂, 叫你的老师去撞墙![69]

TAM   And then I and my friend started talking about the Geylang that we want to rebuild and I said: I want the new Geylang to be like the old Geylang and put in old things from the past also. Like the trolley bus — the kind they have in San Francisco and Melbourne.

DICK   Your trolley bus rail or cable one?

TAM   I think cables are too messy, not nice. So we'll have trolley bus on rail! The trolley bus then can bring us to Gay World.

SAM   Gay World? Why not Happy World?

TAM   Oi, Gay World last time called Happy World hor? OK *lah*, bring back Happy World.

ENG   快乐世界。快乐世界里面有什么?[70]

TAM   快乐世界。快乐, 大家快乐。[71] Happy World of course must make people happy! So inside must have place for people to congregate. 要跳舞就要有舞厅。[72] Must have cabaret! Got dance sure got song so I want 歌台[73] also ... Eh, basketball! I also want a basketball court. Then, 大家可以一起打篮球, 大家。[74] Happy! Erm, adult happy, children must also be happy. So I want ... Ferris Wheel! And Carousel! (*In Hokkien.*) *Gogo bey.*[75] Play, play, play, hungry already *leh*. I want food! *Muah Chee*,[76] 叮叮糖,[77] *kacang putih*,[78] 棉花糖![79] Mm, yummy!

---

[68] Malay: Stupid *lah* that teacher!

[69] Chinese: Hey, get your teacher to bang her head against the wall!

[70] Chinese: Happy World. What was inside Happy World?

[71] Chinese: Happy World. Happy, everyone was happy.

[72] Chinese: There must be a dance hall if people wanted to dance.

[73] Chinese: Performing stage.

[74] Then, all of us can play basketball together, all of us.

[75] *Minnan hua* or *minnan* language; also *chaozhou hua*, or Teochew-Chinese: *Gogo bey*, klopity klop horse. *Gogo* is an onomatopœia, and *bey* means horse.

[76] *Muah Chee* is a Teochew-Chinese style steamed, sticky dough made of glutinous flour. It is cut into small pieces, then coated with sugar and crushed roasted peanuts. Toasted sesame seeds are also sometimes added.

[77] Chinese: 'Ding Ding' maltose candy.

[78] Malay: *kacang putih*, literally, white nuts. It more generally refers to roasted, salted or sweetened peas, peanuts and other types of beans or nuts, traditionally sold wrapped in paper cones.

[79] Chinese: Cotton candy.

Then, the trolley bus goes to Geylang Serai — Geylang Serai must have *serai* what.

DICK   What is *serai*?

TAM   *Serai* is lemongrass *lor*.

ENG   What is lemongrass?

TAM   Lemongrass is *cang mao lor*. Eh! Geylang Kelapa! Geylang Kelapa is over there. Wah, so many coconuts ah. Yah *lah*, Geylang Kelapa must have coconuts what. *Kelapa*[80] 不就是椰子吗? 椰子好, 很多水! 水好, 有水才会旺啊![81] Ah! A river. Geylang must have a river! A river in Geylang. Geylang River. *Sungai*[82] Geylang! Yup, bring back Sungai Geylang.

ONI   (*In Malay.*) Are there going to be *kampungs*[83] next to the river?

TAM   *Kampung* next to the river ah? *Mestilah ada kampung.*[84] If got *kampung*, must have people — fishermen; if got fishermen, must have fishing boats; if got fishing boats, must gave fishing net, then there must be fish in the river *lah*!

ENG   What about Raffles?[85]

TAM   Raffles ah, don't want *lah*, too many Raffles already ... And then I want... I want ...

At this juncture, the 'corpse' of a prostitute — played by ONI — appears, and is carried by an old man.

The following is accompanied by the distant sound of a spiritual song, punctuated by the sound of percussion from a temple.

ONI   When I was young, I avoided walking through the lorongs because I also thought prostitutes were all very bad people. When I later became one myself, I began to know better.

---

[80] Malay: *Kelapa*, coconut.

[81] Chinese: Isn't that coconut? Coconuts are good, they're very juicy. Water is good, with water there will be prosperity.

[82] Malay: *Sungai*, river.

[83] Malay: *kampung*, village.

[84] Malay: *Mestilah ada kampung*, There must be a *kampung* there.

[85] Sir Thomas Stamford Bingley Raffles (1781–1826) is acknowledged by the city-state of Singapore to be its official founder. A reference is being made to the spot on the Singapore River where Raffles first landed in Singapore in 1819.

Yes, there are those who just come to play a fool, and they always make us suffer. But many more are very good people who just need a woman they don't have.

Do you know what happens when a young man goes into a room with a strange woman? Do you know what goes on in a young man's mind and heart when he takes off his clothes to hug a naked stranger woman?

Many of them are very shy, very coy. Many of them tremble; some of them even cry. Like babies, they hug me as if I am their mother.

Many of them want to have the lights on. Some just want to look at my body, but many also want to look into my eyes. And, so, I can also look into their eyes.

Very often we cannot talk because we speak different language. But I can read their heart and their mind through their eyes. And I know why they tremble, why they cry, why they hug me so tight like babies hug their mother.

When I have my monthly, I go to sleep in a temple in the next lorong. There I rest my body, and I spend many hours thinking about those young man who look me in the eye and cry in my bosom.

Now, I can rest my body and think of those young men for ever …

Pause.

Dance Two.

4. Rebuilding Geylang

Second rendering of the Great Durian Fire of Geylang.

WEE   七月七日, 早晨。大火, 芽笼被夷为平地。火起得非常神秘, 火灾区非常奇怪。[86]

DICK   Exactly marked out by Lorong 1 and Gay World, Geylang Serai and Haig Road, Sims Avenue and Guillemard Road.

WEE   芽笼士乃一位德士司机说, 起火的原因很神秘。[87]

---

[86] Chinese: 七月七日 Seventh July, morning. A big fire, Geylang was razed to the ground. The fire started very mysteriously, the disaster area was very strange.

[87] Chinese: 七月七日 A taxi driver in Geylang Serai said, the cause of the fire was very mysterious.

KAMAL   *Waktu dah pagi, tapi langit masih gelap. Saya terdengar bunyi bising …*
         Bombombom. Saya toleh belakang. Eh? Ada durian jatuh dari langit! Banyak
         anjing dan kucing berkerumun. Alangkah terperanjatnya saya melihat ulat
         besar beluar dari biji durian. Ulat-ulat besar itu terus merayap dan meng-
         gigit badan anjing dan kucing semua dengan ganasnya. Darah mengalir
         berkelumuran.[88]

         Selepas itu, darah itu bertukar menjadi api dan ianya mula merebak dengan
         lajunya. Saya toleh belakang. Eh! Anch! Api dah berhenti! Satu Geylang terba-
         kar. Dari Geylang Serai ke Lorong 1, Sims Avenue, Geylang Road sampai
         Guillemard Road. Di dalam, semua hancur, di luar tiada apa-apa. Dari hari itu,
         ianya dipanggil kebakaran durian terbasar di Geylang![89]

         Geylang.

ALL   *Habis.*

WEE   芽笼。[90]

ALL   没有了。[91]

Percussion sounds. JOHNNY and assistant PAT come on beating the gong like street
medicine-sellers.

JOHN   来来来, 人生不要那么悲观。[92]

PAT   Come, come, come, life should not be so tragic.

JOHN   芽笼是块宝地, 你们不要生在福中不知福。

PAT   Geylang is a place of great fortune. You should know how lucky you are!

JOHN   芽笼的消失, 并不一定是坏事。

---

[88] Malay: It is morning already, but the sky is still dark. I heard a loud noise … Bombombom. I
looked behind. Eh? There were durians falling from the sky. A lot of dogs and cats came crowding
over it. I was shocked to see a big worm coming out of the durian. The big worm crawled all over
and bit the bodies of the dogs and cats mercilessly. Blood covered the bodies.

[89] Malay: After that, the blood changed. It turned into a fire and it spread so fast. I looked behind.
Eh! Ah! The fire stopped spreading! The whole of Geylang was on fire. From Geylang Serai to
Lorong 1, Sims Avenue, Geylang Road to Guillemard Road. Inside [Geylang], everything was
destroyed but outside, nothing. From that day it is called the biggest durian fire in Geylang.

[90] Chinese: Geylang.

[91] Chinese: Gone.

[92] Pat directly follows to translate Johnny's Chinese pronouncements.

PAT   Geylang disappearing may not be a bad thing.

JOHN   芽笼被夷为平地, 就象冲了一个凉。

PAT   Geylang burnt is like taking a shower.

JOHN   就象是洗了一个澡。

PAT   Like taking a bath.

JOHN   芽笼的灾难, 有如凤凰涅槃。[93]

PAT   Geylang's tragedy is like *fenghuang niepan*.[94]

JOHN   什么? (*耳语*。)[95]

PAT   Oh … oh … Geylang's tragedy is like phoenix Nirvana.

JOHN   芽笼将会凤凰再生, 重现它的生命力。[96]

PAT   Geylang will rise again like the Phoenix, with extraordinary energy!

JOHN   孔夫子仲尼先生有句千古名言。[97]

PAT   There is a famous saying by Mr Johnny Confucius.

JOHN   嘿, 怎么孔夫子变成 Johnny 啦。[98]

PAT   不然怎样讲? 要Johnny Kong 还是Johnny Confucius?[99]

JOHN   好, Johnny Confucius 比较好听! 孔夫子有句千古名言。[100]

PAT   Johnny Confucius' famous saying!

JOHN   食色性也。食。色。性。也。[101]

---

[93] Geylang's tragedy is like the Chinese phoenix attaining Nirvana.

[94] Nirvana of the Phoenix.

[95] What? (*Whispers in his ear.*)

[96] Geylang as the Chinese Phoenix will experience a rebirth and demonstrate its vitality once again.

[97] The Confucius Kong Zhongni has a saying of ancient wisdom. [Note: The philosopher was born Kong Qiu, with the formal name Kong Zhongni.]

[98] Chinese: Hey, how is it that Confucius became Johnny?

[99] Chinese: Or else how should I say it? Choose, Johnny Kong or Johnny Confucius?

[100] Chinese: OK, Johnny Confucius sounds better! There is a saying of ancient wisdom by Confucius.

[101] Chinese: 'The desire for food and sex is part of human nature.' *Shi. Se. Xing. Ye.* [Note: Johnny emphasises each part of the four-character text.]

PAT　　Oh! Food! Colour! Sex! Also!

LIAN　　食色性也[102] means, 'Food and colour make sex wild.'

JUDY　　No, 食色性也[103] means, 'If you eat food with artificial colour, you become very wild.'

DICK　　No, no, no, 食色性也 means, 'If you eat food with artificial colour you become sexually very wild.'

LIAN　　No, no, no, 食色性也 means 食色性也. You see this man Shise [食色], his surname Ye [也], so 食色性也.

JOHN　　谢谢, 谢谢各位对孔夫子的名言表现了高度的想象力。[104]

PAT　　Thank you. Your interpretation of Confucius is highly original and creative.

JOHN　　芽笼的前途一定光明无比。

PAT　　Geylang's future will be very bright.

JOHN　　各位同胞, 我们都是龙的传人。

PAT　　Dear fellow compatriots. We are all descendants of the dragon.

SAM　　Eh, eh, *penurun naga tuan itu ada kepak atau tidak kepak?*[105]

PAT　　他问说, 你讲的龙的传人是有翅膀的还是没有翅膀的?[106]

JOHN　　我讲的龙的传人包括有翅膀的和没有翅膀的; 只要他认为自己是一条龙, 他就是龙, 是不是龙, 有没有翅膀都没有关系。[107]

PAT　　Got wing or not makes no difference. As long as you declare yourself a dragon descendant, you will be a dragon descendant.

---

[102] *Shi se xing ye*. [Note: The Confucian text is repeated, and Dick and Teck Lian continue playing linguistically with the text in the lines that follow. See note 101.]

[103] *Shi se xing ye*.

[104] Pat directly follows to translate this and the next two lines by Johnny.

[105] Malay: Eh, eh the descendants of your dragon have wings or not?

[106] Chinese: He asked if the descendants of the dragon you mentioned have wings or not.

[107] Chinese: The descendants of the dragon I mentioned include those with wings and those without. As long as he thinks he is a dragon, he is one. Whether one has wings is unrelated to the issue of whether one is a dragon.

KHALID (*In Indian accent.*) Some got dragon, some got *naga*, what about those who don't even have dragon or *naga*, how?

PAT 他讲, 有人有 *dragon*, 有人有 *naga*, 那这些都没有的人怎么办?[108]

JOHN 没有龙, 没有 *naga*, 他有蛇也可以啊。那种大大条的眼睛蛇也可以算嘛。其实, 只要他是一条虫, 不论什么虫, 只要这条虫够大条, 就可以变成龙。[109]

PAT He says, snake also can. The big cobra can also count as dragon. In fact, any worm-looking thing, as long as they get big enough, can be counted as dragon.

JOHN 好了, 各位, 现在我言归正传, 我今天来这里, 主要是为了介绍我的芽笼发展大计划。

PAT To come to my real task. Ladies and gentlemen, I am here today to introduce to you my grand plan for the future of Geylang.

JOHN 食色性也大芽笼。

PAT The Great Geylang Sex and Food Megamall!

SAM Eh, *kawan dari mana? Kawan ada pentingal di Geylang?*[110]

JOHN 哦, 坦白说一句, 我并非芽笼的居民。[111]

TAM Then why are you developing Geylang?

JOHN (气吞河山地。) 因为我买了半个芽笼的地皮。芽笼的主权, 有一半是属于我的! 好, 首先, 让我表明立场, 尽管我有权力为所欲为, 但是, 我很愿意跟你们合作。我知道你们对于过去的芽笼有极大的感情。因此, 我决定了, 你们要保留的东西, 我全部接受, 你们要加上去的东西, 我也全部同意。[112]

YATI *Pasar basah kita?*[113]

---

[108] Pat directly translates what Khalid has just said into Chinese.

[109] Pat will now resume translating what Johnny says.

[110] Malay: Eh, friend where are you from? Friend, have you ever lived in Geylang?

[111] Chinese: To tell the truth, I am not a resident of Geylang.

[112] Chinese: (*In a grand and boastful manner.*) Because I have bought half the land in Geylang. Half of the legal rights of Geylang [now] belongs to me! Allow me therefore to first express my stand, even though I have the power to do whatever I want, I am very willing to cooperate with all of you. I understand that all of you are deeply attached to the Geylang of the past. Hence I have decided to accept all those things you wish to preserve; as for what you hope to add, I will also agree to all requests.

[113] Malay: [What about] Our wet market?

JOHN   保留。你们的湿巴刹, 我计划全面重建。[114]

TAM   My tram?

JOHN   你的电车, 好说好说, 用铁轨的, 用天上电缆的每样给你建一套。[115]

ONI   What about our Happy World? Merry-go-round, indoor stadium, Datuk Rajah nightclub —

DOREEN   叮叮糖, 棉花糖……[116]

JOHN   全部给, 全部给你们。[117]

TAM   My *Sungai* Geylang?

JOHN   古老的芽笼士乃, 我不但愿意重新开掘, 我还要给你重建一座 *kampung,* 任由你们自己装扮成渔夫, 自由自地地划着小舢板, 载着鱼网, 到那满是鱼虾的芽笼河里, 捕鱼玩耍。[118]

PAT   You can have everything.

ALL   Yeah!

After the tremendous cheer, they begin to sense that it is too easy. And everyone quieten down and focus their eyes on JOHNNY, who seems to be the only person who has the answer for that implicit concern.

JUDY   Why are you so nice to us?

JOHN   很简单。我让你们都心满意足了, 你们才会考虑让我心满意足。我是一个很公平很正义的人。孔夫子说, 己所不欲勿施于人。[119]

PAT   As Johnny Confucius say, do not unto others what you would not do unto yourself.

---

[114] Chinese: Preserve. Your wet market. I intend to overhaul it completely.

[115] Chinese: Your tram, that can be negotiated, no matter whether it is the rail system or the overhead cable system, I can build it for you.

[116] Chinese: 'Ding-ding' maltose candy, cotton candy …

[117] Chinese: I will provide everything, everything for all of you.

[118] Chinese: Not only am I willing to revive the old Geylang Serai, I will also rebuild a *kampung* for you, and you will be free to dress up as fishermen, rowing your sampan freely, transporting your fishing nets to Geylang River where it is full of fish and prawns to play with and to catch the fish.

[119] Chinese: It's very simple. Only when I have fully satisfied all of you, will you all consider satisfying me. I am a very fair person who emphasises justice. As Confucius said, do not do unto others what you would not have them do unto you.

YATI   Eh, *apa tujuan tuan pada rancagan besar ini?*[120]

JOHN   你问我的目的啊。很简单, 而且我要说得很透明, 我要在这里展开一项大规模的发展投资, 我要在这块地下有神龙睡觉的宝地, 建设一座前所未有的食色性也大芽笼!

现在, 让我请我的专家顾问们为你们简单的介绍一下这个 Food and Sex Megamall 食色性也大芽笼![121]

DICK   Now, the grand masterplan.

Gay World to Lorong 18 — Sex Palace — 性爱宫殿 — *Panggung Seks.*[122]

Lorong 19 to Lorong 28 — Food and Sex Palace — 性爱美食宫殿 — *Panggung Makanan Dan Seks.*[123]

Lorong 29 to Paya Lebar — Food Palace — 美食宫殿 — *Panggung Makanan.*[124]

First, the Sex Palace.

WEE   异性的性, 同性的性。
多体的性, 单体的性。
真正的性, 想象的性。
代替的性, 虚幻的性。
手工的性, 工具的性。
给予的性, 分享的性。
参观的性, 表演的性。

DICK   Hetero sex, homosex.
Multiple sex, monosex.
Real sex, imagined sex.
Substitute sex, virtual sex.
Manual sex, mechanical sex.

---

[120] Malay: Eh, what is your intention for carrying this big plan?

[121] Chinese: You asked about my motives. They're very simple, and I wish to make them very clear. I wish to invest in a large-scale development project here; I wish to construct an unprecedented Food and Sex Megamall on this piece of treasured land under which sleeps a magical dragon.

Now, allow me to invite my expert consultant to make a short introduction to this Great Geylang Food and Sex Megamall.

[122] Malay: *Panggung Seks*, Sex Hall. [Note: Dick chooses to translate *panggung* as 'palace' rather than 'hall', 'theatre' or 'stage'. In general, what Dick does is to give locations, and then indicate in English, Mandarin-Chinese and Malay what type of 'palace' or 'hall' will go up in the locations.]

[123] Malay: *Panggung Makanan Dan Seks*, Food and Sex Hall.

[124] Malay: *Panggung Makanan*, Food Hall.

Giving sex, sharing sex.
Watching sex, displaying sex.

ALL   What?

DICK   Sexy show like striptease *lah*.

And all these sensual activities are housed in four separate cultural complexes, namely:
The Kamasutra.

WEE   印度经典。[125]

DICK   The Golden Lotus.

WEE   中国经典。[126]

DICK   The Arabian nights.

WEE   阿拉伯经典。[127]

DICK   The Shenandoah — a nudist camp.

WEE   美国经典。[128]

ENG   Now, the food palace.
生吃的美食, 熟吃的美食。
吃肉的美食, 吃素的美食。
讲究的美食, 小民的美食。
坐着吃的美食, 站着吃的美食。
最新鲜的美食, 最臭酸的美食。[129]

DICK   Raw food, cooked food.
Meat food, veg food.
Farmer food, hunter food.
Cuisine food, hawker food.
Family food, banquet food.
Sitting food, standing food.
Fresh food, stale food.

---

[125] Chinese: An Indian classic.
[126] Chinese: A Chinese classic.
[127] Chinese: An Arabic classic.
[128] Chinese: An American classic.
[129] Dick directly follows to translate what Eng has just said into English.

ALL   What?

DICK   Preserved food like cheese *lah*.

           All these culinary pleasures will be housed in four cultural palaces, namely:

           The Butcher's Stable

ENG   杀生大院。[130]

DICK   The Garden of Eden.

ENG   依甸菜园。

DICK   The Roman Colosseum.

ENG   罗马剧场

DICK   The Emperor's Chamber.

ENG   宫廷小厅。
           性和吃, 吃和性。
           性前先吃, 吃前先性。
           奇异的性加吃, 奇异的吃加性。
           野味的吃加性, 野性的性加吃。[131]

DICK   Food and sex, sex and food.
           Food before sex, sex before food.
           Spiced food and sex, spiced sex and food.
           Wild sex with food, wild food with sex.

ALL   What?

DICK   Like skinning a wild rabbit while you have sex *lah*.

JOHN   这就是我的食色性也大芽笼![132]

PAT   The Great Geylang Food and Sex Megamall!

           Yes, yes, the Great Geylang Sex and Food Megamall!

Only now do they comprehend what this man is saying. They are silenced, and anxiously wait to hear the man explain himself. With assistance from his team members, JOHNNY describes his grand plan for Geylang.

---

[130] Chinese: The Butcher's Table. [Note: Eng now follows to translate the Chinese into English for Dick.]

[131] Dick follows by translating what Eng says in Chinese into English.

[132] Chinese: This is my Great Geylang Food and Sex Megamall.

JOHN   从芽笼士乃到繁华世界, 不, 快乐世界, 把20条*lorong*切成40 条小街。这一片宝地上的建筑, 总体来说, 具有非常独特的热带建筑特色。大家放心, 我们要专家研究鉴定, 按照这些建筑的黄金时代的样式全部重建。[133]

YATI   *Semua bangunkan macam zaman lama lulu?*[134]

SAM   If you rebuild everything like old times, how to develop your —

PAT   The Great Geylang Sex and Food Megamall.

ALL   Yeah, where?

JOHN   (*指着说。*) 当然在这里, 在芽笼这里。[135]

ALL   你不是说要保留旧有芽笼的特色?[136]

JOHN   要保留, 也要发展。旧的芽笼, 将再度平地而起, 不过, 我有一个条件, 我可以完全依照大家的愿望重建旧芽笼, 但是, 大家必须同意, 旧芽笼重建后不能搬回去住。[137]

PAT   One condition: you can't go back to old Geylang.

All shocked to hear this.

JOHN   不用怕, 我会再建一个一模一样的芽笼, 在地底下, 请大家到地下去住。地下的芽笼, 将附带一切先进的生活用具。我甚至可以把你们的古代河流天上的太阳都搬到地下去。一切费用由我承担。[138]

PAT   Don't worry, we'll build one for you a copy — underground.

---

[133] Chinese: From Geylang Serai to Gay World, no, Happy World; to cut 20 *lorongs* into 40 smaller streets. On the whole, the buildings on this piece of treasured land possess a unique tropical flavour. Please be assured that we will engage experts to conduct research and assessment, so as to restore the style of these buildings to their heyday.

[134] Malay: All to be built as of the old days?

[135] Chinese: (*Pointing*) Of course, it will be located here, here in Geylang.

[136] Chinese: Didn't you say that you wish to preserve the old Geylang flavour?

[137] Chinese: Preservation should go hand in hand with development. The old Geylang will rise from the ground again. However, I have a condition. I can rebuild the old Geylang in full accordance with everyone's wishes, but everyone must agree that when the old Geylang is rebuilt, you will not move back.

[138] Chinese: Don't worry, I will build an identical Geylang underground and invite everyone to live below the ground level. The underground Geylang will come with all sorts of advanced living items. There, I can even get you the rivers like those in ancient times and the sun in the sky. I will bear all the expenses.

JOHN 而地面上的旧芽笼将成为举世无双的娱乐城。[139]

PAT The Megamall will be on the ground level!

JOHN Now, the report.

WEE Geylang Road 的两边分为单数及双数。从 Gay World 到 Lorong 22, 是Geylang 红灯区的心脏, 有各种各样的身体服务中心。Lorong 22 到 Paya Lebar Road 有 karaoke 及几间比较高档次的, 专门提供外卖的身体服务中心。Paya Lebar Road 直上到 Haig Road 有 shopping centres.

Sims Avenue 这一边, Lorong 1 到 Lorong 23 都是吃的。Lorong 23 到Paya Lebar Road 比较静, 庙堂特别多。Paya Lebar Road.直上, 有 HDB[140] 组屋, Pasar 及 Malay Village.[141]

之后, 那些有信仰的成员纷纷退席, 唱着圣歌带着面具走了。[142]

JOHN 嘿, 我的食色性也大芽笼计划怎么样? 喂喂喂![143]

Dance Three.

5. IT Bubble[144]

BT What do you think of that Geylang Food and Sex Megamall?

GZ 肯定可以发财。[145]

---

[139] Chinese: And the old Geylang on the ground will be an inimitable entertainment complex.

[140] HDB: Housing and Development Board. The state agency responsible for public housing in Singapore.

[141] Chinese: The two sides of Geylang Road will be divided into odd and even numbers. The heart of Geylang's red-light district stretches from Gay World to Lorong 22 and that part will have a variety of 'body servicing' centres. For the stretch from Lorong 22 to Paya Lebar Road, there will be karaoke lounges and a few more posh 'body servicing' centres dedicated to providing takeouts. There will be shopping centres from Paya Lebar Road all the way up to Haig Road.

On this side of Sims Avenue, the stretch from Lorong 1 to Lorong 23 is occupied by eateries. The part from Lane 23 to Paya Lebar Road is quieter, with an unusual number of temples. Beyond Paya Lebar Road, there will be HDB flats, a market and the Malay Village.

[142] Chinese: (*After this, those members with religious faiths walk out of the meeting, one after another. They leave singing religious songs and wearing masks.*)

[143] Chinese: Hey, what do you think of my plans for the Great Geylang Food and Sex Megamall? Hey!

[144] That is, '[The] Information Technology Bubble'.

[145] Chinese: It's sure to make a fortune.

BT   Then why do Geylang people reject it?

GZ   因为这个老板太不懂得含蓄了![146]

BT   Yes, you cannot sell sex here like in New York. You must know the Asian way.

GZ   在这里干这种事, 不能大锣大鼓。[147]

BT   Yeah, for red-light business here, privacy is the best policy.

GZ   所以刚才芽笼人连看都不看就跑了。[148]

BT   The Megamall is a good idea but not good enough. Our Food and Sex service must have more privacy and better productivity.

GZ   是的, 为了让芽笼人生活得更加美满, 我们应该建设一套 '高科技泡泡车'![149]

BT   Yes! The IT Bubble for a better tomorrow in Geylang!

GZ   问题很简单: 芽笼有那么多好吃的好玩的: 春宵苦短, 你一天晚上能享受几样?[150]

BT   So many good F and S in Geylang. How much can you have in one night? You have to run here, run there. No time! No energy!

They draw the audience's attention to the platform with scaffolding on it.

GZ   假使, 大家想象一下: 这辆小车子。是单向玻璃密封的。[151]

BT   A vehicle which you can see outside but no one can look in. Private enough to be anonymous and cozy enough for two.

GZ   它可以带你到芽笼任何地方去吃喝玩乐, 也可以把芽笼任何好吃的东西和好玩的人叫到泡泡车里来享受。[152]

---

[146] Chinese: Because that boss does not understand the merits of being subtle.

[147] Chinese: To conduct such business here, one cannot do it with great fanfare.

[148] Chinese: Hence the Geylang people just now did not even consider the idea and left.

[149] Chinese: Indeed, in order that the Geylang people can have a better life, we should build a system for a high-tech vehicle, the 'IT Bubble'!

[150] Chinese: The problem is very simple: there's so much to eat and do in Geylang, but the night is always too short, how many types of pleasure can you enjoy in one?

[151] Chinese: If this is the case, will everyone please imagine: this small vehicle, enclosed with one-way glass.

[152] Chinese: It can transport you to any place in Geylang for all kinds of pleasure, one can also bring into the IT Bubble any delicious food and interesting characters for enjoyment.

BT   Yes, you can order anything into the bubble or you can go enjoy everything out there.

GZ   泡泡车里有一个 computer。[153]

BT   All your desires are programmed there into the computer. All Geylang pleasures are at your finger tips.

GZ   你想象一下, 整个芽笼布满了泡泡车的网络, 既给您保密, 又节省时间。[154]

BT   This IT Bubble is far superior to the MRT and LRT.[155]

GZ   泡泡车里, 无限的美味和春光, 只供你自己享用![156]

BT   A whole bubble car — full of private, personal pleasure for your senses only.

GZ   由泡泡车进入芽笼的大千世界, 谁也不知道你去什么地方。干什么事情。[157]

BT   You can enter the bubble from anywhere in Geylang. And you decide where to go and what to do. No one else would know the pleasure activities you have chosen.

GZ   示范![158]

BT   Suppose we pick up a gentleman from the Kallang MRT station.

They let the gentleman get up on the platform.

BT   Welcome to the IT Bubble. Please insert your Cash Card.[159]

KH   Cannot use credit card, ah?

---

[153] Chinese: There will be a computer in the IT Bubble.

[154] Chinese: Imagine this: the whole Geylang will be equipped with the IT Bubble network, and it will ensure both confidentiality and the saving of time.

[155] LRT, Light Rail Transit — this is the light rail component of Singapore's rapid transit network, consisting of localised rail systems within public housing estates that then link to the main MRT network. The first LRT line was opened in 1999.

[156] Chinese: There will be unlimited food and erotic pleasures in the IT Bubble, provided for your sole enjoyment.

[157] Chinese: Enter the boundless world of Geylang through the IT Bubble. Nobody will know where you'll go and what you'll do.

[158] Chinese: Demonstrate!

[159] Cash Cards are prepaid debit cards that can be purchased from convenience stores, such as the 7-Eleven stores, or from petrol stations and local banks.

BT　　Sorry sir, strictly by Cash Card only.

KH　　OK. (*Inserts card.*)

GZ　　请用电脑选择您要什么享受。[160]

KH　　Hey, what's this C, F, S?

BT　　C for culture, F for food and S for …

KH　　OK, OK. I know what it's for. For … (*Snickers*) C for culture, aye, Geylang also got culture?

BT　　Geylang's special culture is focused on F and S.

KH　　*Wah*! F and S ah. Come to Geylang surely must try the special culture *lah*. Let's see. Wah! Demi Moore, Michele Pfeiffer, Cindy Crawford also got! OK, OK, one at a time, one at a time. I'll have Demi Moore first. She's got the umph! OK, 'Here', yes. 'In the Bubble', yes, and 'Now'. (*Punches keys fiercely.*) Oh, 'Yes', 'Yes', 'Yes'!

BT　　(*He says, 'Beep!'*) I'm sorry, sir, Demi is only available on Virtual Sex.

KH　　*Alamak*! *Potong*[161] steam, *lah*! Who wants *virtual*? *Chey*! OK, OK, OK. Get me this one … wah a *blonde*? OK, 'This One'. Yes, 'There', 'In Her Own Nest'. Yes, 'Now'. Yes! (*He punches the keys.*)

GZ　　谢谢您的光顾, 马上到达红灯乐园![162]

They reach downstage centre and stop.

BT　　Welcome to the Redcat Pleasure House. Do you wish to have the lights 'On' or 'Off'?

KH　　'On' or 'Off'? (*Undecided. Hesitates. The computer keeps repeating query. Panicks.*) Aye, aye! I don't want to go in. How huh? Hey, I want to cancel! *How to cancel*? Quick tell me how to cancel!

BT　　Just touch the 'Cancel' key.

KH　　OK, OK, 'Cancel'. (*Punches key.*)

----

[160] Chinese: Please use the computer to select your desired pleasure.

[161] Malay: *Potong*, cut; so, less literally, to lose steam.

[162] Chinese: Thank you for your patronage, we will reach the red-light paradise in a minute.

BT   Cancellation acknowledged.

KH   *Heng*[163] eh! Cannot *lah*. I cannot do it. Think I'll try the delivery service. OK, let's see … Wah! So many choices … Local, Thai, White, Yellow, Black, Pink, Blue, Chocolate … *Orange also got*? Okay, I'll have the Orange-coloured one. 'Yes', 'In the Bubble', yes, 'Comprehensive Service', yes '*Now*'!

Dick, in an orange mask, climbs up scaffold at upstage centre.

BT   Your order has arrived, sir.

KH, with back still facing Dick, gets acquainted with Dick's 'property'.

KH   Wah, so nice. So smooth ah. How to turn off the lights, huh?

ET   On the right hand side, sir.

KH puts off lights.

ET   Geylang People, please consider our IT Bubble. Thank you!

KH turns around to look at Dick.

KH   *Ah*! Help!

All exit.

6. Brainwave

LIAN   享乐, 有各种各样。[164]

ONI   *Ada macam cara untuk menggembirakan seseorang.*[165]

JUDY   To give pleasure, we need to understand how it works.

LIAN   让我们仔细再看一遍。[166]

ONI   *Dari mulut, dari tangan, dari seluruh tubuh.*[167]

---

[163] *Minnan hua* or *minnan* language: *Heng*, lucky, fortunate.
[164] Chinese: Enjoyment comes in all forms.
[165] Malay: There are lots of ways to make someone happy.
[166] Chinese: Let us see it again in detail.
[167] Malay: From [using] the mouth, from the hand, from the whole body.

JUDY   It happens in many parts of our body, through the senses.

LIAN   部分的接触, 全身的反应, 但是, 最后, 全部的兴奋都在这里。[168]

JUDY   This is where all the sensations are programmed, and where vibrations are sent out to make the whole body cringe with excitement.

ONI   *Di sinilah, kita memproses kenikmatan dan di sinilah, kita memperbaiki sensasi.*[169]

LIAN   科学家早就发现了, 脑子的运作发出了各种各样的电波, 我们的研究则发现: 每一种快乐都发出不同的脑波形态。[170]

JUDY   It's like saying, every pleasure has a different kind of picture. So if you show this picture to the brain, you will get this vibration; if you show that picture. you will get that vibration.

ONI   *Oleh kerana kenikmatan itu datangnya dari sini, dari otak anda melalui getaran, tanda melahirkan kenikmatan itu. Jadi, kenikmatan besar, getaran besar. Kenikmatan kecil, getaran kecil. Kenikmatan satay, getaran satay. Kenikmatan kopi, geetaran kopi ... Kenikmatan Mel Gibson, getaraannn Mel Gibson. Kenikmatan Fandi Ahmad, getaaraaan Fandi Ahmad ... getaran Fandi Ahmad ... getaran Fandi Ahmad ...*[171]

ONI and JUDY almost go berserk, demonstrating pleasure.

LIAN   OK, OK, OK, 因此我们就想: 与其去建设各种各样的红灯享乐, 与其去经营各种各样的吃喝玩乐, 不如我们把所有的资源投进了科学研究。[172]

---

[168] Chinese: Partial contact, whole body responses, however, in the end, all the excitement is concentrated here.

[169] Malay: It is from here that we process pleasure, and it is from here that we get sensation.

[170] Chinese: Scientists have long discovered that brain operations emit all kinds of electronic waves, and our research has discovered that each kind of happiness emits a different pattern of brain waves.

[171] Malay: As the pleasure comes from here, from the young mind [i.e., the brain] through vibration, you produce the pleasure. Therefore if the pleasure is great, the greater the vibration. Small pleasure, small vibration. The pleasure of satay, satay vibration. The pleasure of coffee, coffee v-ibb ration ... Mel Gibson pleasure, Mel Gibson vibbbbrrration. Fandi Ahmad pleasure ... Fandi Ahmad vibbbbrrration ... [Note: Fandi bin Ahmad (b. 1962) is a Singaporean association football coach and former national team and later professional player whose hey-day was in the 1980s.]

[172] Chinese: OK, OK, OK, therefore we thought, instead of building all sorts of 'red-light enjoyment' or making a business out of all sorts of sensual pleasures, we could pour all resources into scientific research.

JUDY   No building, no call girls, no cowboys, no chefs, no cooks, no IT bubble, no megamall. Instead, we recorded the sensations of enjoying food and enjoying sex in terms of their brainwave patterns.

LIAN   我们投下了巨大的投资, 集合了各种各样直接用脑电波提供各种快感的资料![173]

ONI   *Nah, sekarang kita telah mengumpul semua kenikmatan — kenikmatan ini di dalam sini ... di dalam otak ... wah ... coba anda bayangkan ... Mel Gibson, Robert Redford, Chow Yuen Fatt, Moses Lim, Keanu Reeves, Fandi Ahmad, Princess D ...*[174]

LIAN   沙爹米粉, 黑椒牛扒, 姜葱牛肉, 佛跳墙, 满汉全席……[175]

JUDY   Fish and chips, beef *rendang*, *cha kue tiao*, Tiramisu, fettuccini, escargot ...

They become frantic.

JUDY   Yes, all of these supreme pleasures, fed to you from a single Brainwave Station.

LIAN   我们提供的不只是一个 ‘食色性也大芽笼’, 我们提供的是一个更宏大的东西, 我们要给您一个 ‘食色性也大世界’![176]

ONI   *Dunia kenikmatan semuanya terdapat di Stasiun Gelombang Minda.*[177]

LIAN   生命苦短, 享乐无穷, 找寻欢乐, 要注意质量。[178]

Assistants push platform with scaffolding to downstage centre.

---

[173] Chinese: We made a great investment and gathered a huge amount of material that contributed toward providing a variety of sensations directly through brain waves.

[174] Malay: Well, now we have gathered all the pleasures — the pleasure is in here ... in the brain ... wah ... try to imagine ... Mel Gibson, Robert Redford, Chow Yuen Fatt, Moses Lim, Keanu Reeves, Fandi Ahmad, Princess D ... [Note: Moses Lim (b. 1950) is a Singaporean actor and comedian, probably best known for a role in the Singaporean TV sitcom *Under One Roof* (1994, pilot; 1995–2001, 2003).]

[175] Chinese: Satay bee hoon, black pepper steak, ginger and spring onion beef, the delicacy ‘Buddha Jumps over the Wall’, the ‘Manchu Han Imperial Feast’ ...

[176] Chinese: Not only do we provide ‘Food and Sex in the Great Geylang’, we provide something that is even grander, we wish to provide you with ‘Food and Sex in the Great World’!

[177] Malay: The world of pleasure, all of it can be found on [the] Channel Waves of the Mind.

[178] Chinese: Life is short, enjoyment is infinite, [and to] look for pleasure, one must be mindful of quality.

JUDY   Twenty Lorongs, 40 side streets, how much of Geylang can you reassemble even if you go 40 storeys upwards? What we offer you is an immeasurably larger vision, the Brainwave Station!

Actors climb onto the platform and scaffold, and puts on masks. 'Brain cloth' lowered.

ONI: *Tuan-tuan dan puan-puan, cadangan kami ini serius!*[179]

LIAN: 生活太沉重了。[180]

JUDY: Forget the heaviness of life.

ONI: *Senangkanlah hati anda dengan kenikmatan — kenikmatan dunia selagi anda masih boleh.*[181]

LIAN   我们除了给您提供各种欢乐, 我们也在您的脑波里消除烦恼。[182]

JUDY   We can programme for you the ideal happy life.

ONI   *Hanya kenikmatan, tanpa frustasi.*[183]

LIAN   不用甘榜河流, 不用湿巴刹, 不用电车。[184]

JUDY   Everything is in the brain. And through this brain, we will programme the ideal happiness for you. Don't worry, we'll look after you.

LIAN   房屋不必重建, 不用美男美女, 也不用厨师不用开店。[185]

ONI   *Semua hajat-hajat tuan-tuan dan puan-puan untuk menyenangankan hati bakal dikabulkan, dari Stasiun Gelombang Minda.*[186]

JUDY   Plugged into your ideal Brainwave programme, and it will be like floating in the air, like *nagas* and dragons — the ultimate joys of being alive!

---

[179] Gentlemen and ladies, our proposal is a serious one!

[180] Chinese: Life is too 'heavy'.

[181] Malay: Comfort your heart with this world's pleasures, while you can.

[182] Chinese: Apart from offering you different kinds of pleasure, we will also dispel the worries in your brain waves.

[183] Malay: Only enjoyment, without the frustration.

[184] Chinese: There is no need for *kampungs* and rivers, no need for wet markets, no need for electric cars.

[185] Chinese: There will be no need to rebuild houses, no need for beautiful men and women, no need for chefs, no need for shops.

[186] Malay: All your desires, gentlemen and ladies, to comfort your heart — you will be satiated — from [the] Channel Waves of the Mind.

LIAN   芽笼是神龙出没的地方
            先进的脑波网络站
            应该由你们掀开一个新的纪元。
            你只需要按一按键盘
            文明优雅的生活
            马上在你的网络上出现。[187]

7. Finale

ONI   *Aku hanya mahu sebuah sungai untuk Geylangku.*
          Bersama pohon-pohoon dan rumput-rampai di tepi sungai itu.
          Dan aku hanya mahu ibuku di bawah sebuah pohon di tepi sungai ...
          Mendekapku di dadanya sambil bercerita.
          Derita tentang sebuah pulau ...
          Di pulau itu terdapat sebuah gunung yang tinggi dan sebuah danau yang dalam.
          Di situ, terdapat binatang-binatang yang tercantik, burung-burung yang tercan-
          tik dan ikan-ikan yang tercantik di dunia. Tetapi tiada yang menyentuh bina-
          tang-binatang, burung-burung dan ikan-ikan ini.
          Di situ, semua yang mereka lakukan hanya bernyanyi, berenang dan bermain
          sepanjang hari.[188]

DICK   我只希望芽笼能有一条长长的河流
           河的两岸有绿绿的草地, 有高高的树

---

[187] Chinese: Geylang is the haunt of the magical dragon
The advanced network station for the brain waves
Should be undertaken by all of you to draw the curtain for a new era
You will only need to press the keyboard
A civilised and gracious lifestyle
Will appear immediately on your network.
[188] Malay: I really wish for a river in my Geylang.
With the grass and the trees at the river bank.
And I only long for my mother under the tree at the bank of the river ...
My mother, embracing me in her bosom as she tells a story.
The sufferings of an island ...
There existed a high mountain and a deep lake.
In it, live the most beautiful of animals, the most beautiful of birds, the most beautiful of fishes in the world. But nobody ever even touch the bodies of these animals, the birds and the fish.
There, all they do is sing, swim and play all day long.

我希望有妈妈在树下把我抱在怀里，
跟我讲故事
故事里有一个小岛，有一座高山，有一个大湖
那里有世界上最美的飞鸟，最美的野兽，最美的鱼虾
但是没有人去打猎捕鱼抓鸟
他们一天到晚只会游泳唱歌玩耍。[189]

ONI   Since you can read my brain waves
       You can now hear my hopes and aspirations.

       All I wish to have for my Geylang is a river
       With trees and grass on the river banks
       And I wish my mother is there under the tree, by the river
       Holding me in her bosom and telling me stories
       Stories about an island, with a tall mountain and a deep lake
       Where you can find all the beautiful animals
       All the beautiful birds and
       All the beautiful fishes in the world
       But no people to hunt them down
       All they do is to sing and swim and play all day.

(*End of Play*)

---

[189] Oni will follow with an English-language version of what Dick has just said, as Dick has just followed with a Chinese-language version of what Oni has said in Malay, at the start of scene 7.

The Spirits Play[1]

Characters of the Play

The General
The Mother
The Soldier
The Girl
The Poet

The Setting

A desolate, deserted place in the wilderness.

Stark, sombre colours and irregular light and shadows, perpetually changing, evoking an indescribable, mysterious ambience.

It is night, the realm of spirits.

Night is a world of mysterious wonders: The forms of heaven and earth are fluid; everything has a spiritual dimension; organic and inorganic beings are parts of a continuum; the formed and the formless are one.

The world of spirits is a world in flux.

Scene 1

GENERAL   The leaves must have turned red by now.

            Yes. It's red today.

MOTHER   If it's red today, then it was green yesterday.

---

[1] The English-language version of *The Spirits Play* is co-edited by C. J. W.-L. Wee and Lee Chee Keng.

MAN   Then, it'll be white tomorrow.

GIRL   And then, it'll be black.

MOTHER   Soon, everything will be white.

MAN   All white, as far as your eyes can see.

GENERAL   Yes, everything will soon be white.

MOTHER   As white as snow.

GIRL   As red as blood.

MAN   Or as black.

MOTHER   Yes. All is blue.

GIRL   And again, all is black.

GENERAL   But where's the white?

GIRL   Turned to red.

MOTHER   And blue.

MAN   A patch of blue.

GIRL   A great patch of black.

GENERAL   What about the red?

MOTHER   It has all turned white.

GENERAL   Early in the morning, the sun has made the top of the mountain red.

MAN   No, not the sun.

MOTHER   The red is the rain.

GIRL   No, it's the blood.

GENERAL   Look how the horse gallops, leaving no trace on the snow.

MAN   So dark in the woods, but someone's playing the flute in the middle of the air.

GIRL   Snow is everywhere. Up the top of the tree, there's an apple still waiting.

MOTHER   In the dark of the sea, floating on the crest of the wave, is a flower.

GENERAL   Yes. The snow remains as pure as white.

MOTHER   No, the snow is red.

GIRL   No, the blood is red.

GENERAL   No, the eye is red.

MOTHER   No, the eye is white.

GIRL   No, the face is white.

MAN   No, the face is yellow.

GENERAL   No, the rain is yellow.

MAN   Yes. There's red and white and yellow and blue and black all over the body.

GENERAL   What about the snow? The snow's still white, at least that which is not covered in blood, right?

MAN   It's all blasted, broken, busted, gone.

GIRL   It's rotten, smelly, sunken, torn.

MOTHER   It's passed by, gone through, put out, destroyed.

GENERAL   It's cleared out, gone away, brushed aside, forgotten.

MAN   It's brushed aside? It's forgotten?

MOTHER   It's cleared out, passed by, destroyed, forgotten.

ALL   (*They compete verbally by repeating their respective last lines.*)

Silence. They try hard to reach back to their distant memories.

GENERAL   Yes. This is the day.

Gradually, festive music familiar to them is heard, making them gently sway their bodies as if they all remember a festive event.

Suddenly, snapping out of this moment of intimate recall —

GENERAL   … There they come. (*Sound of approaching planes with bombs being dropped.*)

         … It's now!

Sound of deafening bombing, crowds screaming, fire …

(*End of scene*)

Scene 2

The four of them, General, Mother, Girl and Man, are deep in thought, remembering the past. Then, they drink solemnly.

GENERAL   Another year has gone by. How are you all?

MOTHER   With your blessing, everything is well.

MAN   With your blessing, everything is as it was.

GIRL   With your blessing, every year is the same. Every year is the same.

GENERAL   What else, if not the same?

MAN   The same toast, the same greetings. We think about the past, we talk about the past.

MOTHER   For those who have gone past, what else to talk about but what is already past?

GENERAL   Perhaps we can talk about the sky above, the earth below, the trees and plants around us ... Well, how are they all?

MAN   Yes, another year. How many years now, eh?

GENERAL   Come on, what's the purpose of counting? How is one to count? Even if you could, whom are you counting it for? And for what purpose?

GIRL   Yes, indeed. But then, not to think about it is just as difficult.

MOTHER   Let it go. When life's over, there won't be a 'tomorrow' anymore.

GENERAL   Yes, but then, everyday, the water in the sea still goes up and down, the clouds in the sky still come and go without fail. And the trees and plants keep on growing and dying, growing and dying — they're so very busy! ... Well, if you ask me, I'll say it's all so damned tiring!

MAN   When we were alive, everyday we saluted the sun.

GIRL   Now that we're here, every night we long for the moon.

GENERAL   Well, I think that's quite all right.

MOTHER   It's fine. I think the quietness of it all is very nice.

The silence is so soothing.

GIRL　　　But it's not been this quiet lately.

Over my place, after that ten-day storm, part of the slope fell off ... and some human remains became exposed ...

MAN　　　What? More of our people, near your place?

GIRL　　　Seems they had come much earlier. Everything's scattered about. In bits and pieces. Seems the spirits have all gone astray, disappeared.

MAN　　　That's incredible. All these years, I've always thought we were the only souls here. I thought we were the only lingering spirits around this place.

GENERAL　　Could you tell when and where they were from, or who they were?

GIRL　　　Seems they've been here quite a while. But, honestly, I didn't much care.

GENERAL　　Why not?

GIRL　　　Would it make any difference?

MAN　　　A hell of a difference, it would! Whether they were enemies or —

MOTHER　　You can tell without even asking.

MAN　　　How can you do that?

MOTHER　　They're bound to be somebody's son or daughter.

GIRL　　　But not necessarily anybody's mother or father.

GENERAL　　There are bodies everywhere. Beneath the earth, and beneath the graves; what you can see is just a tiny portion of what you have not seen. Who knows what's there in the woods, under the stones, in the rivers, under the oceans.

MOTHER　　Whoever, wherever, they are bound to be somebody's son or daughter.

GENERAL　　With the blessings from heaven, pray they have all found a place of rest and peace.

MOTHER　　Yes, pray they have all found a place of rest and peace.

Solemnly, they bow to the moon.

The voice of someone singing is heard, stunning them all. Presently, the Man rushes out to find out who could be singing, and where it is coming from.

MOTHER　　Could that be him?

GIRL	Perhaps it is.
GENERAL	Who?
MOTHER	Just a wild guess.
GIRL	It should be him.
GENERAL	Who is it?
MOTHER	He's rather tall and thin.
GIRL	Very quiet and lonely.
GENERAL	But who is it?
MOTHER	He never talks to others.
GIRL	Just keeps on singing to himself.
GENERAL	I've never heard of such a soul.
GIRL	He's from the other side of the mountain.
MOTHER	He's never been to this side of the mountain.
GENERAL	Then who is he?
MOTHER	Yes, it must be him.
GIRL	I'm sure it's him.

The Man re-enters the stage.

MAN	Strange, it's him!
GENERAL	Who is he?
MAN	A poet.
GENERAL	A poet?
MOTHER	That's right.
GIRL	Yes, the poet.
GENERAL	Where's this poet from?
MAN	Sounds like he's from the East.
GIRL	Yes, should be from the East.

MOTHER	Definitely from the East.
GENERAL	Why are you so sure he's from the East?
MOTHER	The song's from the East.
GIRL	It's a folksong from our home country.

Mother and Girl join the singing.

GENERAL	A poet?
MAN	And a reporter.
GENEAL	And a reporter?
MAN	I met him once in HQ. He was sent directly by the General Staff.
GENERAL	Oh, him! ... How come it's him? ... Poet ... and reporter.
MAN	Yes, I've met once before.
GENERAL	Wasn't he called back to HQ before the defensive campaign.
MAN	Yes, it must be the same person.
GENERAL	You saw him just now?
MAN	From a distance.
GENERAL	Did he say anything?
MAN	Not really.
GENERAL	You mean he just kept singing and didn't say anything?
MAN	He was very vague. And a bit confusing.
GENERAL	What exactly did he say?
MAN	He said something like, 'We're going home.'

The women stopped singing. All stunned by these words.

GENERAL	Going home?
GIRL	Going home?
MOTHER	Going home?
MAN	Can we ... really ... go home?

GENERAL   If he is the man you say he is, then it could be true ...

GIRL   But where is home?

MAN   Who's got a home?

MOTHER   Home ... What makes a home?

GENERAL   Home is where the ancestral temple stands. Home is where the tablets of the souls are kept.

GIRL   Home is where there are fruits and orchards.

MAN   Home is where you have rice fields and forests.

MOTHER   Home is where you hear the birds sing and where you do your cooking.

GENERAL   ... How did we get here from home? ... And now, how can we get from here ... to go home? ...

ALL   (*Muttering to themselves.*) Going home ... We're going home? ...

From a distance, the song is again heard. This time, the lyrics come through more clearly —

'Mama, I'm Leaving, Mama'

Mama, I'm leaving, Mama

Mama, I've got the water, Mama

Mama, I've got the firewood, Mama

Mama, keep yourself warm, Mama

Mama, do eat well, Mama

Mama, do sleep well, Mama

Mama, the sun is up, Mama

Mama, I've got to go, Mama

Mama, I've got your photo, Mama

Mama, I'll write to you, Mama

Mama, do take care, Mama

Mama, I'm leaving, Mama

(*End of scene*)

Scene 3

MOTHER   We grew up together as children. We loved playing with each other but we were always quarrelling because we were both very stubborn. I told him he's so short he'd get no wife, and he told me my bad temper would make me an old maid for life. I kept using my sharp tongue until the very day he joined the army. But I regretted the day he went away. How I wished he would come back so I could tell him I had never really hated him for one moment. But, for two full years, he never even wrote me a single letter.

On the first day of winter, heavy fog brought the night early. Just as we were going to bed, there was a knock at the door. It was him, standing there in his army uniform, his seasoned face looking serious and anxious. He seemed to have grown taller. He gave me one intense look and then, without saying a word, he bowed deeply to my Father and my Mother. He said he had just received an honourable mission and was given special leave for a home visit, and he asked for their permission to take me as his wife. We knew immediately that he was selected to join the suicide squad and that this was the last time we would ever see him.

Father and Mother had always dearly liked him. But how could they give their daughter away to a man on the verge of going to his death? I was dead set on marrying him whatever the consequences. I knelt down and begged them. I said if they were to say 'no', I would never ever consider marrying anyone else. So, toasting ourselves with tea instead of wine, we became husband and wife. We never slept a wink; we spent half a night together. Before dawn came, I saw his figure fading away in the thick of the fog.

Come autumn the next year, I gave birth to a son. Oh, how I wished he were there to see the baby. And how I wished he would re-appear in front of me on a foggy night. That he would knock on the door and surprise us all once again. But it could only be a dream. What eventually came with the knocking was the news of his death. No remains. No keepsake. Nothing. For security reasons, they didn't even tell us where and how he perished. I didn't ask, and I didn't cry. In a way, I felt relieved. I knew I didn't have to live in anxiety anymore.

My cool response won me a commendation. The government awarded me the title of 'Model Widow' and hung a plaque in front of our house. On national day that year, I was called to parade with many other widows to the cheers of the crowds lining the streets. But I did not remember hearing anything. Soon after, my son and my parents contracted typhoid. They were all there in the morning when I left for work. But when I got back they were all gone. No one told me. They said that to avoid interrupting production, my factory decided to bury the dead straight away. They said, 'You couldn't have done anything anyway.'

Strange, their death didn't make me sad either. I felt relieved for them, for they had transcended all pain. As for myself, I felt strangely freed. Freed from all ties and responsibilities. And a thought suddenly dawned upon me: I must find my husband. How can I make you understand the longing? How could you understand my yearning? I was married to him for only half a night. How I wished I could at least see him again! To hold him in my arms once more. Even just his body, or just a part of his body! So, one day, without asking anybody's permission, I quietly left. I was on my way in search of my husband. I asked all over. I asked everyone I could think of. After almost a year, I came to this island.

The moment I landed, dead bodies filled my sight. Bodies and bodies. Bony skeletons scattered all over, mostly in soldiers' uniform. But, god help me, which one is my husband? Who knew? Who cared? Every skeleton had a skull. Every skull has two deep hollows, quietly staring at me. Oh my god, which one was my husband? … I walked around. I scouted around, up and down, up and down the island. You have no idea how many dead bodies I had turned over, how many skeletons I'd examined, how many skulls I'd stared at. But there was no trace of him!

Then, one day, suddenly I saw this skull staring back at me, as if it was smiling at me. I was so scared I trembled all over. Yes, it was smiling, and smiling at me like my husband used to smile at me. But then, as I calmed myself and had a closer look at it, and at the others, and yet others. Yes, indeed, they were all smiling at me! Then a strange feeling came over me. Yes, accept it. Accept them. Accept them all. All of them! Accept all of them as my husband! So, from that day onwards, I started to collect the skulls and skeletons, one by one, pile after pile — I'll gather them and then put them to the fire. During the cremation, I gave them, each one of them, the honour due to a husband — I gave them all a wife's tribute to a husband. One by one. Pile after pile, I collected them, I cremated them, I honoured them. Until one day, our troops came to stop me. They told me to stop because they said the fire might draw attention of enemy aircraft and so invite more bombing. But I didn't want to stop. I kept one collecting the bodies, the skeletons, the skulls — one by one, pile by pile, to get them cremated, to give them a wife's remembrance. In the end, they decided to shoot me. And so they shot me!

The General and the Girl have come in. The Poet's song is again heard from the distance.

The Mother responds to the lyrics as they are sung —

MOTHER   ('Mama, I'm leaving, Mama')
              When are you returning, my son?

              ('Mama, I've got the water, Mama')
              Is there still water in the well, my son?

              ('Mama, I've got the firewood, Mama')
              Is there still rice in the urn, my son?

              ('Mama, keep yourself warm, Mama')
              Have you got your cotton coat, my son?

GENERAL   In every soldier's home, we have a mother of courage.

              Behind every soldier's glory, we have a mass of loyal clansmen.

              You are truly our unsung heroes!

The Man rushes in.

MAN   Uncle, uncle, they have discovered another great heap of human remains. Some seven, eight hundred. All from our troops.

GENERAL   All from our troops? ... Some seven, eight hundred!

MAN   A whole great heap, not even buried. The Poet told me to tell you they all died several days before us.

GENERAL   To tell me ... Why does he want you to tell me?

MAN   He didn't say.

The General goes out.

GIRL   Thinking of home?

MAN   No ... my brother's in the army.

GIRL   In that heap?

MAN   So many years now, how can you be sure?

GIRL   Never heard about them all these years?

MAN   So far away. Maybe they had lost all their primal energies.

GIRL   But we are still here!

MAN   You don't understand ... how badly hurt you can get by extreme attrition. You don't understand that a person's primal energies can be totally destroyed ... You have no idea.

GIRL   Tell me. Maybe I can understand.

MAN   No, you won't ... It's so extreme I don't even know how to begin ...

(*End of scene*)

Scene 4

MAN   The day I joined the army, our family was still busy harvesting the rice.

Baba and *Mama* put on their best for our sending-off ceremony. My younger brother and sister stayed to work in the field. The sending-off ceremony put up by the village committee was very rowdy, with drums and cymbals beating all around us. But almost as soon as our truck drove out of the village, everything fell silent. We all strained our eyes looking into the fields, searching for our relatives who hadn't come to the ceremony. There were only kids and old people in the fields. They all stood there, silently looking at us. It was funny that now nobody waved anymore. I could also see my younger brother and sister. They just stood there, just watching us, until we made a turn and disappeared into the hills.

At first, our morale was very high. We overcame every hardship that came upon us; we matched every challenge that was thrown upon us; we followed every order that was handed down to us. We, the new soldiers from the poor mountain villages, we displayed absolute courage, absolute loyalty to the absolute best of our abilities. If the order was to kill, we would kill — hanging, beheading, with ropes, bayonets, swords or bullets; we never hesitated. If the order was to burn, we would burn — houses, crops, man, women, children or old people — anything and everything, anyone and everyone in sight. For the Country, for the Nation, for the Leader, for the Army, no task was impossible, no order was questioned, nothing was spared, no lives were spared, including our very own. We were in the first wave of the landing forces that captured this island. The landing was a surprise attack, but we still suffered heavy casualties, dozens from our company died. After the victory, we had a period of relative quiet and a leisurely life. Then the final battle to defend the island began.

The enemy launched a joint attack from the air, the sea and on land fierce beyond our wildest imagination. Totally surprised, we hurriedly began to withdraw to the mountains behind us. But the enemy just kept on attacking us without relenting, bombing us from the air, land and the sea. Within a week, our force of 200,000 troops was totally disintegrated. We all knew we had to retreat in the opposite direction to the sea, into the depths of the mountains. But, being totally unprepared for the scale of the offensive, we didn't carry enough food with us. Hunger set in within a week and, aggravated by the continuous rain, we entered into a kind of hardship and suffering that none of us had ever known.

Some bodies began to rot so badly that their bones were revealed. Some were so hungry, so exhausted and so badly hurt that they couldn't move or talk anymore. They just sat and laid there looking at us as we walked by. Everyone had long stopped talking. There was only one thought in our minds: Keep going, don't stop, because once you stop, you'd never be able to stand up and walk on again.

Then we began to see more and more dead bodies by the roadside. And the stench would never leave us again. The worst were those who had not yet died. They had only skeletons left, covered with rot and sores all over them, with countless worms crawling all over them — in their eyes, in their mouths, their nose and their ears ... and they were still alive and breathing. Sometimes, you couldn't tell whether it was the man moving or it was the worms moving. When it got dark, the millions of worms on the bodies of the soldiers sent off a kind of silvery radiation, and they guided us like traffic signs. Yes, it was the tens of thousands of dead or dying brothers who were leading us on. But when it was not raining and everything was quiet, we could hear the soft but sure chewing noises of those millions of worms eating into the bodies of our soldier brothers, like silkworms chewing on berry leaves. Oh, it was too horrible, too horrible! Oh you can't imagine how terrifying it was to experience that kind of suffering. People whom you called brothers, with whom you drank and sang and played together, and now you just went past them, as if you didn't see them, not stopping, you just walked past them without stretching our your hand to help them escape suffering and certain death!

But the most incredible thing was that, we began to see groups of bodies in piles, in heaps, in stacks ... But we couldn't care less, we just walked on and on, ignoring all the suffering and dying brothers along the wayside being consumed by hunger, by their wounds, and by the millions of crawling worms eating away at them. They waved at us, they moaned at us, they stared at us, but we never stretched out our hands, we never stopped, we never even looked at them. Oh it was so horrible that I would rather have been shot by enemy bullets or cannon balls. So we just trudged on and on, sometimes even longing for the enemy fire to take us away from the dying brothers, the piles of bodies, the crawling worms ... Oh, the attrition, it was so horrible, so horrible! ...

Sound of machine gun straffing; the Man falls as if he's been hit and killed.

The General is again escorted out by the Girl and the Mother.

GENERAL   You are truly loyal and courageous sons of our motherland, and you are model soldiers whose glorious deeds have enhanced the Military Soul of our Great Army!

MAN   The worms, millions and millions of them. So horrible! And the heaps and piles of bodies. Our poor dead brothers!

GENERAL   All your souls will be taken back to our motherland, to be placed in our Nation's Ancestral Temple, to be venerated for posterity!

MAN   Now my only hope is to be able to go home. This is the time when our harvesting is still ongoing and everybody is working in the field.

MOTHER   Yes. Go back home. Go back to your folks. Go back to the embrace of your woman. Go back to being a son, a husband, a lover. Let us hold you once again and go on living like before ... In a home filled with love and care; in the bosom of a woman soft and warm ... Yes, after the war broke out, our homes had no more men around ... and as the war went on, you men in the war, you have all forgotten what it's like to have a woman ...

GIRL   No, they have not forgotten what it's like to have a woman's body. What they have forgotten is the woman's tenderness, and the woman's love ... Yes, all that's left is the body. No more tenderness, no more love!

(*End of scene*)

Scene 5

GIRL   We were classmates since our first year in high school. I knew he had always liked me. In the spring, we'd go to the gardens; in the summer we'd go fishing, in the autumn we'd go picking fruits, in the winter, we'd go skating. But early one day in our third year, he told me bluntly that he had to end his feelings for me. He said he couldn't make himself go on liking me when our great country was going through such a difficult period in our holy war. He said we shouldn't divert our attention to personal feelings and emotions any longer. He swore that he would never again get involved in personal relationships until our motherland had achieved total victory. And, on the very day he became 16, he withdrew from school, signed on as a soldier, and left home for the front. I was deeply moved and I also joined the army as a nurse, and I was also despatched to the front soon afterwards, finally ending up here on this island. It was about a month before the decisive battle. The whole island was gripped by a state of tense preparedness. It felt as if the fighting could break out any day. Everybody had a heavy heart.

About ten days before the fighting eventually broke out, I was on night duty. At about nine o'clock, three soldiers came into the clinic begging me to go help a few of their friends nearby. I told them to bring them into the clinic but they said they didn't want to leave a record and again begged me to go. Finally, in the company of another nurse, I went out with them carrying with us a first-aid box. We thought they must have got into themselves into trouble by drinking too much liquor or playing too much with women. We never thought for a moment that it could be a trap ... There were actually 18 of them. In a little hut in the woods ... they ... they kept us there until daybreak ...

It was almost noon when we struggled back to the medical centre. We made a report, but although we got the full backing of the chief medical officer, the chief commander made a shocking decision. He wouldn't allow the soldiers to be charged. He said, 'According to military law, soldiers guilty of raping military nurses faced a mandatory death sentence. But because we are anticipating an all-out war to defend the island, this is a very bad time to execute soldiers for an offence of this nature. I don't want the morale of our soldiers adversely affected. No, quash the case!' The soldiers were disciplined with a few slaps and punches by their superior officers and that was the end of it.

The next day, a senior officer from the commander's office came to see us in our barracks. He was a very kind-looking elderly man; he spoke very softly and in a caring manner. He said: 'You have our deepest sympathy and concern. Needless to say, the soldiers' behaviour was utterly despicable and unforgivable. We fully understand your pain and sufferings. However, my dear young sisters, these are unusual and difficult times. If you were to place yourself in a different position, you may see things in an entirely different perspective, and then your feelings and sentiments would be different. Look at it this way: all these soldiers, just as you, are patriotic, good children of our motherland. They, like you, have left their loving families and dear relatives and friends to fight for the defence of the sovereignty, honour and dignity of our nation and leader. The only difference is that, while you are confronted by hardship and danger, they are confronted by injury and death. Daily. Hourly. They have left behind their parents, wives and children. Many of them are not married, and some of them have never felt the touch of a woman, never experienced the pleasure of a woman. For them, is it too difficult to imagine that they do deserve some sensual happiness, some feminine comfort before they march to their deaths? In comparison to their tragedy, don't you think the distress you have experienced is, relatively, very mild? In fact, you may not know this: we actually have thousands of patriotic sisters who fully understand our soldiers' needs, and voluntarily submit themselves to such needs in the various theatres of the war. With the purity of their maidenly hearts and the warmth of their virginal bodies, they gave themselves wholeheartedly to the reinvigoration of the bodies, the hearts and the spirits of our patriotic fighters, so that they would have the highest morale to bravely go forward with great vigour to fight, and to die, for our motherland!'

I was convinced, I was persuaded, I was converted. And I voluntarily withdrew my charges. More than that, I expressed my fervent wish to serve the nation, the leader and the military without reservation. Little did I know that my patriotic expression had immediately earned me greater misfortune. The very next day, I was transferred to another barracks, to a long house of little rooms well protected by barbed wire fencing. This barracks were totally occupied by women with the specific task of entertaining the tired and burnt out body of the soldiers. Their singular mission was to reinvigorate the fighting spirit of the soldiers tasked to die for our motherland.

Yes, I have never seen the tragic scenes of injury, pain and death of your retreating army, but I have seen how our sisters were used and wasted by the long line of scores and scores of soldiers. I had never imagined that anyone could conceive of such a way of using and wasting people. Yes, I have never seen how our dying brothers were eaten away by millions of worms crawling over them. But, my brother, have you ever seen how our sisters suffered under the bodies of men crawling over them one after another, score after score, long line after long line? Unrelenting, never ending, no warmth, no feelings, no tenderness, no love ... Only waste, and waste, and waste. Such inhuman waste! Such inhuman waste!

General and Mother have entered. Now two stagehands enter and help the Girl rise and exit.

GENERAL   Your great contribution will be long remembered by our great nation and leader. We shall forever treasure your lofty spirit of sacrifice.

MAN   (*Enters*) Uncle, uncle. The Poet is coming this way.

GENERAL   Oh, he's here?

MAN   Yes. He said he's looking for someone, and looking for some place!

GENERAL   Oh. Looking for someone. For some place.

Go, invite him over. Ask him to come over here!

Exit Mother, Girl and Man.

(*End of scene*)

Scene 6

The General remembers.

GENERAL   I will never forget the glory of victory. The glory of our victory will always be the very pillar of our pride and honour. I will never forget these proud memories — these proud memories, which will forever nurture the soldier's soul.

The general counter-offensive started before dawn. We had over 200,000 battle-ready, united spirits in extremely high morale. When I realised a heavy fog had covered the entire beachhead, I decided it was a god-given opportunity to launch a surprise assault. So I ordered the advancement of the general offensive by two hours. So, as the moon was till shining somewhere up there in the foggy sky, our forces wrested ten kilometres of coastline in one sudden attack. Everything proceeded according to my strategy, smoothly and efficiently. The vanguard attacked with a powerful thrust; the second line consolidated the gains. Speedily, but steadily, our forces managed to occupy more than one kilometre of the beach front by mid-day — a feat which we had planned to achieve in three days! Immediately, I ordered a respite: take a breather, have a good lunch before we continue the offensive.

Totally underestimating our strength, the enemy crumbled immediately after we released the full power of our onslaught. They suffered heavy casualties, broke into confusion and beat a retreat. But we never relented. Our forces pushed on and on, continuously and mercilessly, for three full days and nights. The enemy was wholly dispirited, and totally annihilated. Some surrendered, most of them were killed. In all, it took us only 20 days to capture this entire island — a campaign we had estimated would take more than two months to complete!

Oh, my dear, respected Grandfather, my dear respected Father, I have always borne your teaching in my heart. I have never tainted the pure and loyal spirit of the military heritage of our great family. I have never forgotten that it was alongside your leather boots that I had learnt how to walk; that it was on your horses' backs that I was taught how to read; and it was by your glorious example that I was inducted into the military, learning the great tradition of loyalty to our great leader, allegiance to our great nation and obedience to our great military force. It was your example that has set me on the way to becoming a good soldier, a good subject, a good son conscious of our eternal glory.

As Commander-in-Chief of the occupation forces, and as ordered by our great leader, I assumed command of the entire island. By my order, a military regime was declared. I then set about demanding the loyalty of the natives, selecting the élites to assist in the rule of the population. A civil code was announced, a native education system was launched using the language of our motherland, and within a month, the great civilisation of our nation was firmly implanted in this newly conquered land. Within six months, the island was officially annexed as our national territory. It was my honour and privilege to report to our great leader that this island of backwardness and barbarity, by the grace of our great nation, had entered the era of civilisation.

Oh my dear respected Father, it was only recently that I have come to deeply understand why, when I fell from a horse as a young boy, you, instead of helping me up, you gave me a severe belting. And then you told me, 'One who can't tame a horse could never be a conqueror.'

Yes, it was at the most glorious moment in my life that I began to understand that only with this kind of aspiration and temperament is one able to inherit the spirit of our superior nation. Bearing this in mind — the teachings of our family, our nation and our army — bearing all these in mind, I initiated a deep-seated education and cultivation programme. I wanted to extract the maximum products from this land, the maximum labour from the natives, the maximum efficiency from the officials and the maximum bravery from the soldiers. With iron discipline, I pushed them to the limits of their capabilities. And, indeed, when the defensive battle finally came, all the elements fell into place!

There were 80,000 soldiers defending the island at the time. They were well prepared, in high morale, and fully committed to defending the island to the last man for the honour of our supreme leader, our beloved country, our superior nation and our invincible army. Long live our great leader! Long live our motherland! Long live our great army! Forever and ever, and ever ...

Totally exhausted, he breathes heavily. With the help of stagehands and under the cover of the darkness of the stage, he disrobes, picks up the walking stick, and re-assumes the identity of an old man.

MAN   (*From inside.*) Uncle, the poet is coming!

GENERAL   Oh, yes. Yes.

The General struggles to exit.

(*End of scene*)

Scene 7

The Poet's voice is heard reading a poem.

POET   'High above me the sky is all blue
All around me there is absolute silence
A single white crane flashes over my head
Painting the entire world with peace and tranquillity'

Now he appears.

POET   I was drawn to writing since I was a boy and I had won the title of 'Wonder Boy of Poetry' at the age of ten. My parents saved every cent they could manage so they could send me to the best school in the capital. I was a very diligent student; I topped the class every year and I won every scholarship there was. I was spotted by the authorities before I finished high school. On graduation, I was immediately appointed cadet reporter in the *Sun Chronicle*.

By then, our patriotic war with the major powers had entered its most intensive phase. The entire nation was firmly united against our enemies. Morale was especially high among the young. Their blood was boiling hot and they competed for the most daring tasks. We deemed ourselves exceedingly proud and privileged in having been born into the age of great national endeavour. As such, I wrote passionately and produced a great number of patriotic poetry. This, for instance:

'A million-strong army marches to the front
A workforce hundred times stronger tills the land
The commander's sword cuts through the air
Rivers and valleys run with enemy's bloody red'

Five months later, the military sent me to the front, on assignment to write on the war as a reporter and a poet, to evoke pride and honour for our real motherland. I was reminded by the leadership of both the newspaper and the military that under no circumstances should I compromise the task of glorifying the aspirations of the patriotic war.

Within six months, I wrote and published 40 field reports and 60 pieces of poetry. With all my passion, I unreservedly glorified our great motherland, our great leader, our great people and our great military. In return, I was repeatedly honoured with citations and rewards. But as time passed, I became more and more uncertain and uneasy. As in this poem:

'Acid smoke has filled the air
Birds have deserted the woods
Neighbours don't laugh any longer
Children cry every night in their nightmares'

GENERAL   Ah, Mr Poet, is that really you? I thought you had gone home to collect your honours. How come you are also here in our midst?

POET   Yes, I did. But I came back after touring several towns and cities to promote our national salvation movement. But I became deeply shocked by what I saw around the country. Because what I saw was far from what I was told. There were so many things I wanted to say which I couldn't say. There were so many questions I wanted to ask but couldn't ask. So I requested to be re-assigned to the front. Here, where everyone is busy preparing for war, this at least allowed me the time and the time to think things over.

GENERAL   But why didn't we get to read your reports again?

POET   Because I stopped writing.

GENERAL   But why?

POET   Because I couldn't write any more.

GENERAL   You couldn't write any more?

POET   To begin with, I had never really written the truth. When I went back home, I suddenly realised what was reported from home was equally false. We were lying to each other in every possible way.

GENERAL   Nonsense! If these were the old days, what you said is more than enough to get yourself convicted by a military court on treason and be summarily executed at once.

POET   It was fortunate that, because the situation was so critical, no one bothered about me. So, as you were all preparing for the final battle to defend the island, I walked away from the army and headed for the top of the hill.

GENERAL   What? You deserted? You deserted!

POET   On the night before, the staff meeting decided that I should, even before the battle had actually began, write a story about how we had totally defeated an enemy vanguard detachment.

GENERAL   Writing about victory, writing reports glorifying our bravery is the sacred mission of a patriotic reporter.

POET   But did we actually fight and win the battle? Was there any real deed of bravery?

GENERAL   Do you doubt the greatness of our nation, of our people, of our military?

POET   Put your hand over your heart, and tell me honestly: did we win any battle at all after the enemy launched their final assault of the island?

GENERAL   The important thing is: what we write about the war must always be encouraging for our national morale. It must never serve to boost the enemy's spirits!

POET   Even going to the extent of cheating and lying to our own people?

GENERAL   We soldiers have a sacred duty, as you reporters also have a sacred duty, to give our people nothing but the best victory and the best news about such victories! So they would be encouraged, so they would become more courageous!

POET   So they would be as corrupted as we were, and so they would die in vain as we did?

GENERAL   Nonsense! To die for the motherland is to die in glory!

POET   Do you dare to say that the battle to defend this island had ended in victory? And all those who died had died in glory?

GENERAL   It was no different from the Great Victory of the Da Tian Island Campaign, the Great Victory of the Huang Yu Island Campaign and the Ma Qing Island Campaign. They were all glorious victories according to your reports. Did you not write those reports?

POET   Yes, I did.

GENERAL   So? What's the difference from our last campaign?

POET   There were no differences. They all ended in total disaster. Total defeat!

GENERAL   No! Your writing was excellent! Beautiful! And that is why our government awarded you citations and rewards, naming you our Patriotic Poet, our Patriotic Reporter!

POET   Yes, I did receive them. And they functioned like blinkers. Like a gag. But when I walked up all the way to the top of the hill, far away from the troops —

GENEAL   And became a deserter!

POET   … when I reached the top of the hill, I began to see the real situation. And it became clear how dangerously positioned we were even before the campaign began. Mr Commander-in-Chief, did you really think we had any chance of winning the battle? Please, tell me, did you really think we were going to win the battle?

MOTHER   What? You, the Commander-in-Chief?

General does not respond.

MOTHER   Then you are the one who ordered them to open fire and had me killed?

General does not respond.

GIRL   Then, you are the one who dismissed my case?

General does not respond.

MAN   And you are the one who ordered the bombing of the bridge and cut off most of our retreating army?

GENERAL   There was only one Commander-in-Chief on this island. And that man is me.

The militaristic man of authority 're-appears' in the person of the General.

GIRL   Oh, Commander-in-Chief, how could you have the heart to allow our soldiers to play upon the bodies of their own sisters with such brutal cruelty, one after another, one after another, as if our bodies were nothing more than toys, totally uncaring that the women under their bodies were being tortured to death by their sexual pleasure.

GENERAL   Yes. That's precisely the point! I didn't want them to look at those who were struggling under their bodies. I didn't want them to see the pain of the women who were giving them pleasure. Let me be very honest with you: I don't give a damn if the women had died while entertaining my soldiers! Do you know why? Let me tell you why. Not because I didn't care about our patriotic sisters, but because I loved my troops more! Because I wanted them to win in battle! Because I want them to let out all their pain and frustrations before I sent them to the front! Because I want them to reward them with carnal satisfaction so that they would march to the front to fight and to die! I wanted them to be in high morale so I would have the best chance of winning in battle! If it helped in some small way to win a battle, I wouldn't hesitate to let my troops fuck to death a hundred women! And if you think this is cruel, then let me ask you: why did you show no remorse but praise us instead when I scored a victory with casualties numbering in the thousands? You tell me: if our soldiers had to suffer death for the sake of winning battles, why couldn't we demand similar sacrifices from our women? Why can't you understand such a simple fact of life?

MOTHER   So, Mr Commander-in-Chief, this is how you teach our children to fight a war?

GENERAL   War is sacrifice. War is death!

POET   But Mr Commander-in-Chief, Do they all deserve to die? Do they all deserve to be sacrificed? You know very well, sir, from the moment the enemy launched the attack, our troops were put on the defensive. Almost immediately, the main column started to run for the hills!

GENERAL   Nonsense! Our great army never ran away from the enemy!

POET   Or maybe you would call it a 'strategic retreat'!

MAN   (*His memories begin to revive.*) Yes, we started to retreat on the morning of the second day of the battle.

POET   Precisely because this great army never permitted any talk of retreat, the troops had never prepared any retreat plan. And when you had to retreat, even your main column of the 80,000-strong army almost immediately got into hopeless confusion. Your ammunition was running low and the retreating forces experienced utter chaos. The enemy were bombarding you from the sea as well as from the air. Casualties were mounting every minute. Within a week, your 80,000-strong army had almost disintegrated, broken into many small groups all running for their lives. But, for the sake of cutting off the enemy so as to protect your commanding units, you prematurely bombed the only bridge that ran up the hills, well aware that the bulk of your remaining troops had not crossed the bridge, knowingly leaving them behind to be slaughtered by the pursuing enemy forces.

Did you know that of the more than 60,000 troops you had deserted on the other side of the bridge, only 1,000 survived? The rest of them had all died either because they were hit by enemy fire, or because they were eliminated summarily by your own officers. More than 50,000 of them, groups and groups, piles and piles. Now only their skeletons and bones are left.

MAN   What? Bones? ... piles and piles and groups and groups of skeletons and bones? You mean, those — ?

POET   Mr Commander-in-Chief, you should know better.

GENERAL   When troops go into battle, the top priority is to protect the command post and the commanding officers, for an army would be leaderless without a commander —

POET   Those groups and groups and piles and piles of skeletons and bones, Mr Commander-in-Chief, what's the meaning of their existence?

GENERAL   Group casualties are not uncommon in major battles.

MAN   But Commander-in Chief, how come they're all in groups and piles?

GENERAL   If they had died in groups and piles, they would have been buried in groups.

MAN   No, they weren't buried! Mr Commander-in-Chief, they were just lying around — in groups and piles!

GIRL   Were they executed by our medical teams?

MOTHER   What? Our medical teams?

GIRL   For those who couldn't be cured, those who couldn't be carried along, sometimes, Command Headquarters would order a summary elimination?

MOTHER   How would they have done the elimination?

GIRL   Mr Commander-in-Chief, you would know best!

MAN   Mr Commander-in-Chief, how did the medical teams carry out the elimination?

GENERAL   ... Those who were beyond cure, and for those who couldn't be carried along, they would have been summarily executed on the spot.

MOTHER   Ah! Ah! *Ah*!

She moans and cries like an animal who has lost her young.

MAN   What did you say, Mr Commander-in-Chief? Those who were beyond cure, those who couldn't be carried along ... summary execution on the spot?

POET   Come on, Mr Commander-in-Chief, it's been more than half a century, do you want to hide the facts any longer?

GENERAL   How can I make you understand. It was a critical battle in a war whose outcome would decide the fate of our motherland. Yes, our troops were put in an
extremely difficult situation. We were not allowed to retreat and we couldn't
surrender! Just before we started the strategic regrouping up the hills,
I received an order from the General Staff Headquarters. It was short and
terse: honour in death, shame in captivity. So, I gave the order: for those who
were unable to move or be moved, and all those who were incapable of exter-
minating themselves, the responsibility rests with the commanding officers to
execute all of them summarily! ...

MOTHER   Oh, my husband, my brothers, my children!

MAN   Oh, my comrades, piles and piles and groups and groups of my comrades!

GIRL   You'd never believe this: the medical teams have executed many, many more
brothers than they have saved!

All three kneel and cry.

POET   Of the more than 70,000 soldiers, not more than 5,000 were killed by the
enemy. All the rest, more than 70,000, had perished because of starvation and
sickness, or were killed by wild beasts, had committed suicide or were poi-
soned or killed by the medical teams or summarily executed by their superiors.
Seventy-thousand men! Seventy-thousand men! Mr Commander-in-Chief, we
didn't lose the campaign to the enemy; we lost it because we drove ourselves
to destruction! We have exterminated ourselves!

GENERAL   Don't make it sound so tragic. There have never been wars without bleeding,
without death. The important thing is: when we were alive, we must live in
glory; when we had to die, we must die in a manner that would encourage our
comrades, leading them onwards to achieve final victory!

POET   But eventually we were led to total defeat.

The others were shocked by the poet's statement.

MAN   Defeat? We lost the war?

POET   Totally and completely.

GENERAL   We? ... We lost the war?

GIRL   How did you know?

POET   Those who came to collect our remains, they were talking about it.

GENERAL   We? ... lost the war? ...
           No no no, that is impossible. Impossible impossible impossible!

GIRL   We really lost the war?

MAN   We were defeated?

MOTHER   You mean all those skeletons and bones ... they all came to nothing?

POET   (*Hugging all of them.*) Yes, yes, yes! Mothers, sisters, brothers, all of you all of us all of them, all these sacrifices have come to nothing! *Nothing!*

GENERAL   Impossible! Impossible! *Impossible!*

           We must keep on fighting! We must never be defeated! We're a superior nation! We have a great leader! We have a great army! Long live! Long Live! Long live! ...

Exhausted and looking flat, he commits suicide.

POET   Look at the way you ended your life, Mr Commander-in-Chief, can we ever win the war?

GENERAL   (*Totally defeated and disillusioned, but still mumbling to himself.*) Long live, long live ...

POET   Unlike you, Mr Commander-in-Chief, all those who died in the wilderness, those tens of thousands of wandering spirits, they were not unhappy. Because they knew the war was finally over. Victory or defeat has no meaning to them. There's only one thought in their minds, 'I want to go home.'

Countless endearing spirits, crying and howling, pass in front of them, as the sky becomes darker and darker.

POET   Look, my Commander-in-Chief, look at yourself. Do you think the sacrifice of all these people could win you victory in war?

        The 300,000 unarmed villagers you massacred on the north coast. The 300-strong self-defence group you mauled in the Black Forest. The civilians you shot, bayoneted, raped, buried alive and burnt to death up in the highlands. And the tens of thousands of your own soldiers who were killed, executed, poisoned or died of disease after you deserted them by destroying the only bridge that could have allowed them to escape enemy assault!

MAN   Oh, my brothers, what, you are all here? ... Company 782, Company 440, Company 395, Companies 529, 434, 277 ...

The atmosphere gets darker and eerier, as if life itself has become formless chaos, removing the difference between the human and the non-human, between the organic and the inorganic, between reality and illusion, between the gods and the demons.

POET   Everything's exterminated. Brothers, sisters, mothers, fathers, clansmen, friends, loved ones, allies, enemies ... everyone, everyone. Mr Commander-in-Chief, how did we become what we have become?

MOTHER   (*As in a delirious state, as if calling the wandering spirits.*)
Go home, go home all of you, whether you've had a woman, whether you've bullied, spoilt or raped a woman, whether you've killed or been killed, everybody's the same — six pieces of wood and a puff of fire. Go home. (*She keeps repeating this.*)

POET   We, allowing ourselves to be butchered, we are like cattle; and we, butchering other people like cattle, we are like wolves.

GENERAL   If you don't behave like a pack of wolves, you will become cattle. If you don't want to become cattle, then you must become wolves. No, we must never become cattle. We'd rather become wolf packs!

MAN   Oh my brothers, you should never have died like this!

GIRL   Oh my sisters, you should never have been sacrificed like this!

MOTHER   With all the sacrifices we've made, the war still ended in our defeat.

GENERAL   No defeat. We could never be defeated. We shall always remain the superior nation, forever powerful, wealthy and strong!

POET   Our people have been so good and hardworking. Our country has been so fertile and rich. How come we have suddenly become so dark and cold, so murderous and cruel. Not even our own brothers and sisters have been spared.

MAN   Whole groups of brothers and comrades, completely wasted to no avail!

GIRL   No feeling, no love, just torture and pain day after day, night after night. Torture and pain!

MOTHER   My husbands, my sons, my fathers, you have all sacrificed yourselves for nothing!

GENERAL   No defeat. We could never be defeated. We shall always remain the superior nation, forever powerful, wealthy and strong!

POET   Enough. Enough! *With a 'bang', he re-enacts his killing of himself.*

All is quiet and still.

GENERAL   ... Now, everything is past. We should look at it with tranquillity and equanimity.

MAN   What else can we say?

MOTHER   And whom can we say it to?

GIRL   And does it make any difference?

GENERAL   Or perhaps we can talk about the cloud up there or the earth down there, or the plants and trees around us.

MOTHER   It may be best to stay silent.

And there is a moment of silence.

MAN   Mr Poet, why are you not speaking?

POET   I don't feel like speaking.

GIRL   Why?

POET   There is nothing left to speak of.

MAN   Why?

POET   What's the use of speaking now?

MOTHER   It is best not to speak. It contributes to tranquility.

GENERAL   Then I will. I'll tell you a story told to me by my grandfather.

In the mysterious darkness of the past, there lived a mythic animal — they called him 'Can'.[2] *Can* was the most vibrant of all living things that ever existed. He was noble, courageous, wise and daringly powerful. He feared nothing; he was completely invincible and nothing could kill him or hurt him. Why? Because he had a gift which no other living thing had ever had: he

---

[2] Or *ts'an*, according to Wade-Giles system of phonetic transcription.

could eat and survive on anything. He could survive on vegetables and fruit, he could survive on meat, he could eat other species and he could eat his own species.

For the sake of survival and propagation, he could even eat his own flesh and blood, including that of his own children and his own parents. In extreme circumstances, he could even consume himself in order to perpetuate his own life. His unique survival power was made possible because his body had this tremendous capacity to regenerate after he had eaten or lost any part of it.

Once, there was a great drought and everything under the sky had been destroyed, and everything that could be eaten had been eaten. All living things had perished except *Can* who was also on the edge of death.

So, *Can*, summoning his extraordinary powers of survival, began by eating his own species. When others had been all been killed and consumed, he began to eat his children. When his children were all consumed, he began to eat his parents. And when his parents had been consumed, he began to eat his spouse. But the great drought still persisted.

Then, he began to eat himself.

He first consumed his feet, then his legs, then his hands, then his arms. But there was still no end to the great drought. So *Can* began to eat his own shoulders and his own torso and his own neck — until there was only his head left. But the end of the great drought was still not in sight. So *Can* began to eat his own head — his ears, his forehead, his nose, his face — until there was only his mouth left — a round hole of his mouth. By then, he had consumed everything under the sky, but the great drought still persisted.

But *Can* had nothing else to eat anymore, and he had no way to sustain his survival. There was only his large open bloody round mouth seemed to stare at the empty, dried world. Because of his extraordinary life force, he kept himself alive for a very, very long time after everything else had perished. But in the end, even he had to die.

But because of the incredible staying power of *Can*, his huge red mouth survived and kept staring at the world with its fearful circular form domineering over all of us — forever inspiring us, encouraging us, edging us to move on, to continue with the lofty struggle of our superior breed ...

Can is our inspiration!
Can is our leading spirit!

There, high up in the sky, appears a round object looking somewhat like a moon that had turned bloody red, stained with grains of a cruel green, while the General was telling his story. It stares threateningly at the world.

The Poet springs up.

POET   I want to tell a story from the East Side.

I want to tell a story from the East Side of our homeland!

In the ancient times of our homeland, they say there lived a mythic bird. They called him *Xiang. Xiang* had a very long neck, a very sharp beak and a very big stomach. *Xiang* was indeed a mythic bird. He didn't eat anything. All he needed to survive was water.

One day, there was a great drought. The sky had no cloud and the earth was baked and cracked, and everything died. Millions upon millions of our folks were on the verge of death. They finished off all the crops; then they finished off all the animals; then they finished off all the fish. But the great drought persisted. So they started to eat all the wild plants they could find. But then the great drought still persisted. So they started to survive only on water. And when all the water had been exhausted, they could wait only to die.

Then, the mythic bird *Xiang* flew in. He stretched his long neck, opened his sharp beak and fragrant water began to flow out. It filled the brooks and it filled the streams. And the stomach of *Xiang* got smaller and smaller. But the great drought still persisted.

So *Xiang* flew over again. He stretched his long neck, opened his sharp beak and the water started to flow out. It filled the ponds, it filled the lakes, it filled the rivers. And *Xiang*'s stomach became flat. But the great drought still persisted.

So *Xiang* flew over again. He stretched his long neck and he opened his sharp beak. But no water flowed out. So, *Xiang* cut off his own neck and drooped his body, and the remaining water in his body poured out, and it filled the last pond, the last brook, the last stream, the last river and the last lake. And then, *Xiang* raised his skinny body, flapped his tired wings and flew away.

Fortunately, the great drought soon began to diminish. But the sad thing was: *Xiang* could never, ever return again.

When I heard the story for the first time as a boy, I wrote a poem:

'High above me the sky is all blue

All around me there is absolute silence
A single white crane flashes over my head
Painting the entire world as peaceful and tranquil'

GENERAL   This is nothing but your fanciful imagination.

POET   That's a fitting description of your own story.

GENERAL   *Can* is our guarding angel! *Can* is the protective god of our military!

POET   *Xiang* is a myth of our homeland! *Xiang* is a part of the folklore from our East Side.

GIRL   *Xiang* is a story which every mother would tell her children.

MAN   *Xiang* is a mythic bird which every boy goes looking for in the mountains.

MOTHER   *Xiang* is a story from our East Side which every father finally forgets ...

GENERAL   *Hahahaha*! (*Most unexpected laughter.*) ... Every father forgets ... Yes. I know the story. And I used to believe it — once.

Everyone is surprised.

          But not anymore. And I don't believe you still do either.

ALL   Yes, we do. We, from the East Side, we still do believe.

GENERAL   Do you?

ALL   Yes, we do. We do!

GENERAL   Do you, really?

ALL   Yes.

GENERAL   Do you *really*?

ALL   Yes.

GENERAL   It's OK if you are telling the story to your children in order to send them to sleep. It's OK if you are telling the story to your students to persuade them to love their folks and the plants and animals in their countryside. But do you really believe the story when it is a matter of *life* and *death*?

ALL   Yes ... yes.

GENERAL   *Please*! Be honest with yourself! Do you *really*?

ALL   ... (*Their mouths are open but no sound is heard.*)

GENERAL   Where were you when the whole nation was mobilised to wage the sacred war
                      to defend our Motherland? Where were you when our entire people were
                      mobilised to strengthen the Army? Where were you when our entire country
                      was united in raising our production in the preparation for war? Where were
                      you when all the cities and countryside demonstrated in support of our decla-
                      ration of war against the enemy? Where were you when each and every one
                      of our families sent forth their able-bodied men to build up our million-strong
                      great army?

*The series of question shock the Mother, the Man, the Girl and the Poet, first into stillness;
then the stillness turns into severe trembling — finally leading them to emit an almost
animalistic cry — as if their inner souls have been stirred and a long-locked beast of the
wild is finally unleashed.*

*Instinctively, impulsively, they begin to undress, revealing bodies painted in primal, savage
colours. They all look the same. Tattoos bear individual designs of a unified primitive style.*

*They show a lightness like spirits, an awesomeness like ghosts, an honesty like children,
a savagery like beasts. And their personalities have been reduced to a basic commonality
of primal instinct.*

BEING A   When the whole nation was mobilised for the sacred war to defend our
                      Motherland, I volunteered to join the army.

BEING B   When the entire people were mobilised to strengthen the army, I sent my
                      sweetheart to the front.

BEING C   When the entire country was united in raising production in preparation for
                      the war, I was doing double shifts in the munitions factory.

BEING D   When all the cities and countryside demonstrated to support our declaration
                      of war against our enemies, I was in the patriotic youth propaganda brigade.

ALL BEINGS   When each and every family sent forth their able-bodied men to make up our
                      million-strong army, we all joined the sending-off parties in joyous celebra-
                      tion. We witnessed their oath-taking, dedicating their lives to the final victory.
                      We applauded them when they swore that they would not want to return alive
                      until the Motherland had totally vanquished its enemy.

GENERAL   Yes. We have all been loyal subjects of our great leader.
                      We have all been unwavering supporters of our great army.
                      We have all been die-hard defenders of the great sacred war.

ALL   Yes, we are loyal subjects of our great leader!
          Yes, we are unwavering supporters of our great army!
          Yes, we are die-hard defenders of the great war of salvation!

GENERAL   (*The General starts to recite first, and then the others join in.*)

          'Oh, such beautiful ponies of war
          Galloping like a flash of light through the air
          Your every hair radiates power and swiftness
          Thundering with a dying will towards the enemy line
          Then you fall like a mountain of strength
          Your eyes streaking fire
          But here your mission ends, dear pony
          I swing my sword to send you to the heavens
          I wash my hand in your blood still warm
          I will make a monument
          In memory of your loyal service

          'We are Men and Women
          Mothers and Daughters
          Brothers and Sisters
          Fighters and Nurses
          Runners and Signallers
          Horses and Dogs
          Pigeons and Rats
          We are all loyal subjects   of the Great Nation
                                           of the Great People
                                           of the Great Leader
                                           of the Great Commander

          'We are all willing to give our blood, our bodies, our lives
          For we know we'd all be worshipped spirits in our ancestral shrine
          Forever and ever, and ever ...'

Practically in a trance — transported to the basic being of their savage instincts.

GENERAL   The great leader shall prevail!

ALL   The great leader shall prevail!

GENERAL   The great army shall prevail!

ALL   The great army shall prevail!

GENERAL   The great war of salvation shall prevail!

ALL   The great war of salvation shall prevail!

GENERAL   We'd rather be a pack of wolves than a herd of cattle!

ALL   We'd rather be a pack of wolves than a herd of cattle!

GENERAL   We must forever be invincible, superior, powerful, wealthy and strong!

ALL   We must forever be invincible, superior, powerful, wealthy and strong!

And they begin to howl and cry, prowl and pry, like a pack of beasts in a bloody, primal feast.

At the climax of their collective 'explosion', there is a sudden round of bombardment, which shocks them and brings them back to stillness. As if they were thrown back into the tranquillity of the beginning. As if they were taken out of a horrible nightmare.

Calmness returns. They get back into the 'spiritly' white robes.

They act as if nothing had happened.

POET   (*Deeply agonised by the feeling of the tragedy.*)

              But ... why have we ... this hardworking, kind, loving people suddenly became a herd of cattle, a pack of wolves overnight? ... Why ... why ... why ...

GENERAL   I would rather we become a pack of wolves rather than become a herd of cattle ... Yes, we must forever be invincible, superior, powerful, wealthy and strong! Forever ... forever ...

The quarrelling comes to nothing ...

MAN   But ... could we still go home?

GIRL   Where there are orchards ...

MAN   ... Rice fields, and sisters and brothers ...

MOTHER   ... Flowers and birds, and kitchens and gardens ...

GENERAL   Where there are ancestral temples and shrines ...

POET   Where there are fragrant water and ... the mythic bird? ...

GENERAL   ... How did we get to where we are in the first place?

              And how can we go back?

ALL   To go back ... to go home ...

POET   I think this, here ... for people like us ... this is more like home.

They mumble on respectively.

(*End of scene*)

Scene 8

GENERAL   The leaves must have turned red by now.

MOTHER   Yes, they must have turned red ... Yes, it's red today.

GIRL   If it's red today, then it was green yesterday.

MAN   Then, it will be white tomorrow.

POET   And then, it will be black.

GENERAL   And the snow?

MOTHER   No, it's the blood. Blood is red.

MAN   No, blood is purple.

GIRL   No, blood is black.

GENERAL   I mean the snow. The white snow!

POET   The snow has also become a bloody red!

GENERAL   Oh, the snow has become a bloody red?

MAN   No, everything's purple.

GIRL   No, everything's black.

MOTHER   All, in black.

GENERAL   Ah ... all, in black.

Multi-coloured leaves begin to fall.

They are suddenly overcome by a deep sense of pain and sadness.

They are totally beyond words.

MAN   It's all blasted, broken, busted, gone.

GIRL   It's all rotten, smelly, sunken, torn.

MOTHER   It's all passed by, gone through, put out, destroyed.

GENERAL   It's all cleared out, gone away, brushed aside, forgotten.

MAN   Brushed aside? Forgotten?

MOTHER   Yes, it's all cleared out, passed by, destroyed, forgotten.

Five spirits, all in tears, looking into the heavens and upon the wilderness, not knowing where to turn to.

While the spirits fade into the shadows, all their brilliant costumes have appeared — bathed in extreme brilliance. As the spirits are overcome by sadness, sobbing and trembling, a canopy of coloured leaves falls down over the brilliant costumes and down to the earth, covering the earth with leaves of red, green, yellow, pink, brown and black.

The leaves keep falling, endlessly falling ... in great abundance ... until darkness draws the play to a final end.

(*End of Play*)

Sunset Rise

Scene 1

A little boy, dressed smartly, enters from stage right.

He walks diagonally across the stage and stops near the centre of the stage.

He bows and invites somebody waiting in the left wing for a dance.

A little girl, prettily dressed, enters from stage left.

She goes to her partner.

Waltz music starts — it is 'Que Sera Sera'[1] — and as this little couple starts waltzing, four more pairs of boys and girls, similarly well dressed, enter from stage right and stage left respectively, and they all dance.

Music changes to 'One Day When We Were Young'.[2]

---

[1] 'Que Sera Sera (Whatever Will Be, Will Be)' was written by Jay Livingstone and Ray Evans in 1956. Doris Day's recording of the song is probably the best-known version, and it was used as the theme song for her TV programme, 'The Doris Day Show' (1968–73).
[2] The song 'One Day When We Were Young' (*'Wer uns getraut'*) is taken from the operetta *Gypsy Baron* by Johann Strauss II. It was adapted by Dimitri Tiomkin for the MGM film *The Great Waltz* (1938), with English-language lyrics by Oscar Hammerstein II. This song is sung by Mary and Salmah at the end of scene 2.

One day when we were young
That wonderful morning in May
You told me you loved me
When we were young one day

Sweet songs of spring were sung
And music was never so gay
You told me you loved me
When we were young one day

Five pairs of well-dressed teenagers enter from stage right, and they waltz.

Five pairs of well-dressed adults waltz in.

The children start to leave the stage, stage left.

Music switches abruptly to disco.

Teenagers and adults disco dance.

Music switches to 'Changing Partners'.[3]

Eight pairs of well-dressed old people waltz in.

Gradually, the teenagers and the adults waltz away, leaving the old people waltzing on stage.

Slowly, some of the partners start to leave.

The song fades.

Five old men and three old women are left alone onstage.

They gaze into the distance.

Lights fade to black.

Voiceover of announcement and a lullaby is played.

You told me you loved me
And held me close to your heart
We laughed then, we cried then
Then came the time to part

When songs of spring are sung
Remember that morning in May
Remember you loved me
When we were young one day

We laughed then, we cried then
Then came the time to part

When songs of spring are sung
Remember that morning in May
Remember you loved me
When we were young one day ...

[3] 'Changing Partners' was written by Larry Coleman and Joe Darion, and it was major hit for Patti Page in 1953.

L The Sunset Rise Old Folks Home wishes everyone of you a very good night. To usher you into a night of sweet dreams, here is Ah Q singing the lullaby for tonight.

Ah Q sings a Cantonese song.

Scene 2

The sound of waves start, and lights go up.

H, with back facing the audience, has already launched into his taichi[4] *exercises.*

JJ jogs in from stage right, then exits stage left.

Z enters from stage right, when B is about to finish his taichi.

H finishes, and facing the audience, bows.

Z recites, and upon completion, gives a bow to greet H a good morning.

JJ moves from stage left to stage right.

H goes to the back of the stage, and Z starts moving chairs.

E enters from stage right.

E Mary! (对 *H*.) 阿娇回来了吗?[5]

JJ moves from stage right to stage left.

H shrugs.

E (对*JJ*.) 阿娇回来了吗?[6] *Mari!*[7]

S (*Wheels herself in from stage right.*) Selamat pagi Ah Eng. *Apa mari mari? Mari mandi. Last night tengoh* TV.[8]

---

[4] *Taichi,* or *taijiquan* ('supreme ultimate fist'), is a type of internal Chinese martial art that is also practised for health concerns, as is the case here.

[5] Chinese: Mary! (*To H.*) Has Ah Q come back? (The translations from Chinese into English in the notes are by Chan Cheow Thia.)

[6] Chinese: (*To JJ.*) Has Ah Q come back?

[7] Malay: *Mari!*, come here!

[8] Malay, interspersed with English: Good morning Ah Eng. Come, come here. Come and have a bath. Last night watched TV.

The sound of waves fade out.

E   TV 有什么好看? 整天打来打去。[9]

S   *Buka*[10] *da lai da hoi* kung fu shows all like that[11] *lah.*[12] Morning, Mr Han; morning Mr Zhang.

JJ moves from stage left to stage right.

S hums, takes out make-up kit, and starts to do herself up.

B apprehensively enters from stage right.

S   Hello! (*S motions him in.*) Welcome!

B gladly walks in. JJ chooses this moment to dash from stage left to stage right, nearly knocking B down.

S   Welcome. You new ah?

B   Hello, my name is Bala.

JJ moves from stage right to stage left.

S   Welcome, Mr Bala, I'm Salmah. This my friend Ah Eng.

B   My name is Bala.

E   早![13]

S   She cannot hear

B   My name is Bala!

E   (*Louder*) 早![14]

---

[9] Chinese: What's there to watch on TV? They just keep fighting and fighting.

[10] Malay: *Buka*, open.

[11] Cantonese-Chinese: *da lai da hoi* (打来打去). In general, combined with the Malay term, *buka*, and the colloquial Singapore English, the entire sentence means: 'There's always fighting in the opening scenes; all kung fu programmes seem to be similar.'

[12] Malay: *lah*, '[A] particle emphasising the word to which it is appended' (*A Malay-English English-Malay Dictionary*, ed. A. E. Coope [revised edn.; London and Basingstoke: Macmillan Education, 1991]).

[13] Chinese: Morning!

[14] Chinese: Morning!

S   Sit down *lah*. Sit down.

JJ moves from stage left to stage right.

B   *To Z.* Hello. My name is Bala.

Z   张。 老张。[15]

They shake hands.

Z   人有悲欢离合, 月有阴晴圆缺, 此事古难全。

     但愿人长久, 千里共婵娟。[16]

B   Thank you. (*Shakes Z's hand.*) Thank you ...

S   You understand, Mr Bala?

B   No.

S   (*Giggles*) One day one poem.

JJ moves from stage right to stage left. Comes to a stop when at stage left.

S   Good morning JJ.

B   (*To JJ.*) Hello, hello sir.

JJ   *Sawadika.*[17]

B   My name is Bala.

JJ   JJ. Guava.

B   What?

JJ   Guava. Taiwan people call guava Bala.

---

[15] Chinese: Zhang. Lao Zhang.

[16] Chinese: Men experience joy and sorrow, partings and reunions; the moon has times of brightness and gloom, as well as periods of waxing and waning. Things are never perfect. I only wish that we will enjoy longevity, to share an appreciation of the moon's beauty, though we are a thousand miles apart. (For assistance with the translations of the poems quoted by Z, the translator made reference to Stephen Owens [ed.], *An Anthology of Chinese Literature: Beginnings to 1911* [New York: W. W. Norton, 1997]; and Victor Mair [ed.], *The Columbia Anthology of Traditional Chinese Literature* [New York: Columbia University Press, 1994]).

[17] Thai: *Sawadika*, Hello.

B   (*Laughs*) You must be from Taiwan?

JJ   No, Thailand.

B   I'm from India.

JJ   Yah. I can see.

B   I was originally from India … But I came to Singapore a long time ago. I'm a teacher. I teach English Literature …

B sits. Z tells him to stand up, arranges the chairs, and then invites him to sit again. J waits for Z to move away before he steals a chair to do exercises at the back.

S   Mr Bala, down here, one Malay. I Malay. Now you come, down here, one Indian. You Indian. Good ah? (*Sees J enter from stage right.*) Eh? Now come another one, bigger one! Mr Bala you got friend.

J   Hello! Good morning! (*Sees B and instinctively walks over, and shakes hands.*)

B   (*In Tamil.*) Do you speak Tamil?

J   (*In Tamil.*) A little bit I'm Malayali.[18]

B   (*In Tamil.*) I'm Tamil.

J   (*In Tamil.*) Then we better speak in English. (*In English.*) I'm Joseph D'costa. Call me Joe.

B   Bala.

E   这两个 *Kiling*[19] 肥肥黑黑的, 是不是两兄弟?[20]

S   She say … you two brothers.

J   No, no, we just met.

B   He's Malayali, I'm Tamil. We don't even speak the same language.

S   But you both look like Indians?

---

[18] Malayali (also spelt 'Malayalee') is the term used to refer to the native speakers of Malayalam, originating from the state of Kerala in India.

[19] Malay: *Kiling*, or sometimes *Kling*, Tamil person. The term can be used in Malaysia and Singapore to refer to Indians in general, and sometimes has a derogatory sense.

[20] Chinese: These two Indians are so fat and dark, are they brothers?

J We are Indians. We can form a political party afterwards. I'm Joseph D'costa. Call me Joe.

S Mr Joe.

J No need 'Mr', just 'Joe' — and your name is?

S Salmah. This one my friend Ah Eng.

J Hello! I'm Joe, Joseph D'costa.

E 早！我补衣的。 一件5角钱。[21]

S Oh, she say, *kalau* your *baju koyak*, she do for you, 50 cents.[22]

J Oh, she's a seamstress! Thank you, *gamsia*.[23]

E 早！[24]

B Joe, meet JJ, he's from Thailand.

J JJ, hi, Joseph D'costa …

JJ shakes his hand without lifting his head, focussing on his exercise.

J Later we'll talk. He's busy.

B That's Lao Zhang.

J Hello, sir, Mr Lao Zhang. I'm Joseph D'costa.

Z (*Shakes hands.*) 张, 老张。

人有悲欢离合, 月有阴晴圆缺, 此事古难全。

但愿人长久, 千里共婵娟。[25]

J Thank you, thank you. What's he saying?

---

[21] Chinese: Morning! I mend clothes, 50 cents for a piece.

[22] Malay, interspersed with English: Oh, she says, if your shirt is torn, she do for you [i.e., will mend the shirt] for 50 cents.

[23] *Minnan hua* or *minnan* language (or Hokkien-Chinese): *gamsia*, thank you.

[24] Chinese: Morning!

[25] Chinese: Zhang, Lao Zhang. Men experience joy and sorrow, partings and reunions; the moon has times of brightness and gloom, as well as periods of waxing and waning. Things are never perfect. I only wish that we will enjoy longevity, to share an appreciation of the moon's beauty, though we are a thousand miles apart.

B   One poem a day, Joe.

S   (*Giggles*) I teach him one.

J sits down opposite B.

J   Say, Bala, did you get any sleep last night?

B   No ... I don't sleep well in a new place *lah* ...

J   I didn't get any sleep at all. There was this pipe leaking in my room, this incessant dripping sound, tap, tap, tap, tap.

An attendant, L, enters from stage left.

L   Hello uncle. Hello. (*Gives B a newspaper.*)

J   What is your name young man?

L   Lee Fatt Ping.

J   Fatt Ping, you see, there's this pipe leaking in my room all night and Uncle cannot sleep. And then Uncle Joe will be very grouchy in the morning.

L   OK, I'll tell my supervisor later. Papers uncle? (*Moves on across the stage.*) *Selamat pagi*! *Cik* Salmah![26]

S   See my lipstick, new colour.

L   *Chantek*![27]

L is stopped by E.

E   啊！ 帮我买这几个号码 ⋯ (给钱)[28]

L   好。[29]

S   Ah Eng buy Toto[30] every week.

---

[26] Malay: *Selamat pagi*! *Cik* Salmah!, Good morning! Miss Salmah!

[27] Malay: *Chantek*, Pretty.

[28] Chinese: Hey! Could you help me buy these numbers ... (*Hands over the money.*)

[29] Chinese: Sure.

[30] Toto is a legal form of gambling in Singapore run by the company Singapore Pools. A buyer picks a minimum of six numbers, and each number needs to be between one to 45. The winning numbers that are drawn will include six numbers, plus an additional number. Four or more numbers on a ticket that may match the numbers that have been drawn qualify the ticket buyer for a monetary prize.

E   Toto 头奖一百万![31]

S   Uh … *kalau menang*[32] … Uh … if win, can get one million.

J   But at her age, what is she going to do with the money if she wins? I'll ask her … Ah Eng?

E   JJ? (*Successfully threads the needle.*) 啊![33]

B   She got it!

All clap for her.

J   Ah Eng … the Toto money, what are you going to do with it?

B   Joe, You can't ask her like that … *Itu duit.* Toto. Toto *duit. Duit*![34]

E   '*Lui*'[35] 啊?[36]

S   Ah! *Lui.* Ah Eng do what? Ah Eng shopping, Ah Eng buy motor car, Ah Eng buy *baju*, Eng buy *rumah*?[37]

E   噢! Toto 的 *lui* 啊?我的孙说他一定要读 Poly。[38] 虽然每个人都说他蠢, 如果我中了, *hambalang* 的钱给我的孙读书。[39]

B   Salmah?

S   She say uh … she say … I dunno what she say. Mr Bala … what she say?

B   She'll give everything to her grandson, a retarded boy.

J   Oh, she has a retarded grandson.

---

[31] Chinese: One million dollars for the top prize of the Toto draw!

[32] Malay: *kalau menang*, if I win.

[33] Chinese: Ah!

[34] Malay: *Itu duit.* Toto. Toto *duit. Duit*!, That's money. Toto. Toto's money. Money!

[35] *Minnan hua* or *minnan* language: *Lui*, money.

[36] Chinese: Ah?

[37] English, interspersed with Malay: Ah Eng shopping, Ah Eng buy motor car, Ah Eng buy garments [or clothing], Eng buy house?

[38] A shortened reference for 'Polytechnic', here possibly the Singapore Polytechnic, as that is arguably the most prominent among the various polytechnic institutes in the city-state.

[39] Chinese: Oh! The money for Toto? My grandchild says he must study at the Polytechnic. Although everyone says he is stupid, if I win, I will give all the money to my grandson for his studies. Cantonese-Chinese: *hambalang*, all/ the entire bulk. The Mandarin–Chinese is mixed with this Cantonese phrase.

B   Thank you, sir. I'm Bala.

J   Joe.

H   Han.

E   那你呢?[40]

B   Think she's asking you what you would do with a million dollars.

J   Me? Well, I'm a bit too old to be painting the town red with it. But I think I'll travel, go to Europe, Paris London, Rome, Venice. Travel. (*Does 'flying' action.*) Travel.

E   哦! 买飞机啊?[41]

H   吃风。[42]

E   噢。 吃风。[43]

J   I spoke for so long and it's *sek fong*.[44]

B   The economy of the Chinese language, Joe.

S   If I had a million dollars, I want to make *filem*.[45] In the *filem*, I the *filem* star.

J   *Macam* Grace Kelly ah?[46]

S   What for Grace Kelly? Saloma. And then my hero P. Ramlee.[47]

B/J   Ahh ... P. Ramlee.

S   Yah ... then if you ask for my autograph, I sure give you.

---

[40] Chinese: What about you?

[41] Chinese: Oh! Buy an aeroplane?

[42] Chinese: Literally 'Eat wind'. Spoken in Mandarin-Chinese, but based on a *Hokkien*-Chinese or *minnan hua* phrase meaning to go for a ride, or in this case, to go on a holiday.

[43] Chinese: Oh. 'Eat wind'.

[44] 'Eat wind' pronounced in Cantonese-Chinese, rather than in Mandarin-Chinese.

[45] Malay: *Filem*, film. A loan word from English.

[46] Malay: *Macam*, Like. So, 'Like Grace Kelly?'

[47] P. Ramlee (1929–1973) was a prominent and extremely popular Malaysian film actor, director, singer, songwriter and producer. He was born in Penang, in what was then British Malaya, and made many films in Singapore with the Shaw Brothers, though he finally returned to Kuala Lumpur in West Malaysia (the former British Malaya, which gained independence from Britain in 1957). Given his contributions to the music and film and industry, he is still considered to be one of *the* major icons of Malay entertainment in Malaysia, Singapore and Sumatra.

S Mr Bala, *kalau*[48] you have one million what you do?

B Me? (*Laughs*) What to do with a million dollars now? They say money should be with you when you have the time. I think I'll do some charity, donate money to the temples. Boring ah? No, I'll book a ticket on a space shuttle, go to the moon! What would you do, JJ, come, sit here. (*Goes over to JJ to invite him to sit.*)

S Mr Bala, JJ no need one million dollars, JJ very *kayu*.[49]

J She says you already have a lot of money.

JJ No more! 全没了![50]

B Never mind, if you had a million dollars?

JJ resumes exercise.

J (*Seeing that this path of enquiry is a deadend with JJ.*) What's the name of the gentleman over there?

B Lao Zhang.

J Good memory Bala. Mr Lao Zhang! What would you do with a million dollars? (*Gestures with one finger.*)

Z 你要我再朗读一遍? (*Gestures with one finger.*) 好。

  人有悲欢离合, 月有阴晴圆缺。[51]

H (*Interrupts*) 老张, 他们问你有一百万你要怎么花?[52]

Z 一百万? 我有一百万? 染头发, 镶牙。[53] 染头发, 镶牙![54] (*Agitated*)

H Dye hair, repair teeth.

---

[48] Malay: *kalau*, if.
[49] Malay: *kayu*, wood. Here it is used colloquially to suggest that JJ is being wooden or stupid, dim-witted.
[50] Chinese: All gone!
[51] Chinese: You need me to read it again? (*Gestures, with one finger.*) Sure. Men experience joy and sorrow, partings and reunions; the moon has times of brightness and gloom, as well as periods of waxing and waning.
[52] Chinese: Lao Zhang, they are asking if you had a million dollars, how you would spend it?
[53] Chinese: A million dollars? If I had a million dollars? Dye my hair, have my teeth crowned.
[54] Chinese: Dye my hair, have my teeth crowned!

J   With one million dollars?

B   Practical fellow huh?

J   Very practical. Mr Bala, what about you, what would you do with a million dollars?

H   I would buy a boat.

J   A boat? That's interesting. And where would you go?

H walks down stage. Sings.

H   一条小路曲曲弯弯细又长
    一直通往迷雾的远方
    我要沿着这条细长的小路
    通往远方找我的老伴。[55]

H bows.

L   *Heng*[56] 啊! 开一下门![57]

Attendant wheel in a dead body from stage right. Then exits stage left.

All stand except S. Z bows.

E   阿娇! 好啦, 整天什么声音都不出。 有事都不出声……好啦, 现在想出声都没声出啦。Mary, Mary! 她有没有交代身后事? (*M* 摇头。) 我什么都交代好了。 只要我的孙记得帮阿嬷来插一只香就得了。 阿嬷会保佑你的, 孙。[58]

M   Her funeral, most important, her grandson must be there.

Ah Eng suddenly leaves in a hurry.

M   Diapers. Wet. You all new is it? Welcome. I'm Mary. I live here one year already. Here, we're all good friends.

---

[55] Chinese: A meandering path, narrow and long, / that stretches all the way towards the hazy, distant land. / I wish to walk along this long narrow path / leading toward the distant land to look for my wife.

[56] *Minnan hua* or *minnan* language: *Heng*, Lucky.

[57] *Heng* ah! Open the door! The latter phrase is in Mandarin–Chinese.

[58] Chinese: Ah Q! Well, usually there isn't a word from you the entire day, not even when there are problems. Well, now there won't be any sound from you even if you want to speak. Mary, Mary! Did she not leave word about matters after she's gone? (*M shakes her head.*) I have left instructions for everything. As long as my grandson remembers to come and burn joss sticks for Grandma. Grandson, Grandma will bless and protect you. Note: E is addressing the cadaver.

B   My name is Bala.

J   Joe.

M   Ah Q passed away, this morning 4 o'clock. 今天早上4点走的。[59]

M   Your first day and this happens. But don't worry: not every day like that.

B   Well, I suppose we all have to go one day.

J   Er, Mary, does the home make arrangements?

M   Yes.

J   Because I have some instructions about how to be sent off. I just want them to give me a simple send-off. No fuss. Maybe even a party for whoever's left.

M   Just tell the office. (*Gets her gardening tools.*)

B   You know they say you know when it's your time to go ... Simple is good, Joe. Simple is good. But there must be flowers. Jasmines and incense. And four fellows to carry me to the hearse. And on the third day, after I'm cremated, just throw my ashes into the sea.

Z   人有悲欢离合, 月有阴晴圆缺。[60]

M   老张, 他们不是在说这个, 他们在谈死后要选择什么样的葬礼。[61]

JJ hops up. Runs, stage right.

Z   我们有得选择吗?[62]

M   有! 当然有。[63]

Z   我们可以选择吗?[64]

M   可以。 可以。[65]

---

[59] Chinese: Left this morning at four o'clock.
[60] Chinese: Men experience joy and sorrow, partings and reunions; the moon has times of brightness and gloom, as well as periods of waxing and waning.
[61] Chinese: Lao Zhang, they are not talking about this, they are discussing the choices of funerals after they've passed.
[62] Chinese: Do we get to choose?
[63] Chinese: We do! Of course we do.
[64] Chinese: Can we choose?
[65] Chinese: Possible. Possible.

s   If I go, I go Thursday night *lah*. No tear. Only pray.

M   Yah, no tears. Me, I want a white funeral.

s   (*Wheels herself slightly down stage.*) *Kalau saya pergi, saya mahu pergi malam Jumaat, lepas Maghrib. Kalau saya pergi, tolong telepon kawan-kawan saya, anak saya, supaya mereka dapat menziarahi saya untuk kali terakhir. Esok paginya, mandikanlah saya dan bungkuskanlah badan saya dengan kain kapan yang putih dan bersih. Bas jenazah akan bawa saya ke Pusara Aman di Chao Chu Kang. Di situ, toIong jangan manangis, kerana setiap detik air mata akan memberatkan pemergian saya.* [66]*

    Saya cuma minta disedakahkan Surah Al-Fatiha ...:[67]

    Bismillah Ar-Rahman Ar-Raheem
    Al-hamdu lillahi Rabb il-'alamin Ar-Rahman Ar-Raheem
    Maliki yawmi-d-Din
    Iyya-ka na'budu wa iyya-ka nasta'in
    Ihdina-sirat al-mustaqim
    Sirat al-ladhina an'amta 'alai-him
    Ghair il-Maghdubi 'alai-him wa la-d-dallin.[68]
    Amin.

Lights fade to black.

Announcement is made and lullaby is to be sung.

L   Tonight's lullaby is by Mary and Salmah. 'One Day When We Were Young.'[69]

M and S sing.

---

[66] Malay: If I go, I wish it were a Friday night, after the Maghrib [the evening, just after sunset] prayer. If I go, please call my friends, and my child, so they can visit me one last time. The next morning, cleanse me and wrap my body in a clean white shroud. The bus [i.e., the hearse] will take me to the Aman Cemetery in Chao Chu Kang. While there, please don't cry, because every tear will increase the burden of my leaving.

[67] Malay: I just ask that the *Surah Al-Fatiha* be read ...:

[68] Arabic: In the name of Allah, the Most Beneficent, the Most Merciful.
Praise be to Allah, Lord of the Worlds:
The Most Beneficent, the Most Merciful:
Owner of the Day of Judgement.
Thee alone we worship; Thee alone we ask for help.
Show us the straight path:
The path of those whom Thou hast favoured;
Not (the path) of those who earn Thine anger nor of those who go astray.

[69] See note 2 for the lyrics of 'One Day When We Were Young.'

Scene 3

H is playing 《故乡》[70]
Lights go up.
B is dozing.
E gargles.
B wakes.
E picks her teeth.
S enters from stage left with a lot of food.

S   Eee! What you doing? Ah Eng!

E   鱼骨啊。 *Ikan* 的骨![71]

S   *Tulang ikan?*[72] *Aiyoh*!

E wheels over. S struggles forwards. E offers S a needle.

S   You *gila*![73] Tissue, tissue. *Satu, dua, tiga*![74] (*Pulls out bone.*)

Z enters, arranges chair at stage right.

E   谢了。[75] (*Sees bag of food.*) 谁 *tengoh* 你?[76]

S   *Saya chuchu tengoh.*[77]

E   我的孙几个月都没有来看我，我的儿子说没有空。[78]

S   *Aiyah*, Ah Eng … *makan lah, makan. Kueh, bandung. Makan lah, makan.*[79]

E   我的孙喜欢吃那个。 好吃。[80]

---

[70] Chinese: 'Hometown.'
[71] Chinese: Fish bones. The bones of fish [stuck in me]. Malay: *Ikan*, Fish.
[72] Malay: *Tulang ikan?*, Fish bone?
[73] Malay: *gila*, mad, crazy.
[74] Malay: *Satu, dua, tiga*!, One, two three!
[75] Thanks.
[76] Chinese: Who came to see you? Malay: *tengoh*, to look.
[77] Malay: *Saya chuchu tengoh*, My grandson came to look for me.
[78] Chinese: My grandson has not visited me for a few months already; my son says he is not free.
[79] Malay: *Aiyah*, Ah Eng … eat, eat. Cake, *bandung*. Eat, eat. (*Bandung* is a milk drink flavoured with rose cordial, which then gives the drink a pink colour.)
[80] Chinese: My grandson likes to eat that. Delicious.

z   (*Discovers that B is reading.*) 你也喜欢看书?[81]

B   Book, yes. *Shu*.[82] This is an English book.

z   这是诗歌华文诗歌······ 人有悲欢离合······[83]

B   Poetry! This is poetry too! This is Shakespeare.

z   莎士比亚?[84]

B   *Sha shi bi ya?*[85] Shakespeare! You know, I used to be a teacher, I used to teach this to my students.

z   Teacher? 老师? 我也是老师。[86] I teacher too!

B   Really!

The two are elated; they shake hands.

B   I was a good teacher you know, and I can still teach. I show you.

B arranges chairs as his prop.

B   I will read a section from *Hamlet*. Sit down please.

z   哈姆乐特![87]

B   Hamlet! Yes! I will read the part: 'To be or not to be, that is the question.'

z   玛丽? 他要念哈姆乐特的哪一段?[88]

M   Which part?

B   To be or not to be, that is the question.

M   要还是不要, 就是这个问题。[89]

---

[81] Chinese: You also like to read?
[82] Chinese: Mandarin-Chinese: *Shu*, Book.
[83] Chinese: This is poetry, Chinese poetry ... Men experience joy and sorrow, partings and reunions ...
[84] Chinese: Shakespeare?
[85] Chinese: Shakespeare, in transliteration.
[86] Chinese: Teacher? I am also a teacher.
[87] Chinese: Hamlet!
[88] Chinese: Mary? Which part of *Hamlet* will he be reading?
[89] Chinese: Want or not to want, this is precisely the question. A deliberately crass translation is offered here by M.

H   生存还是毁灭……[90]

M   To live or to destroy ...

B   *Yes*!

Z   那是莎士比亚最有名的著作! 好! 好![91]

B   To be, or not to be — that is the question.
Whether is nobler in the mind to suffer
The slings and arrows ...

Z   这手势可以再大一点。[92]

Z corrects B's gesture, and B submits.

B   Whether 'tis nobler in the mind to suffer
The slings and arrows of outrageous fortune
Or to take arms against the sea of troubles,
And by opposing end them?

Z   (*Claps*) 好! 很好![93]

B   Thank you! Thank you!

Z   我也来一段。[94]

M   He also want to read.

B   Which part?

M   哪一段?[95]

Z   生存还是毁灭……[96]

M   Same part.

Z   生存还是毁灭, 这真是一个值得思考的问题。

---

[90] Chinese: To be or not to be ...
[91] Chinese: That is Shakespeare's most famous work. Excellent! Excellent!
[92] Chinese: This hand gesture can be slightly bolder.
[93] Chinese: Good! Very Good!
[94] Chinese: Let me try to read a part.
[95] Chinese: Which part?
[96] Chinese: To be or not to be ...

默然忍受欺人命运的箭伤抢挑，
还是拔起刀，向着无边大海般的磨难搏斗去，一了百了！[97]

The two are ecstatic, they shake hands. They start reciting simultaneously. Upon finishing, they embrace.

B   Now you sit down. Sit down and teach.

Z sits, mumbles to himself, and is relaxed.

B   Teach. Teach! Sit down and teach. Teach.

Z gets up.

B   No, what are you doing? Sit! Lao Zhang?

Z is stunned. He gets up quickly and bows.

Zhang bows to B, shuffles away, exits stage left.

B   Hey. what's the matter, Lao Zhang? Lao Zhang? Mr Han. What's the matter?

H   你跟他说。 在文革的时候他就是这样被人家审问。[98]

M   It reminds him of the interrogation during the Cultural Revolution.

H   他连老婆都赔了。[99]

M   He even lost his wife.

B   Oh my god ... I thought he was admiring my teaching. I was just trying to encourage him.

Han takes to his harmonica again. Plays 《草原之夜》[100]

JJ enters, followed by Joe.

---

[97] To be, or not to be? That is the question —
Whether 'tis nobler in the mind to suffer
The slings and arrows of outrageous fortune,
Or to take arms against a sea of troubles,
And, by opposing, end them?
[98] Chinese: You tell him [i.e., Bala]. During the Great Cultural Revolution of China he [i.e., Lao Zhang] was interrogated exactly like this.
[99] Chinese: He even lost his wife.
[100] Chinese: 'Night on the Grassland.'

B puts chair back in place and retreats to a chair that is at stage right.

JJ   Joe, come, quick. I am going to kick your *kacang*.[101]

J   Yeah, yeah, we'll see, we'll see …

S hums to H's music, mesmerised; she looks for somebody to talk to but all the old folks seem to be busy, except B.

S   Mr Bala, Mr Bala, Mr Han music romantic. I think Mr Han very romantic. Are you romantic, Mr Bala?

B   Me? No *lah*. I'm not romantic.

S   Come on Mr Bala, you can tell Salmah.

B   No, you see, I didn't even pick my own bride! My parents picked her for me from India. The first time I saw her face was on my wedding day.

S   So romantic!

B   But, you know, I was so tired from the journey back that … (*lowers voice in embarrassment*) fell asleep on my wedding night! (*Laughs*)

S   *Alamak*,[102] Mr Bala!

B   Not very romantic ah? But, we took care of each other, you know? She took care of me, I took care of her … I made sure she had everything she needed, and we were happy. But there was no romance *lah*. That time there was no romance *lah*.

S   You bluff. You don't want to tell me right? I go and ask Mr Han. I ask you another day. (*Wheels over to H.*) Mr Han, oh, Mr Han! Are you romantic? Come on Mr Han, you can tell Salmah.

H gets up, gazes at a faraway ocean and starts to play 《可爱的家庭》.[103]

S   *Aiyah*, why nobody want to talk to me? Ah Eng, oh Ah Eng, Ah Eng romantic talk ah? Ah Eng romantic talk ah?

M   她问你以前有没有拍拖?[104]

---

[101] Malay: *kacang*, nut.
[102] Malay: *Alamak*, expression of surprise.
[103] Chinese: 'A Lovely Family'.
[104] Chinese: She asked if you had dated anyone in the past.

E   *Choy*! 都七老八十还问这么恶心的事。[105]

M   那你年轻时有没有拍拖?[106]

e   最多不是拉一下手……[107]

M   Got! Hold hand.

S   Hold hand? So boring! Ah ... JJ most romantic. JJ tell SaImah, you no need tell me, I tell you all JJ got three wives. One, two, three, three wives. *Tiga*![108]

J   Three wives? No wonder you are so skinny ... Actually, I also heard that he's so romantic he has three wives and one *angmoh*[109] boyfriend!

JJ is enraged. He jumps up and throws the chess pieces at J.

J   Hey, I'm just joking. Hey!

JJ storms off, stage right.

S   Joe! *Betul*[110] *lah*.

J   It's true?

B   Joe, I think you might have hit a raw nerve.

J   You mean he's a ...

S   JJ, *macam* like my boyfriend. Everyday *mara, mara,*[111] angry angry.

B   Ah ... Salmah, are you romantic?

S   Me, my love story *tujuh hari*[112] ... seven days seven night also cannot finish. Cannot tell you all now. What about you Mr Joe. They say big people big romance. Are you romantic?

J   Where you hear all these nonsense from?

---

[105] Chinese: *Choy*! She's already so old and still raises such disgusting questions.

[106] Chinese: Well, did you date anyone when you were young?

[107] Chinese: At most we held each other's hands ...

[108] Malay: *Tiga*, Three.

[109] *Minnan hua* or *minnan* language: *angmo*, red hair. A shortened form for *angmo kow*, red-haired monkey — a derogatory reference to white people.

[110] Malay: *Betul*, Correct.

[111] Malay: *mara*, angry.

[112] Malay: *tujuh hari*, seven days.

S   Come on *lah* Joe, you can tell Salmah.

J   Oh yes, I'm very romantic. I once fell madly and passionately in love. It was the day I came here.

S   *Siapa*[113] Joe?

J   With Mary! Who else? But she's too old for me. You know, a fellow like me needs a spring chicken. If she was 20 years younger I'll surely tackle her.

S   You want spring chicken? You take my friend Ah Eng *lah*!

J   No, no I'll pass.

B   Mary, what about your love story?

M   You want to hear love story? I tell you all a great romantic story.

S   Your story?

M   A very romantic story. Once there was this woman, who loved this man for 40 years.

J   Nothing special about that, my own parents were married for 52 years.

M   But this couple was never married.

      The man was already married.

      He had a wife and three children. For 40 years, his wife and three children never knew. They also had an agreement. That is, if one day the man cannot take care of her anymore, it would be the end of their relationship. Forty years later, this day came. The man suffered a stroke and was paralysed. And he couldn't take care of her anymore. And that was the end of their story.

S   Mary ... it's you right?

M   (*Laughs*) Do I look like a romantic woman to you? Me? (*Walks down stage right to her plants again.*)

B   Then tell us Mary, who is this woman?

M   Either a very romantic woman or a very stupid woman. Depends on how you look at it.

J   Bala, come, let's have a game.

B   So, Joe, what's the score between you and JJ?

---

[113] Malay: *Siapa*, who.

J   Fifty to zero, poor fellow hasn't won a game yet.

S wheels herself forwards to where M is.

s   Mary, the woman in the story? I think she very stupid.

H starts playing on the harmonica the song 'Swanee River'.[114]

Lights fade to black.

---

[114] A song by Stephen Foster (1826–1864), composed in 1851. Also known as 'Old Folks at Home':

Way down upon de Swanee Ribber,
Far, far away,
Dere's wha my heart is turning ebber,
Dere's wha de old folks stay.
All up and down de whole creation
Sadly I roam,
Still longing for de old plantation,
And for de old folks at home.

Chorus
All de world am sad and dreary,
Eb-rywhere I roam;
Oh, darkeys, how my heart grows weary,
Far from de old folks at home!

All round de little farm I wandered
When I was young,
Den many happy days I squandered,
Many de songs I sung.
When I was playing wid my brudder
Happy was I;
Oh, take me to my kind old mudder!
Dere let me live and die.

One little hut among de bushes,
One dat I love
Still sadly to my memory rushes,
No matter where I rove.
When will I see de bees a-humming
All round de comb?
When will I hear de banjo strumming,
Down in my good old home?

Scene 4

Lights go up.

B, M and H have not moved from their last positions. H wraps up 'Swanee River'.

B   Mary.

M   Yah?

B   Can I ask you a question?

M   Sure.

B   Was he also a good gardener?

M   Who?

B   The man in your story, was he a good gardener?

M   Yes, he was a wonderful gardener. Any plant in his hands will surely bloom.

B   So, they must have done a lot of gardening together.

M   Yes, they did. They couldn't go out a lot, so they were at home most of the time. They did everything at home. They listened to music, eat, drink, dance ... He was a wonderful cook. He taught her how to eat cheese and drink red wine. And she, she liked to cut his hair for him. She would make him sit on the stool in the toilet and she would cut his hair. Then he would let her hair down and he would massage her very tenderly ...

      Then they would make love. When they woke up, they would do more gardening together.

B   Was the relationship very difficult for the woman?

M   Yes, sometimes. She was often lonely, lonely on new year's eve, new year's day, Christmas, birthdays, weekends. So many lonely nights knowing he was with his wife. She left a few times but each time she went back to him ... Why? Life was better with him than without him. Despite everything, he was always there for her. When she was sad, he was there to comfort. When she was happy, he was there to share her joy with her. He was there even when he was not there.

B   Did she have any regrets? (*Walks over to sit down beside M.*)

M   She wanted a baby very very much. But they waited too long and by then it was too late.

B   When he fell sick, did she ever visit him?

M   Yes. She was at the hospital everyday. He was in intensive care for three days. His family was with him 24 hours a day. She couldn't go in so she waited and waited and waited for three days to go and see him. On the fourth day, she went in. He was lying on the bed. He was slightly better but he still couldn't move but he could say a few words. She went up to him and held his hands. She asked him: 'Is this the end?'

我们讲好的。 我现在不能动了。 我的家人每天都在, 他们会看到你的……这 40 年来, 我很快乐。 我们一直埋怨时间不够, 其实已经很多了。 每一天都可以很美, 一小时都可以很美乐, 一分钟都可以很美。 我们就这样吧。[115] So they decided, that was the end of their story. And so she left. A promise is a promise.

B   You are a very strong woman, Mary.

M   (*Smiles, gets up to go to the back.*) I'm sure your wife must have been a very strong woman.

B   She was. But you wouldn't say so, looking at her. She was very small-sized. I used to say her arms were like longbeans. But she could do a lot of work. Every morning, she would get up at the crack of dawn and do all the housework. Cooking, cleaning, washing, preparing the altar. Then at 5.45 sharp, she would put on her clean sari, well-ironed, and wait for me to come home with a cup of coffee. Everyday without fail. And, I took care of her, good care of her. One day, I even wanted to get her flowers! It was her birthday.

She loved white jasmines, packed tightly into small garlands. Those sold along Serangoon Road. And she would put it in her hair. And her hair would have the fragrance of the flowers. That day I left work early and went down to Serangoon Road to get jasmines. But that day, they were all sold out! It was a prayer day or something. So I didn't get her any flowers. Sometimes, sometimes I still get the smell of jasmines in her hair. Nobody teaches you how to love.

M   Bala, do you think I'm a bad woman?

B   No Mary ... I think you are a beautiful woman. Just a little bit stupid sometimes.

---

[115] Chinese: We had a spoken agreement. I am now bed-ridden. My family is around every day, they will see you ... I have been very happy for the past 40 years. We have always complained of insufficient time, but in fact, we already had a lot. Every day can be beautiful, just like every hour, and every minute. Let's keep it this way.

H   Mary, 爱一个男人, 一个有家庭有孩子的男人, 40年不变, 我看你是够痴情的了。 他呢, 媒妁之言, 父母之命, 一辈子老老实实, 也真是难能可贵。[116]

M   He said, you're a loyal man and I'm a crazy woman.

B   What about you, Mr Han?

M   那你呢?[117]

H smiles and picks up his harmonica, plays 《可爱的家庭》.[118]

Lights fade to black.

Announcement is made and lullaby is played.

L   Tonight's lullaby is by JJ

JJ   *(JJ sings a few lines of a Thai song but he ends abruptly and says:)* 哎呀, 不会唱了啦![119]

Scene 5

The sound of waves is heard.

H is playing on his harmonica.

Lights go up.

M is gardening. B is sitting apart from the group. Salmah is dozing. Eng is sewing.

E   Salmah! Salmah!

M wakes S.

S   *Apa*[120] Ah Eng?

---

[116] Chinese: Mary, to love a man, a man who has family and kids, for forty years changing your heart, I think you can really be considered passionate. And that man, to observe the command of his parents and listen to the matchmaker, and behave honestly all his life, is also truly commendable.
[117] Chinese: What about you?
[118] Chinese: 'A Lovely Family'.
[119] Chinese: *Aiya*, I don't know how to continue singing!
[120] Malay: *Apa*, what.

E   好了。[121]

S   *Chantek* ah, Ah Eng. (*Puts blouse to herself.*) Nah, *satu, dua, tiga, empat, lima* ...[122] (*Gives coins to E.*)

E   不用了。[123]

S   Ah Eng sew my clothes for me, Ah Eng must take the money.

E   不要。 你请我吃 *makan* 我不收你钱。[124]

S   Bala, *baju koyak*.[125] You sew for him you also take his money.

E   Bala 是 Bala 吗。[126]

S   Ah, Salmah, Salmah *lah*!

E   我都说不要了![127]

S   Ah Eng! Take it! (*Seemingly in the heat of an argument.*)

J   (*Enters, holding bananas.*) Children, children, what's all the commotion about? I could hear you all from outside.

S   Ah Eng dun want to take my 50 cents.

J   Never mind *lah*. She's your friend. Come *lah*, have some bananas. Come, Mary, Bala, Ah Eng.

S   Ah ... *Obat datang!*[128]

JJ enters with three glasses of water.

B   Ah ... medicine time.

JJ gives the water to M, J and B.

---

[121] Chinese: It's done.

[122] Malay: *satu, dua, tiga, empat, lima* ..., one, two, three, four, five ...

[123] Chinese: There's no need.

[124] Chinese: I don't want it. You gave me *makan* (Malay: *makan*, to eat; or, here, perhaps 'a treat'), I won't take your money.

[125] Malay: *baju koyak*, dress is torn.

[126] Chinese: Bala is a different case. What is said, literally, is: 'Bala is Bala.'

[127] Chinese: I already said there's no need.

[128] Malay: *Obat datang*, medicine is coming.

S   Down here, me most healthy, no need *obat*. My friend Ah Eng also.

J   Bala, why are you counting your pills for? No need to count, I'll beat you hands down. I have one for high blood pressure, one for high blood sugar, one for high cholesterol, one for high uric acid and one for high ... I don't even know what this is for.

E   这个人越肥吃越多药。 好看不好吃! 等我帮你煎一些药。[129]

M   She say, all this no use. She boil Chinese medicine for you.

B   Mary, how are your headaches?

M   Not so good. I've got to see Dr Tan tomorrow. How's your blood pressure?

B   Oh, it's OK, it's OK as long as I eat the medicine. Joe, should you be eating these bananas?

J   Look, it's just one banana, not the whole damn tree. What's your problem?

B   You know, these bananas remind me of the best *pisang goreng*[130] in Singapore. The best *goreng pisang* in Singapore was at Rex cinema.

J   Mackenzie Road[131] *pisang goreng*. When it was still around, I would go buy two *goreng pisang*, wallop them during the show and then come out and have a bowl of *cendol*[132] behind the alley there.

B   But, you know where they had the best *cendol* in the world? Not in Singapore, but in KL,[133] Jalan Alor[134] there.

J   Oh, yes, that's good, but that's not the best. You know where they have the best *cendol*? Here ... (*Blows his nose.*) Ha! Ha!

---

[129] Chinese: The fatter this person is, the more medicine he takes. These medicines may look good but they don't taste good! I'll boil some medicine for you.

[130] Malay: *pisang goreng*, fried banana.

[131] A road close to Serangoon Road in Singapore that still has a number of restaurants and food stalls on it; there also used to be a major bus terminus on the road.

[132] Malay: *cendol*, a dessert that can be found in Indonesia, Malaysia, Singapore and even Burma. The main ingredients consist of coconut milk, little (usually described as) worm-like slivers of jelly made from rice flour (coloured green with food colouring often derived from the *pandan* leaf), shaved ice and palm sugar.

[133] KL, Kuala Lumpur, the capital city of the Federation of Malaysia, located in a Federal Territory inside the state of Selangor on the west coast of West Malaysia.

[134] Jalan Alor is a street in Kuala Lumpur, adjacent to Jalan Bukit Bintang, that is famed for food.

S   *Eee*!

E   *Choy*!

J   Nothing there *lah*. Just joking!

M   Dirty fellow!

B   Why do they think that when you get older, they say you have to stop your chilli? No salt.

J   No sugar.

B   No spice.

J   No oil.

B   No chilli.

B/J   No taste!

M   Why do you think that ever since I come here, I'm all skin and bones. Look!

J   Yah Mary, same problem here.

       You know Socrates once said — a life without chilli is not worth living.

B   Socrates said that?

J   Socrates Mareemuthu from the curry shop!

M   You know what I miss most, I miss the chilli from the *Yong Tau Foo*[135] shop in Chinatown. I used to go there every Sunday and eat the *Yong Tau Foo* just for the chilli.

S   You eat *Yong Tau Foo* just for the chilli? Then you must eat my *Lontong*[136] just for my chilli. My *Lontong*, put *tauhu, tepek, telor, serondeh*.[137] And then put my chilli.

---

[135] *Yong Tau Foo* is a Hakka-Chinese dish which can come either in soup form, or without soup, and with or without noodles. The main ingredients used are vegetable and fish paste.

[136] *Lontong* is a Malay dish: compressed rice is wrapped inside a banana leaf, then cut into small cakes, and served as a replacement of steamed rice. Often, *Lontong* is a dish in itself, with the rice cut into pieces and served with a coconut-based vegetable stew called *Sayur Lodeh* — this is probably what is referred to, in this instance.

[137] Malay: *tauhu, tempeh, telor, serondeh*, soya bean cake, fermented soya bean, egg, hot coconut spread.

E   我的孙喜欢 *Lontong*.[138]

B   What, Mary?

M   Her grandson also like *Lontong*.

S   Next time *Hari Raya*[139] I cook for all of you!

B   But, you know the best chilli is chicken rice[140] chilli! You put the chilli in the rice, and then you mix them all up and then ...

S   Mr Bala you like chicken rice, chicken rice chilli? Mary, you tell him.

M   You like chicken rice? You lucky man, Mr. Han here makes wonderful chicken rice.

S   We call him the Chicken Rice Man!

B   Really? Mr Han, I hear you make good chicken rice; tell us how do you make good chicken rice. Tell us.

Old folks gather at table, stage right.

H   Very complicated.

M   Mr Han. 跟他们讲啦, 你讲华语啦。 来, 我也想听。[141]

H   煮鸡饭, 最重要是要选对鸡。[142]

M   Must choose the right chicken.

H   很多人以为, 童子鸡, 处女鸡最好。[143]

M   People say virgin chicken is the best.

B/J   Virgin chicken?

H   错的。[144]

---

[138] Chinese: My grandson likes *Lontong*.
[139] Malay: *Hari Raya*, or *Hari Raya Puasa*. This is the Muslim celebration that signifies the end of the fasting season of Ramadan. *Hari Raya Puasa* is the term used in Singapore and Malaysia. Elsewhere, it would be known as *Eid-ul-Fitr*, *Eid al-Fitr*, *Id-ul-Fitr*, or *Id al-Fitr*.
[140] Chicken rice is a Hainanese-Chinese dish.
[141] Chinese: Tell them, you speak Chinese. Come, I would also like to listen.
[142] Chinese: The most important thing in making chicken rice is to choose the chicken appropriately.
[143] Chinese: Many think that unmated chickens are the best.
[144] Chinese: That's wrong.

M   Wrong.

H   其实最好是少妇鸡。[145]

M   Huh?

H   少妇鸡。[146]

M   Actually the best is young married woman chicken.

H   好像刚生过一两个孩子的女人，丰满极了。[147]

M   Like a woman, after having one or two children, very voluptuous.

H   重两公斤。[148]

M   Weigh about two kilograms. The chicken *lah*.

H   鸡皮底下和屁股有一层黄黄的脂肪。这种鸡用来煮鸡饭，味道特别好。[149]

M   Under the skin and around the backside got one layer of fat, best.

H   我们家乡有一句话：   (*In Hainanese-Chinese.*) 鸡肥，脚都香。[150]

M   Huh?

H   鸡肥脚都香。[151]

M   If chicken fat, chicken legs also fragrant.

J   Hey, why are you looking at me?

   You know, Han, I'll never look at a plate of chicken rice in the same way again.

B   But the chilli? What about the chilli?

H   The chilli. 辣椒更不能马虎。   要选最新鲜的红辣椒。[152]

---

[145] Chinese: In fact, the best chickens are young female chickens that have mated.

[146] Chinese: Young female chickens that have mated.

[147] Chinese: Like a woman who has just given birth to one or two children, very plump and fleshy.

[148] Chinese: Weighs two kilograms.

[149] Chinese: With a yellow layer of fat under the skin and at the buttocks. To use such chickens for making chicken rice, the taste will be extremely good.

[150] Chinese: There's a saying in our hometown: If the chicken is fat, even the [thin] chicken legs will be fragrant. (The 'saying' is to be spoken in Hainanese–Chinese and not in Mandarin–Chinese.)

[151] Chinese: If the chicken is fat, even the [thin] chicken legs will be fragrant.

[152] Chinese: The chilli must not be compromised; one must choose the freshest red chillis.

M   Must choose the most fresh red chilli.

H   很多的姜。[153]

M   A lot of ginger.

H   蒜。[154]

Garlic.

把它们盅碎。[155]

M   Pound into pieces.

H   加一点盐。[156]

M   Add a bit of salt.

H   一点点糖。[157]

M   A little bit of sugar.

H   还有一点酸柑汁。[158]

M   Add some lime juice.

H   最重要是要加一点鸡油，搅均匀。[159]

M   Most important must add some chicken fat and then stir it together.

H   Best chicken rice chilli.

B   Best chicken rice chilli! (*They shake hands.*) Thank you Mr Han, Thank you. (*The old folks disperse from the table.*) Must use virgin chicken.

J   No, Bala, you weren't listening. Virgins are no good: you have to use the young married ones.

B   Yes ... what about frozen chicken, can I use frozen chicken?

H shakes his head.

---

[153] Chinese: Lots of ginger.
[154] Chinese: Garlic.
[155] Chinese: Pound them into small pieces.
[156] Chinese: Add a little salt.
[157] Chinese: A little bit of sugar.
[158] Chinese: And a little lime juice.
[159] Chinese: Most importantly, add a little chicken fat and stir well.

H   *Kampong*[160] chicken is the best.

S   *Ayam*[161] *kampong*? (*Giggles hysterically.*) *Ayam kampong* chicken cook best, but *tangkap* not best you know? Last time, I make *filem* in a *kampong* and there was one chicken, *lari sini, lari situ. Lari, lari, lari.* This one my *rumah* and this is my *tingkap*, *apa tingkap* Joe? Window. That one, my hero *tingkap*. He *ketok ketok* bottle because he want to meet me but we cannot any how meet. He want to come my house and eat *nasi ayam*, but got no *ayam*. We make *filem lah*. Here make *filem*. Come, I need *ayam*. Mr Joe, you be my *ayam kampong*.[162]

E   什么啊?[163]

M   拍戏啊。[164]

J   You want me to be a chicken? No, I can't, because you know what? I'm not a virgin.

S   Come on, Joe.

J   No *lah*, chickens have feathers, I have hair.

S   Today we see chicken have hair.

J   No, no …

S   Come on Joe, I will be the chicken but I the *filem* star …[165]

J   Okay, okay, don't nag me. When this woman starts nagging, she never stops.

S   OK, Joe, Make chicken *bunyi*.[166] Ah, practice.

---

[160] Malay: *Kampong*, village. So, 'kampong chicken' — a village-reared chicken — is the equivalent of a free-range chicken.

[161] Malay: *Ayam*, chicken.

[162] Salmah speaks in a combination of Malay and colloquial Singapore English: Village chicken? (*Giggles hysterically.*) Village chicken cook best, but to catch not best [or it is not easy] you know? Last time, I make a film in a village and there was one chicken, run here, run there. Run, run, run. This one my house and this is my window, what is *tingkap* Joe? Window. That one, my hero's window. He knocks bottle[s] because he want[s] to meet me but we cannot any how meet. He want[s] to come my house and eat chicken rice, but [I] got no chicken. We make [a] film *lah*. Here make a film. Come, I need [a] chicken. Mr Joe, you be my village chicken.

[163] Chinese: What's going on?

[164] Chinese: They're making a film.

[165] Come on Joe, I would play the part of the chicken but I am playing the part of the film star …

[166] Malay: *bunyi*, produce the sound. So S means: OK, Joe, Make the sound of a chicken.

J   Cockakoo!

S   No, girl chicken.

J   Oh ... Pok pok pok pok.

S   *Jalan.*[167]

J   (*Walks*) Pok pok pok pok.

S   Shake.

J   (*Shakes*) Pok pok pok pok pok.

E   好像啊![168]

S   I need hero. Mr Bala, Mr Bala P. Ramlee.

J   Come on Bala, at least you're P. Ramlee, I'm just a chicken!

S   Mr Bala, you *ketok ketok*[169] two bottle, because you want to meet me. Camera there.

J waves at the camera.

S   OK. We make *filem*. Mary, you in. charge of music. OK? Camera!

Cha-cha-cha music comes on.

S   *Abang, mari lah masok!*[170] I have no *ayam* to *masak!*[171]

B   *Tangkap*[172] *lah*!

S and B chase J around the table.

Sharon enters.

J walks over to S where SH is. J dances with SH.

S   Eh! *Ini filem saya.*[173] Stop music! (*The music stops.*)

---

[167] Malay: *Jalan*, Walk.
[168] Chinese: This is so real!
[169] Malay: *ketok*, knock.
[170] Malay: *Abang, mari lah masok!*, Brother (literal meaning, but here meaning 'Sweetheart'), come enter!
[171] Malay: *masak*, cook.
[172] Malay: *Tangkap*, Catch; so '*Tangkap lah*!': 'Go and catch a chicken then!'
[173] Malay: *Ini filem saya*. This is my film.

Shh *ini*?[174]

SH   Hello, Salmah!

S   You *balik sini*?[175]

SH   I come back see you. You making *filem* hah? Let me do my business first OK?

Hello! I'm from CAC. Comprehensive After Care. I'm here to introduce you a special kind of service. This service is for all the senior citizens like you. This special kind of service includes all the necessary documentation, all the rites and rituals, deposition of the client and the procurement of a final resting place. I know people have been doing this for ages. But with today's globalisation and all the advance technology, my company has come up with many new possibilities. For example, if you want to find a resting place not only in Singapore, but also in the neighbouring countries as well. Or, maybe China, Taiwan, India ... Or if you want to go to the other parts of the world also can. Australia, Europe, America, maybe even Africa!

E   Sharon 啊! 你又回来了?[176]

SH   阿英! 你还在啊?[177]

E   我不在我在哪里?[178]

SH   好, 好。 我们公司是专门为我们老人家服务的。 你可以留在这里, 你也可以回唐山。[179]

E   Sharon 啊, 我跟你讲过多少次了? 我交代我的姐妹做了。[180]

SH   交代? 你交代什么? 我知道你实怕的。 你不用怕的。 你怕! (*To M.*) 不用怕的, hor。 我们准备好好, 那我们走的时候就不用怕。 避免我们的孩子为了这件事有什么纠纷。[181]

---

[174] Malay: *ini*, this.

[175] Malay: You *balik sini*? You return here?

[176] Chinese: Sharon! You came back again?

[177] Chinese: Ah Eng! You're still around?

[178] Chinese: If I'm not around, where will I be?

[179] Chinese: Good, good. Our company devotes our services exclusively to our old folks. You can stay here, or you can also return to China.

[180] Chinese: Sharon, how many times do I have to tell you? I have instructed my sisters to do it.

[181] Chinese: Instruct? What did you instruct? I know you are scared. You don't have to be. You are scared! (*To M.*) There's no need to be scared, hor. If we prepare well, we won't need to be scared when we go. It will prevent our children from going into dispute over this matter.

M 我安排好了。[182]

SH 你安排什么?[183]

M 要坐什么车, 穿什么衣服我什么都安排好了。 谢谢你。[184]

SH 好, 好。 有安排就好。[185] (*To S.*) No matter who you are, one day you will have to go there. So to prevent our children fight over this thing, ah, we must prepare.

S Sharon, Sharon, how many times I tell you, my mosque do, you cannot.

SH Yah, forget *lah*. (*To B.*) You Indian?

B Yes.

SH You burn?

B *Huh*?

SH You burn, then you scatter your ashes over the river, over the sea, right?

B Yes.

SH Now with my company, you can choose to scatter your ashes not only into the sea and into the river. You can scatter them over the grassland, over the mountain and even the desert!

B I'm very impressed. Do you have a business card?

SH Yah, sure, sure!

B I'll call you ... you don't call me.

SH Better can early, OK?

B I think it is better to can later. Right? (*Laughs*)

J (*Laughs, and mumbles.*) Can earlier or later ...

SH (*To Z.*) 这位先生你在看书啊? 很有学问哦? 不过也是要去的啦。 我是来介绍我们公司的服务的。[186]

---

[182] Chinese: I have made arrangements.
[183] Chinese: What have you arranged?
[184] Chinese: What vehicle to take, what dress to wear, I have arranged everything. Thank you.
[185] Chinese: Good, good. As long as you have made arrangements.
[186] Chinese: This gentleman, are you reading? You must be very knowledgeable. But one day you will also be gone. I am here to introduce the services of my company.

Z   买过，买过。 我自己买一份，儿子在美国又给我买好一份。 两份保险。[187]

SH   不是，你误会了。 我不是卖保险的。 我是卖身后安乐服务。[188]

Z   身后?[189]

SH   对，身后安乐服务。[190]

Z   那有没有一个评价。[191]

SH   我们的价钱很公道的。 我们不会骗老人家的。[192]

Z   不是价钱，评价，身后的一个评价。[193]

SH   我们可以帮你一个估价。[194]

Z   不是价钱，盖棺定论。[195]

SH   你要什么样的棺木我们都有。 你要檀香的，白玉的都有。[196]

Z   不是棺木。盖棺定论，一个公道的结论![197]

SH   是，你要怎樣安排我们都······[198]

Z   盖棺定论![199]

H goes over to calm him down.

M enters with L.

L   Auntie Sharon, 你还记得我吗?[200]

---

[187] Chinese: Bought already. I bought one, my son bought me another one in America. Two insurance policies.

[188] Chinese: No, you have misunderstood. I don't sell insurance, I sell post-mortality comfort services.

[189] Chinese: Post-mortality?

[190] Chinese: Yes, post-mortality comfort services.

[191] Chinese: Is there an evaluation?

[192] Chinese: Our price is very reasonable. We won't cheat old folks.

[193] Chinese: I am not talking about price, but evaluation, an evaluation after one's death.

[194] Chinese: We can help you get a valuation.

[195] Chinese: It's not about price, it's about 'closing the coffin and reaching a final judgement'.

[196] Chinese: We have all kinds of coffins, whichever you want. Whether it is made of sandalwood or white marble, we have them.

[197] Chinese: Not coffin, but a final judgement after closing the coffin, a fair judgement!

[198] Chinese: Sure, whatever arrangement you wish we can …

[199] Chinese: A final judgement!

[200] Chinese: Do you still remember me?

SH 哦?[201]

L 你又来推销东西啦? 你记得吗? 你答应我不要在做这种东西了。 你已经回家了。 你已经不住在这里了。[202] (*To old folks.*) She used to live here. (*Does a circle motion with finger around his temple.*)

我已经打了电话给你的儿子, 他们很快就会来接你。 我们去那里休息好吗? 来, 来。[203]

SH (*Leaves, and looks at B.*) Early better or later better?

I think early better.

H takes to playing harmonica again. He plays 'Swanee River'.

The sound of waves starts.

Lights fade to black.

Announcement and lullaby are heard.

L Tonight's lullaby is by Bala: 'Tom Dooley'.[204]

---

[201] Chinese: Huh?
[202] Chinese: You're here to do promotion again? Do you remember? You promised me that you won't do this anymore. You have gone home already. You don't live here anymore.
[203] Chinese: I have called your son; they will come and get you soon. Let's go there to take a rest, shall we? Come, come.
[204] 'Tom Dooley' is a folk song from North Carolina in the USA that is based on an 1866 murder. The Kingston Trio in 1958 made a hit recording of the song.

I met her on the mountain
I swore she'd be my wife
I met her on the mountain
And I stabbed her with my knife

Chorus
Hang down your head, Tom Dooley
Hang down your head and cry
You killed poor Laura Foster
Poor boy, you'Sre bound to die

Tonight I'll pick my banjo
I'll pick it on my knee
When this time comes tomorrow
It'll be no use to me

B sings 'Tom Dooley'.

Scene 6

The sound of waves starts.

J enters from stage right, holding newspaper; stops.

J goes to sit down at table, stage left, and puts newspaper down on top of the chess set.

JJ enters from stage right and walks across, wrapped up in his own thoughts. He then walks back to Joe.

Observes, and then taps Joe on the shoulder.

JJ   Who?

     Who?

J   You know, everyday I check these pages. Recently, I see so many old friends. But I didn't expect to see her. I haven't seen her in almost 30 years. (*Takes out photo from wallet.*)

JJ   Beautiful ... girlfriend?

J   She was my missed opportunity.

JJ   Girlfriend huh?

     Cry, cry! (*JJ holds Joe's hands. J breaks down.*) I understand. When Jimmy died, I also cried. Cry.

When this time comes tomorrow
I reckon where I'll be
In some lonesome valley
A-hangin' from a white oak tree

Oh, what my mother told me
Is about to come to pass
That drinkin' and those women
Would be my ruin at last

This time tomorrow
Reckon where I'll be
If it hadn't been for Grayson
I'd a-been in Tennessee

J regains composure slightly.

J   I was young, I made one error of judgement. I lost everything, my career, this woman, I was too ashamed to face her.

JJ   Never married?

J   (*Shakes his head.*) But she did. Please, not a word of this to anyone, please. (*Wipes his face.*)

JJ bows in respect. Joe keeps photo back in wallet.

J   Let's play a game. I'll go first. I need to take my mind off this ...

JJ   No, I have to go. (*JJ walks away.*)

J   Where you going? Please come back, please.

JJ   Do you know where's guava? Guava ... Bala, your friend.

J   You want Bala? No, I don't know where he is.

JJ   How come you don't know? You are both Indians!

J   What kind of ridiculous logic is that? Where's Monty?

JJ   Who's Monty?

J   The Thai gardener.

JJ   I don't know.

J   How can you not know? You are both Thais. Same stupid logic. Come on, JJ. Sit down and have a game please.

JJ   No, I need guava to write important letter to insurance company.

J   I can write it for you. Come.

JJ   No, you cannot. You no good. Bala English teacher, he good.

J   I've worked in the legal service for many years. I'll write it for you.

JJ   Legal service? You lawyer?

J   I was, a long time ago.

JJ   I don't trust lawyers. Lawyers cheat. Lawyers lie.

J   *What?*

JJ   Lawyers cheat, lawyers lie.

J   Are you saying I'm going to cheat you?

JJ   I dunno.

J   What do you mean you don't know?

JJ   You lawyer, now no more. Did you cheat?

J   Don't be ridiculous. Give me the letter.

JJ   Did you cheat?

J   Do you want the letter written or not?

JJ   You cheat huh? You cheat!

J   Who are you to call me *a cheat*? Have you slept with a man? You have got two wives, you fathered children, you cheated on your wives! Do they know you are homosexual?

JJ   *What did you call me?*

M enters.

Both stop when they realise Mary's presence, standing between them.

M   Joe, put these flowers on the table. JJ, 把这些放在桌子上。[205]

Both oblige, after which, Joe packs up his Dum set,[206] picks up newspaper, looks at it and leaves via stage right. Walking past JJ, Joe looks at him and puts a finger on his lips. Mary starts moving plants around. On seeing her difficulties, JJ offers to help.

JJ   来来来。(*Bends down to lift up potted plants.*) 不自量力。(*Mumbles to himself.*) 这么重, 怎么搬的动? 放哪里?[207]

M   放这里。[208]

JJ   (*Grumbles as he works.*) 没有力就不要种这么重的花。[209]

---

[205] Chinese: JJ, put these on the table.
[206] Dum set: a board game.
[207] Chinese: Here, let me do this. [Literally, 'come, come, come.'] (*Bends down to lift up potted plants.*) You overestimate your own ability (*Mumbles to himself.*) How can you possibly move this when it's so heavy? Where should I put this?
[208] Chinese: Leave it here.
[209] Chinese: If you don't have the strength, don't cultivate such heavy plants.

M   不, 还是放这里比较好。[210]

JJ   你想好好! 这里那里。 这个很重的。 要放这里刚才把车子推到这里不是好了。[211]

M   这两盆放后面。[212]

JJ   你想好好啊![213]

M   想好了啦。[214]

JJ   要放后面车子推去那里做什么。 啊……啊……没有位了。[215]

M   移一移不就有位了。[216]

JJ   你很像我大老婆, 什么事都不要先想好好就叫人家做。[217] (*Puts the pot down.*)

M   我看你比老婆还要罗嗦。[218]

JJ   好心没好报。[219]

After a while, M settles down at a stool in front of her plants and JJ sits at the table in deep thought, with pen and paper.

M   你看我这盆花, 很像 Joe, 不用我怎样施肥还是长得胖胖的。 这盆就很像你。 无论我怎样施肥还是干巴巴的。 刚才为什么吵架?[220]

JJ   那个 Joe 咯。 不懂又装懂。 这封信很重要的。[221]

---

[210] Chinese: No, it's better to have it here instead.

[211] Chinese: Do consider carefully! One time here, another time there, this is very heavy. If you want to have it here, we should have pushed the trolley here just now.

[212] Chinese: Leave those two pots at the back.

[213] Chinese: Do consider carefully!

[214] Chinese: I've thought through already.

[215] Chinese: If you wish to leave them at the back, why did you push the trolley there? Ah … ah … there's no space left.

[216] Chinese: If we move this by a little, there would be space.

[217] Chinese: You are so much like my oldest wife; she would summon people to do things without first thinking thoroughly.

[218] Chinese: I think [you are] more naggy than than your wife.

[219] Chinese: Kindness doesn't beget kindness.

[220] Chinese: Look at this potted plant of mine, it greatly resembles Joe, it looks so well-nourished without me having to fertilise it much. This pot greatly resembles you, regardless of how I fertilise it, it is still emaciated. Why did you quarrel just now?

[221] Chinese: That Joe, acting as if he knows when he's ignorant. This letter is very important.

M　家里的信?[222]

JJ　不是啦, 他们哪里会写信给我? 我没有钱了, 全部当我是死的。 是 Jimmy 留给我的保险费。[223]

M　哦。 你以前那个男朋友?[224]

JJ　他全部都给我, 全部![225]

M　JJ, 下礼拜我们又要开 party 了咧, 你去不去? 你很没有用的咧。 上几次你都没有去。[226]

JJ　我不去。[227]

M　这次 Mr Han 要煮鸡饭 Salmah 要煮 *Lontong* 咧。[228]

JJ　吃吃吃。 再吃就跟那两个印度人一样, 尤其是那个Joe.[229]

M　还有好听的音乐。[230]

JJ　我不听音乐的啦。[231]

M　还可以跳舞。[232]

JJ　我又不会跳。[233]

M　不会不是学咯。[234]

JJ　要学我早就学了。[235]

---

[222] Chinese: A letter from home?

[223] Chinese: No, how is it possible that they will write me a letter? I am broke, all of them treat me as if I'm already dead. It's the insurance money that Jimmy left me.

[224] Chinese: Oh, your boyfriend in the past?

[225] Chinese: He gave it all to me, everything!

[226] Chinese: JJ, we are going to have another party again next week, would you want to go? You are useless, you never attended the past few parties.

[227] Chinese: I won't be going.

[228] Chinese: Mr Han will be cooking chicken rice and Salmah will be cooking *Lontong* this time.

[229] Chinese: Eat and eat and eat. If you eat some more, you will be like those two Indians, especially that Joe.

[230] Chinese: There will also be great music.

[231] Chinese: I don't listen to music.

[232] Chinese: We can also dance.

[233] Chinese: I don't know how to.

[234] Chinese: Learn if you don't.

[235] Chinese: I would have learnt much earlier if I had wished to.

M   你们做生意的不会跳舞的吗?[236]

JJ   只有我的三老婆会。 还有 Jimmy。 不过他都是跳那种……摇摇摇的。 也不知道在跳什么。[237]

M   现在学也不会太迟啊。 要不要我教你?[238]

Clears tools to one side.

M   我教你, 很容易的。三拍的。 Bom cha cha. 站起来。 (*JJ looks around.*) 没有人看你啦。 不要懒惰。 站起来, 站起来![239]

JJ stands up.

M   女孩子的手放在男孩子的肩膀上。 男孩子的手放在女孩子的腰上, 另外一只手捉住女孩子的手。[240]

M moves forward to hold JJ's hands but he takes a step back. M continues dancing.

M   看脚。 男孩子的脚先向前 bom cha cha ……跟着我。[241] (*JJ does steps. Mary puts her hands on JJ. JJ resists, backs away.*)

       OK, 来。[242] (*Lifts up chair.*)

Both dance with chair. JJ keeps looking at his feet while he dances. Soon, JJ begins to relax and starts to enjoy the dance.

The rest of the old folks enter and look on, amused. Z, B, S from stage right; E, H from stage left. Realising their presence, JJ stops. Everyone claps, and JJ gets anger and feels humiliated. JJ tries to rush out via stage right but is held back by B. More clapping to encourage JJ.

B   Where are you going? That was good!

---

[236] Chinese: You don't know how to dance when you are a businessman?
[237] Chinese: Only my third wife can dance, and Jimmy, but he danced … that keeps shaking. I don't know the name for the dance.
[238] Chinese: It's not too late to learn now, do you want me to teach you?
[239] Chinese: Let me teach you, it's very easy. Three beats. Bom cha cha. Get up. (*JJ looks around.*) Nobody will see you, don't be lazy. Get up, get up!
[240] Chinese: The girl places one of her hands on the boy's shoulders. One of the boy's hands is placed at the girl's waist, and the other hand clasps that of the girl.
[241] Chinese: Look at the legs. The boy's leg takes a step forward first … bom cha cha … follow me.
[242] Chinese: OK, come.

JJ stops as he spots a young girl standing outside, by the fence.

A   He11o,-I'm-Alicia-Tan-from-Shing-Yi-Secondary-School.-I-am-doing-a-project.-Can-I-come-in-and-ask-you-all-a-question?

ALL   Come in first, come in!

A   (*Runs in.*) I'm-Alicia-Tan.-I'm-from-Shing-Yi-Secondary-School.-I'm-doing-a-project,-can-I-ask-you-all-one-question?

Puzzled silence.

M   Girl, one more time, slower.

A   (*Slower*) I am A-licia Tan, from Shing Yi Se-con-da-ry School. I am doing a project.

       Can I come in and ask you all a question?

M   Can, can, come in come in. (*Takes chair for A.*) (*To Z.*) 学生，来访问我们。[243]

Old folks watch intently as A takes out notebook, pencil, microphone and Walkman,[244] *one by one, and lays them on the table. JJ hurries over to take his letter back.*

A   (*To Salmah.*) See, same colour. The question I want to ask is ... what is the meaning of life?

Puzzled silence.

A   What is the meaning of life? (*B translates for S.*)

       生命的意义是什么?[245]

E   讲什么?[246]

A   阿婆! (*Goes over and speaks in Cantonese-Chinese.*) 你不会讲华语哦? 生命的意义在哪里?[247]

E   什么在哪里?[248]

---

[243] Chinese: A student, came to interview us.
[244] Walkman: A reference to the Sony Walkman.
[245] Chinese: What is the meaning of life?
[246] Chinese: What did you say?
[247] Chinese: Old Lady! (*Goes over and speaks in Cantonese-Chinese.*) You can't speak Chinese? Where is the meaning of life?
[248] Chinese: What is where?

A 作人有什么意思?[249]

E 作人没什么意思, 就是命咯![250]

A 没了?[251]

E 没了![252]

A looks at M, questioningly.

M Ask that uncle there

B Uncle JJ.

A Uncle, 你好! 作人有什么意义?[253]

JJ (*Speaks in Teochew-Chinese.*) 等等等![254]

A Huh?

JJ 等等等![255]

A 等什么?[256]

JJ Wait, wait, wait!

M 哎呀, 你胡说八道啦你。[257]

B You wait *lah*, you wait. Go and ask Mr Han there. Mr Han.

A Uncle Mr Han, 你会讲华语吗?[258]

H nods.

A 生命有什么意义?[259]

---

[249] Chinese: What is the point of living?
[250] Chinese: There is no point, it's just destiny.
[251] Chinese: Nothing else?
[252] Chinese: Nothing else!
[253] Chinese: How are you? What the point of living?
[254] Chinese: Wait, wait, wait! (This utterance should be spoken in Teochew- or *Chaozhou*-Chinese, and not in Mandarin–Chinese.)
[255] Chinese: Wait, wait, wait!
[256] Chinese: For what?
[257] Chinese: *Aiya*, you are talking nonsense.
[258] Chinese: Do you speak Chinese?
[259] Chinese: What is the meaning of life?

H   作人千万不要亏欠任何人。 尤其是你最心爱的人。 要不然你会后悔一辈子。[260]

A   不知道你说什么。[261]

H   你再活多几年你就会明白了。[262]

A   那不是要等到下个世纪?[263]

A, disappointed, dangles and swings her microphone. S motions her over.

S   I speak *Melayu*.[264]

A   Huh?

M   Bala translate.

A gives the microphone to B.

S   *Hidup itu sebuah pentas.*

B   Life is a stage.

S   *Awak pelakun.*

B   You are an actor.

S   *Saya pelakun.*

B   She is an actor

S   *Api saya bintang filem.*

B   But she is a film star.

A   Really ah?

B   Yah!

S   Wait, wait, haven't finish.

Pelakun boleh main banyak watak.

---

[260] Chinese: Don't be in debt to anyone in life, especially the person you love most, or else you will regret it forever.

[261] Chinese: I don't know what you are talking about.

[262] Chinese: You will understand after living for a few more years.

[263] Chinese: Doesn't that mean that I have to wait until the next century?

[264] Malay: *Melayu*, Malay.

B　An actor can play many roles.

S　*Tapi Hidup ... kita main satu kali.*

B　But in life you only play once.

S　*Awak masih muda kalau ada peluang.*

B　You are young, if you get a chance.

S　*Jangan ditolak.*

B　Don't push it away

S　*Awak chantek.*

B　You are very pretty.

A　You really movie star?

S　Yah *lah*!

A　Can you sign my autograph? I collect movie star autograph.

S　Can!

M　她说，人活着，有机会不可以放弃。[265]

A puts her Walkman into S's lap and hurries to get her autograph book from her bag. S autographs the book and puts her lips to the book.

A　Wah ... See, I got autograph. (*Shows the book off.*)

S　Thank you. Now ask Mr Bala ...

B　Girl, let me ask you, what is the meaning of the sun?

A　To shine, lor.

B　Yes! Clever girl.

A　I know.

B　The meaning of the sun is to shine. Then the meaning of life is to live!

M　他说，人要认真地活。[266]

---

[265] Chinese: She said that when one must not give up opportunities in life.
[266] Chinese: He said that one must live seriously.

A   First uncle say wait, second uncle say wait long long, now your answer so short, how to do project like that?

S   You ask Aunty Mary.

A   Must say long long, ah.

M   Aunty say for you. Meaning of life ... Now you young, anything you want to do you go and do. You want to eat, you eat, you want to drink, you drink. You happy, you laugh! Not happy, you scream, you cry. One day you grow up, you fall in love, you love, with all your heart. Cannot half half. Just love. No love, no meaning.

A   Wah, so long, very difficult to write. Can summarise?

M   Teacher, teacher, you summarise.

A   That uncle again?

B   The meaning of life is to love, laugh, enjoy. Now you go and ask that uncle there.

M   人活着，要有爱，要开心。[267]

A   Yeah, last one, can go home.

   Uncle, 生命有什么意义？[268]

Z   生命的意义？[269]

   人生自古谁无死留取丹心照汗青，你懂吗？来，坐下。[270]

   人吃饭，是为了活着，可是我们活着不是为了吃饭。　我们活着是为了别人活得更美好。中国古时候有个文学家叫司马迁的说过：人故固有一死，或重于泰山，或轻于鸿毛。　为人民的利益而死就比泰山还重。　为法西斯卖力，为剥削人民和压迫人民的人去死，就比鸿毛还轻！她就真的死了你知道吗？她是怎么死的你知道吗？她是被她的学生活活打死的。他们像疯狂似的打她骂她斗她。　她为了我的书，为了我们的尊严……[271]

---

[267] Chinese: One must have love and be happy in life.

[268] Chinese: What meaning does life hold?

[269] Chinese: Meaning in life?

[270] Chinese: 'Who was ever spared from Death? Allow me to leave a loyal heart shining in the pages of history.' Do you understand? Come, sit down.

[271] Chinese: One eats to live, but we do not live to eat. We live in order to give others a better life. There was a famous literary figure in ancient China by the name Sima Qian who said: While everyone for certain has to die, the significance of the deaths differs. Some are as great as Mount Tai, others are as trivial as birds' feathers. Dying for the sake of people's interests would be heavier than

Z, agitated, chases after A. B helps A to pack up and leave. H and M try to calm Z down.

Attendant enters from stage right. Whispers into M's ear.

M   Who?

L   You have a phone call from Mr Lee Choon Huat.

M   I've got *a phone call*! *I've got a phone call*! From that stupid man! (*Rushes off.*)

S   What? Mr Bala?

B   That stupid man finally called that stupid woman!

The sound of waves starts.

Lights fade to black.

Lullaby is heard.

All sing 'You are my Sunshine'.[272]

---

the weight of Mount Tai; dying for fascism, for the sake of oppressors who exploit people would be lighter than the weight of birds' feathers! And did you know? She really died. Did you know how she died? She was beaten to her last breath by her students. They beat her, admonished her, criticised and denounced her publicly, as if they were insane. For the sake of my books, our dignity …

[272] 'You Are My Sunshine', written by Jimmie Davis and Charles Mitchell, was first recorded in 1939.

The other night dear, as I lay sleeping
I dreamed I held you in my arms
But when I awoke, dear, I was mistaken
So I hung my head and I cried.

Chorus
You are my sunshine, my only sunshine
You make me happy when skies are grey
You'll never know dear, how much I love you
Please don't take my sunshine away.

I'll always love you and make you happy,
If you will only say the same.
But if you leave me and love another,
You'll regret it all some day.

You told me once, dear, you really loved me
And no one else could come between.

Scene 7

Lights up.

The old folks have a feast, eating probably chicken rice. Z, J and JJ arrange chairs into a semi-circle first.

J   Right, everybody hurry up and settle down. Mary, we have a surprise for you. But, before that, let's hear from our guest of honour. Speech, speech, speech!

M   Thank you everybody. First, let me say that the food was excellent. Thank you, Mr Han, for the wonderful chicken rice.

Everybody claps.

M   And Salmah's *Lontong*, and the wonderful chilli.

J   Never mind the food, Mary, what we want to know is the conclusion to your romantic story! Are all his parts still working?

M   Yes, I've met him. He's a totally new man. And all his parts are working, thank you. I'm happy just to see him again. To hear his voice, touch his hair, eat together with him, smell the flowers with him, listen to the waves together. 我去看过他，他已经可以自己走动了。 讲话也差不多恢复了。 我跟他说，能够再见，很好，不能再见，也好。 是你的时间，要好好珍惜。 不是你的时间，也不用勉强，也不用难过。[273]

Z   你能够这样想很好。[274]

But now you've left me and love another;
You have shattered all of my dreams.

In all my dreams, dear, you seem to leave me
When I awake my poor heart pains.
So when you come back and make me happy
I'll forgive you dear, I'll take all the blame.

You are my sunshine, my only sunshine
You make me happy when skies are grey
You'll never know dear, how much I love you
Please don't take my sunshine away.

[273] Chinese: I have been to visit him. He can walk on his own already. He has also recovered his speaking ability. I told him, it's great that we can meet again; it's OK even if we don't. It's your time, you must treasure it well. If it's not your time, you need not force things to happen or feel sad.
[274] Chinese: It's great that you can think of it this way.

M   I told him, maybe because we had so little time together, so all the more we treasure the time we had. All the more we know we must be happy. We also know that we must let other people be happy and let other people enjoy him. And I told him, if I go first, I want a white funeral, because I didn't get a white wedding.

J   Right, so who will start the ball rolling first?

S   You *lah*, Joe.

B   Joe!

J   You all plotting against me ah? You know, Mary, when Bala first told me the news that you were going to meet the man you love, I was happy for you but at the same time selfishly sad for myself. I was like you once, in love, but I didn't have the courage to see it through. As a result, for much of my life, I was alone, lonely, no family, few friends most of whom have left me by now. I gave up on life a long time ago. I actually came to this place to die, because I didn't want to die alone outside. The last thing I expected was to make new friends. You don't know how much I envy you … You know what? I talk too much. I have a little something for you. (*Goes and gets a hat.*) I know you'll be doing a lot of gardening under the sun … so I got you this to shield your pretty face. These flowers are fake OK, don't water them. (*Kisses M's hand.*) Thank you. (*Everybody claps.*)

J   Right, who's next?

S   My friend Ah Eng.

J   Ah Eng, you've been volunteered.

Everybody claps.

E   你今大很美阿英祝福你。 你有人等, 有人在外面等你, 有人等你就是好。 我唱一首我儿子和孙子最喜欢听的歌。[275]

M   She's going to sing her son and grandson's favourite song.

E   好久没唱了。

    月光光，照地堂
    虾仔你乖乖睡落床
    明早阿爸要补鱼网

---

[275] Chinese: You are very beautiful today. Ah Eng offers you her best wishes. You have someone waiting, someone is waiting for you outside. It's good that you have someone waiting for you. I'll sing a favourite song of my son and grandson.

阿爷他放牛上山岗
啊······[276]

She stops abruptly, and walks away, embarrassed.

All clap.

J   Lao Zhang?

z   Mary, 我为你感到高兴。 感谢你一直以来的照顾。 要分别了, 我想送你一首我最喜欢的诗歌。

明月几时有, 把酒问青天。
不知天上宫阙, 今夕是何年。
我欲乘风归去, 又恐琼楼玉宇, 高处不胜寒。
起舞弄清影, 何似在人间!
转朱阁, 低绮户, 照无眠。
不应有恨, 何事长向别时圆?
人有悲欢离合, 月有阴晴圆缺,
此事古难全。
但愿人长久, 千里共婵娟。
但愿人长久, 千里共婵娟。[277]

---

[276] Chinese: I have not sung it for a long time.

The moon cast her glow on the floor
The little one, you sleep adorably in the bed
Pa will mend the fishing net tomorrow morning
Grandpa, he will take the cows grazing up in the mountain ridges.
Ah …
[277] Chinese: Mary, I am happy for you. Thank you for taking care of me all this while. As we part, I would like to dedicate a favorite poem of mine to you.

How long has the moon been up in sky? With wine in my cup I ask the blue sky.
And I wonder in those palaces of Heaven, what year this evening is?
I would like to ride there on the wind, but fear that the richly decorated jade palace is up so high that I could not bear the cold.
I rise and dance, playing with my shadows; what can be compared with being in the mortal world!
Moving through the red pavilion, down the exquisite doors, shining upon the sleepless.
I should not harbour regret, but why is the moon always full when people part?
Men experience joy and sorrow, partings and reunions; the moon has times of brightness and gloom, as well as periods of waxing and waning.
Things are never perfect.
I only wish that we will enjoy longevity, to share an appreciation of the moon's beauty, though we are a thousand miles apart.

All clap. B stands to congratulate Z.

J   Bala, since you're so eager to go next?

B   Mary, as you know, I was a teacher; I've read many books. But in all the books that I've read, I've never found the lesson that you taught me: that is, to love and to love now. I don't have much of value, except this book of poems. I'll like to share a poem with you. It's by one of my favourite poets, W. B. Yeats.

Z   叶磁, 叶慈的诗, 好好。[278]

B   'When You are Old'
    When you are old and grey and full of sleep,
    And nodding by the fire, take down this book,
    And slowly read, and dream of the soft look
    Your eyes had once, and of their shadows deep;

    How many loved your moments of glad grace,
    And loved your beauty with love false or true,
    But one man loved the pilgrim soul in you,
    And loved the sorrows of your changing face;

    And bending down beside the glowing bars,
    Murmur, a little sadly, how Love fled
    And paced upon the mountains overhead
    And hid his face amid a crowd of stars.

All clap. B gives poetry book to M.

J   Who's next? JJ, your turn.

All clap.

JJ stands. Walks to the centre of semi-circle. Raises his hands, looks at M.

M smiles and gets up. She steps into JJ's arms, and rests her hands on him, preparing to dance. JJ puts his hand around her waist. They dance. JJ looks down at his feet the whole time. Just as they are getting into the swing of things, JJ looks into M's eyes. He is stunned. He backs away.

JJ   花, 我会帮你照顾你的花。[279]

M   JJ said he will take care of all my flowers!

I only wish that we will enjoy longevity, to share an appreciation of the moon's beauty, though we are a thousand miles apart.
[278] Chinese: A poem by Yeats, good, good.
[279] Chinese: Flowers, I will help you take care of your flowers.

All clap.

J   Chicken rice man?

All clap.

H   Mary, 我很羡慕你。 你就要跟心爱的人见面了。 以前我很少说话不过在离别前我想告诉你我心中的一个秘密。[280]

M   Mr Han is going to tell us a secret!

B   A secret, Mr Han! What is it? Tell us!

H   我也曾经相爱过。 她是我的妻子。 我们在一起生活了30多年, 可是她却突然走了。 在她病重的时候, 我才发现, 原来她早就患了癌症。 我永远也不会原谅我这个过失。 我完成了她的意愿, 把她的骨灰撒到海里去, 就在前面。 这么多年来我只有一个愿望; 我希望很快就可以去到她的身边。 我要跟她在夕阳下再恋爱一次, 比上一次更投入比上一次更热情, 更多的关怀。 我要在夕阳下无微不至地照顾她, 我要在夕阳下拥抱她亲吻她, 直到永远永远……[281] (*H looks out at the faraway ocean.*)

M   Mr Han is the real romantic. He wants to join his wife under the sunset. His wife's ashes, there. (*Points to the sea.*) He wants to fall in love with his wife again, this time even more serious even more passionate.

H bows.

All clap.

J   And now, last but not least, hailing all the way from Kampong Rambutan in Malaya,[282] can you manage the drum roll Bala, we have our very own Cathay Kris movie star, *Salmah*! Salmah … Salmah … Salmah …

All clap excitedly.

S   Mary, today I feel sad because you leave. But I also happy because today your chance. I also had chance. I can sing, I can dance, I can act. But because of family,

---

[280] Chinese: Mary, I am very envious of you. You are about to meet the one you love. I seldom talk about the past, but before leaving, I wish to tell you a secret.

[281] Chinese: I have been in love. She was my wife. We lived together for over 30 years, but she left suddenly. I only discovered when she was extremely sick that she had cancer much earlier. I will never forgive my negligence. I fulfilled her wishes by scattering her ashes into the sea, right in front [of us]. For so many years I have only a single wish; I hope I can return to her side very soon. I want to fall in love with her once again under the evening sun, and this time it will be more engaged, more passionate and with more concern. I want to take care of her under the evening sun, under which I want to hug and kiss her, forever and ever …

[282] Kampong Rambutan in Malaya: the name of a place for mad people.

because of leg ... pain, now no more chance love. But today we don't sad. I sing for you Mary. (*Stands*)

Getaran jiwa melanda hati ku.
Tersusun nada irama dan lagu.
Walau hanya sederhana
Tapi tak mengapa.
Semoga dapat mengbangkitkan
Serdalah oh wahai insan.
Tak mungkin hilang irama dan lagu
Bagaikan kembang sentiasa bermadu.
Andai dipisah lagu dan irama,
Lemah tiada berjiwa hampa.[283]

All clap.

Mary starts to feel great discomfort; she seems to have difficulty breathing. She goes into mild convulsions.

E   Mary! 不要吓我, Mary! 叫 Missy 啊![284]

J   I'll go get the nurse. (*Starts to walk away.*) Fatt Ping!

M   No ...

B   Joe, stay!

M   Bala, remember you said that when the moment comes, you'll know? I think my moment has come.

B   Should we call him over?

M   He doesn't need to see me like this. We enjoyed our best moments together and that is good enough for me.

---

[283] The vibrations from my heart
Arranging the tune and the song
Even if it is just so humble
It doesn't matter
Hopefully, it can enliven!
Be conscious oh man
It will never be lost, the tune and the song
As the blooms, perennial honey
If the tune and the song is divorced
Weak, without soul – emptiness.
[284] Chinese: Mary! Don't frighten me, Mary! Call Missy [the nurse] ah!

Bala, let my hair down. He likes my hair down.

Remind him, I want a white funeral, no tears. Just flowers, white flowers and songs and smiles ... Please sing for me ...

H takes out his harmonica.

M goes into more violent convulsions.

B takes her into his arms, holds her close.

M's grasp relaxes.

S and E weep.

H   啊英，不要哭啦。[285]

B   She said no tears. (*Looks at H.*)

H blows his harmonica.

ALL   You are my sunshine, my only sunshine.
       You make me happy, when skies are grey.
       You never know dear, how much I love you,
       So please don't take my sunshine away.

Faster and louder.

       You are my sunshine, my only sunshine.
       You make me happy when skies are grey.
       You never know dear, how much I love you,
       So please don't take my sunshine away.

JJ gets up and takes one pot of white flowers and puts it in front of M.

       You are my sunshine, my only sunshine.
       You make me happy, when skies are grey.
       You never know dear, how much I love you,
       So please don't take my sunshine away.

Music drowns their singing. Lights fade to blackout.

(*End of Play*)

---

[285] Chinese: Ah Eng, don't cry.

One Hundred Years in Waiting[1]

by

Haresh Sharma and Chong Tze Chien, with Kuo Pao Kun

Dramatis Personæ

MADAM TAN (Chen Cui Fen), Dr Sun Yat-sen's second wife
JASON, an actor
AH HO, Madam Tan's servant
MRS SUN, Dr Sun's first wife
DIRECTOR
ENSEMBLE

1. Jason

Houselights fade. Spotlight on Jason on stage.

JASON   Hi, Jason Leong. I'm here to audition. Erm, for the part of Dr Sun Yat-sen.[2] I've prepared a monologue. Kuo Pao Kun's *The Coffin is Too Big for the Hole*. No need? Oh ... This is just a screen test ... Sorry. What do I know of Sun Yat-sen? Er ... He's like a friend of Wong Fei Hong right? Wrong. But I

---

[1] Permission to perform this play must be obtained from Haresh Sharma (c/o The Necessary Stage, 278 Marine Parade Road, Marine Parade Community Building, #B1-02, Singapore 449282), Chong Tze Chien (c/o The Finger Players, One-Two-Six Cairnhill Arts Centre, 126 Cairnhill Rd, #03-01/02, Singapore 229707) and Goh Lay Kuan (c/o The Theatre Practice, 155 Waterloo Street, Stamford Arts Centre, #02-08, Singapore 187962).

[2] Sun Yat-sen (1866–1925) was a Chinese revolutionary, and is often referred to as the 'Father of the Nation'. He played an important role in the overthrow of the Qing dynasty during the Xinhai Revolution — the Chinese Revolution of 1911. Sun was the first provisional president of the new Republic of China, set up in 1912. He lived abroad in exile for many years; he was an exile in Japan, Europe, the USA and Canada, raising money for his revolutionary party and to support uprisings in mainland China.

saw the film. *Adventures of Gong Fu Master Wong Fei Hong.*[3] You mean this is not a martial arts movie? Er, yes, I have the script ... (*Reads*) 'An Incomprehensible Love — The Untold History of Dr Sun Yat-sen.' Can I just say that I like the script already ... erm ... even though I haven't read it yet. But 'The Untold History' — add new perspectives to history! History is nothing more than a matter of opinion. I mean, history changes as governments change! (*Laughs*) Oh I know! Why don't we have a ghost story ... where dead people come back to life and see what's going on, and then get a heart attack and die again! And then they ... — sorry? Oh, OK ... I'll just get on with the screen test. Er ... What do I do?

Lights come on upon the whole stage. Ensemble slowly 'wakes up' and starts walking towards Madam Tan's chair. After a while, Madam Tan and Ah Ho walk to the chair. It is late at night. Madam Tan sits, holding on to a watch. Ah Ho walks and sees her. She is holding a glass of milk. She looks at her for a moment.

While the scene is going on, the Director comes out, passes out 'Sun Yat-sen' clothes to Jason, who changes into them. The Director takes Jason's clothes and exits.

2. Madam Tan and Ah Ho

MDM TAN   Ah Ho? What are you doing? Still never sleep?

AH HO   四姑,[4] you also still never sleep

MDM TAN   What time is it?

AH HO   You want milk?

MDM TAN   I ask for the time, you give me milk. You drunk, is it?

AH HO   I never drink only a little bit. (*Smiles*) 四姑,[5] so many years you never take out the watch. Why now you must take out? Look at the time so much no

---

[3] This is possibly a reference to *Once Upon a Time in China II* (1992), which featured both the folk hero Wong Fei Hong (1847–1924) — in Mandarin the name would be Huang Feihong — and Dr Sun Yat-sen in it; it was directed by the Hong Kong film-maker, Tsui Hark. Wong was a martial-arts practitioner and teacher, a traditional Chinese medicine physician and a revolutionary. He has become the subject of numerous films and television series.

[4] Chinese: Here Fourth Aunt — Madam Tan, as she is addressed by Ah Ho; this also occurs in other parts of the play. The translations from Chinese into English in the notes are by Chan Cheow Thia.

[5] See footnote 4.

good. Just look outside can already. Got sun means day time. Now got moon. Means night time. Nah. Drink and then go and sleep OK? So many nights you never sleep properly.

MDM TAN   Every night I dream of something floating in the sky.

AH HO   *Aiyoh*! Why you must say something floating in the sky? I give you milk, just say thank you and drink!

Ah Ho leaves the glass of milk behind and is about to leave.

MDM TAN   If I don't tell you, I tell who?

AH HO   You always shout at me.

MDM TAN   If I don't shout at you, I shout at who?

AH HO   Don't shout. I so nice to you, give you milk.

MDM TAN   I'm also nice to you.

AH HO   Very nice, very nice. Tomorrow I die, you sure cry.

MDM TAN   When I die, I will leave nothing to you.

AH HO   Don't talk so big. You have nothing to give me.

MDM TAN   I have this. When he gave this to me, I ask him, 'Why'? He said, 'For all you have done'. I said, 'Is this all I am worth? A watch?' Then he said, 'I know it will never be enough, but this is all I can afford. This is all I have.'

Madam Tan suddenly hyperventilates. Ah Ho quickly goes to hold her.

MDM TAN   He's dying, he's dying … We … we must pack our bags … go to Peking. He needs … he needs my help. Our country is still divided. The revolution …

AH HO   Shh … shh …

She gives the glass to Madam Tan. She takes it and drinks the milk.

AH HO   You want to go and visit 孙夫人?[6] Huh? Tomorrow we can go … Long time we never see her. Remember last time she come here … stay for one month. Very nice hor … Want? Want to go and see her … She also sure thinking about us. (*Slight pause.*) Sleep. OK? Tonight you sleep properly. Tonight you

---

[6] Mrs Sun.

have sweet dreams ... about ... about the seaside ... when you grow up that time ... you run at the beach. Then you lie down on the sand ... close your eyes ... and dream ... about tomorrow ... a beautiful tomorrow ...

Pause. Ah Ho exits with the glass of milk. Lights remain on Madam Tan and Mrs Sun. Pause.

MDM TAN   What time is it? (*No response.*) What time is it? (*No response.*) *What time is it?*

3. Video: Funeral

Video begins. It is Dr Sun Yat-sen's funeral. People are crying. It is like a newsreel. After a while, the spotlight is on Jason again. He is dressed — and looks like — Dr Sun Yat-sen. He is sitting, looking at the script. He is reading Dr Sun's will in English, together with the video.

JASON   'For forty years I have devoted myself to the cause of the National Revolution, the object of which is to raise China to a position of independence and equality. The experience of these forty years has convinced me that, to attain this goal, the people must be aroused and that we must associate ourselves in a common struggle with the peoples of the world who treat us as equals.' Sun Yat-sen, Last Will, 11th March, 1925.

Lights on Madam Tan, She is sitting, looking at her watch.

Jason finishes reading the will.

4. Ensemble #1 — This is Not a Government

Lights on Ensemble, behind Madam Tan.

P   This is not a government.

WM   This is a dynasty.

J   My great grandfather fought in the war.

WS   My brothers were buried alive.

N   My sisters were raped and decapitated.

HZ	I carry the weight of my ancestors on my shoulders.
JX	I bear the burden of their pain and suffering.
T	Their ghosts tell me to act.
HL	To act now.
WG	I do not fear death.
GX	I do not fear torture.
P	Electrocute me with your power.
WS	Disembowel me with your pride.
WM	I shall not speak.
N	I shall not sleep.
HZ	I shall not eat.
JX	I must act.
T	I must act.
ENSEMBLE	I must act. I must act.

5. Day One: Ah Ho and Madam Tan

N: Day One!

Madam Tan is looking at her watch. Ah Ho runs in. The pace is fast.

AH HO   (*In Chinese.*) We must prepare the funeral. Must say good-bye to the doctor. (*Shouts to the others.*) Candles! Must have candles! Take from upstairs. We got no money to make banners. Tell everyone they must give money to make banners. Wreaths. We need wreaths. Put them outside the villa, in the streets … tell everyone the doctor is dead. (*Pause. In English.*) Madam Tan, the funeral is ready. I will call Nanking. They must send the body here. Madam Tan, this is Penang. He will come back to Penang.

MDM TAN   Who says?

AH HO   He stay here before!

MDM TAN   He stay everywhere. Why here so special? (*Slight pause.*) Now, stop all this. We are not his family. We are not his relatives.

AH HO   You are his second wife.

MDM TAN   You know I was only pretending to be his wife to hide his true identity. I was only acting. Remember when he became president? Who was beside him? Mrs Sun, not me. And now his widow is Song Qingling, not me. I was his comrade, Ah Ho, his comrade. Not his wife.

AH HO   A funeral ... we must say good-bye to Dr Sun.

MDM TAN   I said good-bye a long time ago.

6. Day Two: Jason Handphone[7] #1

Hz   Day Two!

Lights on Jason. He is on the phone.

JASON   Yah, Val! So surprising right? I got the role! Especially after the big boo boo I made during the auditions. So *embarrassing*! I thought Sun Yat-sen was a gong fu master or something. You know like Chow Yun-Fat in *Crouching Tiger, Hidden Dragon*? Trust me to base my research on some cheap Hong Kong flick.[8] I must do my research properly this time. This is a serious film. Eh Val, is it 'Soon' or 'Sun'? The director keeps saying 'Sun', but the make-up artist keeps saying 'Soon'. (*Slight pause.*) Val, why are you still like that? I'm sorry we have to postpone the wedding. But I can't possibly spend the next few weeks filming and get married at the same time. (*Slight pause.*) But I couldn't say no, right? I mean, this is my big break. My only break in like 15 years! Look, we've gone through before. Can we just move on? The moment this ends, OK? Choose any date you want. I promise. OK? Yup ... bye ...

He hangs up. Pause.

---

[7] Or mobile/cell phone.

[8] *Crouching Tiger, Hidden Dragon* (2000) is a *wuxia* (martial arts) film directed by Lee Ang and featured an international cast of ethnic Chinese actors, including Chow Yun-Fat, Michelle Yeoh, Zhang Ziyi and Chang Chen. It was an American-mainland Chinese-Hong Kong-Taiwanese co-production made with a budget of US$17 million.

7. Day Three: Jason and Director #1

T   Day Three!

Director enters.

DIRECTOR   Hey, hey, hey, three more days to shooting!

JASON   Eh! Director! I've been doing a lot of research and the script is ... — how come the scriptwriter is not around?

DIRECTOR   The scriptwriter is history. No pun intended. I'm the director. I call the shots. When we start shooting ...

JASON   I keep dreaming about this man. And that ... that Madam Tan ... There's hardly anything written about her.

DIRECTOR   Exactly! Which is why we can make it all up! I already have everything in my head. The climax! It is very important. The good-bye scene between him and her.

JASON   Erm, according to my research there wasn't a good-bye scene. He was already in Nanking. She was supposed to go but decided not to in the end.

DIRECTOR   Like, do I care? We must have a good-bye scene. Every love story has a good-bye scene.

JASON   That's the other thing. It wasn't a 'love' story. They were ... well, they were partners in the revolution.

DIRECTOR   Who cares about the revolution? Jason, I want love. I want the love! The incomprehensible love between this man and this peasant comrade woman person.

JASON   Then all my questions ... there are things I still don't understand.

DIRECTOR   Remember, there'll be a lot of waiting ... waiting for the lights to be ready, or for the rain to stop. I can't let you go. You have to be around all the time, just in case you're needed. It's in the contract.

JASON   What about my questions? What if I can't get him, understand him ...?

DIRECTOR   You're an actor. Just act. Three more days, Jason! *Three more days!*

8. Day Four: Ah Ho

P   Day Four!

Lights on Ah Ho.

AH HO   (*In Chinese.*) His spirit … we can have his spirit. They said spirit will come
           home on the seventh day. (*Shouts*) Dr Sun's spirit is coming back! Nanking
           can have his body. We can have his spirit! We must prepare for his return!
           Find all of his clothing and things he used before. Display them in the hall!
           We must remind him of the days he has spent here! If his spirit is still with us,
           the revolution will not die! The revolution will never die!

9. Day Five: Jason Handphone #2

WS   Day Five!

Lights on Jason. He's talking on the handphone.

JASON   What do you mean you have to go to Hong Kong? Then our flat how? You're
           supposed to get the keys tomorrow. (*Slight pause.*) Yah, I know it can wait
           for a week. But that will just delay the renovations. They're supposed to start
           the renovations next week. OK, fine whatever. (*Slight pause.*) What's it this
           time? Another conference? … Predictable. No, nothing. Er, so, you just call
           me when you get back. Shooting starts tomorrow, so … yup, whatever …

He hangs up. Pause.

10. Day Six: Madam Tan and Ah Ho

JX   Day Six!

Lights on Madam Tan and Ah Ho.

MDM TAN   Why are the mirrors in my room covered with cloth?

AH HO   When Mr Sun's spirit come back, he cannot see the mirror. If not he will get
           scared. I also put salt on the floor and pull the bedsheets tight tight. Then we
           will know whether … —

MDM TAN   — Remove the cloth.

AH HO   But Madam Tan, we will scare ... —

MDM TAN   But but but. I say remove the cloth. He is a Christian. He is in heaven. He is not coming back.

AH HO   People say he will come back.

MDM TAN   Then let him come back in their house. Not here.

AH HO   You inside very pain ah Madam Tan?

MDM TAN   Don't talk to me today OK? Today you don't talk to me!

AH HO   See, people are already coming ... waiting outside. They all want to see Dr Sun one more time.

MDM TAN   And what if he doesn't come back? Then what?

AH HO   They will see what they want to see. Dr Sun give them hope. Last time he say, must always have hope. Even when the revolution everytime fail, people die ... he say don't give up. Remember?

MDM TAN   You don't tell me what he said. I live with him for 17 years. I know everything he said.

AH HO   Madam Tan, the people outside ... they are waiting for their saviour. They are full of hope. They are waiting because ... because the revolution not yet finish.

MDM TAN   Tell the people that their saviour is dead. He is dead! And not in a hundred years will he come back. Not in a hundred years will there be another like him!

11. Day Seven A: Mrs Sun (First Appearance)

H   Day Seven!

Mrs Sun walks down the stairs.

MRS SUN   翠芬，一直以来，你就是这样的愤怒。[9]

---

[9] Chinese: Cui Fen, all along you have been so angry.

MDM TAN   I am not angry, Mrs Sun. I am at peace.

MRS SUN   为什么要的那么多。[10]

MDM TAN   I don't want anything.

MRS SUN   时间应该会使伤口愈合。死应该是一种结束而不是一个开始。[11]

MDM TAN   Why are you here?

MRS SUN   不要再等待了。去争取吧。你是一个战士，既然他都已经不在了，你更应该......[12]

MDM TAN   — Yes. Thank you. Thank you very much. Thank you for coming … but you were not what I was looking for. Good-bye.

Mrs Sun walks away. Pause.

11. Day Seven B: Ah Ho Disguises as Dr Sun

WM   Day Seven!

Ah Ho enters, dressed as Dr Sun.

AH HO   Madam, er … *Cui Fen*! *It is the seventh day*! I am here! *How are you*? I am dead but happy! You eat already?

MDM TAN   No, that Ah Ho's cooking taste like earthworms

AH HO   Hahaha … Er, I have come to tell you that … er … that I have come!

MDM TAN   Thank you. Now you may go.

AH HO   Thank you, thank you. Yes … it is a long journey … to come back here. But before I go, I must say …

MDM TAN   You don't have to say anything, Yat-sen. I am fine.

AH HO   Sorry … for letting you go.

----

[10] Chinese: Why do you want to have so much?
[11] Chinese: Time should heal the wounds. Death should bring an end to this, not a beginning.
[12] Chinese: Don't wait any longer. Fight for it, you are a fighter. Since he is no longer around, all the more you should … —

MDM TAN	Enough.
AH HO	I regret my actions.
MDM TAN	Enough.
AH HO	If I live my life again, I want my wife more than my country.
MDM TAN	*Enough*! (*Pause*) Day … seven …

11. Day Seven C: Jason and Director #2/Madam Tan

Director comes in and goes to Jason.

DIRECTOR	OK, Jase, it's time for lights, camera and *action*! First scene, funeral. You don't look dead enough.
JASON	Well, I feel it.
DIRECTOR	Get into the coffin, Jason, and break a leg! Countdown to the shoot! Don't think, Jason. Just be. Just be him.

Director exits.

JASON	I will. I am. Jason Leong *is* the doctor. I *am* Dr … —
MDM TAN	My watch. It has stopped.
JASON	'Sun' or 'Soon'?

11. Day Seven D: Dr Sun

ENSEMBLE	*Day Seven*!

Pause. Music starts. Jason stands up. We see a 'complete' Dr Sun — in full costume, make up and accessories. Pause. Madam Tan turns to look at him. They look at each other for a while.

12. Video

VIDEO	What did he like?

Or dislike?
What was his voice like?
Did he like animals?
Was he lonely?

His favourite colour was white,
his favourite meals, simple.
He liked things clean.
He liked books and revolution more.
Women less.

What was she like?
Did she dream?
What did she eat?
Did she pray?
Did she have friends?

She was a simple woman.
She made bombs for the revolution.
She cooked for the men and travelled with him.
She worked, she served.
She did not pray.

Did he love her?
Did she miss him?
Did he regret?
Did she cry?
Did he return?
Did she wait?

13. Dr Sun and Madam Tan #1

Flashback. Church. Their first meeting. Madam Tan stands by Dr Sun and looks at him, but doesn't know what to say.

DR SUN   Yes?

MDM TAN   No ... I ...

Pause

DR SUN   The sermon is over.

MDM TAN	Yes. But I can still hear the message. It hasn't left this church. (*Pause*) I am ... my name is ... Cui Fen
DR SUN	Nice to meet you. I am ... —
MDM TAN	— I know. Erm, I know who you are. I have heard you speak. Many times.
DR SUN	And?
MDM TAN	Your name is offensive to some.
DR SUN	And?
MDM TAN	I would like to be part of your revolution.
DR SUN	Do you know what you're getting yourself into?
MDM TAN	Yes. No. (*Slight pause.*) The red devils are cruel. They nailed their God to the cross. If they rule over China, we would be nailed to the cross as well.
DR SUN	Don't you fear death?
MDM TAN	No.
DR SUN	I do.
MDM TAN	Why?
DR SUN	A dead man cannot start a revolution. I am not God. I can't save people's souls by dying.
MDM TAN	Then let me join you. I ... I won't let you die.

14. Monologues

Lights cross-fade to Mrs Sun. The following is a series of monologues, interspersed with texts spoken by the Ensemble.

N	The Revolution of Life.
MRS SUN	17岁，我进了孙家。打从那天起，我就没有什么机会侍候他。他总是很忙。每一次送逸仙出门，我只能够默默地望着他。心里一直有一句话想问他：你，什么时候回来？可我从来没有开口。像我们这样的女子，是不会过问丈夫的事。[13]

---

[13] Chinese: I was 17 when I was accepted into the Sun family. Since that day, I never had many opportunities to serve him. He was always very busy. Each time I sent Yat-sen off, I only watched

WM   That there are three classes of men.

J   One. Pre-seeing. They are extremely intelligent people, creators and inventors.

WG   Two. Post-seeing. They neither create nor invent. They follow and imitate. They are promoters.

P   Three. Non-seeing. They can learn nothing. They can only act. They are executors.

JASON   This is the third time we've postponed the wedding. The first ... we sort of had jitters ... didn't know whether we were ready and all that. The second. Val is a lawyer. But really, she's an activist. You know, when they study in America, they all become activists. So she travels a lot ... human rights conferences, NGO meetings. I think she's trying to change the world. So, the second time was because she had to go for a two-week conference that clashed with the wedding. So postpone. And now ... now this.

T   The Revolution of Rights

AH HO   I got 11 brother and sister. I am number nine. Sometimes my father don't remember who born first, who eat already who haven't. My neighbour, Ah Heng, ask my father ... say he want to marry me. My father say anything can. One day Ah Heng and I see this man talking about revolution in the school hall. Ah Heng tell me he want to follow this man, this Dr Sun Yat-sen. I say OK because my father always say you marry who you must follow who.

WG   That all men are by nature equally free and independent, and have certain inherent rights.

HL   The right to an enjoyment of life and liberty, with the means of acquiring and possessing property, and pursuing and obtaining happiness and safety.

JX   The right to freedom under laws of their own making.

HZ   The right to do anything that does not harm another.

MRS SUN   我不知道他什么时候回来，但我知道他永远不会留下来。我不知道他在哪里，但我知道他永远不会在我身边。我不知道他忙些什么，但我知道他永远不会为我而忙。我不知道他心里在想什么，但我知道他永远不会为我牵挂。[14]

---

him silently. There was always a question I would like to ask. When will you be back? But I never did. Women like us do not ask about the affairs of our husbands.

[14] Chinese: I didn't know when he would return, but I knew he would never stay. I didn't know where he was, but I knew he would never be by my side. I didn't know what he was busy with, but

WM   The Revolution of Freedom.

AH HO   So I follow Ah Heng go Penang and follow Dr Sun. Then I meet Madam Tan. Wah, she know everything, everybody listen to her. One day got big dinner. Whole day we cook because the man all coming back from don't know where. But we wait and wait nobody come back. Then Madam Tan say that they all catch by the emperor. Ah Heng also. Everyday I wait because I think Ah Heng and I only just marry, how can he go away never come back. Some more I never even see his body. If I see his body … — (*She is at breaking point.*)

J   That the people must not take a rebellious attitude towards the government.

JX   That is not their right.

GX   That is not freedom.

WM   That is not democracy.

JASON   I used to help Val out when … well, when I was a 'struggling actor' — which was until last week. She had like research work, websites, forums … I knew she was happy when I was helping her. But I thought, OK, I help you, you … you stay with me. Fair exchange, right?

WG   Rights are not about an individual, but a community.

GX   Freedom is not about autonomy, but control.

MRS SUN   一年, 两年, 十年, 我尽心尽力的照顾一家大小, 偶尔打开他留下来的地图, 想着他会在这里, 这里, 还……[15]

HZ   A strong government is not about power, but capacity.

P   A strong government is not about authority, but ability.

JASON   When I first met her, I knew she was the one. Maybe it was because her birthday is one day after mine. I don't know. But there was something about her. Maybe it was just me. I never really asked her how she felt. But I never thought I needed to …

N   Power is not equal to capacity.

I knew he would never be engaged for my sake. I didn't know what he was thinking, but I knew he would never miss me.

[15] Chinese: One year, two years, ten years … I did my best to take care of the family, and sometimes, I would open the map he left behind, and think that he might be here, here, or …

J   Authority is not equal to ability.

AH HO   Now I take care of Madam Tan. Sometimes I a bit scared, but don't know what. Now everything finish already. At night if I can sleep, everything is OK.

WS   One word can mean two things.

HZ   Look not at the word.

N   Look at the meanings.

MDM TAN   A few days after we met, he brought me to the sea. You will not be happy with me, he said. Think carefully. You may dedicate your life to me, but I will not dedicate it to you. He looked out at the sea, and was silent for a long time. Then he spoke. In my village, when I was young, it took 47 steps for me to get from my house to the sea. Over here it takes 22. Has the sea come closer? Or have my feet become bigger? There were mountains behind my village. Here there are hills. Have the mountains becomes smaller? Or have I become bigger? In my childhood, the world was a map. Now it is a journey.

             My dear, find a man who will worship you, who will carry you across muddy puddles. Find a man who has smaller strides, who journeys home to you every night.

             I left him and went for a walk. I walked on the sand. With every step, the sea climbed higher up my legs. I stopped. I could continue to walk ahead, and feel the water quickly engulf me. I could walk away from the sea, towards my little home. I could turn back and walk towards a man who I could dedicate my life to, but who I could not grow old with. I stopped for a moment, as the sea nudged at my feet to decide.

WS/P/T   Fundamentals of National Reconstruction.

HL/WG/HZ   Plans for National Reconstruction.

P/GX/JX   The Three Principals of the People.[16]

N   The revolution has not ended.

---

[16] *The Three Principles of the People*, or the *San-min* Doctrine, is Sun Yat-sen's political philosophy developed to help make China a free, prosperous and powerful nation. The three principles are often translated and presented as *nationalism, democracy* and *the livelihood of the people*.

15. Ah Ho and Madam Tan

Pause. Ah Ho enters. She sits by Madam Tan for a moment. She looks at Madam Tan's feet. She then massages her feet.

AH HO   Lucky we no need to tie the feet, hor?[17] (*Slight pause.*) Like 孙夫[18] ... walk very slow ... (*Slight pause.*) But your feet very small. No need to tie also can. Mine very big. See? But yours very hard. This part very hard ... —

MDM TAN   Ow! Ah Ho! What are you *doing*?

AH HO   Why 四姑?[19] You thinking about what?

MDM TAN   Thinking about nothing. Thinking about sleeping. Drinking milk and going to sleep.

AH HO   Madam Tan, cannot drink milk. Cannot sleep. 孙先生[20] come back, how?

MDM TAN   Last time people come to this villa to plan revolutions. Always new people ... new faces. All the old faces never come back because they all die in the revolution.

AH HO   Like my Ah Heng.

MDM TAN   Yah ... Every year, new faces replace the old faces ... (*Slight pause.*) Now he is gone. Other people must replace him. Then next time, when we go, others will replace us.

AH HO   Replace us for what ah?

MDM TAN   I don't know ... to fight ... to plan other revolutions ... (*Slight pause.*) We must not think about old ghosts, Ah Ho. New faces ... we must think about new faces ...

---

[17] The reference here is to foot binding, or in Chinese.
[18] That is, Mrs Sun.
[19] Fourth Aunt, or Madam Tan.
[20] That is, Dr Sun.

16. Video — Old People #1

Pause. Cross-fade to an interview on video with three or more older people. They speak in different Chinese dialects.

OLD ONE   我们组织了一个团体。不是, 不是, 不是正式的团体。不过因为我们大家都有共同点, 所以决定聚一聚。[21]

OLD TWO   当博物院开幕的时候, 我们将会主办有史以来最大的聚会。全区域的革命同志和他们的后代都会来。是是, 全世界。他们都会回来, 都会回来庆祝。[22] Their people are dying at home and they are still alive. It's not good.

OLD ONE   You feel you owe the dead an answer because you are not suffering.

17. Flashback #1 — Mrs Sun Visits (30 Days)

Cross-fade to Ah Ho and Madam Tan. Flashback scene — Mrs Sun's first visit to them.

AH HO   *Ah*! 孙夫人[23] coming, 孙夫人[24] *coming*!

MDM TAN   Remember what I told you ah … don't look at her feet.

AH HO   OK, I know … my mother's feet also was bound. Very smelly!

MDM TAN   A woman's bound feet are like her private parts. Cannot anyhow see, cannot anyhow touch.

AH HO   Yah, I know, I know

MDM TAN   And, Ah Ho, you don't talk rubbish in front of her. She is his wife. The Real wife!

AH HO   OK *lah*,[25] OK *lah*. You think you very cultured is it?

---

[21] We've formed a group. No, no, not a formal organisation … It's only because we have something in common that we've decided to come together.

[22] At the opening of the museum, we will be organising the largest gathering in history. Revolutionary comrades and their descendants from all regions will be attending. Yes, from all over the world. They will return, they will, to celebrate.

[23] That is, Mrs Sun.

[24] That is, Mrs Sun.

[25] Malay: lah, '[A] particle emphasising the word to which it is appended' (*A Malay-English English-Malay Dictionary*, ed. A. E. Coope [revised edn.; London and Basingstoke: Macmillan Education, 1991]).

Mrs Sun enters. There is a silence for a moment. She walks very slowly. Pause. Ah Ho and Madam Tan rush to bring a seat to her.

MRS SUN   谢谢。[26]

MDM TAN   First time come here. Anything you want we will get for you.

MRS SUN   水。[27]

AH HO   Ah.

Ah Ho exits.

MDM TAN   (*To Mrs Sun.*) Actually we have coconut water. You want to try?

(*Ah Ho comes in with a basin of water.*)

AH HO   孙夫人,[28] I put in your room OK?

(*Pause. Mrs Sun and Madam Tan look at each other.*)

MRS SUN   (*To Ah Ho.*) 一杯可以喝的水。[29]

AH HO   Orr.

MDM TAN   (*To Ah Ho.*) Just get her some water! Water! (*To Mrs Sun.*)

Ah Ho exits.

MDM TAN   It is safe here, you don't have to be afraid.

MRS SUN   逸仙离开中国的时候，那些清兵有来追杀我们。幸亏他们去错了村子。[30]

MDM TAN   Dr Sun will be home soon. He's giving speeches outside.

MRS SUN   他跟我在一起的时候，难得开口说话。现在一说话就口若悬河。14年了，他改变了真多。是因为我他才那么沉默，还是你改变了他？[31]

Ah Ho enters.

---

[26] Chinese: Thank you.

[27] Chinese: Water.

[28] That is, Mrs Sun.

[29] Chinese: Water that I can drink.

[30] Chinese: The Qing soldiers came after us when Yat-sen had left China. Luckily, they went to the wrong village.

[31] Chinese: When he's with me, he seldom speaks. Now when he speaks, he's so eloquent. It has been 14 years, he's changed so much. Was it me that made him so taciturn, or did you change him?

MDM TAN   Ah Ho, get the pineapples. (*To Mrs Sun.*) It's Dr Sun's favourite fruit in Penang.

Ah Ho exits.

MRS SUN   14年来，我无时无刻不在为他操心。我想他身边需要有个人，可以照顾他，一个细心体贴的......[32]

MDM TAN   (*Shouts to Ah Ho.*) *Make sure you bring the nicer pineapple, ah*! And the durians! *Bring the durians*! (*Slight pause.*) Yah. We all help him. But you must understand. These are important matters. If he doesn't do all this, who will do it?

MRS SUN   他可以叫别人代劳，不是吗？一切亲力亲为，最后自己的母亲去世连家也回不了。[33]

MDM TAN   He was very sad when she passed away. But ...

MRS SUN   他的心里有家吗？都这么多年了。有吗？还是他有一个人......[34]

Ah Ho enters with some fruit.

MDM TAN   Ah Ho! Er ... I go and get the ...

Madam Tan exits.

AH HO   (*In Chinese.*) This one pineapple. This one durian. (*Pause. Mrs Sun is uncomfortable.*) Er ... you want to eat? (*Mrs Sun shakes her head.*) Er ... tie the feet like that very painful hor? (*Slight pause.*) Last time my mother also tie. Very smell ... — er, painful. (*Slight pause.*) My mother say I also must tie. But dunno why never tie. (*Slight pause.*) Hehe ... if I tie, I cannot walk like this. I must walk like this. (*She tiptoes on her clogs.*) Very difficult hor ...

Madam Tan enters. She screams when she sees ah Ho.

MDM TAN   Ah Ho! (She hits her a few times.) What are you trying to do?

AH HO   Aw! I show her how to ... —

---

[32] Chinese: Over these 14 years, I have been constantly worried for him. I think he needs someone by his side, someone who is considerate and can take care of him ...

[33] Chinese: He could have asked someone to share his load, couldn't he? He would do everything himself, and in the end, he couldn't return home even when his mother passed away.

[34] Chinese: Does home have a place in his heart? It has been so many years. Does it? Or does he have someone ...

MDM TAN   Never mind! I don't want to know. (*To Mrs Sun.*) I'm sorry. (*To Ah Ho.*) You clear all this … (*To Mrs Sun.*) I'm sorry.

Ah Ho exits.

MDM TAN   I told him that I will take care of you.

MRS SUN   我已经跟他说了纳你为妾。……[35]

MDM TAN   I'm just doing my part for the revolution.

MRS SUN   我已经跟他说了纳你为妾。[36]

Just then, Ah Ho enters with a glass of water.

AH HO   *Concubine? Madam Tan! Congratulations!*

MDM TAN   Shut up! (*To Mrs Sun.*) Mrs Sun, you must be very tired from your long journey. Why don't you go and rest?

Ah Ho helps Mrs Sun offstage.

AH HO   (*To Mrs Sun.*) You want water? (*To Madam Tan.*) Concubine ah …?

Madam Tan is still a little flustered. Slowly, she starts to clear the space. Suddenly, the scene changes. It is 15 days later. Madam Tan breaks into the next scene.

MDM TAN   Faster, faster … I'm late *already*!

Ah Ho and Mrs Sun enter.

AH HO   四姑,[37] you don't faster faster *lah*. She cannot walk as fast as you, you know.

MDM TAN   Yah, yah, I always forget.

AH HO   She here 15 days already, can still forget.

MDM TAN   I have to rush back, Ah Ho. Some people are coming. We are supposed to meet to talk about the money for the next uprising!

MRS SUN   你们先走吧，我知道怎么回家。我自己回去行了。[38]

MDM TAN   Can you walk a little faster?

---

[35] Chinese: You are really very suitable for him.
[36] Chinese: I have already told him to take you in as his concubine.
[37] Chinese: Fourth Aunt — Madam Tan as she is addressed by Ah Ho.
[38] Chinese: Run along. I know how to get home; it's alright that I go back on my own.

MRS SUN   你先走吧……哦，我还要买些护身符。[39]

AH HO   Yah, yah, this amulet very nice. (*To Madam Tan.*) Ah … you go *lah* … I walk with her.

MRS SUN   保佑逸仙。[40]

MDM TAN   He is a Christian.

MRS SUN   还是很灵验的。这些年来，我每天为他念经拜佛还有买这些灵符，他才能安然无恙。[41]

AH HO   Yah, yah, come we buy the (*in Chinese*) amulet. Madam Tan, you … —

MRS SUN   其实我得买很多很多给那些牺牲的人。[42]

MDM TAN   Buy! Just buy! Buy for all the heaven and all the hell and all the gods and all the demons! Look at you! Just look at you! You are … you are an embarrassment to women. You and the whole generation of you … Look what the monarchy has done to you. Look! Every time I look at you I am more convinced … that everything you are … is everything that I don't want.

AH HO   Madam Tan! How can you speak to her like *that*?

MRS SUN   翠芬你告诉我……那你到底要什么？[43]

MDM TAN   I want freedom … equality … man, woman … I want a successful revolution. I want people to have a roof over their head, food on their table. Not poverty. Not monarchy. Not war.

MRS SUN   在这世界上，免不了有贫穷有战争，就像生老病死，就好像夫妻，有时相聚有时分离，就好像情侣，有的相爱有的不。[44]

MDM TAN   I am talking about the country here, not about love. Not about your husband.

---

[39] Chinese: Do make a move first … I still want to buy some talismans.

[40] Chinese: To bless Yat-sen.

[41] Chinese: They're still very effective. He's been safe and healthy because all these years, I have been chanting scriptures and praying to the Buddha every day, as well as buying these talismans.

[42] Chinese: Actually, I'll need to buy many more for those who had sacrificed.

[43] Chinese: Cui Fen, tell me … what is it that you want?

[44] Chinese: It cannot be avoided that in this world, there'll be poverty and war. It's like the life of man: one goes through old age and sickness between birth and death. It's also like husband and wife who have times of separation and times of reunion; as it's like couples among whom some are in love and some are not.

MRS SUN   你没有丈夫, 你不会懂的。[45]

MDM TAN   Yes, I don't have a husband!

MRS SUN   我丈夫离开我14年了, 革命……这一场革命。[46]

MDM TAN   The revolution! The revolution! You know how many people have died for the revolution?

MRS SUN   翠芬, 那些死去的人。他们也有父母, 他们也都是别的女人的丈夫。难道逸仙真的那么与众不同吗? 为什么? 为什么? 为什么我走到哪里, 到处都充满了哀痛、死亡。人们一个个地倒了下去, 就为了他。还有你, 你的所谓的革命![47]

MDM TAN   Blood is necessary.

MRS SUN   你鼓励他, 怂恿他。(顿)那你想要什么? 万古流芳? 还是想当皇后?[48]

MDM TAN   I have no time for this. I must go.

She is about to walk off.

AH HO   I want to buy this. This pillow. It will make us sleep, make us dream. Dream someone you love sleep beside you every night. This pillow will give us rest, give us strength … spirit to go on. I want to buy this pillow for you … and for you … and for me and for our Dr Sun.

Pause. Ah Ho exits. Pause. Madam Tan and Mrs Sun look at each other. They move slowly. Suddenly, the scene changes. It is 15 days later. They break into the next scene.

AH HO   Wah! So fast one month already. When you come, your bag not so heavy. Now very heavy! Mrs Sun, when you come back again?

(She puts the bag down. Madam Tan and Mrs Sun look at each other. There is a good-bye scene. Ah Ho takes the suitcase and exits. Mrs Sun exits.)

---

[45] Chinese: You don't have a husband, you won't understand.

[46] Chinese: My husband has left me for 14 years, revolution, this revolution …

[47] Chinese: Cui Fen, those people who died, they have parents as well. They were also husbands of other women. Is Yat-sen really that special? Why? Why? Why is it that everywhere I go, each place is full of grief and death? People collapse, one by one, all for the sake of him, and you, and what you call the 'revolution'!

[48] Chinese: You encourage him and urge him. (Pause) What do you want? A great reputation that will be remembered forever? Or to become the empress?

18. Ensemble #3 — It Takes Ten Uprisings

Cross-fade to Ensemble.

HZ   It takes 10 uprisings to change a government.

HL   The first will end in mass arrest.

GX   The second will run out of ammunition.

WS   The third will be overpowered.

N   The fourth will once again run out of ammunition.

WM   The fifth will be outnumbered.

P   The sixth will retreat.

JX   The seventh will once again run out of ammunition.

J   The eighth will, yes, run out of ammunition.

T   The ninth will be overpowered.

WG   The tenth will succeed.

Pause.

J   Lives would be lost, tears would be shed, martyrs would be honoured, govern-
            ments would change.

WM   And new uprisings will begin.

19. Jason Handphone #3

Cross-fade to Jason on his seat. He is on his handphone. He is in shorts and a T-shirt.

JASON   ... I said I'm fine, all right? Yes, I'm tired. It's all this waiting, shooting, wait-
            ing, make-up, waiting ... and I ... — I just don't feel any support OK? (*Slight
            pause.*) But what exactly is the *problem*? Huh? Why are you ... — I thought
            you were OK about postponing the wedding. Why are you still bringing it *up*?
            Look Val, there's something really wrong here, OK? I'm depending on you to
            get the renovations sorted out ... *No, it can't wait!* Everything is settled. We
            got the bloody keys! Just tell them to start! What's the use of having a damn
            flat when it's *empty*? (*Slight pause.*) No! No! No, you are *not* going to

another conference. You are not ... — Yes, I am unreasonable. I'm sick of being sensitive to your needs all the time. What about my needs? If you want to go and change the world so much, I'm not going to wait for you, OK? I'm not going to wait for you. No, don't hang up! Fine hang up. But don't bother calling back cos I'm not going to answer!

20. Flashback #2 — New Year's Eve, Tokyo

He hangs up. As he looks at his handphone, the lights come on, and shine on Madam Tan. She is holding onto a kimono ... Looking into a mirror, she has a smile on her face. She takes off her clothes and tries on the kimono.

The spotlight remains on Jason throughout this scene. He tries to call Val back.

Ah Ho enters and look at Madam Tan for a moment. She suddenly pretends to be a Japanese maid.

AH HO   Ah so! Madam Tan! You wear kimono *neh*!

Ah Ho helps Madam Tan put on the kimono.

AH HO   This kimono is the style of the empress. (*Makes 'samurai' sound.*)

MDM TAN   It is very grand.

AH HO   Yes, very grand-o. Today is new year eve. 1899. 31 December. We have party. Very nice to dance *neh*!

MDM TAN   Yes ... I'm going to dance all night ...

AH HO   Madam Tan ... your husband is a great man.

MDM TAN   Yes. Yes, he is.

AH HO   But why you never bring Ah Ho-o. She is very nice. (*Does a 'samurai' laugh.*) But, Madam Tan, this kimono is not the real one. The kimono of the real empress is 50 times more heavy and 100 times more beautiful. This is imitation *neh*.

MDM TAN   When does the party start? I want to go to the party!

AH HO   No party *neh*! The men are talking and drinking. Woman must wait! (*Slight pause.*) You are in revolution, madam?

MDM TAN   Yes! I … my husband and I … we are going to free China … we are going to eradicate the Qing Dynasty!

AH HO   Long live the emperor! Eh? Long live Sun Yat-sen! And *Madam Tan*! (*'Samurai' laugh.*) Today is last day of old year, old century. Fortune teller tell me I will be famous actress. *Sakura … sakura …*[49] Madam, you look like empress. Empress *Madam Tan*! (*Continues acting and singing.*) Tomorrow, the sun will rise to a new beginning. But tonight you must dance with the one you love. *Sakura, sakura …*

Ah Ho continues singing. She dances away with Madam Tan's clothes.

MDM TAN   Where are my clothes? Ah Ho? (*Speaks quickly.*) I am not a real revolutionary. I am an imitation. He is not even my husband. An … imitation of a husband. When I was a girl, my big dream was to go to Singapore. Now I am in Tokyo. I am in Tokyo, celebrating a new year, celebrating the start of a new century. Nothing seems real. My clothes … I need my clothes.

Madam Tan is only in her undergarments.

MDM TAN   Is he waiting for you, Madam? (*Slight pause.*) No, I am. I am waiting for him.

21. Jason and Director #3/Madam Tan and Ah Ho

Jason, who has been trying to call Val, suddenly turns to look at the mirror. Both Madam Tan and he put on their clothes, looking at each other. The Director and Ah Ho enter into their respective places on stage.

JASON   (*Having a conversation with the Director, but with the lines directed to Madam Tan.*) Did he love her? *Did he love Madam Tan?*

DIRECTOR   Is it really important?

MDM TAN   (*Having a conversation with Ah Ho, but with the lines directed at Jason.*) Do you often think about Ah Heng?

AH HO   Think so much also for what right? Think also cannot change anything.

---

[49] Japanese: Cherry blossom. *'Sakura Sakura'* is a traditional folk song that depicts spring, the season of cherry blossoms.

JASON	Why did they leave each other? Why did they separate? Did they love each other?
DIRECTOR	Must two people be together, to love each other?
MDM TAN	Some people have fire in them ... to fight ... to change ... What happens when the fire dies?
AH HO	No, Madam Tan. The person can go away, can die. But the fire ... the fire no need to die. (*Slight pause.*) You must cover the mirror. When ghost come, no good to see the mirror.
JASON	Why did he let her go?
DIRECTOR	Why did she?
MDM TAN	Milk ... where's my milk Ah Ho?
AH HO	Milk can make you sleep. But milk cannot make you forget.

Lights on Madam Tan and Ah Ho blackout. The mood changes.

JASON	I need answers. I don't know what to do if ... —
DIRECTOR	— You're an actor. Find your motivation. (*Slight pause.*) Look, it's all in the script. Just play it. Let the script speak for ... —
JASON	— But I don't understand him. Why did he just let her go ... just let her slip away. And why didn't she want to go ... why didn't she want to be with him?
DIRECTOR	*Why are you asking me so many questions?* Just act *lah*! It's not difficult to act. You were a theatre student right? Do one of your acting exercises. Like, if Sun Yat-sen were alive today, what would he do differently? Would he surf the net or start a website to canvass for funds? Or what would he do for leisure? And, like, if he were a fruit, what fruit would he be?
JASON	No! It's not about all that. It's about here (*touches his heart*) ... how we connect ... how do I play him ... how do I be him, if I can't even understand him!
DIRECTOR	You know ah ... actually I casted you because ... because I think you're quite cute *lah*. (*Slight pause.*) There were three of you ... shortlisted. But you ... Jason, when your face is framed ... beautiful ... (*Slight pause.*) Women ... and some men ... will fall in love with you. We can sell your photographs. Framed photographs of Jason Leong ... every household, every office will want one. And it'll all be because of me ... me, Jason ... the wind beneath your wings ...
JASON	(*Pause*) You know ... I think, maybe I should just imagine him as a fruit.

22. Video — The Last Farewell Letter

AN EXTRACT:

The last farewell letter
By Lin Jue Min
To his wife

He participated in the 9th uprising in Canton
And together with 71 others
He died.

My dear Yi Qing
This letter is my farewell to you.
As I write this letter,
I am still a man in this world;
but when you read it,
I would have become a ghost,
A ghost of the next world.

My love for you is so deep
I am able to die
for all under heaven to bear witness
so that they too
can realise their love for their loved ones

How many couples in history are reunited?
How many have happy endings?
How many people have died or separated

When they do not deserve to die or be separated?
That is why I have decided to die for a cause
That is why I will die without regret

I have never believed in ghosts
But I now wish I had
So, when I am dead
I will be able to stay
By your side

Read what is said.
The unspoken

The unwritten
The unsaid
Will forever remain
In your imagination

23. Flashback #3 — Dr Sun and Mrs Sun

Pause. Lights on Mrs Sun. Flashback. Dr Sun walks to Mrs Sun. Mrs Sun and Dr Sun are sitting together in a car. She is holding a tiffin carrier. There is silence. It is a little awkward.

DR SUN   I don't know when I'm coming back. (*Pause*) Here is some medicine. In case the children get sick. (*She looks hesitant.*) It's Western. Western medicine is good. (*She takes the medicine.*) Do you need money? (*She shakes her head. Pause. He gives her some money. She takes it.*) It's not that I don't want to bring you. But my work …

MRS SUN   我明白的, 那是你的事业……[50]

DR SUN   You don't have to get off. I will … I will just go …

Pause. She gives him the tiffin. He takes it. They look at each other for a while. Then he leaves.

24. Flashback #4 — Dr Sun and Madam Tan

Dr Sun gets onto the ship. Madam Tan is there. Flashback to another time.

MDM TAN   I've never been to Tokyo.

DR SUN   You'll like it. They're having a big party. For the new year.

MDM TAN   I hope I don't get seasick. (*Slight pause.*) I love the sea. I love the sea, the sky … Even at night, when it looks dark and dangerous.

DR SUN   I've never seen you like this

MDM TAN   Like what?

---

[50] Chinese: I understand, you work for the cause …

DR SUN   Like this. Standing. Looking. Admiring. You're always moving around, work-ing, fixing something or cooking a meal …

MDM TAN   I'm happy. That I'm with you.

DR SUN   We've travelled so much, Where are we? Where is our home? Who are our families? (*Pause*) When I first met you, you were only a village girl. Now … (*Slight pause.*)

MDM TAN   Yes. Now. Don't talk about the past. Don't talk about the future. I only want now.

DR SUN   Now? Now I can barely recognise my face in the mirror. I've taken on so many names, so many disguises, what's my real name? (*Pause*) It's senseless. It's all senseless.

MDM TAN   Let's make a pact. Anytime you feel weak, I will be strong for you. Anytime I feel weak, you in turn will be strong for me.

DR SUN   That is a pact I have made a long time ago

25. Flashback #5 — Mrs Sun and Madam Tan/Ah Ho

Pause. Mrs Sun and Madam Tan walk to each other. They are sitting on a train. Flashback to another time.

MRS SUN   翠芬，你能陪我一起去，真的是太好了。他们说总统就职典礼那天要有夫人在身边。我们都是他的妻子。我……我是他孩子的母亲，你是革命的母亲。我有我的丈夫，你有你的革命。翠芬，这次你能跟我一起去，真的是太好了。(顿)什么站口啦？[51]

MDM TAN   I have to get off.

MRS SUN   什么？[52]

MDM TAN   I'm sorry. But I have to get off. I'm sorry. This is not my future.

---

[51] Chinese: Cui Fen, it's really great that you can go with me. They say that the wife should be present at investiture ceremony of the president. We are both his wives. I … I am the mother of his children; you are the mother of the revolution. I have my husband; you have your revolution. Cui Fen, it's really great that you can go with me for this occasion. (*Pause*) What station is this?
[52] Chinese: Why?

MRS SUN   你知道你在说什么吗?[53]

MDM TAN   I can't go on.

MRS SUN   不, 翠芬, 算我求求你, 跟我一起去好吗? 我真的不能单独面对他⋯⋯翠芬⋯⋯[54]

(Madam Tan walks away. She goes to her space. Lights fade on Mrs Sun.)

(Madam Tan looks at her watch. Ah Ho enters.)

26. Jason Handphone #4

Lights comes up on Jason. He's on the phone.

JASON   Erm … it's me … *(Slight laugh.)* Don't even know where you are. Are you in Singapore? Hong Kong? London? Anyway, call me when you get this message. *(He's about to hang up.)* Look, there's a lot at stake here. OK? I know you listen to my messages. I just need to know. You want out? You really want out? Then tell me! Just call me and tell me! Or leave a message. You don't want to speak to me, then leave a message. *(Pause)* I did a really good scene yesterday, you know … and I … I thought of you. *(Slight pause)* But, I … I'm not ready to give up, OK? I'm not about to give you up …

27. Ensemble #4 — When I Sleep, I Dream

The Ensemble enters. While the following takes place, Ah Ho rolls out a mat. Madam Tan lies down. Madam Tan looks at Ah Ho. Ah Ho sits by her side.

Jason has finished. He hangs up. He looks at his handphone.

HZ   When I sleep, I dream of nothing.

WG   When I read the newspapers, I want to migrate.

JX   I stopped reading.

WS   When I walk, I look at the reconstruction of a state.

---

[53] Chinese: Do you know what you are saying?

[54] Chinese: Please, Cui Fen, take it that I'm begging you. Come with me please? I really can't face him alone … Cui Fen …

HL   When I travel, I always come home.

GX   When I eat, I watch the news.

T   I stopped watching.

N   When I fall, I get up.

P   When the sun shines, it's hot.

WM   When it rains, it pours.

28. Video — Old People #2

Video begins.

OLD FOUR   My grandfather poured all of his money into the revolution. My grandmother was very mad at him because of that. She asked him: 'You have one meeting with this Sun Yat-sen character and you sell away all your rubber plantations to fund his revolution.' My grandfather went bankrupt and became a beggar. I heard he died of tuberculosis in the end. He gave money to a doctor but had no money to see a doctor in the end.

OLD FIVE   我是陈汉的后代。他是孙先生的园丁。以前他经常把孙先生最爱吃的南洋水果带给他吃！他会说：'享受你劳动的成果吧'。[55]

OLD SEVEN   (*In Hokkien-Chinese or* minnan hua.) 我是明泰的后代。他是其中一位捐款给革命的生意人。最后他破产，什么也没有只剩下一条命。他就把命奉献给革命，在黄冈起义战后死了。[56]

OLD FOUR   Some of us have good memories. Others, not so good. But we are united, in a way. We are united because we have families that lived together … They lived and worked together at a certain period of time. Very different from now.

---

[55] Chinese: I am a descendant of Chen Han. He was a gardener of Dr Sun. He used bring to Dr Sun his favourite fruits from Nanyang. He would say, 'Do enjoy the fruits of your labour!'

[56] Chinese: I am a descendant of Ming Tai. He was a businessman who donated to the revolutionary cause. He became bankrupt in the end; was left with absolutely nothing except his life. With that he dedicated himself to the revolution, and died after the Huanggang Uprising.

OLD FIVE 对，现在……人们比较关心的是衣食住行……人要过得开心一点就是要照顾自己，家人。我们以前的人有一种使命感……一种欲望……现在没有这种感觉了。[57]

OLD SIX Don't worry so much about government and all that. You can get into trouble. Just do your own thing, be good to your wife and children ... All these words — sacrifice, revolution, honour... they are all old words ... and like any old thing, they must die.

29. Ensemble — Blindfolded and Shot

During the last part of the video, each member of the Ensemble blindfolds himself/herself. At the last line of the video, they are 'shot', and all collapse.

Blackout.

Interval.

30. Chinese Opera

Lights come on to reveal a Chinese opera. It goes on for a while. The following text scrolls on the video screen:

Stage plays and operas were used to publicise the revolution. In 1904, Chen Shaobai, one of the 'Four Outlaws/Desperadoes' and Li Qitang formed a revolutionary theatre group, 'Cai Nan Ge', which staged plays with strong revolutionary sentiments in Hong Kong and Macau. The company was disbanded after two years due to financial difficulties. Plays also toured Singapore and Malaya. These included 'Xu Xin Assassinates En Ming', 'General Xiong Fi Martyred at Pomegranate Flower Pagoda', 'The Martyrdom of Qui Jin' and 'Zhang Liang Attempts to Assassinate Emperor Qin Shi Huang'.

VIDEO 来了，适才间别母别妻情千万，俺这里，丈夫有泪不轻弹，别家堂，怕只怕，时光已晚。劳太子, 岸边长候我羞惭。大鹏展翅恨天低，催动征骑把路赶。只见易水滔滔腾白浪, 白衣白甲白旗幡。速下雕鞍, 共向良朋饯别盏。荆轲参见太子。[58]

---

[57] Chinese: Yes, these days ... people are more concerned with the basic necessities of life ... Leading a happier life means that one has to take care of oneself and one's family. We in the past have a sense of mission ... A certain desire ... There aren't such sentiments anymore.

[58] Chinese: Here I come. I have just bid an emotional farewell to my mother and wife. A man does not shed tears easily. Leaving my ancestral home, I am worried that it is late. I will be ashamed to keep the Crown Prince waiting for me on the river bank at length. Like the Great Bird that spreads

31. Jason and Director #4

The opera continues. It is the climax of the show. There is an assassination or death. The emperor addresses the audience as he is dying.

EMPEROR　　Beware ... the dragon is bleeding ... It's not his blood but yours ... Even the heavens have migrated. They will no longer shield you ... If earthquakes still shake the ground ... if floods still cover the fields ... if corruption still prevails ... if anger still occupies your mind ... if sadness still remain inside ... then nothing has changed ... The emperor is dead. But there will be new emperors ... I will rise ... I will return!

He suddenly gets up. Everyone gasps. Then he collapses and dies.

Director and Jason enter.

DIRECTOR　　Chinese opera in English is *so* not easy to do. (*Slight pause.*) Anyway, I thought about what you said ... you know, research and all that. Which was why I decided to bring you here — Island of the Sun. It's a little theme park in honour of Dr Sun. It'll only be officially opened next year ... but I'm like the arts and entertainment consultant, so ...

JASON　　That explains the tackiness.

DIRECTOR　　Look, history is boring. Need to dress it up with some entertainment. Like this part — Viva la Villa. Rent a Dr Sun Villa, each faithfully recreated to look like Dr Sun's real villas in Shanghai, Hong Kong, Japan and wherever he went. Rent a villa, and we'll throw in two aromatherapy amahs — trained ones, from China. Or maybe Macau. And here Revolution Nation! Where you can ... —

JASON　　— What's this? 'No Chinese and dogs allowed?'

DIRECTOR　　Oh ... this is ... Empress Dowager *lah* ... she went to sub-let parts of China to the Europeans ... So those areas ... no dogs and Chinese allowed. The tourists love these things ... But the no dog rule stays *lah*. Some things are just not welcomed.

---

its wings and feels restricted by the sky, I wish the journey could be faster covered as I spur my horse along. One could see the river Yi surging with waves, and the bank teeming with white robes, white armour and white flags. I dismount hastily to toast my worthy friends farewell. Jing Ke pays his greetings to the Crown Prince.

JASON   You brought me here because you thought I could learn something.

DIRECTOR   Yah. You see, like this hi-tech entertainment centre — Boxer Rebellion 2001. The kids become the boxers, and they will have boxing gloves to fight the imperialists ... the *enemies*!

JASON   Yah, but the bullets from the *guns* killed the boxers.

DIRECTOR   Yes, but the boxers thought they could defeat the guns with their bare fists. So Boxer Rebellion 2001 is paying a tribute to their courage.

JASON   That's stupidity! Not courage! And why are you reinforcing this almost *a hundred years later*? (*Slight pause.*) Look, can we just go? I need to learn my lines for the good-bye scene.

DIRECTOR   Jason, we can't use our modern eyes to judge the past.

As the scene goes on, lights come up on Madam Tan and Ah Ho. Madam Tan is fast asleep. Ah Ho pulls a blanket over her. She looks at Madam Tan for a while before she exits.

JASON   You know, I don't have any other eyes.

DIRECTOR   I'm trying to help you OK? All those things you said ... 'it's about here' (*touches his heart*) ... how ... how you want to *understand* him ... how you want to *be* him. So ... *be*!

JASON   There is no 'be'. There is only 'act'. Nothing is real. My clothes are my costumes. My age is my make-up. I cry when I say that the revolution is not complete because it's my line. Oh look! Isn't that his villa in London? See Dr Sun drink a cup of tea. Take a few steps more! Paris! See Dr Sun eating French loaf! Turn left! Japan! Dr Sun dances under the peach blossom! Has the world grown smaller or have Dr Sun's footsteps grown bigger? Why is it that Dr Sun can't find his way out? Has his home grown so small or has he grown so big that he missed his home?

DIRECTOR   — Jason! Jason, I know you are under a lot of stress. Erm ... the make-up artists have been talking to me ... about your, er ... personal problems... (*Slight pause.*) I don't want to replace you ... because we've been doing good work ... and I ... Jason, I ... —

Jason's handphone rings.

JASON   *Val*! Yes! Yes! No, I'm not at the shoot. I'm — er, it's difficult to explain ... No, no, I'm sorry! Val, I love you, and ... (*laughs*) I thought you were going to leave, and … (*Laughs*) No, at first I kept telling myself it was just a fight … like how we *always* fight. But when you didn't call … (*Slight pause.*) No, the shoot has been going great … no, I can't today. We've got to … — No, I really can't! Yes, you took time off, but … — (*Director makes a motion.*) Hey, Val, hang on …

DIRECTOR   Um, why don't you take the afternoon off.

JASON   But we're supposed to do the … —

DIRECTOR   — Yah, yah, yah … the whatever. Go. She's waiting for you.

JASON   Then the crew …?

DIRECTOR   Screw the crew! Just go!

JASON   I owe you one.

DIRECTOR   …

JASON   (*On the phone.*) Val! I'm coming … yes, *now!* (*Slight pause.*) OK, we're not going to fight, right? I mean, if we're going to grow old together, then we' can't be fighting forever. Our kids will put us in a home! (*He starts to walk away.*) I knew you couldn't bear to let me go … (*Laughs*) What do you call it …

Director is alone. Pause.

DIRECTOR   Faith. I think it's called faith.

32. Flashback Seven — Ten Revolutions in Ten Minutes

Madam Tan suddenly wakes up.

J   Ten revolutions.

ENSEMBLE   Ten revolutions in ten minutes.

P   *Number one. 1895. The Bomb*

Dr Sun us trying to fix a bomb. Madam Tan is sitting.

DR SUN   What do you do with this? (*No response.*) I've made this bomb before, but … (*He continues trying.*) The wires. I can never remember the wires. How many more of these explosives do we have left? We should start making some new … You can teach me. I know you taught me before, but …

MDM TAN   It's over. We lost. Everyone has been killed. And by sunrise we will too.

DR SUN   The wires. If I just know which wire goes here and — (*Madam Tan gets up and walks away.*) People shouldn't die for nothing. (*She stops.*) We are small. Our guns don't work properly. Home-made bombs. Not enough ammunition. We are small. Like a little mouse. Trying to fight a big bear. But one day ... one day, we will grow, we'll be big enough ... maybe not as big as a bear. But big enough. (*Slight pause.*) Big enough.

Pause. She turns and goes to him.

MDM TAN   This wire ... and this wire ... should cross with this wire.

WM   *Number two. 1900. Departure.*

DR SUN   I have to go. The ship is leaving.

MDM TAN   I can't do this anymore.

DR SUN   There's no time. I have to go!

MDM TAN   Then go! Go! *Go!* (*Slight pause.*) Escape. Run. Hide. I will face the widows myself. I will explain to the children why their fathers are never coming back. While I ... while *we* ... are still alive. Look! Completely unhurt. Not a scratch. Not one scratch.

DR SUN   We made some mistakes. Before the next uprising, we need to get more support from the overseas Chinese. I'll have to travel. A lot. (*He's about to go, then he stops.*) If you don't want to continue ... I won't hold it against you.

MDM TAN   If I don't continue, I will die.

J   *Number three. 1907. Fatigue.*

Madam Tan is sitting still. Dr Sun is pacing.

DR SUN   It was supposed to work. It was supposed to work. What happened? I don't know what happened. Why didn't it work? It was close. We were close. Don't you think so? Don't you think we were close? (*He goes to her.*) Speak to me. Why don't you speak to *me*? (*He holds her. She is limp.*) We knew this was going to happen. But we're almost there. The ... the revolution made a strong, a very strong impact. The troupes. They liked you. They, they, they said that you were an inspiration. They admired your ... — (*Pause*) Please ... please speak to me. Say something ... please ...

MDM TAN   I want to go away … Shall we go away? … We can … we can adopt … two or three children … go … somewhere quiet … somewhere … far away … like a normal family …

Dr Sun holds her up. He caresses her. He kisses her. They hug.

WS   *Number four. 1907. A Quiet Meal.*

MDM TAN   Dinner.

DR SUN   Mm …

MDM TAN   Very simple.

DR SUN   Mm …

MDM TAN   A lot of new people want to join.

DR SUN   Mm …

MDM TAN   And I hear some of the tin and rubber merchants want to contribute.

DR SUN   Mm …

MDM TAN   I spoke to the sailor's union. They're smuggling more weapons for us.

DR SUN   Mm …

MDM TAN   The next one should be soon. We must ride on everyone's anger. People are waiting to do something.

Pause. Madam Tan goes to him.

MDM TAN   They want to hear your 'Three Principles' and your 'Five Constitutional Rights'.

DR SUN   Mm …

MDM TAN   You must eat, OK? Then you will be strong.

Dr Sun grabs her and sobs.

WG   *Number five. 1907. Each Day They Wonder.*

They are both sitting separately, looking away from each other. Long pause.

GX   *Number six. 1907. She Sleeps Peacefully.*

She's sleeping. He goes to her. He sits by her feet. He strokes her hair. He brushes his cheek against her head. He touches her feet. He looks at his hands. He gets up and walks away, facing away from her. She opens her eyes. Pause.

DR SUN   We have failed.

Pause.

G   *Number seven. 1908. Fever.*

Dr Sun is sitting. Madam Tan stands behind him, dabbing his forehead with a cloth. She feels his neck.

MDM TAN   I think the fever has gone down.

DR SUN   Yah. I feel much better. Why don't you go to bed?

He leans his head back against her.

MDM TAN   Why don't you rest? Your mind … —

DR SUN   — My mind. My mind.

MDM TAN   Let your mind rest. That's why your head is burning. What are you thinking about?

DR SUN   I don't know. Everything. Everything. The past. The future. Death.

She holds his head tight.

MDM TAN   Don't think. Just sleep. (*Slight pause.*) Just sleep.

HL   *Number eight. 1908. Failure. Failure. Failure.*

MDM TAN   I told you it wasn't the right time! They weren't prepared. They weren't ready for action. Why do we have to repeat the same mistake *every time*?

DR SUN   It's not the same. It looks the same, but it's not.

MDM TAN   It is the same. We didn't have enough men, we didn't have enough guns, we didn't have enough ammunition. It is always the same mistake!

DR SUN   Every seeming failure brings us closer to the success of the revolution

MDM TAN   It is not seeming. We have failed. Over and over. We've been doing this for how many years? How many years? How long more do we have to go on? Until every strand of hair on my head turns white? Until there are a hundred wrinkles on my face? I'll still do it. I will still do it.

DR SUN   Cui Fen, was there ever a revolution without repeated failure, killing and destruction? Was there ever a revolution without sacrifices and martyrs?

(*Slight pause.*) Remember Tan Si Tong? He was executed by the Empress Dowager for leading the 100-day Reformist Movement.[59] He could have escaped to freedom like Kang Youwei[60] and Liang Qichao.[61] But he chose martyrdom. Remember what he said in his will?

MDM TAN   Every revolution must be baptised with blood

DR SUN   Yes. So we too must be prepared to shed our blood. We, Cui Fen. You. And I.

MDM TAN   I have been prepared. From the first day I met you.

Pause.

N   *Number nine. 1910. He Smiles Just Before He Leaves.*

He is slowly and calmly packing a suitcase. She gets clothes and passes them to him in an orderly manner. After he finishes, he closes the bag, picks it up, smiles and walks off.

HZ   *Number ten. 1911. Success.*

They are facing each other. She smiles. She nods slowly. Pause. She smiles. He breathes heavily. They cry. They hold hands. Their heads meet. They part. He gives her the watch. He leaves.

33. Video — Old People #3

Pause. Cross-fade to video.

OLD THREE   I think we will have a party when we meet. We will all go to the villa ... see what it looks like now ...

---

[59] The Hundred Days Reform (11 June 1898–21 September 1898) was a failed attempt by the Qing Emperor at educational, political and cultural reform within China, undertaken in the wake of the Chinese defeat during the First Sino-Japanese War of 1895. The reform was supported by Kang Youwei (see next note) and Kang's supporters.
[60] Kang Youwei (1858–1927) was a Chinese scholar and a leader of the 1898 Reform Movement. He was a key figure in the intellectual development of modern China. Kang was a believer in constitutional monarchy and, controversially, wanted to re-model the country after Meiji-era Japan. During the last years of the Qing Dynasty and the early years of the Republic of China, he promoted Confucianism as an antidote against 'moral degeneration' and indiscriminate Westernisation.
[61] Liang Qichao (1873–1929) was an influential literary scholar who was also a young radical reformer and a journalist.

OLD FIVE	Sometimes I ask why we doing this. We are not special. Our ancestors are the special ones. So I ask... why do we meet? It's like a funny club ... people who are very different ... and we come together. In the past, our ancestors, they were people with a cause, a mission. That's why they came together ...
OLD THREE	不，这样也好。让这些回忆继续下去。现在我的孙女儿也开始对这些事感兴趣。她开始写下我们家的家谱。她还说要到中国去。你看, 不错嘛…… 连年轻人都有兴趣。[62]
OLD FOUR	你的孙子有兴趣。我的都是一群饭桶。没有梦想, 没有愿望。只会吃喝嫖赌。[63]
OLD FIVE	Our people are still not united. Our country is still not free. Sometimes I feel I want to continue ... I want to ... — I don't know. We must do something. What for just sit down, drink coffee and talk about the past? Right or not? We must do something. But I don't know what. We are old. What can we do?

34. Bizarre Revolution

Lights on Ensemble.

WG	Revolution of the soul.
GX	What time is it?
JX	Day One.
T	I'm in a dark trench, I can't see!
N	Maybe it's not dark. Maybe we're blind.
HL	Maybe we're not blind. Maybe we're asleep.
HZ	Maybe we're not asleep. Maybe we're in our graves.
WG	Revolution of the mind.
WM	What time is it?
JX	Day Two.

---

[62] Chinese: No, this is also good. Let these memories live on. My granddaughter has begun to take an interest in these matters. She is starting to record our family tree. She even said that she wants to visit China. See, isn't this good? ... Even the young people are interested.

[63] Chinese: Your grandchildren are interested. Mine are good-for-nothings. No dreams, no hopes. They only know how to indulge in vices.

HZ	Why did it take ten dynasties to realise something was wrong?
HL	Why did it take 107 emperors to realise that they are not chosen by god?
WS	Why must it take eight barbaric imperialists to pillage our country before we realise there is a bigger world outside China?
N	Why?
WG	Revolution of the heart.
P	What time is it?
JX	Day three.
WG	By oppression and judgment he was taken away like a lamb to the slaughter. After the suffering of his soul, he will see the light of life and be satisfied. I will give him a portion among the great, and he will divide the spoils with the strong, because he poured out his life unto death, and was numbered with the transgressors. For he bore the sin of many, and made intercessions for the transgressors.
J	'... From the sixth hour until the ninth hour darkness came over all the land. About the ninth hour, Jesus cried out in a loud voice, "My God, my God, why have you forsaken me?"'
WG	Revolution of the spirit.
N	What time is it?
JX	Day four.
P	This is not a government.
WM	This is a dynasty.
J	My great grandfather fought in the war.
WS	My brothers were buried alive.
N	My sisters were raped and decapitated.
HZ	This is not a government.
HL	This is a dynasty.
GX	We can't sleep.
P	We can't eat.

HL/JX	We must act. We must act.
WG	Revolution of the past.
P	What time is it?
JX	Day five.
P	I have asked him to take you as his concubine.
HZ	Tomorrow the sun will rise to a new beginning.
J	Everything that you are, is everything that I don't want.
T	I have to get off. This is not my future.
WM	I'm the one that's down here. While you're just up there.
P	You are an embarrassment to women. You and the whole generation of you.
N	Tonight you must dance with the one you love.
WG	Revolution of the present.
WS/WM	What time is it?
JX	Day six.
J	One hundred years, and nothing has changed.
WG	The sea has risen, the ice has melted, the moon is a leap away.
P/T	But nothing has changed.
N	Because of you.
WM	Because you embody all that self-sacrificial shit that is oh so brave … so loyal … like a woman should be, while a man is loyal to bigger values like country and liberty.
HZ	One hundred years … —
ENS	— and nothing has changed.
T	We are still slaves. Slaves to our ideals, desires, greed and hopes. The enemy is no longer outside but living within us.
GX	It's *you*. You. Nothing has changed because of you.
WG	Revolution of the future.

WM　　　What time is it?

ENS　　　Day Seven.

MDM TAN	ENSEMBLE
It is two thousand and one.	Day seven
When I woke up today, my body ached.	Day seven
My shoulders have started to slouch.	Day seven
Yesterday, I rode a horse, and sent messages of warning.	Day seven
I travelled on a steamship, and visited friends and allies.	Day seven
Tomorrow I will turn into an ape.	Day seven
It is two thousand and one.	Day seven
I have seen boys killed as they tried to stop tanks.	Day seven
I have seen girls raped and decapitated	Day seven
for no reason except pleasure, boredom and madness.	Day seven
I have seen common men worshipped as emperors.	Day seven
It is two thousand and one.	Day seven

35. Madam Tan and Ah Ho

As Madam Tan continues saying 'It is two thousand and one', she clutches the watch and hyperventilates. Ah Ho rushes to her.

AH HO　　　Madam Tan! Madam Tan! What happen?

MDM TAN　　What time is it? What time is it?

AH HO　　　Not yet twelve o'clock

AH HO	MDM TAN
I think you sleep better …	
Don't think OK?	I can't sleep Ah Ho. I can't sleep!
don't think what day what time …	Is he here?
he come he don't come …	The mirrors … the watch
you sleep, OK? You sleep …	I still have the watch
Don't think about him	I can't
Madam Tan, no	I can't Ah Ho
I'm sorry. OK? I'm sorry	Is he here? Where is he?
I try. I try to make you happy	Is it day seven? What day?
Don't care, OK? No need already	Don't go. Are you going?
Don't want already. I see you …	Sit with me, Ah Ho

so many days never sleep properly,
never eat properly ...
Why he do this to you?
Why, Mdm Tan, why?
Why? Why must think so much?
Why you not happy? What you do wrong?
Why do you want? What do you want?

I can't breathe. There's ...
There's something ...
It's me, Ah Ho. It's me.
I'm doing this to myself.
I'm doing it to myself.
I don't know what to do. I don't know,
Ah Ho ... I don't know ...

They hold each other and cry.

36. Jason and Director #5

Lights come up on Jason and the Director. They are rehearsing, reading from the script.

DIRECTOR I cannot go with you.

JASON But you must. You must! I made a dress for you. To wear at ... —

DIRECTOR — No! I don't belong there.

JASON Don't you love me?

DIRECTOR I have loved you from the very moment I laid eyes on you. And I will keep that love till the day I die. (*Slight pause.*) Eh, for this good-bye scene tomorrow ah ... I want to do it in one take.

JASON *One take?* OK, OK, I'll try. OK? For *you!* (*Slight pause.*) Er, director ... you know ... you've been really ... Anyway, I wanted to say thanks and ... Oh! I have to rush off right tomorrow? Val and I are going away. So I can't attend the party. So ... anyway ... (*Takes out a gift.*) For you! (*He gives it.*) Open it! (*Director does so.*) It says 'Best Director'.

Pause

DIRECTOR Just make sure you do the scene well ... Good-bye scenes are always the hardest.

Jason's handphone rings. As Jason speaks, we the Director take out the present. It's a watch.

JASON Hey *Val!* Guess what? The director says you can watch the good-bye scene tomorrow. Then we can go straight to the airport. Oh, but I *have* to take off my make up first cos I ... — Huh? What do you mean? You're kidding right?

But I thought … — No, no, no, no, wait … What job? What do you mean UN job? What about the wedding? (*Laughs*) OK, Val, joke's over. Tomorrow we're going to … — No! *I don't say that*! *I need you*! I need you Val … Val, we have a flat … we have a flat under our name … *Hello? How?* How is this blackmail? Val, you can't just run off to China to be an activist. We are getting married, OK? We are going to move in to our new flat, OK? We are going to have children, *OK*! *We are going to grow old together, Val, grow old together*!

Long pause.

JASON   I made a dress for you. To wear at the Presidential Ceremony. I need you. (*Slight pause.*) Be with me. Be with me forever.

DIRECTOR You know I can't. Our love … our love can only exist when it is veiled, when it is a secret, private, unspoken. Our love can only exist when there is a revolution. And that revolution has ended.

JASON   *No*! No, it's not. Don't go to China. (*Slight pause.*) I'll die. I'll die without you.

DIRECTOR No Jason, you won't. And she won't die without you either.

37. Madam Tan and Mrs Sun

They look at each other. Pause. Lights on Madam Tan and Ah Ho, who is sleeping. Lights come up on Mrs Sun.

MRS SUN   Cui Fen …

MDM TAN   I don't know what to do. I don't know what to say. It's almost a hundred years later, and I'm still waiting. (*slight pause*) I can't breathe, *Dajie*,[64] I can't breathe …

MRS SUN   翠芬，你想不想知道大总统就职典礼舞会的情况？舞会上很热闹。每个人见了我们都说"恭喜大总统。恭喜大总统夫人。"跳舞的人真多。音乐很大声。[65]

MDM TAN   Music … what music?

---

[64] Chinese: Big sister.
[65] Chinese: Cui Fen, do you wish to know what it was like at the ball held after the Investiture Ceremony? The scene was very lively. Everyone we met said, 'Congratulations, my Great President; congratulations, my First Lady.' Many people were dancing, and the music extremely loud.

MRS SUN   我不认识是什么音乐。好像是古典的。[66]

MDM TAN   — the waltz! When we were in Tokyo at the New Year's Party, in 1899, he taught me how to waltz. We danced and danced, turning and turning until the room was spinning. As we danced, he whispered softly to me his dreams and ambitions. How he wanted our own country to be like Japan — so we too could dance and enjoy the peace, prosperity and beauty in our own country. I was so moved. I couldn't say anything. I was living a dream that couldn't have been more beautiful … and for all my remaining years I waited … I waited for this dream, this wonderful dream, to turn into reality.

Long pause.

MRS SUN   你的一生够丰富多彩啦。那是一般的女人连做梦都不敢想的。你不知道我多么羡慕你。你能说能做、能办事能打仗一凡是男人能做的你都能做。可是作为一个女人，你缺少的是他的陪伴；那是每一个女人都最渴望的。这一点，我太了解了。我和他做夫妻那么久，他多数时间都不在我身边。可是我没有选择。我只能做一个贤妻良母；我只能做一个孝顺的媳妇。[67]

MDM TAN   No, no, I never regretted it! All my life, and even now! (*Slight pause.*) But, at the time, I was so afraid that he would send someone down to fetch me. Because if he had insisted, I would probably have given in and gone to him. But he didn't. (*Slight pause.*) *Dajie*, I loved him until the day I died. I still do. But I could never have faced the world as his second wife standing next to you! And I would never snatch that right and honour away from you! Do you understand, *Dajie*? It would have gone against everything we dreamed about.

MRS SUN   作为一个女人，我可以明白。可是作为他的妻子，我不要明白。我要过的日子，跟你的不同。如果我跟你一个想法，那我的日子就更加痛苦难挨了。所以我才那么佩服你。可是，有时候我又那么可怜你。大总统就职典礼你没去，他非常失望。晚上舞会，逸仙穿上大总统的礼服，帅极了。你知道，我一生最光荣骄傲的是能做孙

---

[66] Chinese: I don't know the music, it seems to be classical.

[67] Chinese: Your life is colourful enough. It is one that ordinary women would not even dare to dream of. You don't know how envious I am of you. You can speak up and also take action, you can also complete tasks and fight battles — you can accomplish all that a man is also capable of. However, as a woman, what you lack is his company, that is what every woman craves. I understand that too well. I was man and wife with him for so long; he wasn't by my side most of the time. But I have no choice. I can only be a virtuous wife and mother; I can only be a filial daughter-in-law.

中山的夫人！可是那天晚上，我多么希望我不是他的妻子。因为我发现穿在我身上那件衣服是为你量身订做的。[68]

MDM TAN   I so loved him, adored him, worshipped him. I was his companion, his confidante, his *lover*! But I just couldn't go back to him. It wasn't right for the new China — the new China we fought and died for had no place for a relationship like ours. The new China needed new men and new women. (*Pause*) Maybe we were too idealistic. Did we force our ideals on others? When the thousands and millions cried for change, cried for help, cried for a leader to lead the revolution, were they just being selfish? If not, why have they now become as cruel, as inhuman as their previous oppressors? I have waited and waited. When will the change come?

MRS SUN   翠芬，我没念过书，不懂事。可是我觉得，人是不会变的。像你们这样的革命党，你们都是大好人。可是你们太理想了。你们走得太快太远啦。你可以带着你的链表，上下古今走遍全世界。可是我想，不论你走到什么时代、什么地方，你能见到的人大概是一样的。老实说，我小时候见到的人，跟我老了的时候见到的人，没有多大的改变。翠芬，你可以等。也可以去了再来。可是你要等的还是等不到。你还是会孤伶伶的一个人。也许，这就是你们革命党的命运。逸仙跟你，你们都是一个样子。50年，100年。什么都不会变。你一直等下去吗。?[69]

---

[68] Chinese: As a woman, I can understand; but as his wife, I don't wish to understand. The life I wish to lead is different from yours. If I share your thinking, my life would be even more insufferable. That is why I admire you, but sometimes I pity you. He was very disappointed that you didn't attend the Investiture Ceremony. He was so handsome at the evening ball, in his ceremonial dress as the Great President. You should know that the proudest achievement of my life is to be Sun Yat-sen's wife! However, I wished so much that I wasn't his wife that evening, for I found out that the dress I was wearing was tailored for you.

[69] Chinese: Cui Fen, I have not been to school, there are many things I don't understand. However, I fell that people will not change. Revolutionaries like you all, all of you are extremely good people. But you are all too idealistic, you people walk too fast and too far. You can bring along your wind-up watch and travel back and forth in time and anywhere in the world. However, regardless of which era you travel to, or where you go, the people you meet will be almost the same. To tell the truth, comparing people whom I met when I was young to those I met when I've grown older, there aren't any great changes. Cui Fen, you can wait, you can leave and return again. However, what you have been waiting for still hasn't arrived. You will still be alone. Perhaps this is the destiny of you revolutionaries. You and Yat-sen, both of you are of the same mould. Fifty years, one hundred years, nothing will change. Do you wish to continue waiting?

MDM TAN　　Yes! I will! *I will!* I was an ignorant girl from Penang before I met him. It was *he*, his *ideas*, his *actions*, his *struggles*, his *life* and his *death* that have made my life meaningful. It broke my heart to give him up in Macau. But giving up this wait would have denied my whole life, my whole existence! No, *Dajie*, I can't. I may be waiting for the impossible, dreaming a fantasy. But I can't give up! I can't give up my dream. It's the last thing I have. What else is there for me, if I give up my dream? Can you tell me? What else is there? What else is there?

Pause

MRS SUN　　你跟逸仙真像。[70]

They are together. Madam Tan is calm.

MDM TAN	CHORUS
I have endured all this.	
Silently, painfully, I have endured.	It is 2001.
But what I can't endure is that	
history refuses to go away.	It is 2001.
What we have given our life to eradicate,	
what millions others have given their life	
and their blood to change … keeps coming back.	It is 2001.
What we thought we had revolutionised	
with blood, and death, and destruction.	
They keep coming back.	It is 2001.
Or they keep repeating.	It is 2001.
Why?	It is 2001.
So many lives	It is 2001.
So many lives	It is 2001.
Was it worth it?	It is 2001.

Madam Tan and Mrs Sun start walking away, to the back. Chorus continues repeating their line.

CHORUS　　It is 2001. And nothing has changed!

---

[70] Chinese: You and Yat-sen are so alike.

38. Ah Ho/Madam Tan/Jason and Recorded Text

Ah Ho suddenly wakes up.

AH HO   Madam Tan, wake up. It is twelve o'clock. Seven day already! Seven day *already*! Madam Tan, *seven day already*!

Pause. Voiceover begins. In the meanwhile, the Director comes out and gives Jason's clothes back to him. Jason changes and gives his Dr Sun clothes back to the Director. Director exits. Jason crosses over to Madam Tan's chair.

VOICEOVER
I don't know what the word is. It is an emotion, yet it is not emotional.
Maybe the word is pride.
You are proud of the people around you,
Above you
And below you.
And they too are proud of you.
You have pride in yourself
Your work
Your beliefs ...

Maybe the word is peace.
Your mind, your village and your country are not in conflict.
Peace is not the opposite of war.
It is not an opposite.
It is not an opposition.
It is a necessity.

Lights come up on Madam Tan, standing in the box, behind a gauzy sheet.

Maybe the word is unity.
The story of the three sticks that cannot be broken if they are together.
But unity is a defence.
A people,
A country,
Is always united against other people,
Other countries.

Jason is at Madam Tan's chair. He holds the script.

Maybe the word is not pride
But arrogance;
Not peace

But settlement;
Not unity
But anonymity.

Jason cries.

39. Video — Old People #4

Cross-fade to video sequence.

OLD EIGHT   I was sleeping in the hall when I sensed something. I opened my eyes and I am telling you I really couldn't believe my eyes. I swear I saw Dr Sun's spirit. And Madam Tan was with him. The both of them walked out of the door hand in hand. When I wanted to give chase, they just disappeared into the night. It was the most amazing thing that I have ever seen.

OLD NINE   Yes, I saw them. I was outside the villa, smoking, when I saw two white figures. I have a third eye you know? I see such things everyday. So at first I didn't really bother. Then I thought I recognise one white figure as Madam Tan. I stared hard and true enough, it was her. And when I saw who was beside her, I tell you, I cried like a baby. It was Dr Sun.

Waltz music begins.

OLD EIGHT   I don't believe in emperors, I don't believe in gods, I don't believe in ghosts. I believe man controls his own fate. No hell, no heaven, it's just us. That's what the revolution proved. That night, I saw Dr Sun's spirit and Madam Tan. I am certain that I didn't imagine it. I saw what I saw.

OLD NINE   They are fated. Right? Fated to be together

OLD EIGHT   Or maybe ... Maybe that's what we want. We want to believe in unity.

Video cross-fades to image of revolutionaries.

40. Finale

Music soars to its loudest. Sounds of distant machine guns gets louder, overwhelming the music. Sound of clock ticking.

Blackout.

(End of Play)

Production Information

The Coffin is Too Big for the Hole
First directed in English by Kuo Pao Kun at the Marine Parade Library, Singapore, 16 November 1985. Produced by Practice Performing Arts School.

No Parking on Odd Days
First directed in English by Kuo Pao Kun at the Shell Theatrette, Singapore, 3 June 1986. Produced by Practice Performing Arts School.

Kopitiam (The Coffee shop)
First directed by Kuo Pao Kun, Lin Jinxiong and Lim Jen Erh at the Victoria Theatre, Singapore, 6 June 1986. Produced on the behalf of 23 Chinese-language drama groups: Singapore Amateur Players; Singapore I-Lien Dramatic Society; Practice Performing Arts School; Southern Arts Society; Life Drama Society; Youth Players; Chuen-Lei Literature and Arts Association; Singapore Broadway Playhouse; Singapore Creative Dramatic Society; Lian He Bao Drama Group; Rediffusion Play Group; People's Association Cultural Section Drama Unit; Singapore Broadcasting Corp. Children's Workshop; Singapore Chin Kuan Huay Kuan Drama Group; Nanyang Fang Shee Drama Group; Singapore Foochow Association Drama Group; Singapore Hui Ann Association Drama Group; Tung Ann Association Drama Group; Singapore Polytechnic Chinese Language Society; National University of Singapore Chinese Society; Ngee Ann Polytechnic Cultural Activity and Social Service Club; Nanyang Technological Institute Chinese Society; and National Library Central Lending Chinese Youth Club.

Day I Met the Prince
First directed in English by Roger Jenkins for a tour of Singapore schools, March 1989. Produced by Singapore Theatre Repertory Showcase (STARS).

Mama Looking for Her Cat
Multilingual play first directed by Kuo Pao Kun at the Singapore Conference Hall, 10 August 1988. Produced by Practice Theatre Ensemble.

The Silly Little Girl and the Funny Old Tree
First directed in English by Kuo Pao Kun at the Victoria Theatre, Singapore, 12 August 1989. Produced by Practice Theatre Ensemble.

0Zero01
Multilingual play first directed by Kuo Pao Kun at the Guinness Theatre, The Substation, Singapore, 6 December 1991. Produced by Practice Theatre Ensemble.

The Evening Climb
Multilingual play first directed by Kuo Pao Kun at the Victoria Theatre, Singapore, 3 June 1992. Produced by Practice Theatre Ensemble.

Lao Jiu — The Ninth Born
First directed in English by Ong Keng Sen at the Drama Centre, Singapore, 14 April 1993. Produced by Theatre Works (Singapore) Ltd.

Descendants of the Eunuch Admiral
First directed in English in Singapore by Ong Keng Sen at the Victoria Theatre, 3 June 1995. Produced by Theatre Works (Singapore) Ltd.

The Eagle and the Cat: A Monodrama
First directed in English by Kuo Pao Kun at the Jubilee Hall, Singapore, 30 April 1997. Produced by The Theatre Practice.

Geylang People in the Net
Multilingual play first directed by Kuo Pao Kun at the Victoria Theatre, Singapore, 21 August 1997. Produced by The Theatre Practice.

Sunset Rise
Multilingual play first directed by Kuo Pao Kun at the Victoria Theatre, Singapore, 7 June 1999. Produced by The Theatre Practice.

The Spirits Play
First directed in English as a performance conceived in collaboration between Japanese performance artists and Singapore actors by Ong Keng Sen at the Battle Box, Fort Canning Park, Singapore, 16 August 2000, as *The Spirits Play: Six Movements in a Strange House.* Produced by Theatre Works (Singapore) Ltd.

One Hundred Years in Waiting
Multilingual play first directed by Wong May Lan and Alvin Tan at the Victoria Theatre, Singapore, 2 June 2001. Produced by The Theatre Practice and The Necessary Stage.

The Complete Works of Kuo Pao Kun

| Volume FOUR | Plays in English |

Global Publishing

General Editor	Quah Sy Ren
Editor	C. J.W. -L. Wee
Commissioning Editor	Liang Wern Ling
In-house Editor	Zheng Danjun
Creative Director	Tan Kay Ngee
Graphic Designer	Ong Guat Teng
Typeset by	Stallion Media
Co-published by	The Theatre Practice
	155 Waterloo Street, Stamford Arts Centre
	#02-08, Singapore 187962
	www.practice.org.sg
	Global Publishing
	5 Toh Tuck Link, Singapore 596224
	www.globalpublishing.com.sg
	65-64665775
	chpub@wspc.com
Distributed by	Global Publishing
	(An Imprint of World Scientific Publishing Co. Pte. Ltd)
Printed by	World Scientific Printers
First Edition	September 2012
ISBN	978-981-4139-46-5 (pbk)
Copyright	© 2012 Goh Lay Kuan
	except *One Hundred Years in Waiting* © 2012 Haresh Sharma, Chong Tze Chien and Goh Lay Kuan

This book is sponsored by National Arts Council.

郭宝崑全集

The Complete Works of Kuo Pao Kun

总编辑　柯思仁　　General Editor　Quah Sy Ren

第一卷
华文戏剧①　1960/1970年代
主编：柯思仁、潘正镭

Volume ONE
Plays in Chinese ①　The 1960s and the 1970s
Edited by Quah Sy Ren and Pan Cheng Lui

第二卷
华文戏剧②　1980年代
主编：柯思仁、潘正镭

Volume TWO
Plays in Chinese ②　The 1980s
Edited by Quah Sy Ren and Pan Cheng Lui

第三卷
华文戏剧③　1990年代
主编：柯思仁、潘正镭

Volume THREE
Plays in Chinese ③　The 1990s
Edited by Quah Sy Ren and Pan Cheng Lui

第四卷
英文戏剧
主编：黄万灵

Volume FOUR
Plays in English
Edited by C.J.W.-L. Wee

第五卷
翻译戏剧
主编：张夏帏

Volume FIVE
Plays in Translation
Edited by Teo Han Wue

第六卷
评论
主编：陈鸣鸾

Volume SIX
Commentaries
Edited by Tan Beng Luan

第七卷
论文与演讲
主编：陈鸣鸾

Volume SEVEN
Papers and Speeches
Edited by Tan Beng Luan

第八卷
访谈
主编：陈鸣鸾

Volume EIGHT
Interviews
Edited by Tan Beng Luan

第九卷
生活与创作图片
主编：林春兰、陈鸣鸾

Volume NINE
Life and Work: A Pictorial Record
Edited by Lim Soon Lan and Tan Beng Luan

第十卷
年表与资料汇编
主编：韩咏红

Volume TEN
Chronology and Bibliography
Edited by Han Yong Hong

关于**实践剧场** ▌ **About** The Theatre Practice

在戏剧家郭宝崑（已故）及舞蹈家吴
丽娟的催生下，新加坡第一个双语
剧团诞生了！

成立于1965年，比新加坡还年长一月
有余，**实践剧场**是本地戏剧界和文化
界历史最久、最为重要的组织之一。
走过半个世纪，历经几代努力，跟跟
跄跄、风风雨雨。

多年来，**实践剧场**以其双语的优势，
以"扎根本土、放眼世界、求同存
异、追求和谐"为理念，不断介绍
经典作品，却又鼓励原创；不断注入
本地色彩，却又放眼全球。自成立以
来，**实践剧场**便以艺术教育为己任，
将无数课程和演出带到校园，熏陶
了几代的新加坡人。

迈入新的世纪，**实践剧场**面临新的开
始和挑战，努力以叫好叫座的演出，
不计回报的创新，尝试为新加坡剧
坛添砖加瓦。如今翘首未来，叫人不
禁期待！

实践剧场为非牟利组织，主要经费来
自政府与民间的赞助。

Co-founded by Goh Lay Kuan and the late Kuo Pao Kun in 1965, **The Theatre Practice** has etched out a pivotal and long-cherished spot in local theatre and cultural history. We have painstakingly ridden out the storms of the last half-century, found ourselves indebted to the staggering contributions of generations gone by, and emerged stronger than ever.

Through the years, **The Theatre Practice** has marched forward upon the strength of our bilingualism, while pursuing the ideals of "staying firmly rooted to the local, expanding our awareness of the world at large, seeking commonalities yet accepting differences, and embracing one and all in harmony". We continually introduce classic gems, while also encouraging original creations; we strive to inject local flavour in our pieces, while also keeping ourselves open to the infinite possibilities in the global arena. From the very beginning, **The Theatre Practice** has been a pioneer in Arts Education, bringing countless workshops and performances into schools, and nurturing several generations of Singaporeans.

Forging into the new century, **The Theatre Practice** awaits fresh beginnings and challenges. We will spare no effort in presenting highly acclaimed quality productions, and see no limits in exploring original, experimental works — as we aim to steadily build upon the foundations of Singapore theatre. Let us welcome the future in eager anticipation, for there is much to look forward to!

The Theatre Practice is a nonprofit organisation and relies on government, public and private support to continue its work in the local and global community.

155 Waterloo Street #02-08 Stamford Arts Centre, Singapore 187962 www.practice.org.sg UEN/IPC No. 198801755D